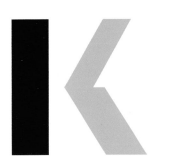

How to access your on-line resources

Kaplan Financial students will have a MyKaplan account and these extra resources will be available to you online. You do not need to register again, as this process was completed when you enrolled. If you are having problems accessing online materials, please ask your course administrator.

If you are not studying with Kaplan and did not purchase your book via a Kaplan website, to unlock your extra online resources please go to www.en-gage.co.uk (even if you have set up an account and registered books previously). You will then need to enter the ISBN number (on the title page and back cover) and the unique pass key number contained in the scratch panel below to gain access.

You will also be required to enter additional information during this process to set up or confirm your account details.

If you purchased through the Kaplan Publishing website you will automatically receive an e-mail invitation to register your details and gain access to your content. If you do not receive the e-mail or book content, please contact Kaplan Publishing.

Your code and information

This code can only be used once for the registration of one book online. This registration and your online content will expire when the final sittings for the examinations covered by this book have taken place. Please allow one hour from the time you submit your book details for us to process your request.

D1438532

Please scratch the film to access your unique code.

Please be aware that this code is case-sensitive and you will need to include the dashes within the passcode, but not when entering the ISBN.

KAPLAN
PUBLISHING

CIMA

Subject F2

Advanced Financial Reporting

Study Text

Published by: Kaplan Publishing UK

Unit 2 The Business Centre, Molly Millars Lane, Wokingham, Berkshire. RG41 2QZ

Notice

Kaplan Publishing's learning materials are designed to help students succeed in their examinations. In certain circumstances, CIMA can make post-exam adjustment to a student's mark or grade to reflect adverse circumstances which may have disadvantaged a student's ability to take an exam or demonstrate their normal level of attainment (see CIMA's Special Consideration policy). However, it should be noted that students will not be eligible for special consideration by CIMA if preparation for or performance in a CIMA exam is affected by any failure by their tuition provider to prepare them properly for the exam for any reason including, but not limited to, staff shortages, building work or a lack of facilities etc.

Similarly, CIMA will not accept applications for special consideration on any of the following grounds:

- failure by a tuition provider to cover the whole syllabus

- failure by the student to cover the whole syllabus, for instance as a result of joining a course part way through

- failure by the student to prepare adequately for the exam, or to use the correct pre-seen material

- errors in the Kaplan Official Study Text, including sample (practice) questions or any other Kaplan content or

- errors in any other study materials (from any other tuition provider or publisher).

Acknowledgements

We are grateful to the CIMA for permission to reproduce past examination questions. The answers to CIMA Exams have been prepared by Kaplan Publishing, except in the case of the CIMA November 2010 and subsequent CIMA Exam answers where the official CIMA answers have been reproduced.

Trade Marks

The IFRS Foundation logo, the IASB logo, the IFRS for SMEs logo, the "Hexagon Device", "IFRS Foundation", "eIFRS", "IAS", "IASB", "IFRS for SMEs", "NIIF" IASs" "IFRS", "IFRSs", "International Accounting Standards", "International Financial Reporting Standards", "IFRIC", "SIC" and "IFRS Taxonomy".

Further details of the Trade Marks including details of countries where the Trade Marks are registered or applied for are available from the Foundation on request.

This product contains material that is ©Financial Reporting Council Ltd (FRC). Adapted and reproduced with the kind permission of the Financial Reporting Council. All rights reserved. For further information, please visit www.frc.org.uk or call +44 (0)20 7492 2300.

British Library Cataloguing-in-Publication Data

A catalogue record for this book is available from the British Library.

ISBN: 978-1-78740-713-8

Contents

Page

Syllabus area F2A: Financing capital projects

Syllabus area F2B: Financial reporting standards

Syllabus area F2C: Group Accounts

Syllabus area F2B continued: Financial reporting standards

Syllabus area F2C continued: Group accounts

Syllabus area F2D: Integrated reporting

Syllabus area F2E: Analysing financial statements

Introduction

This document references IFRS® Standards and IAS® Standards, which are authored by the International Accounting Standards Board (the Board), and published in the 2020 IFRS Standards Red Book.

How to use the Materials

These official CIMA learning materials have been carefully designed to make your learning experience as easy as possible and to give you the best chances of success in your objective tests.

The product range contains a number of features to help you in the study process. They include:

- a detailed explanation of all syllabus areas

- extensive 'practical' materials

- generous question practice, together with full solutions.

This Study Text has been designed with the needs of home study and distance learning candidates in mind. Such students require very full coverage of the syllabus topics, and also the facility to undertake extensive question practice. However, the Study Text is also ideal for fully taught courses.

The main body of the text is divided into a number of chapters, each of which is organised on the following pattern:

- **Detailed learning outcomes.** These describe the knowledge expected after your studies of the chapter are complete. You should assimilate these before beginning detailed work on the chapter, so that you can appreciate where your studies are leading.

- **Step-by-step topic coverage.** This is the heart of each chapter, containing detailed explanatory text supported where appropriate by worked examples and exercises. You should work carefully through this section, ensuring that you understand the material being explained and can tackle the examples and exercises successfully. Remember that in many cases knowledge is cumulative: if you fail to digest earlier material thoroughly, you may struggle to understand later chapters.

- **Activities.** Some chapters are illustrated by more practical elements, such as comments and questions designed to stimulate discussion.

- **Question practice.** The text contains three styles of question:

    - Exam-style objective test questions (OTQs).

    - 'Integration' questions – these test your ability to understand topics within a wider context. This is particularly important with calculations where OTQs may focus on just one element but an integration question tackles the full calculation, just as you would be expected to do in the workplace.

    - 'Case' style questions – these test your ability to analyse and discuss issues in greater depth, particularly focusing on scenarios that are less clear cut than in the objective tests, and thus provide excellent practice for developing the skills needed for success in the Management Level Case Study Examination.

- **Solutions.** Avoid the temptation merely to 'audit' the solutions provided. It is an illusion to think that this provides the same benefits as you would gain from a serious attempt of your own. However, if you are struggling to get started on a question you should read the introductory guidance provided at the beginning of the solution, where provided, and then make your own attempt before referring back to the full solution.

If you work conscientiously through this Official CIMA Study Text according to the guidelines above you will be giving yourself an excellent chance of success in your objective tests. Good luck with your studies!

Quality and accuracy are of the utmost importance to us so if you spot an error in any of our products, please send an email to mykaplanreporting@kaplan.com with full details, or follow the link to the feedback form in MyKaplan.

Our Quality Co-ordinator will work with our technical team to verify the error and take action to ensure it is corrected in future editions.

Icon explanations

 Definition – These sections explain important areas of knowledge which must be understood and reproduced in an assessment environment.

 Key point – Identifies topics which are key to success and are often examined.

 Supplementary reading – These sections will help to provide a deeper understanding of core areas. The supplementary reading is **NOT** optional reading. It is vital to provide you with the breadth of knowledge you will need to address the wide range of topics within your syllabus that could feature in an assessment question. **Reference to this text is vital when self-studying.**

 Test your understanding – Following key points and definitions are exercises which give the opportunity to assess the understanding of these core areas.

 Illustration – To help develop an understanding of particular topics. The illustrative examples are useful in preparing for the Test your understanding exercises.

 Exclamation mark – This symbol signifies a topic which can be more difficult to understand. When reviewing these areas, care should be taken.

New – Identifies topics that are brand new in subjects that build on, and therefore also contain, learning covered in earlier subjects.

 Tutorial note – Included to explain some of the technical points in more detail.

Study technique

Passing exams is partly a matter of intellectual ability, but however accomplished you are in that respect you can improve your chances significantly by the use of appropriate study and revision techniques. In this section we briefly outline some tips for effective study during the earlier stages of your approach to the objective tests. We also mention some techniques that you will find useful at the revision stage.

Planning

To begin with, formal planning is essential to get the best return from the time you spend studying. Estimate how much time in total you are going to need for each subject you are studying. Remember that you need to allow time for revision as well as for initial study of the material.

With your study material before you, decide which chapters you are going to study in each week, and which weeks you will devote to revision and final question practice.

Prepare a written schedule summarising the above and stick to it!

It is essential to know your syllabus. As your studies progress you will become more familiar with how long it takes to cover topics in sufficient depth. Your timetable may need to be adapted to allocate enough time for the whole syllabus.

Students are advised to refer to the examination blueprints (see page P.13 for further information) and the CIMA website, www.cimaglobal.com, to ensure they are up-to-date.

The amount of space allocated to a topic in the Study Text is not a very good guide as to how long it will take you. The syllabus weighting is the better guide as to how long you should spend on a syllabus topic.

Tips for effective studying

(1) Aim to find a quiet and undisturbed location for your study, and plan as far as possible to use the same period of time each day. Getting into a routine helps to avoid wasting time. Make sure that you have all the materials you need before you begin so as to minimise interruptions.

(2) Store all your materials in one place, so that you do not waste time searching for items every time you want to begin studying. If you have to pack everything away after each study period, keep your study materials in a box, or even a suitcase, which will not be disturbed until the next time.

(3) Limit distractions. To make the most effective use of your study periods you should be able to apply total concentration, so turn off all entertainment equipment, set your phones to message mode, and put up your 'do not disturb' sign.

(4) Your timetable will tell you which topic to study. However, before diving in and becoming engrossed in the finer points, make sure you have an overall picture of all the areas that need to be covered by the end of that session. After an hour, allow yourself a short break and move away from your Study Text. With experience, you will learn to assess the pace you need to work at. Each study session should focus on component learning outcomes – the basis for all questions.

(5) Work carefully through a chapter, making notes as you go. When you have covered a suitable amount of material, vary the pattern by attempting a practice question. When you have finished your attempt, make notes of any mistakes you made, or any areas that you failed to cover or covered more briefly. Be aware that all component learning outcomes will be tested in each examination.

(6) Make notes as you study, and discover the techniques that work best for you. Your notes may be in the form of lists, bullet points, diagrams, summaries, 'mind maps', or the written word, but remember that you will need to refer back to them at a later date, so they must be intelligible. If you are on a taught course, make sure you highlight any issues you would like to follow up with your lecturer.

(7) Organise your notes. Make sure that all your notes, calculations etc. can be effectively filed and easily retrieved later.

Progression

There are two elements of progression that we can measure: how quickly students move through individual topics within a subject; and how quickly they move from one course to the next. We know that there is an optimum for both, but it can vary from subject to subject and from student to student. However, using data and our experience of student performance over many years, we can make some generalisations.

A fixed period of study set out at the start of a course with key milestones is important. This can be within a subject, for example 'I will finish this topic by 30 June', or for overall achievement, such as 'I want to be qualified by the end of next year'.

Your qualification is cumulative, as earlier papers provide a foundation for your subsequent studies, so do not allow there to be too big a gap between one subject and another. For example, F2 *Advanced financial reporting* builds on your knowledge of financial accounting from F1 *Financial reporting* and BA3 *Fundamentals of financial accounting* and lays the foundations for long term financing and weighted average cost of capital usage within F3 *Financial strategy*.

We know that exams encourage techniques that lead to some degree of short term retention, the result being that you will simply forget much of what you have already learned unless it is refreshed (look up Ebbinghaus Forgetting Curve for more details on this). This makes it more difficult as you move from one subject to another: not only will you have to learn the new subject, you will also have to relearn all the underpinning knowledge as well. This is very inefficient and slows down your overall progression which makes it more likely you may not succeed at all.

Also, it is important to realise that the Management Case Study (MCS) tests knowledge of all subjects within the Management level. Please note that candidates will need to return to this material when studying for MCS as it forms a significant part of the MCS syllabus content.

In addition, delaying your studies slows your path to qualification which can have negative impacts on your career, postponing the opportunity to apply for higher level positions and therefore higher pay.

You can use the following diagram showing the whole structure of your qualification to help you keep track of your progress. Make sure you seek appropriate advice if you are unsure about your progression through the qualification.

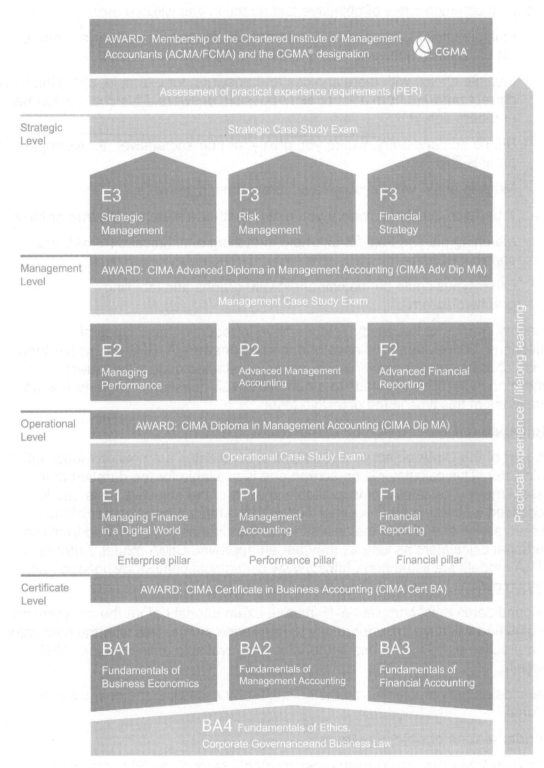

Objective test

Objective test questions require you to choose or provide a response to a question whose correct answer is predetermined.

The most common types of objective test question you will see are:

- Multiple choice, where you have to choose the correct answer(s) from a list of possible answers. This could either be numbers or text.

- Multiple choice with more choices and answers, for example, choosing two correct answers from a list of eight possible answers. This could either be numbers or text.

- Single numeric entry, where you give your numeric answer, for example, profit is $10,000.

- Multiple entry, where you give several numeric answers.

- True/false questions, where you state whether a statement is true or false.

- Matching pairs of text, for example, matching a technical term with the correct definition.

- Other types could be matching text with graphs and labelling graphs/diagrams.

In every chapter of this Study Text we have introduced these types of questions, but obviously we have had to label answers A, B, C etc. rather than using click boxes. For convenience, we have retained quite a few questions where an initial scenario leads to a number of sub-questions. There will be no questions of this type in the objective tests.

Guidance re CIMA on-screen calculator

As part of the CIMA objective test software, candidates are now provided with a calculator. This calculator is on-screen and is available for the duration of the assessment. The calculator is available in each of the objective tests and is accessed by clicking the calculator button in the top left hand corner of the screen at any time during the assessment. Candidates are permitted to utilise personal calculators as long as they are an approved CIMA model. Authorised CIMA models are listed here: https://www.cimaglobal.com/Studying/study-and-resources/.

All candidates must complete a 15-minute exam tutorial before the assessment begins and will have the opportunity to familiarise themselves with the calculator and practise using it. The exam tutorial is also available online via the CIMA website.

Candidates may practise using the calculator by accessing the online exam tutorial.

Fundamentals of objective tests

The objective tests are 90-minute assessments comprising 60 compulsory questions, with one or more parts. There will be no choice and all questions should be attempted. All elements of a question must be answered correctly for the question to be marked correctly. All questions are equally weighted.

CIMA syllabus 2019 – Structure of subjects and learning outcomes

Details regarding the content of the new CIMA syllabus can be located within the CIMA 2019 professional syllabus document.

Each subject within the syllabus is divided into a number of broad syllabus topics. The topics contain one or more lead learning outcomes, related component learning outcomes and indicative knowledge content.

A learning outcome has two main purposes:

(a)   To define the skill or ability that a well prepared candidate should be able to exhibit in the examination.

(b)   To demonstrate the approach likely to be taken in examination questions.

The learning outcomes are part of a hierarchy of learning objectives. The verbs used at the beginning of each learning outcome relate to a specific learning objective, e.g.

Calculate the break-even point, profit target, margin of safety and profit/volume ratio for a single product or service.

The verb '**calculate**' indicates a level three learning objective. The following tables list the verbs that appear in the syllabus learning outcomes and examination questions.

The examination blueprints and representative task statements

CIMA have also published examination blueprints giving learners clear expectations regarding what is expected of them.

The blueprint is structured as follows:

- Exam content sections (reflecting the syllabus document)

- Lead and component outcomes (reflecting the syllabus document)

- Representative task statements.

A representative task statement is a plain English description of what a CIMA finance professional should know and be able to do.

The content and skill level determine the language and verbs used in the representative task.

CIMA will test up to the level of the task statement in the objective tests (an objective test question on a particular topic could be set at a lower level than the task statement in the blueprint).

The format of the objective test blueprints follows that of the published syllabus for the 2019 CIMA Professional Qualification.

Weightings for content sections are also included in the individual subject blueprints.

CIMA VERB HIERARCHY

CIMA place great importance on the definition of verbs in structuring objective tests. It is therefore crucial that you understand the verbs in order to appreciate the depth and breadth of a topic and the level of skill required. The objective tests will focus on levels one, two and three of the CIMA hierarchy of verbs. However, they will also test levels four and five, especially at the management and strategic levels.

Skill level	Verbs used	Definition
Level 5 Evaluation How you are expected to use your learning to evaluate, make decisions or recommendations	Advise	Counsel, inform or notify
	Assess	Evaluate or estimate the nature, ability or quality of
	Evaluate	Appraise or assess the value of
	Recommend	Propose a course of action
	Review	Assess and evaluate in order, to change if necessary
Level 4 Analysis How you are expected to analyse the detail of what you have learned	Align	Arrange in an orderly way
	Analyse	Examine in detail the structure of
	Communicate	Share or exchange information
	Compare and contrast	Show the similarities and/or differences between
	Develop	Grow and expand a concept
	Discuss	Examine in detail by argument
	Examine	Inspect thoroughly
	Interpret	Translate into intelligible or familiar terms
	Monitor	Observe and check the progress of
	Prioritise	Place in order of priority or sequence for action
	Produce	Create or bring into existence
Level 3 Application How you are expected to apply your knowledge	Apply	Put to practical use
	Calculate	Ascertain or reckon mathematically
	Conduct	Organise and carry out
	Demonstrate	Prove with certainty or exhibit by practical means
	Prepare	Make or get ready for use
	Reconcile	Make or prove consistent/compatible

Skill level	Verbs used	Definition
Level 2 Comprehension What you are expected to understand	Describe	Communicate the key features of
	Distinguish	Highlight the differences between
	Explain	Make clear or intelligible/state the meaning or purpose of
	Identify	Recognise, establish or select after consideration
	Illustrate	Use an example to describe or explain something
Level 1 Knowledge What you are expected to know	List	Make a list of
	State	Express, fully or clearly, the details/facts of
	Define	Give the exact meaning of
	Outline	Give a summary of

Information concerning formulae and tables will be provided via the CIMA website, www.cimaglobal.com.

SYLLABUS GRIDS

F2: Advanced Financial Reporting

Analysing and communicating insights about the performance of the organisation

Content weighting

Content area	Weighting
A Financing capital projects	15%
B Financial reporting standards	25%
C Group accounts	25%
D Integrated reporting	10%
E Analysing financial statements	25%
	100%

F2A: Financing capital projects

For selected strategic (capital investment) projects to be implemented, funds must be sourced at the right cost and at the right time. This is a key role of the finance function and shows how it enables the organisation to create value. This section looks at the sources and types of funds and how much they cost.

Lead outcome	Component outcome	Topics to be covered	Explanatory notes	Study text chapter
1. Compare and contrast types and sources of long-term funds.	Compare and contrast: a. Long-term debt b. Equity finance c. Markets for long-term funds	• Characteristics of different types of shares and long-term debts • Ordinary and preference shares • Bonds and other types of long-term debt • Operations of stock and bond markets • Issuance of shares and bonds • Role of advisors	What are the types of funds that can be used to finance medium to long-term projects? What are their unique and shared profiles and under what conditions are they suitable for organisations seeking long-term funds? What is the impact of these funds on the risk profile of organisations? Where can these funds be sourced? What are the criteria that organisations must fulfil to access funds from these sources?	1
2. Calculate cost of long-term funds.	Calculate: a. Cost of equity b. Cost of debt c. Weighted average cost of capital	• Cost of equity using dividend valuation model (with or without growth in dividends) • Post-tax cost of bank borrowing • Yield to maturity of bonds and post-tax cost of bonds • Post-tax costs of convertible bonds up to and including conversion	What is the cost of each type of funds? What is the cost of the total funds used by the organisation to fund its projects? How can the organisation minimise the cost of funds whilst ensuring the availability of adequate funds at the right time and at the same time maintaining an appropriate risk profile?	2

F2B: Financial reporting standards

The finance function is responsible for narrating how organisations create and preserve value. Different types of narratives are used for different audiences. Financial reporting is used for external stakeholders. This section examines the building blocks for constructing the narratives in the financial statements. It covers the key financial reporting standards on which the financial statements will be based.

Lead outcome	Component outcome	Topics to be covered	Explanatory notes	Study text chapter
1. Explain relevant financial reporting standards for revenue, leases, financial instruments, intangible assets and provisions.	Explain the financial reporting standards for: a. Revenue b. Leases c. Provisions d. Financial instruments e. Intangible assets f. Income taxes g. Effect of changes in foreign currency rates	• IFRS 15 – Revenue from Contracts with Customers • IFRS 16 – Leases • IAS 37 – Provisions, Contingent Liabilities and Contingent Assets • IFRS 9 – Financial Instruments • IAS 32 – Financial Instruments: Presentation • IAS 38 – Intangible Assets • IAS 12 – Income Taxes • IAS 21 – Effect of Changes in on Foreign Exchange Rates	How should important elements of the financial statement be treated in the books? What principles should underpin these? How do financial reporting standards help to ensure this? Using financial reporting standards terminology this part will be looking at issues in recognition and measurement. The most important issues will be considered here.	6 5 7 3 8 9 10
2. Explain relevant financial reporting standards for group accounts.	a. Explain the financial reporting standards for the key areas of group accounts	• IAS 1 – Presentation of Financial Statements • IAS 27 – Separate Financial Statements • IAS 28 – Investment in Associates and Joint Ventures • IFRS 3 – Business Combinations • IFRS 5 – Non-current Assets Held for Sale or Discontinued Operations • IFRS 10 – Consolidated Financial Statements • IFRS 11 – Joint Arrangements	What are the key principles that should govern the preparation of group accounts? How are they reflected in financial reporting standards? The approach should focus on the aspects of group accounts that are essential for discussions with the rest of the business. Therefore, the emphasis should be on awareness creation and basic understanding of the technical elements.	11-16

F2C: Group accounts

Organisations sometimes acquire or merge with other organisations to improve their strategic performance, position and prospects. The performance and position of combined operations are reported through group accounts. This section covers the application of the relevant financial reporting standards to prepare group accounts. The topics covered are those that are essential to conducting conversations with different parts of the business about the performance of the group and its component parts.

Lead outcome	Component outcome	Topics to be covered	Explanatory notes	Study text chapter
1. Prepare group accounts based on IFRS.	Prepare the following based on financial reporting standards: a. Consolidated statement of financial position b. Consolidated statement of comprehensive income c. Consolidated statement of changes in equity d. Consolidated statement of cash flows	• IAS 1 – Presentation of Financial Statements • IAS 27 – Separate Financial Statements • IAS 28 – Investment in Associates and Joint Ventures • IFRS 3 – Business Combinations • IFRS 5 – Non-current Assets Held for Sale or Discontinued Operations • IFRS 10 – Consolidated Financial Statements • IFRS 11 – Joint Arrangements	This is about the preparation of basic group accounts applying the financial reporting standards learned in the previous section. Basic understanding of the technical issues is required. Thus, it should cover the rules of consolidation, goodwill, foreign subsidiaries, minority interests and associated companies. These should be placed in the context of the organisation's strategy as executed through mergers and acquisitions and the setting up of subsidiaries. In addition, it can be linked to the performance management of responsibility centres.	11-16
2. Discuss additional disclosure issues related to the group accounts.	Discuss disclosure requirements related to: a. Transaction between related parties b. Earnings per share	• IAS 24 – Related Party Disclosures • IAS 33 – Earnings Per Share	What other issues should be disclosed outside the financial statements? Why? Again, the focus is on building awareness and basic understanding of the technical issues in order to equip finance professionals to conduct meaningful discussions with the rest of the organisation about the performance, position and potential of the organisation.	17 4

F2D: Integrated reporting

In a multi-stakeholder world, there has been a call for broader forms of reporting to cover wider audiences and issues of concern to them. The International Integrated Reporting Framework developed by the International Integrated Reporting Council (IIRC) is one of the most influential frameworks that seeks to fulfil this role. This section introduces candidates to the Framework and its components.

Lead outcome	Component outcome	Topics to be covered	Explanatory notes	Study text chapter
1. Discuss the International <IR> Framework activities.	a. Describe the role of the International Integrated Reporting Council. b. Explain integrated thinking. c. Discuss the International <IR> Framework.	• Context of integrated reporting • International Integrated Reporting Council • Integrated thinking • International <IR> Framework • Benefits and limitations of the Framework	This section looks at the International <IR> Framework as a means of addressing the need for wider forms of reporting in a multi-stakeholder world. It introduces the role of the IIRC and uses the concept of integrated thinking as the foundational concept of the International <IR> Framework. It also discusses the Framework, its benefits and limitations.	18
2. Explain the Six Capitals of Integrated Reporting.	Explain the measurement and disclosure issues of: a. Financial capital b. Manufactured capital c. Intellectual capital d. Human capital e. Social and relationship capital f. Natural capital	• Definition of the six capitals • Measurement and disclosure issues relating to the six capitals	The six capitals are a key part of the International <IR> Framework. This section defines the six capitals and explains the measurement and disclosure issues relating to them.	18

F2E: Analysing financial statements

The analyses of financial statements enable organisations to explain their performance and to compare their performance and prospects over time and against others. It can show how vulnerable they and their business models are to disruption. This section shows how these analyses are conducted and their limitations.

Lead outcome	Component outcome	Topics to be covered	Explanatory notes	Study text chapter
1. Analyse financial statements of organisations.	Analyse financial statements to provide insight on: a. Performance b. Position c. Adaptability d. Prospects	• Ratio analysis • Interpretation of ratios • Reporting of ratios along the dimensions of the Gartner Data Analytics maturity model – descriptive, diagnostic, predictive and prescriptive • Link to organisation's business model	The financial statements narrate how organisations create and preserve value using financial numbers. Analyses of financial statements allows finance professionals to go beyond the numbers and put the narrative into everyday business language to facilitate discussions and collaboration with the rest of the organisation. The analysis could be based on the Gartner Data Analytics model which presents information as descriptive, diagnostic, predictive and prescriptive. Thus, it will cover hindsight, insight and foresight into the organisation's performance, position, resilience (or adaptability) and prospects. The analyses can be linked to the organisation's business model.	19
2. Recommend actions based on insights from the interpretation of financial statements.	a. Recommend actions	• Linkages between different areas of performance • Predictive and prescriptive ratios • Impact of recommendations on wider organisational ecosystem	Draw logical conclusions from the analysis. The focus is mainly predictive and prescriptive areas of data analytics. The recommendations should also be organisation wide and must encompass the ecosystem. A link with the business model framework in E2 is essential.	19

| 3. Discuss the limitations of the tools used for interpreting financial statements. | Discuss:

a. Data limitations

b. Limitations of ratio analysis | • Quality and type of data used

• Comparability – both in segment and internationally | What are the limitations of the data and techniques used in the analyses of financial statements? How do they affect the recommendations? How could they be overcome? | 19 |

Long term finance

Chapter learning objectives

Lead	Component
A1: Compare and contrast types and sources of long term funds	Compare and contrast: (a) Long-term debt (b) Equity finance (c) Markets for long-term funds

1 Session content

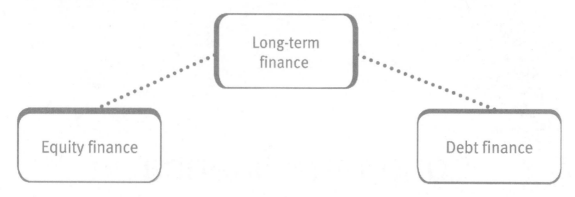

2 Introduction

Syllabus area F2A 'Financing capital projects' is covered in the first two chapters of this text. Financing capital projects makes up 15% of the syllabus. It consists of two main areas – sources of long term finance (Chapter 1) and the cost of long-term funds (Chapter 2).

Sources of long term finance

Long-term finance is typically considered to consist of methods of finance that will be held or settled over periods of greater than 12 months from the date of issue. Short-term finance was covered in F1 (and is not testable in F2) and consists of financing methods settled within 12 months from the date of issue.

If a company has a large cash surplus, it may be able to afford to undertake new investment projects without having to resort to external sources of finance.

However, if external funds are required, the company might raise finance from the following sources:

1   The capital markets:

  –   new share issues, for example by companies obtaining a listing on a stock market for the first time (thus selling their shares)

  –   rights issues

  –   issues of marketable debt.

  A company must be quoted/listed on a recognised stock exchange in order to be able to raise finance from the capital markets.

2   Banks and finance houses - borrowings such as long-term loans or short-term loans, including bank facilities (revolving credit facilities (RCFs) and money market lines).

  NB Short-term finance methods have been tested in F1 and are not testable in F2 but are mentioned here for completeness.

3   Government and similar sources – government grants, charitable grants

In general, these financing methods can be considered either equity or debt sources.

3 Equity finance

Equity is another name for shares or ownership rights in a business.

Important terminology

Share – a fixed identifiable unit of capital in an entity which normally has a fixed nominal value, which may be quite different from its market value.

Shareholders receive returns from their investment in shares in the form of dividends, and also capital growth in the share price.

Ordinary shares

Ordinary shares (sometimes also referred to as 'equity shares') pay dividends at the discretion of the entity's directors. The ordinary shareholders of a company are the owners of the company and they have the right to attend meetings and vote on any important matters.

On a winding-up of a company, the ordinary shareholders are subordinate to all other finance providers (i.e. they receive their money last, if there is any left after all other finance providers have been paid).

Preference shares

Preference shares are shares that pay a fixed dividend, which is paid in preference to (before) ordinary share dividends, hence the name.

Also, on a winding-up of a company, the preference shareholders are subordinate to all the debt holders and creditors, but receive their pay-out before ordinary shareholders.

More details on preference shares

Comparison of preference share dividends with debt and with ordinary shares

Preference vs ordinary shares

Preference shares pay a fixed proportion of the share's nominal value each year as a dividend. This is why they are often considered to behave in a way which is more similar to debt finance (fixed annual returns) rather than ordinary shares (variable dividend at the discretion of the directors).

Preference vs debt finance

However, unlike interest on debt finance, preference share dividends are paid out of post-tax profits, so there is no tax benefit to a company of paying preference share dividends.

Also, there are certain circumstances (e.g. where a company has insufficient distributable profits) when the company will be given permission to not pay its preference share dividends in a year. This is not the case with debt interest, which is an obligation every year, whether or not the company can afford to make the payment.

The lack of tax relief on dividends mentioned above explains why preference shares are relatively unattractive to companies compared with bank borrowings and other forms of fixed rate security such as bonds.

However, they do have some appeal to risk-averse investors looking for a relatively reliable income stream.

Different types of preference shares

There are four types of preference shares:

- **cumulative preference shares**, for which dividends must be rolled forward if the company has insufficient reserves to be able to pay a dividend i.e. if a dividend is not paid in year 1, that dividend has to be paid in year 2 along with the 'normal' dividend for year 2

- **non-cumulative preference shares**, for which missed dividends do not have to be paid later. There is no roll forward of dividends

- **participating preference shares**, which give the holder fixed dividends plus extra earnings based on certain conditions often linked to performance (in a similar way to ordinary shares)

- **convertible preference shares**, which can be exchanged for a specified number of ordinary shares on some given future date.

Also, note that some preference shares are **redeemable**, meaning that holders will be repaid their capital (usually at par) at a pre-determined future date.

Example of convertible preference shares

Convertible preference shares are fixed-income securities that the investor can choose to turn into a certain number of ordinary shares after a predetermined time span or on a specific date.

The fixed-income dividend offers a steady income stream and some protection of the investor's capital. However, the option to convert these securities into ordinary shares gives the investor the opportunity to gain from a rise in the share price.

Convertibles are particularly attractive to those investors who want to participate in the rise of hot growth companies while being insulated from a drop in price should the ordinary share price growth not live up to expectations.

If a company were to issue some 5% $10 nominal value preference shares at par, convertible to ordinary shares in five years' time, the investor would receive a fixed amount of $0.50 each year for the first five years.

In five years' time, the investor would have the choice to keep the preference shares or convert to a number of ordinary shares. The conversion ratio would have been set when the preference shares were first issued. For example it could be 1:3, i.e. each preference share could be converted into 3 ordinary shares.

In this example, the investor would be keen to convert if the ordinary shares on the conversion date were worth more than $3.33 ($10/3) as the return is higher than the amount paid in the original investment.

For example, if the ordinary share price growth has been impressive and the shares are actually worth $4.50 each on the conversion date, the investor could trade a single preference share (value $10) for 3 ordinary shares worth $13.50 in total.

Capital markets

The shares in a listed, or quoted, company will be traded on a capital market.

Capital markets (or stock markets) must fulfil both primary and secondary functions.

Primary function:

The primary function of a stock market is to enable companies to raise new finance (either equity or debt). Through the stock market, a company can communicate with a large pool of potential investors, so it is much easier for a company to raise finance in this way, rather than contacting investors individually.

Note that in the UK, a company must be a plc before it is allowed to raise finance from the public on the stock market.

Secondary function:

The secondary function of a stock market is to enable investors to sell their investments to other investors. A listed company's shares are therefore more marketable than shares of an unlisted company, which means that they tend to be more attractive to investors.

Listed v private companies

Private vs public companies

A limited company may be 'private' or 'public'. A private limited company's disclosure requirements are lighter, but for this reason its shares may not be offered to the general public (and therefore cannot be traded on a public stock exchange). This is the major distinguishing feature between a private limited company (Ltd) and a public limited company (plc). Most companies, particularly small companies, are private.

Private limited company (Ltd in UK terminology)

A private company limited by shares, usually called a private limited company, has shareholders with limited liability and its shares may not be offered to the general public, unlike those of a public limited company (see details below).

'Limited by shares' means that the company has shareholders, and that the liability of the shareholders to creditors of the company is limited to the capital originally invested, i.e. the nominal value of the shares and any premium paid in return for the issue of the shares by the company. A shareholder's personal assets are thereby protected in the event of the company's insolvency, but money invested in the company will be lost.

The company will have "Ltd" after its name to indicate its status as a private company.

Public limited company (plc in UK terminology)

A public limited company is a limited liability company that may sell shares to the public. It can be either an unlisted company, or a listed company on the stock exchange. The company will have "plc" after its name to indicate its status as a public limited company.

A stock exchange listing

When an entity obtains a listing (or quotation) for its shares on a stock exchange this is referred to as a flotation or an Initial Public Offering (IPO).

Advantages of a listing

- Once listed, the market will provide a more accurate valuation of the entity than had been previously possible.

- Creates a mechanism for buying and selling shares in the future at will.

- Raise profile of entity, which may have an impact on revenues, credibility with suppliers and long-term providers of finance.

- Raise capital for future investment.

- Makes employee share schemes more accessible. Some employers offer their staff share save schemes or access to share options as part of the employees' salary package which enable employees to benefit financially if the company performs well. The financial benefit is obtained through appreciation of share prices. These schemes are easier to offer if the entity is listed.

Disadvantages of a listing

- Costly for a small entity (flotation, underwriting costs, etc.)

- Making enough shares available to allow a market, and hence loss of at least some control of the original owners.

- Reporting requirements are more onerous.

- Stock exchange rules for obtaining a quotation can be stringent.

UK capital markets

There are two important capital markets in the UK:

- the full Stock Exchange – a market for larger companies. Entry costs are high and scrutiny is very high for companies listed on the 'full list', but the profile of a Stock Exchange listed company's shares is very high, so the shares are extremely marketable

- the Alternative Investment Market (AIM) – a market for smaller companies, with lower associated costs and less stringent entry criteria.

The operation of stock exchanges

Prices of shares on the stock exchange are determined by the forces of supply and demand in the market. For example, if a company performs well, its shares become attractive to investors. This creates demand which drives up the price of the shares.

Conversely, investors who hold shares in an underperforming company will try to sell those shares, creating supply in the market. This drives down the price of the shares.

The role of advisors in a share issue

Investment banks usually take the lead role in share issues and will advise on:

- the appointment of other specialists (e.g. lawyers)
- stock exchange requirements
- forms of any new capital to be made available
- the number of shares to be issued and the issue price
- arrangements for underwriting
- publishing the offer.

Stockbrokers provide advice on the various methods of obtaining a listing. They may work with investment banks on identifying institutional investors, but usually they are involved with smaller issues and placings.

Institutional investors are investors from large organisations or institutions e.g. pension funds. Institutional investors have little direct involvement other than as investors, agreeing to buy a certain number of shares. They may also be used by the entity and its advisors to provide an indication of the likely take up and acceptable offer price for the shares. Once the shares are in issue, institutional investors have a major influence on the evaluation and the market for the shares.

Registrars to an issue will provide administrative functions such as collecting and processing applications from potential investors, monitoring payments made to and from investors and providing advice regarding share issues to stock exchanges, investors and issuing entities.

Public and Investor relations will work with the entity to ensure communications regarding the share issue are transparent, informative and are understandable to those investing. If successful, the work of public and investor relations could improve the uptake of the share issue and increase the market value of the issued shares.

Reporting accountants will provide advice regarding the impact on the financial statements of any potential shares issues. They must consider the wider ramifications upon the economic decisions of the users of the financial statements caused by the potential share issues e.g. implications on loan covenants.

Underwriters are financial institutions that help corporations raising finance by taking on the risk associated with a new issue and attempting to promote the new share issue to 3rd party investors. The underwriters retain part of the proceeds from raising the finance in return for bearing the risk.

4 Methods of issuing new shares

The three most commonly used methods of issuing new shares are:

- an IPO (initial public offering) or flotation
- a placing
- a rights issue (see section 5).

An IPO is suitable when an entity seeks a listing on a stock market for the first time.

Placings and rights issues are relevant for entities that already list their shares on a stock market and are seeking further financing through a new share issue.

Initial public offering (IPO)

IPOs occur when a company seeks to be listed on a stock market for the first time. These offers may be of completely new shares or they may derive from the transfer to the public of some or all of the shares already held privately.

Shares are offered for sale to investors, through an issuing house. The offer could be made:

- at a fixed price set by the company
- via a tender offer.

For a tender offer, investors are invited to tender for new shares at their own suggested price. All shares being offered are sold at the best price that would generate the required finance.

 Further information on tenders and IPO's

Tender offers

A tender offer is an alternative to a fixed price offer. Under a tender offer, subscribers tender for the shares at, or above, a minimum fixed price. Once all offers have been received from prospective investors, the company sets a "strike price" and allocates shares to all bidders who have offered the strike price or more. The strike price is set to make sure that the company raises the required amount of finance from the share issue.

Once the strike price has been set, all bidders who offered the strike price or more are allocated shares, and they all pay the strike price irrespective of what the original bid was.

Example of a tender offer

Bragg Co needs to raise $20m to invest in a new project. The company has asked investors for tender offers and the following offers have been received:

Maximum price offered ($ per share)	No of shares requested at this price ((in millions)
2.0	5.0
2.2	4.1
2.4	1.9
2.6	3.2

The strike will be set at the highest possible level that generates the required amount of finance. This is to make sure that the company does not issue more shares than it has to. This ensures that the dilution of the existing shareholders' holding is kept to a minimum. If Bragg Co sets the strike price at $2.60, only 3.2 million shares will be issued, raising $8.32m in total ($2.60 × 3.2m). This is not acceptable since $20m is needed.

If Bragg Co sets the strike price at $2.40, 5.1m shares will be issued (being 1.9m to the people who bid $2.40 and 3.2m to the people who bid $2.60). Therefore the total finance raised will be $2.40 × 5.1m = $12.24m. Again, not sufficient.

If Bragg Co sets the strike price at $2.20, 9.2m shares will be issued (being 4.1m to the people who bid $2.20, 1.9m to the people who bid $2.40 and 3.2m to the people who bid $2.60). Therefore, the total finance raised will be $2.20 × 9.2m = $20.24m. This is now enough to satisfy Bragg Co's financing requirements.

Hence, to ensure that $20m is raised from the tender offer, the strike price would be set at $2.20 and any investor who bid $2.20 or more would be allocated shares at the strike price of $2.20.

Placing

Shares are placed directly with certain investors (normally institutions) on a pre-arranged basis.

In this type of issue the shares are not offered to the public, but the issuing house will arrange for the shares to be issued to its institutional clients. This method is very popular, being cheaper and quicker to arrange than most other methods. However, it does not normally lead to a very active market for the shares after flotation.

5 Rights issues

A rights issue is where new shares are offered for sale (typically at a discounted price) to existing shareholders only, in proportion to the size of their shareholding.

The right to buy new shares ahead of outside investors is known as the 'pre-emption rights' of shareholders. Note that the purpose of pre-emption rights is to ensure that shareholders have an opportunity to prevent their stake being diluted by new issues. Pre-emption rights are protected by law, and can only be waived with the consent of shareholders.

Rights issues are cheaper to organise than a public share issue.

An issue price must be set which is:

- low enough to secure acceptance of shareholders, but
- not too low, so as to avoid excessive dilution of the earnings per share (see chapter 4 for further detail on earnings per share).

 Rights issues – further detail

Definition

A rights issue may be defined as:

- Raising of new capital by giving existing shareholders the right to subscribe to new shares in proportion to their current holdings. These shares are usually issued at a discount to market price.

Explanation

In a rights issue, the entity sets out to raise additional funds from its existing shareholders.

The entity does this by giving existing shareholders the opportunity to purchase additional shares. These shares are normally offered at a price lower than the current share price quoted. The entity cannot offer an unlimited supply at this lower price, otherwise the market price would fall to this value. Accordingly, the offer they make to the existing shareholders is limited. For example they may offer one new share for every four held.

> ### Selection of an issue price
>
> In theory, there is no upper limit to an issue price but in practice it would never be set higher than the prevailing market price (MPS) of the shares, otherwise shareholders will not be prepared to buy as they could have purchased more shares at the existing market price anyway. Indeed, the issue price is normally set at a discount on MPS. This discount is usually in the region of 20%. In theory, there is no lower limit to an issue price but in practice it can never be lower than the nominal value of the shares. Subject to these practical limitations, any price may be selected within these values. However, as the issue price selected is reduced, the quantity of shares that has to be issued to raise a required sum will be increased.
>
> ### Selection of an issue quantity
>
> It is normal for the issue price to be selected first and then the quantity of shares to be issued. The effect of the additional shares on earnings per share and dividend cover should be considered (these ratios will be covered later). The selected additional issue quantity will then be related to the existing share quantity for the issue terms to be calculated. The proportion is normally stated in its simplest form, for example, 1 for 4, meaning that shareholders may subscribe to purchase one new share for every four they currently hold.

Market price after issue

- After the announcement of a rights issue there is a tendency for share prices to fall.

- The temporary fall is due to uncertainty about:
    - consequences of the issue
    - future profits
    - future dividends.

- After the actual issue the market price will normally fall again because:
    - there are more shares in issue (adverse affect on earnings per share), and
    - new shares were issued at market price discount.

'Cum rights'

When a rights issue is announced, all existing shareholders have the right to subscribe for new shares, and so there are rights ('cum rights') attached to the shares, and the shares are traded 'cum rights'.

'Ex rights'

On the first day of dealings in the newly issued shares, the rights no longer exist and the old shares are now traded 'ex rights' (without rights attached).

Theoretical prices/values

Theoretical 'ex rights' price is the theoretical price that the class of shares will trade at on the first trading day after issue. It is calculated as follows:

$$\frac{(N \times \text{cum rights price}) + \text{Issue price}}{N + 1}$$

N = number of shares required to be held in order to receive one rights issued share (e.g. 1 for 4 rights issue, N = 4).

Illustration 1 – Rights issue
Lauchlan plc has 2m $1 ordinary shares in issue, with a current market value of $5 per share. It offers a 1 for 4 rights issue at $4 per share.

TERP

The cum rights price = $5

Issue price = $4

N = 4

Therefore, TERP = [(4 × $5) + $4]/5 = $4.80

NB. The calculation of TERP would not be a requirement to an exam question within syllabus area F2A1. It is included here for illustration purposes only. However, it will be revisited in chapter 4 EPS and the calculation could be a question as part of syllabus area F2C2.

Implications of a rights issue

(a) From the viewpoint of the shareholders:

- they have the option of buying shares at a preferential price
- they have the option of withdrawing cash by selling their rights
- they are able to maintain their existing relative voting position (by exercising the rights).

(b) From the viewpoint of the company:

- it is simple and cheap to implement
- it is usually successful ('fully subscribed')
- it often provides favourable publicity.

6 Debt finance

This is the loan of funds to a business without conferring ownership rights. The funding will create an obligation for the business to repay the capital and interest repayments based on the specific terms of the arrangement. The key features of debt financing are:

- Interest is paid out of pre-tax profits as an expense of the business.

- It carries a risk of default if interest and principal payments are not met.

Security – charges

To reduce its exposure to risk, the lender of funds will normally require some form of security against which the funds are advanced. This means that, in the event of default, the lender will be able to take assets in exchange of the amounts owing.

There are two types of 'charge' or security that may be offered/required:

1   **Fixed charge** – The debt is secured against a specific asset, normally land or buildings. This form of security is preferred because, in the event of liquidation, it puts the lender at the 'front of the queue' of creditors. An individual's mortgage works in the same fashion as a fixed charge for a business.

2   **Floating charge** – The debt is secured against underlying assets that are subject to changes in quantity or value e.g. inventory. The floating charge can cover any other assets that are not already subject to fixed charges. This form of security is not as strong as fixed securities offer earlier repayment on liquidation of the borrower. However, floating charges still provide 'preferred creditor' status, meaning that the lender is higher in the list of creditors than if no security was present.

Covenants

A further means of limiting the risk to the lender is to restrict the actions of the directors through the means of covenants. These are specific requirements or limitations laid down as a condition of taking on debt financing. They may include:

1   **Dividend restrictions** – Limitations on the level of dividends a company is permitted to pay. This is designed to prevent excessive dividend payments which may seriously weaken the company's future cash flows and thereby place the lender at greater risk.

2   **Financial ratios** – Specified levels below which certain ratios may not fall, e.g. debt to net assets ratio, current ratio.

3   **Financial reports** – Regular accounts and financial reports to be provided to the lender to monitor progress.

4   **Issue of further debt** – The amount and type of debt that can be issued may be restricted.

Examples of long-term debt finance – terminology

Bank finance

Loans

Banks typically provide short-term and long-term debt finance to businesses and individuals. Short-term are typically repayable within 12 months. Long-term repayable after 12 months. The banks will lend money which will be repayable at a pre-determined date (or dates) in the future. Interest will be also need to be paid to avoid defaulting on the loan based upon the specific terms negotiated.

Bonds

A bond is a debt security, in which the issuer owes the holders a debt and is obliged to pay interest and/or to repay the principal at a later date i.e. a bond is a formal contract to repay borrowed money with interest at fixed intervals.

Thus a bond is like a loan: the issuer is the borrower, the holder (or investor) is the lender. Bonds provide the borrower with external funds to satisfy long-term funding requirements.

Bonds and shares are both securities which can be traded in the capital markets, but the major difference between the two is that shareholders have an equity stake in the company (i.e. they are owners), whereas bondholders have a creditor stake in the company (i.e. they are lenders). Another difference is that bonds usually have a defined term, or maturity, after which the bond is repaid (known as being redeemed), whereas shares may be outstanding indefinitely.

Debt capital markets – further detail

Issuing debt finance (bonds) in the capital markets enables an entity to borrow a large amount of finance from (potentially) a wide range of potential investors.

The bond market can essentially be broken down into three main groups: issuers, underwriters and purchasers.

Issuers

The issuers sell bonds in the capital markets to fund the operations of their organisations. This area of the market is mostly made up of governments, banks and corporations.

The biggest of these issuers is the government, which uses the bond market to help fund a country's operations. Banks are also key issuers in the bond market, and they can range from local banks up to supranational banks such as the European Investment Bank. The final major issuer is corporations, which issue bonds to finance operations.

Underwriters

The underwriters within the bond market are typically investment banks and other financial institutions that help the issuer to sell the bonds in the market.

In most cases, huge amounts of finance are transacted in one offering. As a result, a lot of work needs to be done to prepare for the offering, such as creating a prospectus and other legal documents.

In general, the need for underwriters is greatest for the corporate debt market because there are more risks associated with this type of debt.

The underwriters can place the bonds with specific investors ('bond placement'), or they can attempt to sell the bonds more widely in the market. Alternatively, under a medium term note (MTN) programme, the issuer (via the underwriter) can issue debt securities on a regular and/or continuous basis.

Purchasers

The final players in the bond market are those who purchase the bonds. Purchasers can include any type of investor e.g. every group already mentioned including individuals.

Governments play one of the largest roles in the market because they borrow and lend money to other governments and banks. Furthermore, governments often invest in bonds issued by other countries if they have excess reserves of that country's money as a result of trade between countries. For example, Japan is a major holder of U.S. government debt, such as U.S. gilts.

7 Other sources of finance

Retained earnings/existing cash balances

An entity can use its current cash balances to finance new investments.

There is a common misconception that an entity with a large amount of retained earnings in its statement of financial position can fund its new investment projects using these retained earnings. This is not the case.

An entity can only use internal sources of finance to fund new projects if it has enough cash in hand.

The level of retained earnings reflects the amount of profit accumulated over the entity's life. It is not the same as cash.

Sale and leaseback

This means selling good quality fixed assets such as high street buildings and leasing them back over many years (25+). Funds are released without any loss of the use of the assets.

Any potential capital gain on the assets is forgone.

Sale and leaseback is a popular means of funding for retail organisations with substantial high street property e.g. Tesco, Marks and Spencer.

Grants

These are often related to technology, job creation or regional policy. They are of particular importance to small and medium-sized businesses (i.e. unlisted). Their key advantage is that they do not need to be paid back.

Grants can be provided by local governments, national governments, and other larger bodies such as the European Union.

Debt with warrants attached

A warrant is an option to buy shares at a specified point in the future for a specified (exercise) price. Warrants are often issued with a bond as a sweetener to encourage investors to purchase the bonds.

The warrant offers a potential capital gain where the share price may rise above the exercise price.

The holder has the option to buy the share on the exercise date but can also choose to sell the warrant before that date with no impact on the bond. The warrant and bond are considered as separate items once issued.

Convertible debt

This is similar to attaching a warrant to a debt instrument (as described above) except that the option to convert to shares (the warrant) cannot be detached and traded separately.

With convertible debt, the debt itself can be converted into shares at a predetermined price at a date or range of dates in the future. For example, a $1m loan has an option to convert into 10 new shares for every $100 of loan in 3 years' time.

This has the effect of giving the debt holder a potential capital gain over and above the return from the repayment of the debt. If the value of the shares is greater than value of the debt on the exercise date, then conversion should be made by the investor. If the share value is lower than the debt value, the investor should retain the debt until maturity.

Venture capital

This is finance provided to young, unquoted profit-making entities to help them to expand. It is usually provided in the form of equity finance, but may be a mix of equity and debt.

Venture capitalists generally accept low levels of dividends and expect to make most of their returns as capital gains on exit. A typical exit route is an IPO or flotation, which enables the venture capitalist to sell his stake in the entity on the stock market.

Business angels

Business angels are similar to venture capitalists. Venture capitalists are rarely interested in investing in very small businesses, on the grounds that monitoring progress is uneconomic.

Business angels are wealthy investors who provide equity finance to small businesses.

Test your understanding 1 (further OTQs)

1 _____ preference shares are those for which dividends must be paid in a following year if they are not paid in the current year. _____ preference shares give the holder fixed dividends plus extra earnings based on certain conditions being achieved.

Select the correct words to complete the above sentences, from the following options:

convertible, cumulative, irredeemable, participating, redeemable

2 Capital markets fulfil two functions, one of which is to enable investors to sell investments to other investors.

Is this the primary function or secondary function? Select the correct answer below.

A   Primary function.

B   Secondary function.

3 When fixing security, a lender of funds will prefer a f_____ charge.

Select the correct word to complete the above sentence, from the following options:

fixed, floating

---

8 Chapter summary

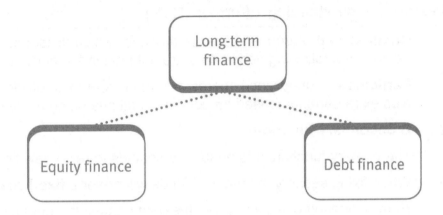

Test your understanding answers

Test your understanding 1 (further OTQs)
1 **Cumulative** preference share are those for which dividends must be paid in a following year if they are not paid in the current year. **Participating** preference shares give the holder fixed dividends plus extra earnings based on certain conditions being achieved. 2 **B Secondary function** The primary function is to enable companies to raise new finance. 3 When fixing security, a lender of funds will prefer a **fixed** charge. **Note:** a floating charge secures the debt against the underlying assets that are subject to changes in quantity and value whereas a fixed charge is against a specific asset. Therefore a fixed charge is preferable as, in the event of a liquidation, the lender would have a right to the specific asset secured. The fixed charge holder would be paid earlier than a floating charge holder.

Cost of capital

Chapter learning objectives

Lead outcome	Component outcome
A2: Calculate cost of long term funds	Calculate: (a) Cost of equity (b) Cost of debt (c) Weighted average cost of capital

1 Session content

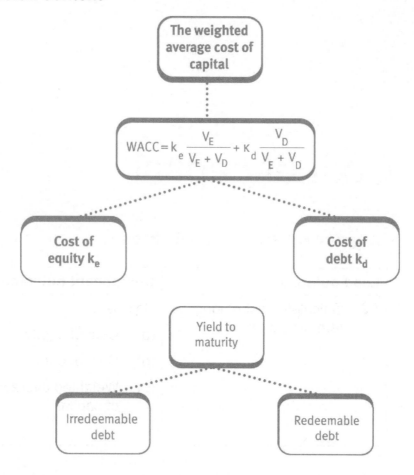

2 Introduction

The weighted average cost of capital (WACC) measures the average cost of an entity's finance. Entities often use the WACC as a discount rate in net present value (NPV) calculations.

The WACC is derived by first estimating the cost of each source of finance separately (e.g. ordinary shares, debt, preference shares) and then taking a weighted average of these individual costs, using the following formula:

$$k_0 = k_e \left[\frac{V_E}{V_E + V_D}\right] + k_d \left[\frac{V_D}{V_E + V_D}\right]$$

k_0 = WACC

3 The cost of equity – k_e

The cost of equity is the rate of return that ordinary shareholders expect to receive on their investment. The main method of computing k_e is the dividend valuation model (DVM).

The dividend valuation model (DVM)

The DVM states that the current share price is determined by the future dividends, discounted at the investors' required rate of return.

$$P_0 = \frac{d}{k_e}$$

where k_e = cost of equity

d = is the constant dividend

P_0 = the ex div market price of the share

This is a variant of the formula for a PV of a perpetuity.

We can re-arrange the formula to get the one below:

The dividend valuation model with constant dividends

$$k_e = \frac{d}{P_0}$$

DVM – further detail

The DVM is a method of calculating cost of equity.

This model makes the assumption that the market price of a share is related to the future dividend income stream from that share, in such a way that the market price is assumed to be the present value of that future dividend income stream.

This is known as the fundamental theory of share valuation.

Cum div and ex div share prices

The ex dividend ('ex div') value of a share is the value just after a dividend has been paid. Occasionally in questions, you may be given a share price just before the payment of a dividend (a 'cum div' price). In this case, the value of the upcoming dividend should be deducted from the cum div price to give the ex div price.

For example, if a dividend of 20 cents is due to be paid on a share which has a cum div value of $3.45, the ex div share price to be entered into the DVM formula is $3.45 – $0.20 = $3.25.

Illustration 1 – k_e with constant dividends

The ordinary shares of Jones plc are quoted at $4 per share. A dividend of 30 cents is about to be paid. There is expected to be no growth in dividends.

Required:

Calculate the cost of equity.

Solution

$$k_e = \frac{30}{400 - 30} = 8.1\%$$

Test your understanding 1 (OTQ style)

The ordinary shares of Smith plc are quoted at $12 per share. A dividend of 75 cents per share is about to be paid. There is expected to be no growth in dividends.

Required:

Calculate the cost of equity. Give your answer to 1 decimal place.

Introducing growth

The dividend valuation model with constant growth

$$k_e = \frac{d_1}{P_0} + g$$

NB. This formula is provided in the formulae sheet within the exam.

or

$$k_e = \frac{d_0(1 + g)}{P_0} + g$$

Where:

g = a constant rate of growth in dividends

d_1 = dividend to be paid in one year's time

d_0 = current dividend

P_0 = the ex div market price of the share

Illustration 2 – k_e with constant dividend growth

The ordinary shares of Jones plc are quoted at $4 per share. A dividend of 30 cents is about to be paid. The expected growth rate of dividends is 5%.

Required:

Calculate the cost of equity.

Solution

$$k_e = \frac{30 \times 1.05}{400 - 30} + 0.05 = 13.5\%$$

 Test your understanding 2 (OTQ style)

The ordinary shares of Smith plc are quoted at $12 per share. A dividend of 75 cents per share is about to be paid. The expected growth rate in the dividend is 8%.

Required:

Calculate the cost of equity. Give your answer to 1 decimal place.

Estimating growth within the DVM

The growth rate used in the cost of equity calculation will not always be provided within the information relating to the question. It may be required to be separately calculated.

Two main methods to calculate dividend growth are examinable. They are:

- the averaging method

- the growth model based upon the profit retention rate.

NB. The examiner may also give you the growth rate within questions. You will not always be expected to calculate the growth.

1 **Averaging method (Historical method)**

$$g = \sqrt[n]{\frac{d_o}{d_n}} - 1$$

Where d_o = current dividend

d_n = dividend n years ago

NB. This formula is provided in the formulae sheet within the exam.

Illustration 3 – k_e and the averaging method for dividend growth

A company paid a dividend of 8 cents per share eight years ago. The current dividend is 13 cents. The current share price is $2.76 ex div.

Required

Calculate the cost of equity (state your answer to 1 decimal place)

Solution

To work out growth

$g = (13/8)^{1/8} - 1 = 0.0626 = 6.26\%$

NB. To the power of 1/8 is equal to the 8th root.

To work out the cost of equity

$K_e = (13 \times 1.0626/276) + 0.0626 = 0.1126 = 11.3\%$

2 Growth model based upon the profit retention rate

$$g = r \times b$$

Where:

g = dividend growth rate

r = percentage rate of return the company receives on its investment

b = proportion of funds retained (aka proportion of profits not distributed as dividends).

NB. This formula is provided in the formulae sheet within the exam.

Assumptions of the growth model based on retention rate

The rationale behind the model is that an increase in the level of investment by a company (caused by profits not paid out as dividends) will give rise to increases (and therefore growth) in future dividends.

The two key elements in determining future dividend growth will be the rate of reinvestment by the company (aka, the rate of retained profits) and the required return generated by the investments.

There are a number of assumptions required to apply this model:

- the entity must be fully financed by equity

- the retained profits are the only source of additional investment

- a constant proportion of each year's earnings is retained for reinvestment

- projects financed from retained earnings earn a constant rate of return.

Illustration 4 – k_e and growth using profit retention rate

The ordinary shares of Klopp are quoted at $7.00 cum div. A dividend of 50c is just about to be paid. The company has an annual return on reinvested funds of 12% and each year pays out 70% of its profit after tax as dividends.

Required:

Calculate the cost of equity. Give your answer to 2 decimal places.

Solution

Firstly work out the growth rate

$g = r \times b = 12\% \times 30\% = 3.6\%$

NB. 70% of the profits are paid as dividends meaning 30% of the profit is retained.

Then work out the cost of equity

$k_e = [(d_0 \times (1 + g)/P_0] + g$

$= [0.5 \times 1.036/(7 - 0.5)] + 0.036$

$= 11.57\%$

The cost of preference shares

Preference shares usually pay a constant level of dividend, which is quoted as a percentage of nominal value. Hence, the cost of preference shares (k_p) can be calculated using a formula very similar to k_e assuming constant dividends (no growth). The formula is:

$$k_p = \frac{d}{P_0}$$

d = is the constant dividend

P_0 = the ex div market price of the share

k_p = the cost of preference shares

4 The cost of debt – k_d

The cost of debt is the rate of return that debt providers require on the funds that they provide.

The value of debt is assumed to be the present value of its future cash flows.

Features of debt

1 Interest on debt is tax deductible and hence interest payments are always considered net of tax

2 Debt is always quoted in $100 nominal units or blocks.

3 Interest paid on the debt is stated as a percentage of nominal value. This is known as the coupon rate. The amount of interest payable on the debt is fixed. The interest paid is calculated as the coupon rate multiplied by the nominal value of the debt. Interest paid is not the same as the cost of debt.

4 Debt is redeemable (repaid) at par (nominal value) or at a premium or discount.

5 Interest can be either fixed or floating (variable) on borrowings, but bonds normally pay fixed rate interest.

k_d for bank borrowings

The cost of debt for bank borrowings is simply $k_d = r (1 - T)$

where:

   r = annual interest rate in percentage terms

   T = corporate tax rate

k_d for irredeemable, or undated, bonds

It is highly unusual for a bond to be irredeemable but, if it were, the cost of debt could be calculated as follows:

$$k_d = \frac{i(1 - T)}{P_0}$$

Where:

i = interest paid each year (per $100 of bond)

T = marginal rate of tax

P_0 = ex interest market price of the bonds, normally quoted per 100 unit nominal

Note that **this formula can also be applied** to **redeemable bonds** where the redemption value is equal to the current market price or as an approximation for **long-dated debt**.

NB. This formula is provided in the formulae sheet within the exam.

For bonds trading at par, P_0 is the nominal value and so this formula can be simplified to $k_d = r(1-T)$, where r is the interest rate, expressed in percentage terms.

Illustration 5 – k_d for long-dated bonds

The 10% long-dated bonds of an entity are quoted at $130 ex int. Corporation tax is payable at 30%.

Required:

Calculate the net of tax cost of debt. Give your answer to 1 decimal place.

Solution

$$k_d = \frac{10(1 - 0.30)}{130} = 5.4\%$$

Test your understanding 3 (OTQ style)

The 8% long-dated bonds of an entity are quoted at $127 ex int. Corporation tax is payable at 25%.

Required:

Calculate the net of tax cost of debt. Give your answer to 1 decimal place.

The internal rate of return (IRR)

Definition

The IRR is the discount rate which gives a zero NPV.

Calculation

It can be estimated by working out the net present value (NPV) at two different interest rates (L, the lower rate, and H, the higher rate) and then using the following (linear interpolation) formula:

$$L + \left(\frac{NPV_L}{NPV_L - NPV_H}\right)(H - L)$$

This formula does appear in your formula sheet provided in the exam.

k_d for redeemable bonds

The k_d for redeemable bonds is given by the IRR of the relevant cash flows associated with the bond.

The relevant cash flows would be (assuming that there is no one year delay in the tax saving):

Year	Cash flow	
0	Market value of the bond (or nominal value if being issued or is trading at par)	(P_0)
1 to n	Annual interest payments net of tax	$i(1 - T)$
n	Redemption value of the bond	RV

There are three steps to ensuring an accurate computation:

1   Identify the cash flows. Note that the interest payments should be included net of tax when calculating the cost of debt for bonds from the viewpoint of the issuer.

2   Choose 2 discount factors and calculate two NPVs (preferably one providing a negative NPV and one providing a positive NPV).

3   Calculate the IRR.

NB Discount factors and cumulative discount factors are provided via tables in the examination.

Illustration 6 – k_d for redeemable bonds

An entity has some 10% bonds quoted at $95.00 ex int redeemable at par in five years' time. Corporation tax is paid at 31%.

Required:

Calculate the entity's cost of debt.

Solution

Cash flows

Year 0	$95.00
Year 1 – 5	$10 (1 – 0.31) = $6.90
Year 5	$100.00

Discounting

Year	Cash flow	Disc. fact. @ 6%	Present value	Disc. fact. @ 10%	Present value
0	(95.00)	1	(95.00)	1	(95.00)
1 – 5	6.90	4.212	29.06	3.791	26.16
5	100.00	0.747	74.70	0.621	62.10
Total			+8.76		–6.74

$$IRR = 6\% + \left[(10\% - 6\%) \times \frac{8.76}{(8.76 + 6.74)} \right] = 8.26\%$$

Test your understanding 4 (OTQ style)

An entity has 8% bonds quoted at $92.00 ex int redeemable at par in three years' time. Corporation tax is paid at 27%.

Required:

Calculate the entity's cost of debt. Give your answer to 2 decimal places.

The cost of convertible bonds

Convertible bonds offer the investor a choice of cash or shares on the redemption date.

In practice, particularly if the value of the cash or share option are very similar, some investors will choose cash for liquidity reasons, whereas other investors may choose shares, hoping for large dividend returns in the future.

In order to calculate the cost of convertible bonds, we make a simplifying assumption that all investors will make the same decision.

Illustration

Consider a 10% $100 bond which is redeemable at par in 5 years, or convertible into 10 shares at that time. The bond is issued at par. The current share price is $8.60 and historically, dividends (and hence share prices) have grown at 5% per annum. The tax rate is 20%.

Step 1 – Work out which conversion option is likely to be used

To decide which option is likely to be chosen by investors, we compare:

- the value of the cash option, that is $100 (redemption at par)

- the value of the conversion option, i.e. $10 \times (\$8.60 \times 1.05^5) = \$109.76$.

Hence, it is assumed that all investors will choose the conversion option.

Step 2 – Determine the cost of capital

The cost of the convertible debt is calculated in a similar way to the cost of redeemable debt but the value of the highest conversion option is used as the cash flow at redemption.

It is the IRR of:

Year	Cash flow	$
0	Market value of the loan	(P_0)
1 to n	Annual net interest payments	$i(1 - T)$
n	**The higher of the cash and the conversion option**	C

Cash flows

Year 0	$100.00
Year 1 – 5	$10 (1 – 0.2) = $8
Year 5	$109.76

IRR

Year	Cash flow	Disc. fact. @ 5%	Present value	Disc. fact. @ 10%	Present value
0	(100.00)	1	(100.00)	1	(100.00)
1 – 5	8	4.329	34.63	3.791	30.33
5	109.76	0.784	86.05	0.621	68.16
Total			+20.68		–1.51

$$IRR = 5\% + \left[(10\% - 5\%) \times \frac{20.68}{(20.68 + 1.51)}\right] = 9.66\%$$

Cost of the convertible debt is 9.66%

---

5 Weighted Average Cost of Capital (WACC)

The weighted average cost of capital (WACC) is the average cost of the entity's finance (equity, bonds, bank loans, and preference shares) weighted according to the proportion each element bears to the total pool of funds.

In the analysis so far carried out, each source of finance has been examined in isolation. However, the practical business situation is that there is a continuous raising of funds from various sources. These funds are used, partly in existing operations and partly to finance new projects. There is not normally any separation between funds from different sources and their application to specific projects.

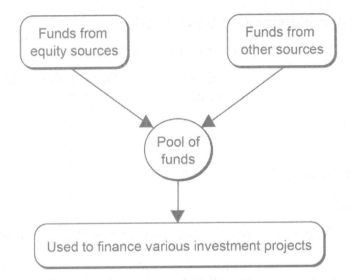

In order to provide a measure for evaluating these projects, the cost of the pool of funds is required. This is referred to as the weighted average cost of capital (WACC).

The general approach is to calculate the cost of each source of finance, then to weight these according to their proportion in the financing mix.

Procedure for calculating the WACC

Step 1 Calculate weights/proportions for each source of capital based upon market values.

Step 2 Estimate the cost of each source of capital.

Step 3 Multiply the weight/proportion of each source of capital by the cost of that source of capital (step 1 x step 2).

Step 4 Sum the results of step 3 to give the weighted average cost of capital.

Formula – given in the assessment

$$k_0 = k_e \left[\frac{V_E}{V_E + V_D} \right] + k_d \left[\frac{V_D}{V_E + V_D} \right]$$

Alternative WACC formula

Using market values for a firm with equity, debt and preference shares in its capital structure, the WACC would be:

$$k_0 = \frac{k_e V_e + k_P V_P + k_d V_d}{V_e + V_P + V_d}$$

where Ve, Vp and Vd are the market values of equity, preference shares and debt respectively.

Test your understanding 5 (OTQ style)

Rebmatt Co has a capital structure as follows.

	Cost of capital %	Book value $m	Market value $m
Bank loans	6	5	5
Bonds	10	8	5
Ordinary shares	15	18	30

Required:

Calculate Rebmatt's WACC. Give your answer to 2 decimal places.

Test your understanding 6 (integration question)

The following is an extract from the statement of financial position of Gate Co at 30 September 20X4:

	$
Ordinary shares of 25 cents each	250,000
Reserves	350,000
7% preference shares of $1 each	250,000
15% long-dated bonds	150,000
Total long-term funds	1,000,000

The ordinary shares are currently quoted at $1.25 each, the bonds trading at $85 per $100 nominal and the preference shares at 65 cents each. The ordinary dividend of 10 cents has just been paid, and the expected growth rate in the dividend is 10%. Corporation tax is at the rate of 30%.

Required:

Calculate the weighted average cost of capital for Gate Co. Give your answer to 1 decimal place.

Problems with the computation of WACC

The sources of finance to include

The above examples have concentrated on the cost of long-term finance. Firms also raise finance from short-term sources, e.g. overdrafts, short-term loans, trade credit etc. It is possible to calculate a cost for short-term finance. Therefore, consideration is required as to whether short-term finance should be included in WACC calculations. The usual argument is that the weighted average cost of capital is a tool for appraising long-term investments and as these should only be financed by long-term funds then the costs of short-term funds should be excluded. However, if it is clear that short-term finance is being used to fund long-term projects, then it should be included.

Loans without market values

Bank loans do not have market values in the same way as bonds. As a result, weightings in WACC will be calculated using book values of loans as an approximation of market value.

Cost of capital for small entities

There are important factors which are relevant to the cost of capital of small entities:

- If the entity is unquoted, then obtaining the cost of finance is much more difficult.

- The lack of liquidity offered by the entity's securities, plus the smaller size of the entity, tend to make finance more expensive.

When can WACC be used as a discount rate?

The WACC is often used as a discount rate when using net present value or internal rate of return calculations. However, this is only appropriate if the following conditions are met:

1   The capital structure is constant. If the capital structure changes, the weightings in the WACC will also change.

2   The new investment does not carry a different business risk profile to the existing entity's operations. Basically, the new investment is not a significant departure in strategy and is similar in nature to the typical projects carried out by the entity.

3   The new investment is marginal to the entity. If we are only looking at a small investment then we would not expect any of k_e, k_d or the WACC to change materially. If the investment is substantial it will usually cause these values to change.

6 Yield to maturity (YTM)

The yield to maturity

So far in this chapter we have seen how the WACC requires calculation of the cost of equity (k_e) and the cost of debt (k_d). The cost of equity and the cost of debt is considered from the perspective of an entity raising finance.

This section will cover the calculation of the yield to maturity (aka the yield on debt).

The yield to maturity is very similar to the calculation of k_d. The main difference is that the yield to maturity is calculated from the **investor's** perspective (the entity/person PROVIDING the finance).

An investor who purchases a traded debt instrument (e.g. a bond) receives a return, known as a 'yield', in the form of the annual interest (or 'coupon') payments and, if the debt is redeemable, the final redemption payment. Before making the investment, the investor will be interested in determining the percentage return. This will allow the investor to make an informed decision as to whether they consider the investment worthwhile. It also allows comparison against other similar investments. This return is also known as the 'yield to maturity' (YTM), or 'redemption yield', on the bond.

YTM is defined as the effective average annual percentage return to the investor, relative to the current market value of the bond.

As investors do not obtain tax relief from any interest received, YTM is calculated using pre-tax interest receipts. This means that tax is not deducted from any interest received within the YTM calculation.

NB. This is another major difference between YTM and the cost of debt (k_d) calculation. As previously noted, k_d will consider post-tax interest within its calculation. Tax is deducted from interest within k_d calculations.

If the bond is irredeemable, the YTM calculation is very simple. However, YTM becomes more complex if the bond is redeemable.

Yield on irredeemable debt

For irredeemable debt:

YTM = (annual interest received/current market value of debt) × 100%

The yield calculation is always calculated in units of $100 nominal value of bond.

Illustration 7 – YTM for irredeemable bonds

Knife plc, a UK listed company, has some 5% coupon, $100 nominal value, irredeemable bonds in issue, which have a current market value of $95.

Required:

Calculate the yield to maturity for these bonds.

Solution

YTM = (annual interest/current market value) × 100%

= (5/95) × 100% = 5.26%

Note that the coupon rate is applied to the nominal value to calculate the annual interest, but otherwise, the nominal value is not used in the calculation.

Test your understanding 7 (OTQ style)

Fork plc, a UK listed company, has some 7% coupon, $100 nominal value, irredeemable bonds in issue, which have a current market value of $93.50.

Give your answer to 2 decimal places.

Required:

Calculate the yield to maturity for these bonds.

Yield on redeemable debt

YTM for redeemable debt = the internal rate of return (IRR) of the bond price, the annual interest received and the final redemption amount.

This ensures that the yield calculation incorporates a return in the form of the final redemption amount as well as the annual interest amounts.

Illustration 8 – YTM for redeemable bonds

Knife plc also has some 7% coupon, $100 nominal value bonds in issue, which are redeemable at a 10% premium in 5 years. The current market value of the bonds is $98.

Required:

Calculate the yield to maturity for these bonds.

Solution

The yield to maturity for these redeemable bonds is found by taking the IRR of the current market value (98 at t_0), the annual interest (7 per annum from t_1 to t_5), and the redemption amount (110 at t_5), as follows:

Time	$	DF 5%	PV	DF 10%	PV
t_0	(98)	1	(98)	1	(98)
$t_1 - t_5$	7	4.329	30.30	3.791	26.54
t_5	110	0.784	86.24	0.621	68.31
			18.54		(3.15)

Hence IRR = 5% + [(10% − 5%) × 18.54/(18.54 + 3.15)] = 9.27%.

Test your understanding 8 (OTQ style)

Fork plc also has some 4% coupon, $100 nominal value bonds in issue, which are redeemable at a 7% premium in 3 years. The current market value of the bonds is $95.

Give your answer to 2 decimal places.

Required:

Calculate the yield to maturity for these bonds.

Test your understanding 9 (further OTQs)

1   KM plc has 500,000 $1 par value shares in issue that are trading at $1.35. It has recently paid a dividend of $60,000. Dividends are expected to grow by 5% per annum.

　　The cost of equity is:

　　A　8.9%

　　B　9.3%

　　C　14.3%

　　D　15.2%

2　CG has in issue 6% irredeemable debentures currently quoted at $92 per $100 nominal value. CG pays corporate income tax at a rate of 20%.

　　Calculate the post-tax cost of debt. Give your answer as a percentage to one decimal place.

3   RP's cost of equity is 12% and the yield on its debt is 7%. Its debt to equity ratio is 3:2 based on book value and 5:3 based on market value. The corporate income tax rate is 25%.

Calculate the weighted average cost of capital (WACC). Give your answer as a percentage to one decimal place.

4   Joe plc, a UK listed company, has 6% coupon, $100 nominal value, irredeemable bonds in issue, which have a current market value of $96.25.

Calculate the yield to maturity for these bonds. State your answer to two decimal places.

5   Sofia plc has 5% coupon, $100 nominal value bonds in issue, which are redeemable at an 8% premium in 5 years. The current market value of the bonds is $94.

Calculate the yield to maturity for these bonds. State your answer to two decimal places. Use discount rates of 5% and 10% to determine your answer.

7   Chapter summary

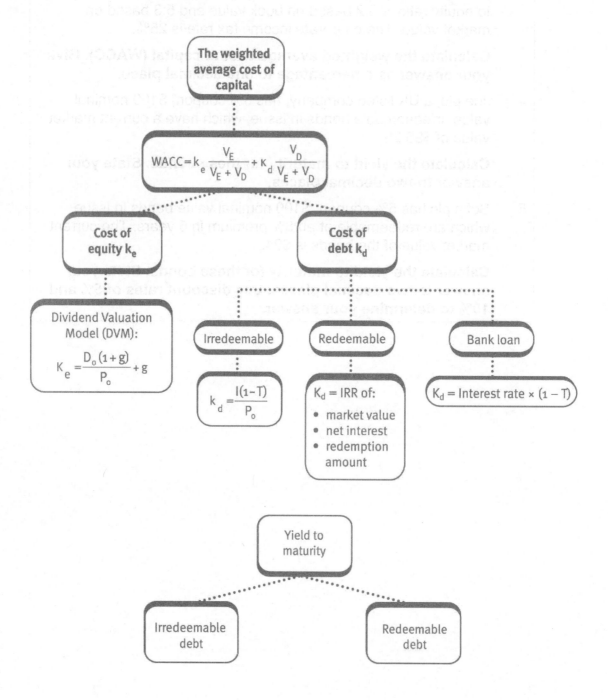

Test your understanding answers

Test your understanding 1 (OTQ style)

$$k_e = \frac{0.75}{12 - 0.75} = 6.7\%$$

Test your understanding 2 (OTQ style)

$$k_e = \frac{0.75 \times 1.08}{12 - 0.75} + 0.08 = 15.2\%$$

Test your understanding 3 (OTQ style)

$$k_d = \frac{8(1 - 0.25)}{127} = 4.7\%$$

Test your understanding 4 (OTQ style)

Cash flows

Year 0	$92.00
Year 1 – 3	$8 (1 – 0.27) = $5.84
Year 3	$100.00

Discounting

Year	Cash flow	Disc. fact. @ 5%	Present value	Disc. fact. @ 12%	Present value
0	(92.00)	1	(92.00)	1	(92.00)
1 – 3	5.84	2.723	15.90	2.402	14.03
3	100	0.864	86.40	0.712	71.20
Total			+10.30		–6.77

$$IRR = 5\% + \left[(12\% - 5\%) \times \frac{10.30}{(10.30 + 6.77)}\right] = 9.22\%$$

Test your understanding 5 (OTQ style)

The calculation is carried out as follows:

Source	Market value (MV)		Cost of capital	Weighted cost
	$m	Proportions (Individual MV/Total MV of finance)		%
Bank loans	5	0.125	× 6% =	0.75
Bonds	5	0.125	× 10% =	1.25
Ordinary shares	30	0.75	× 15% =	11.25
Total MV of finance	40	1.00		13.25

WACC = 13.25%

Test your understanding 6 (integration question)

Solution:

Market values of the securities:

Equity = 1,000,000 × $1.25 = $1,250,000

Preference = 250,000 × $0.65 = $162,500

Bonds = 150,000 × 85% = $127,500

So total market value = 1,250,000 + 162,500 + 127,500 = $1,540,000

Cost of equity (k_e) =

$$\frac{10 \times 1.1}{125} + 0.10 = 18.8\%$$

Cost of preference shares (k_p) =

$$\frac{7}{65} = 10.8\%$$

Cost of bonds (k_d) = i(1 − T)/P$_0$

$$\frac{15(1 - 0.3)}{85} = 12.4\%$$

Weighted average cost of capital

Source	Market value $000	Proportions (Individual MV/Total MV of finance)	Cost of capital	Weighted cost %
Equity	1,250	0.812	× 18.8% =	15.3
Preference shares	162.5	0.106	× 10.8% =	1.1
Bonds	127.5	0.083	× 12.4% =	1.0
Total MV of finance	1,540	1.00		17.4

WACC = 17.4%

Test your understanding 7

YTM = (annual interest/current market value) × 100%

= (7/93.5) × 100% = 7.49%

Test your understanding 8

Year	$	DF 5%	PV	DF 10%	PV
0	(95)	1	(95)	1	(95)
1–3	4	2.723	10.89	2.487	9.95
3	107	0.864	92.45	0.751	80.36
			8.34		(4.69)

Hence IRR = 5% + [(10% − 5%) × 8.34/(8.34 + 4.69)] = 8.20%

Test your understanding 9 (further OTQs)

1   **C   Cost of equity = 14.3%**

$$k_e = \frac{12 \times 1.05}{135} + 0.05 = 14.3\%$$

Dividend per share = $60,000/500,000 = $0.12

Dividend has already been paid so don't deduct it from market price of share (price is already ex div)

2   **Post-tax cost of debt = 5.2%**

(6 × 0.8)/92 = 5.2%

3   **WACC = 7.8%**

WACC = ((7 × 0.75) × 5/8) + (12 × 3/8) = 3.3 + 4.5 = 7.8%

NB the yield on the bond is not the same as the cost of debt. Yields give the interest return pre-tax. Cost of debt must be considered post tax therefore cost of debt was 5.25% (7 x 0.75).

4   **6.23%**

YTM = (annual interest/current market value) × 100%

= (6/96.25) × 100% = 6.23%

5   **8.0%**

Year	$	DF 5%	PV	DF 10%	PV
0	(94)	1	(94)	1	(94)
1–5	5	4.329	21.65	3.791	18.96
5	108	0.784	84.67	0.621	67.07
			12.32		(7.97)

Hence IRR = 5% + [(10% − 5%) × 12.32/(12.32 + 7.97)] = 8.04%

Financial instruments

Chapter learning objectives

Lead outcome	Component outcome
B1: Explain relevant financial reporting standards for revenue, leases, financial instruments, intangible assets and provisions	Explain the financial reporting standards for: (d) Financial instruments

1 Session content

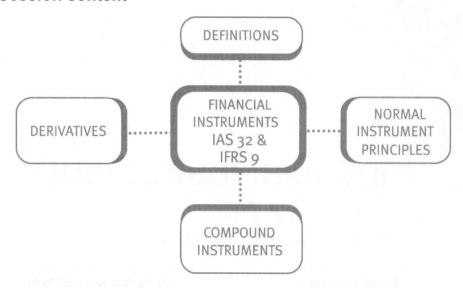

2 Introduction

Syllabus area F2B covers 'Financial reporting standards'. Chapter 3 and Chapter 5 to 10 inclusive cover topics that fall under this syllabus area. Financial reporting standards makes up 25% of the F2 syllabus.

The first financial reporting standards covered in this chapter are relevant to the accounting of financial instruments.

Definitions

 A **financial instrument** is **'any contract that gives rise to a financial asset of one entity and a financial liability or equity instrument of another entity'** (IAS 32, para 11).

Think of financial instruments as anything that can be used to finance a business.

As seen in chapter 1, businesses can **raise** finance for themselves via debt or equity. When raising finance, an entity may use financial liabilities and equity instruments.

Businesses can also **provide** finance for other entities e.g. banks giving loans to customers, companies acquiring bonds/debentures. When providing finance an entity will create a financial asset.

'A **financial asset is** any asset that is:

- **cash**

- **an equity instrument of another entity**

- **a contractual right to receive cash or another financial asset from another entity**

- **a contractual right to exchange financial instruments with another entity under conditions that are potentially favourable'** (IAS 32, para 11).

Examples of financial assets are:

- Investments in ordinary shares of another entity

- Investments in debentures/loan stock/loan notes/bonds i.e. lending money to another entity.

 'A **financial liability** is any liability that is a contractual obligation:

- **to deliver cash or another financial asset to another entity**

- **to exchange financial instruments with another entity under conditions that are potentially unfavourable'** (IAS 32, para 11).

Examples of financial liabilities include:

- Issue of debentures/loan stock/loan notes/bonds i.e. borrowing money from another entity

- Trade payables

- Loans from financial institutions.

 An **equity instrument** is **'any contract that evidences a residual interest in the assets of an entity after deducting all of its liabilities'** (IAS 32, para 11).

An example of an equity instrument would be:

- an issue of ordinary shares.

Accounting standards

There are three accounting standards that deal with financial instruments:

- IAS 32 *Financial instruments: presentation*
- IFRS® 7 *Financial instruments: disclosures*
- IFRS® 9 *Financial instruments.*

IAS 32 deals with the classification of financial instruments and their presentation in financial statements.

IFRS 7 deals with the disclosure of financial instruments in financial statements. **This standard is not examinable in the F2 syllabus.**

IFRS 9 deals with how financial instruments are measured and when they should be recognised in financial statements.

IFRS 9 is effective for annual periods beginning on or after 1 January 2018. IFRS 9 supersedes IAS® 39 *Financial instruments: recognition and measurement*, the stipulations of which are no longer examinable.

Why issue a new accounting standard?

In recent years, there has been a huge growth worldwide in the variety and complexity of financial instruments in international financial markets.

The impact of recent corporate scandals (e.g. Enron, Parmalat) and the global economic crisis were felt by individuals and businesses alike. Financial instruments, and the accounting of which, were right at the heart of these significant events.

In the aftermath of the economic crisis, numerous concerns about the accounting practices used for financial instruments were raised which led to demand for changes to the accounting standards. Problems included the following:

- there had been significant growth in the number and complexity of financial instruments
- accounting standards had not developed in line with the growth in instruments
- financial instruments were found to be overstated and unrealised losses were not recognised
- companies could choose when to recognise profits on instruments in order to smooth overall profits.

As a result, IFRS 9 was issued which introduces robust new classification rules for financial instruments and adopts a more prudent accounting approach aimed at reducing the risks described.

3 Classification of financial instruments in the issuing entity

IAS 32 Financial instruments: presentation provides the rules on classifying financial instruments as liabilities or equity.

 Presentation of liabilities and equity

The **issuer** of a financial instrument must classify it as a financial liability or equity instrument on initial recognition according to its substance.

Financial liabilities

The instrument will be classified as a liability if the issuer has a contractual **obligation:**

- to deliver cash (or another financial asset) to the holder

- to exchange financial instruments on potentially unfavourable terms.

Equity instruments

A financial instrument is only an equity instrument if there is no such contractual obligation.

 Illustration 1 – Preference shares

> The above definitions ensure that substance over form is reflected and that any obligations are correctly presented as liabilities.
>
> Consider the classification of redeemable preference shares. Legally they are called shares, however, if we consider their characteristics, a different interpretation could be applied.
>
> The entity receives an inflow of cash upon their issue, it then makes annual payments based on a percentage of the nominal value of the 'shares' and, at a specified point in the future, the cash is repaid. From a commercial perspective, they are just like a loan. As a result, the substance dictates that they should be classified as debt instruments.
>
> Even if the preference shares are not redeemable, they are still typically considered to be liabilities if they are 'cumulative'. This means that there is a contractual obligation to pay the preference dividends in a future period if they cannot be paid out in the current year.

Interest, dividends, losses and gains

- The accounting treatment of interest, dividends, losses and gains relating to a financial instrument follows the treatment of the instrument itself.

- For example, dividends paid in respect of preference shares classified as a liability will be charged as an expense (finance costs) through profit or loss.

- Dividends paid on shares classified as equity will be reported in the statement of changes in equity through retained earnings.

Offsetting a financial asset and a financial liability

IAS 32 states that **'a financial asset and a financial liability may only be offset in very limited circumstances. The net amount may only be reported when the entity:**

- **has a legally enforceable right to set off the amounts, and**

- **intends either to settle on a net basis, or to realise the asset and settle the liability simultaneously'** (IAS 32, para 42).

4 Recognition and measurement of financial instruments

IFRS 9 *Financial instruments,* provides guidance on when financial instruments should be recognised in the financial statements and how they should be measured.

Initial measurement of financial instruments

 IFRS 9 *Financial instruments* says that a financial instrument should be initially recognised at its **fair value**.

Subsequent measurement of financial instruments

Issued equity instruments (where the entity issues shares to raise finance) are not re-measured after initial recognition.

Subsequent measurement of other financial instruments depends on how that particular financial instrument is classified.

This text will cover the initial recognition and subsequent treatment of financial liabilities and financial assets in turn, starting below with financial liabilities.

5   Financial liabilities

NB. An entity will **raise** finance by **ISSUING** bonds/loan stock/debentures. This creates a financial liability.

 Exam scenarios regarding financial instruments often include terminology that initially can seem daunting. Below is an example of a typical financial liability and the subsequent table includes an explanation of some of the terminology used.

'An entity issues 5% $100 debentures at a discount of 4%. The debenture is redeemable after 5 years at a premium of 10%.'

Term	Definition	Equivalent from example
Par value	Headline value of a debenture/bond. Can also be described as the nominal value.	$100
Coupon rate	Minimum interest repayment per annum based on par values.	5% × $100 = $5 interest repayment each year (in cash)
Discount	If the loan is issued at a discount, the cash amount received from the loan is less than the par value.	Discount of 4% = 4% of $100 = $4 The amount initially received would be $96.
Redemption date	Date of repayment of capital element of loan aka the maturity date.	5 years
Premium	Extra amount repayable at redemption date based on par values.	$10 10% premium on par value of $100 = repayment of $110 (premium of $10)
Effective interest rate	The rate of interest that spreads the total finance costs, including discounts, premiums and coupon rate repayments, across the life of the loan at a constant rate.	None given but it can be determined via an internal rate of return calculation. In exam questions the effective interest rate will be given.

Initial measurement of financial liabilities

 IFRS 9 *Financial instruments* says that a liability should be initially recognised at its **fair value**.

Directly attributable transaction costs (e.g. professional fees directly related to the issue or acquisition of a financial instrument) are capitalised unless classified as fair value through profit or loss.

Capitalised transaction costs are deducted from the liability.

If the financial liability is classified as fair value through profit or loss, then transaction costs are expensed within the statement of profit or loss.

Subsequent measurement of financial liabilities

Subsequent measurement of financial liabilities depends upon the classification of the financial liability. There are two possible categories of financial liability.

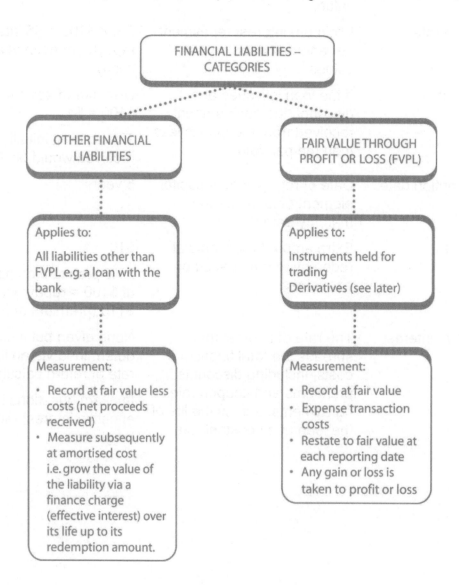

Amortised cost

- Financial liabilities will normally be measured as at the year-end at amortised cost. The amortised cost in the first year of a liability is the amount initially recorded, plus interest, less repayments.

- The interest will be charged on the outstanding balance at the effective rate. This is the internal rate of return of the instrument.

The simplest way to prepare a working for amortised cost is to use the following table.

Year	Opening balance	Effective interest % (P/L)	Coupon paid %	Closing balance (SFP)
	$	$	$	$
1	X	X	(X)	X
2	X	X	(X)	X
3	X	X	(X)	X

The opening balance in year 1 is the net proceeds (i.e. after deduction of any discounts and issue costs):

- Dr Cash

- Cr Liability

Effective interest is calculated on the opening balance each period and is charged to the statement of profit or loss (P/L):

- Dr Finance costs (P/L)

- Cr Liability

The coupon paid is the coupon percentage multiplied by the par/nominal value of the debt:

- Dr Liability

- Cr Cash

The closing balance is the amortised cost shown on the statement of financial position (SFP) at the reporting date.

Illustration 2 – amortised cost (effective rate = coupon rate)

A company issues 5% loan notes at their nominal value of $20,000. The loan notes are repayable at par after 4 years.

Initial recognition

When the loan notes are issued:

Dr Bank $20,000

Cr Loan notes $20,000

Financial statement extracts over the 4 year term

Note: Because the loan is repayable at par (face/nominal) value of $20,000, the coupon rate is equal to the effective rate.

Statement of profit or loss (P/L)

Year	1	2	3	4
	$	$	$	$
Finance costs **(W1)**	(1,000)	(1,000)	(1,000)	(1,000)

Statement of financial position (SFP)

Year	1	2	3	4
	$	$	$	$
Non-current liabilities	20,000	20,000		
Current liabilities			20,000	0

(W1) Amortised cost table

Year	Opening balance	Effective interest 5% (P/L)	Coupon paid 5%	Closing balance (SFP)
	$	$	$	$
1	20,000	1,000	(1,000)	20,000
2	20,000	1,000	(1,000)	20,000
3	20,000	1,000	(1,000)	20,000
4	20,000	1,000	(1,000)	20,000

The notes are repaid at par ($20k) at the end of year 4 = balance of 0.

Illustration 3 – amortised cost (effective rate not equal to coupon rate)

A company issues 0% loan notes at their nominal value of $40,000 at the beginning of the year. The loan notes are repayable at a premium of $11,800 after 3 years. The effective rate of interest is 9%.

Required:

(a) What amount will be recorded as a financial liability when the loan notes are issued?

(b) What amounts will be shown in the statement of profit or loss and statement of financial position for years 1–3?

Solution

(a) When the loan notes are issued:

Dr Bank	$40,000
Cr Loan notes	$40,000

(b) Financial statement extracts

Statement of profit or loss (P/L)

Year	1	2	3
	$	$	$
Finance costs **(W1)**	(3,600)	(3,924)	(4,276)

Statement of financial position (SFP)

Year	1	2	3
	$	$	$
Non-current liabilities	43,600		
Current liabilities		47,524	0

(W1) Amortised cost table

Year	Opening balance	Effective interest 9% (P/L)	Coupon paid 0%	Closing balance (SFP)
	$	$	$	$
1	40,000	3,600	–	43,600
2	43,600	3,924	–	47,524
3	47,524	4,276	–	51,800
			(51,800)	0

The loan notes are repaid at par i.e. $40,000, plus a premium of $11,800 at the end of year 3.

Test your understanding 1 (integration question)

A company issues 5% redeemable preference shares at their nominal value of $10,000. The preference shares are repayable at a premium of $1,760 after 5 years. The effective rate of interest is 8%.

Required:

Explain how the instrument should be classified in accordance with IAS 32 *Financial instruments: Presentation*.

What amounts will be shown in the statement of profit or loss and statement of financial position for years 1–5?

Test your understanding 2 (integration question)

Fratton issues $360,000 of redeemable 2% debentures at a discount of 14% on 1 January 20X5. Issue costs were $5,265. The debenture will be redeemed on 31 December 20X7 at par. Interest is paid annually in arrears and the effective interest rate is 8%.

Required:

Show the effect of the transaction on the statement of financial position and statement of profit or loss for the three year term of the debenture.

Test your understanding 3 (OTQ style)

A company issues 4% loan notes with a nominal value of $20,000.

The loan notes are issued at a discount of 2.5% and $534 of issue costs are incurred.

The loan notes will be repayable at a premium of 10% after 5 years. The effective rate of interest is 7%.

Required:

The value recorded on initial measurement of the loan notes is:

A $18,966

B $19,466

C $19,500

D $20,034

Test your understanding 4 (OTQ style)

An entity issues 3% bonds with a nominal value of $150,000. The bonds are issued at a discount of 10% and issue costs of $11,450 are incurred.

The bonds will be repayable at a premium of $10,000 after 4 years. The effective rate of interest is 10%.

The initial recognition of the bonds was correctly recorded by the entity at $123,550. However the entity has not re-measured the bonds and has instead expensed the interest paid to the statement of profit or loss.

Required:

Calculate the carrying amount of the bonds that should be presented in the statement of financial position at the end of year 1.

6 Presentation of compound instruments

 A **compound instrument** is a financial instrument that has characteristics of both equity and liabilities.

Convertible bonds are compound instruments. They are currently debt but can be converted into equity shares at certain points in the future.

From the convertible bond issuer's (the entity raising the finance) perspective, a potential cash payment or a share issue looms on the horizon.

The financial reporting conundrum presented with convertible bonds is should the issuer classify it as a liability or an equity instrument? The answer is to show a bit of both!

Upon initial recognition, IAS 32 requires compound financial instruments to be split into their component parts:

- a financial liability (the debt) – measured as the present value of the future cash flows, including redemption, using a discount rate that equates to the interest rate on similar instruments without conversion rights

- an equity instrument (the option to convert into shares) – calculated as the balancing figure.

The liability and equity elements must be shown separately in the financial statements. The equity balance would be held as a separate reserve within the statement of financial position. It is commonly held under the heading of 'Other components of equity' and is separate from share capital and share premium.

Subsequently, the liability component is measured at amortised cost and the equity component remains unchanged.

Any transaction costs would be pro-rated between equity and liability components based on the relative proportion of their values.

Convertible bonds: extra information

Why issue a convertible bond?

As already seen in earlier chapters, the bondholder (who buys the bond) has the prospect of acquiring cheap shares in an entity, because the terms of conversion should be generous. Even if the bondholder wants cash rather than the shares, they will be likely to accept the conversion and then sell the shares at market price to make a profit.

This ability to partake in the benefits of share appreciation provides an added incentive that may encourage bond holders to invest in the convertible bonds. As a result, the addition of the conversion option may improve the issuer's chances of raising the finance required through issuing the bond.

In exchange for the option to convert, the bondholders normally have to accept a below-market rate of interest, and will have to wait some time before they get the shares that form a large part of their return. There is also the risk that the entity's shares will under-perform, making the conversion unattractive. In this case, the bond holder will simply wait for the cash receipts from the bond.

Illustration 4 – Compound instrument

On 1 January 20X1, Daniels issued a $50m three year convertible bond at par.

- There were no issue costs.

- The coupon rate is 10%, payable annually in arrears on 31 December.

- The bond is redeemable at par on 1 January 20X4.

- Bondholders may opt for conversion. The terms of conversion are two 25 cent shares for every $1 owed to each bondholder on 1 January 20X4.

- Bonds issued by similar companies without any conversion rights currently bear interest at 15%.

- Assume that all bondholders opt for conversion in full.

Accounting treatment

On initial recognition, the method of splitting the bond between equity and liabilities is as follows:

- Calculate the present value of the debt component by discounting the cash flows at the market rate of interest for an instrument similar in all respects, except that it does not have conversion rights.

- Deduct the present value of the debt from the proceeds of the issue. The difference is the equity component.

1 Splitting the proceeds

The cash payments on the bond should be discounted to their present value using the interest rate for a bond without the conversion rights i.e.15%.

Date		Cash flow	Discount factor @ 15%	Present value
		$000		$000
20X1–X3	Interest	5,000	2.283	11,415
01/01/X4	Redemption	50,000	0.658	32,900
Present value = the liability component				44,315
Equity (balancing figure)				5,685
Net proceeds of issue				50,000

The journal entry required to record the issue is:

Dr Bank	$50m
Cr Financial Liability	$44.315m
Cr Equity (bal fig) – other reserves	$5.685m

2 Subsequent remeasurement of liability component

	Opening balance	Effective interest rate 15%	Payments	Closing balance
	$000	$000	$000	$000
20X1	44,315	6,647	(5,000)	45,962
20X2	45,962	6,894	(5,000)	47,856
20X3	47,856	7,144*	(5,000)	50,000

* Note that the effective interest in 20X3 is rounded (due to the discount factors having only been applied to 3 decimal places) to ensure that the closing balance equals the redemption amount of $50 million. Without the adjustment, finance costs would be $7,178.

Note: The equity component is not remeasured after initial recognition.

3   **The conversion of the bond**

The carrying amounts at 1 January 20X4 are:

	$000
Equity – other reserves	5,685
Liability – bond	50,000
	55,685

The conversion terms are two 25c shares for every $1, so $50m × 2 = 100m shares, which have a nominal value of $25m. The remaining $30.685 million should be classified as the share premium, also within equity. There is no remaining liability, because conversion has extinguished it.

The journal entry on conversion would be:

Dr Liability	$50m
Dr Equity – other reserves	$5.685m
Cr Share capital	$25m
Cr Share premium	$30.685m

Test your understanding 5 (integration question)

An entity issues 2% convertible bonds at their nominal value of $36,000 on 1 January 20X1.

The bonds are convertible at any time up to maturity into 120 ordinary shares for each $100 of bond. Alternatively, the bonds will be redeemed at par after 3 years. Similar non-convertible bonds would carry an interest rate of 9%.

The entity is preparing its financial statements for the year-ended 31 December 20X1. They are not sure how to record the convertible bonds and have credited the £36,000 cash received to non-current liabilities and recognised the interest paid in the year as a finance cost.

Required:

(a) Prepare the journal entry that should have been applied to correctly record the initial recognition of the convertible bonds on 1 January 20X1.

(b) Prepare extracts from the statement of profit or loss and statement of financial position for the year ended 31 December 20X1.

(c) What are the journal entries required to correct the entity's accounting records in the year ended 31 December 20X1?

Test your understanding 6 (OTQ style)

A company issues 4% convertible bonds at their nominal value of $5 million on 1 January 20X3.

Each bond is convertible at any time up to maturity into 2 ordinary shares for every $1 bond. Alternatively, the bonds will be redeemed at par after 3 years.

The market rate applicable to non-convertible bonds is 6%.

Required:

Complete the following journal entry required to record the initial recognition of the convertible bonds on 1 January 20X3. Give your figures to the nearest $000:

	$000
Dr Bank	5,000
Cr Financial Liability	
Cr Equity	

Test your understanding 7 (OTQ style)

A company issues 100,000 5% convertible bonds with a nominal value of $100 each on 1 January 20X0.

Each bond is convertible at any time up to maturity into 120 ordinary shares for every $100 bond. Alternatively the bonds will be redeemed at par after five years.

The market rate of interest for a similar five year term bond with no conversion option is 7%.

Upon initial recognition, the liability component of the bond was correctly calculated and recognised as $9,180,000 and the equity component was $820,000.

Required:

Calculate the carrying amount of the liability component that would be shown in the statement of financial position at 31 December 20X0. Give your answer to the nearest $.

7   Financial assets

An entity that **provides** finance to another entity will account for a financial asset.

Finance can be provided through equity or debt financial assets.

If an entity **ACQUIRES** shares, it will own an equity financial asset.

If an entity **ACQUIRES** bonds/debentures/loan stock, it will own a debt financial asset.

Initial measurement of financial assets

 IFRS 9 *Financial instruments,* says that a financial asset should be initially recognised at its **fair value** (which is typically the cost of the asset).

Directly attributable transaction costs (e.g. professional fees directly related to the issue or acquisition of a financial asset) are capitalised unless the financial asset is classified as fair value through profit or loss.

Capitalised transaction costs are **added** to the asset.

If the financial asset is classified as fair value through profit or loss, then transaction costs are expensed within the statement of profit or loss.

Subsequent measurement of financial assets

The subsequent measurement of financial assets depend upon how the financial assets have been classified.

Classification depends upon whether the financial asset is an equity financial asset or a debt financial asset.

Subsequent measurement of investments in equity financial assets

If an entity **ACQUIRES** shares, it has an equity financial asset.

The subsequent treatment of an equity financial asset depends upon its categorisation. There are two options for categorising equity financial assets.

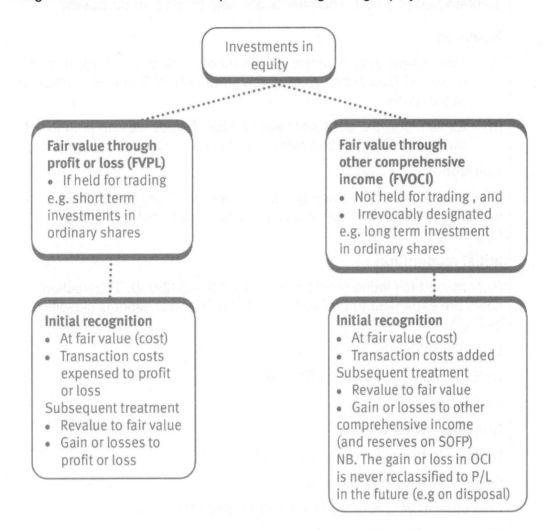

Classification as FVPL is considered the default for equity financial assets.

Illustration 5 – Accounting for equity financial assets

A company invested in 10,000 shares of a listed company in November 20X7 at a cost of $4.20 per share. Transaction costs relating to the investment were $1,300. At 31 December 20X7, the shares have a market value of $4.90. The shares are held for trading purposes.

Required:

(a) Prepare extracts from the statement of profit or loss for the year ended 31 December 20X7 and a statement of financial position as at that date.

(b) Explain how the treatment would differ if there was no plan to sell the shares and the company opts to use the FVOCI designation.

Solution

The financial assets are equity financial assets. They are classified as fair value through profit or loss as the shares are held for trading purposes.

Initial recognition

Recorded at fair value (cost) = 10,000 × 4.2 = $42,000. Transaction costs are expensed to profit or loss as the financial asset is classified as FVPL.

Dr FVPL $42,000

Dr Expense – Finance cost $1,300

Cr Cash $43,300

Subsequent treatment

Revalue to fair value at the year-end.

Gains or losses to profit or loss

Fair value at year end = 4.9 × 10,000 = $49,000

Gain = 49,000 – 42,000 = $7,000

Dr FVPL financial asset $7,000

Cr P/L $7,000

Statement of profit or loss

	$
Gain on financial assets	7,000
Finance cost	(1,300)

Statement of financial position

	$
Current assets	
Investments	49,000

(b)   The equity financial asset has been designated as fair value through other comprehensive income (FVOCI) as the shares are not held for trading and the irrevocable designation has been applied.

Initial recognition

The transaction costs would be added to the financial asset upon initial recognition rather than being expensed, therefore the initial asset would be recognised at an amount of $43,300.

To record the purchase of the shares

Dr FVOCI financial asset $43,300

Cr Cash $43,300

Subsequent treatment

As at the year end, the FVOCI financial asset should be revalued to fair value with gains or losses taken to other comprehensive income (OCI). A FVOCI reserve would be held in equity on the statement of financial position.

The asset would be recognised as non-current on the statement of financial position and the subsequent gain of $5,700 (49,000 – 43,300) would be taken to reserves and shown as other comprehensive income in the statement of profit or loss and other comprehensive income.

Dr FVOCI financial asset $5,700

Cr Equity/OCI $5,700

It would be presented in other comprehensive income as an item that may not be reclassified subsequently to profit or loss.

Test your understanding 8 (OTQ style)

MNB acquired 100,000 shares in AB on 25 October 20X0 for $3 per share. The investment resulted in MNB holding 5% of the equity shares of AB. The related transaction costs were $12,000. AB's shares were trading at $3.40 on 31 December 20X0. The investment has been classified as held for trading.

Required:

The journal entry required to record the change in fair value of the investment in shares at 31 December 20X0 is:

A   Dr Investment $28,000   Cr Profit or loss $28,000

B   Dr Investment $28,000   Cr Reserves/Other comprehensive income $28,000

C   Dr Investment $40,000   Cr Profit or loss $40,000

D   Dr Investment $40,000   Cr Reserves/Other comprehensive income $40,000

Subsequent measurement of investments in debt financial assets

If an entity ACQUIRES debentures/loan notes/bonds, it is a debt financial asset.

There are three classifications of debt financial assets:

- Amortised cost
- Fair value through other comprehensive income (FVOCI)
- Fair value through profit or loss.

At initial recognition, an entity can designate a debt financial asset as either FVOCI or at amortised cost dependent upon the outcome of two tests:

- The business model test
- The contractual cash flow test.

The business model test

To determine the category of debt financial asset, the **business model test** considers the entity's strategies regarding investments in debt.

Does the entity invest in debt financial assets with an intention to keep financial assets, to sell them to other investors or do they expect to hold some and sell some of the financial assets?

The contractual cash flow test

The contractual cash flow test states that the contractual terms of the debt financial asset give rise to cash flow receipts that are **solely** repayments of:

- principal (the capital element of the debt),and
- interest on the principal amount outstanding.

If the cash flows received are deemed to consist of cash flows relating to anything else, then the financial asset does not comply with the contractual cash flow test and **the fair value through profit or loss (FVPL)** category should be used (see below).

For example, investments in convertible bonds are often issued at lower than market value interest rates to compensate for the bond holder having the option to redeem the loan in the form of cash or shares. The cash flows are also considered payment for the extra choice of method of redemption. As a result convertibles do not comply with the contractual cash flow test as payment is received for something other than capital and interest.

Amortised cost

An investment in a debt financial asset is classified and measured at amortised cost if:

- the entity's business model is **to hold and collect all** of the asset's contractual cash flows, **and**

- the terms of the financial asset create the receipt of cash flows that are solely repayments of interest and principal amount outstanding (in other words, it passes the contractual cash flow test).

Fair value through other comprehensive income (FVOCI)

An investment in a debt financial asset is classified and measured at fair value through other comprehensive income if:

- the entity's business model is to **hold some** of the assets until maturity **and** to **sell some** of the financial assets, **and**

- the terms of the financial asset create the receipt of cash flows that are solely repayments of interest and principal amounts outstanding (it passes the contractual cash flow test).

If the entity considers holding some of the financial assets to maturity and selling some of the financial assets as being integral to the business model of the entity, the FVOCI model should be used. For example, holding financial assets yet selling financial assets to raise funds to take advantage of other investments with better returns.

 If the entity sells a debt financial asset due to unforeseen circumstances (e.g. an increase in credit risk leading to the sale of the financial asset), the intention of the entity may not have been to sell. This would not necessarily qualify as an intention to hold some and sell some of the debt financial assets. The amortised cost classification would still be applicable as the entity's business model is still to hold until maturity. Sales are infrequent and incidental.

Fair value through profit or loss (FVPL)

If no designation as either amortised cost or fair value through other comprehensive income has occurred, the debt financial asset is classified and measured at fair value through profit or loss.

Debt financial asset accounting: Summary

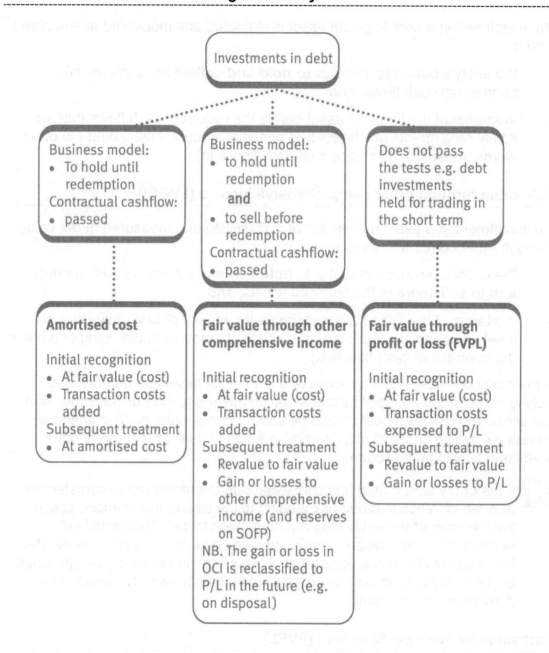

Amortised cost

- The amortised cost of an asset equals: initial cost plus interest less cash received.

- The interest will be charged at the effective rate. This is the internal rate of return of the instrument.

The simplest way to prepare a working for amortised cost is to use the following table:

Year	Opening balance	Effective interest % (P/L)	Cash received (coupon) %	Closing balance (SFP)
	$	$	$	$
1	X	X	(X)	X
2	X	X	(X)	X
3	X	X	(X)	X

The opening balance in year 1 is the total investment (cash invested plus transaction costs):

- Dr Asset

- Cr Cash

Effective interest is calculated on the opening balance and is credited to the statement of profit or loss (P/L) as finance income:

- Dr Asset

- Cr Finance income (P/L)

The coupon received is the coupon percentage multiplied by the face value of the instrument:

- Dr Cash

- Cr Asset

The closing balance is the figure for the statement of financial position (SFP) at the reporting date.

Test your understanding 9 (integration question)

JS Co invests $5,000 in 10% debentures at the start of the year. The debentures will be repaid at a premium at the end of their term. The business model applied by JS is to hold the debentures until this time. The effective rate of interest is 12%.

Required:

Prepare extracts from the statement of profit or loss and statement of financial position for years 1 and 2 of the instrument's term.

Fair value through other comprehensive income (debt investments)

If classified as a debt FVOCI financial asset, the business model will be both to hold and sell the financial assets.

The FVOCI financial asset will be measured as at the year-end using fair value with gains or losses recorded in other comprehensive income (OCI) and equity in the statement of financial position.

The debt financial asset still earns interest income and will receive coupon rate interest repayments. The interest income is calculated based upon the figures as if the debt financial asset were classified at amortised cost.

The revalued fair value amounts do not affect the interest income.

Please note that calculations of FVOCI financial asset values are specifically excluded from the syllabus. You need awareness of the category but you will not need to calculate values within the financial statements for FVOCI debt financial assets.

Test your understanding 10 (Integration question)

On 1 January 20X1, Tokyo bought a $100,000 5% bond for $95,000, incurring issue costs of $2,000. Interest is received in arrears. The bond will be redeemed at a premium of $5,960 over nominal value on 31 December 20X3. The effective rate of interest is 8%. The fair value of the bond was as follows:

31/12/X1 $110,000
31/12/X2 $104,000

Required:

Explain, with calculations, how the bond will have been accounted for over all relevant years if:

(a) Tokyo planned to hold the bond until the redemption date.

(b) Tokyo intends to sell the bond in the short term.

The requirement to recognise an impairment on debt instruments held at amortised cost is to be ignored.

8 Derivative financial instruments

 Definition of derivatives

According to IFRS 9 *Financial instruments,* a derivative is a financial instrument that **derives its value from the value of an underlying asset, price, rate or index.**

 Characteristics of a derivative

A derivative has all of the following characteristics:

- Its value changes in response to changes in the underlying item

- It requires little or no initial investment

- It is settled at a future date.

Underlying items are typically found in volatile and unpredictable market places where prices/values are easily accessed. Underlying items include equities, bonds, commodities, interest rates, exchange rates and stock market and other indices.

Derivative financial instruments include futures, options, forward contracts, interest rate and currency swaps.

 The risks associated with derivatives

- Derivatives were originally designed to hedge against fluctuations in agricultural commodity prices on the Chicago Stock Exchange. It was noted that they also could be used by risk takers purely in a speculative manner. For instance, a speculator would pay a small amount (say $100) now for the contractual obligation to buy a thousand units of wheat in three months' time for $10,000. If, in three months' time, one thousand units of wheat costs $11,000, then the speculator would make a profit of $900 (11,000 – 100 – 10,000). This would be a 900% return on the original investment over 3 months, which is one of the attractions of derivatives to speculators. But if the price had dropped to $9,000, then the trader would have made a loss of $1,100 (100 + 1,000) despite the initial investment only having been $100.

- This shows that losses on derivatives can be far greater than the historical cost carrying amount ($100 cost in this example) of the related asset. Therefore, shareholders need to be given additional information about derivatives in order to assess the entity's exposure to loss.

- In most cases, entering into a derivative is at little or no cost. Therefore, it is important that derivatives are recognised and disclosed in the financial statements as they have very little initial outlay but can expose the entity to significant gains or losses.

Recognition and measurement

All derivatives are accounted as **fair value through profit or loss (FVPL).**

A derivative's gains (or losses) fluctuate as the underlying item's price moves. On the date of initial recognition, no price movements would have occurred so fair value is typically nil (as long as there is no cost of entering the derivative).

At each reporting date, the derivative is restated to fair value and recorded as a financial asset or financial liability on the statement of financial position. Any gains/losses are taken to the statement of profit or loss.

Types of derivative

- **Forward** – the obligation to buy or sell a defined amount of a specific underlying asset, at a specified price at a specified future date.

- **Forward rate agreements** – a contract to fix the interest charge on a floating rate loan.

- **Futures contracts** – the obligation to buy or sell a standard quantity of a specific underlying item at a specified future date.

- **Swaps** – an agreement to exchange periodic payments at specified intervals over a specified time period.

- **Options** – the right, but not the obligation, to buy or sell a specific underlying asset, at a specified price, on or before a specified future date.

Types of derivatives – further detail

Forward contracts

The holder of a forward contract is obliged to buy or sell a defined amount of a specific underlying asset, at a specified price at a specified future date.

For example, a forward contract for foreign currency might require £100,000 to be exchanged for $150,000 in three months' time. This is the same as stating that the entity is buying $150,000 at an exchange rate of $1.5:£1 in 3 months.

If the rate of exchange in 3 months was $1:£1, then $150,000 could be bought at £150,000. By entering the forward to buy at $1.5:£1, the entity makes a gain on the derivative of $50,000. They pay £100,000 in the contract but would have had to pay £150,000 without the contract. By being in the derivative, they save $50,000. This $50,000 gain would be recorded as a financial asset within the financial statements.

If the rate in 3 months was $2:£1, the entity would make a loss of $25,000. By being in the forward contract, the entity pays £100,000. They would pay £75,000 to buy the $150,000 without the forward contract. This loss would be recorded a financial liability of $25,000.

Forward currency contracts may be used to minimise the risk on amounts receivable or payable in foreign currencies. These risk management strategies are called hedge arrangements and are outside the scope of the F2 syllabus.

Forward rate agreements

Forward rate agreements can be used to fix the interest charge on a floating rate loan.

For example, a company has a $1m dollar floating rate loan, and the current rate of interest is 7%. The rates are reset to the market rate every six months, and the company cannot afford to pay more than 9% interest. The company enters into a six month forward rate agreement (with, say, a bank) at 9% on $1m. If the market rates go up to 10%, then the bank will pay them $5,000 (1% of $1m for 6 months) which, in effect, reduces their finance cost to 9%. If the rates only go up to 8% then the company pays the bank $5,000.

Futures contracts

Futures contracts oblige the holder to buy or sell a standard quantity of a specific underlying item at a specified future date. Futures contracts are very similar to forward contracts. The difference is that futures contracts have standard terms (off-the-shelf) and are traded on a financial exchange, whereas forward contracts are bespoke (tailor made) and are not traded on a financial exchange.

Swaps

Two parties agree to exchange periodic payments at specified intervals over a specified time period. For example, in an interest rate swap, the parties may agree to exchange fixed and floating rate interest payments calculated by reference to a notional principal amount. This enables companies to keep a balance between their fixed and floating rate interest payments without having to change the underlying loans.

Options

These give the holder the right, but not the obligation, to buy or sell a specific underlying asset on or before a specified future date.

An option to buy is called a call option. An option to sell is described as a put option.

If the option is in the money (the entity makes a gain), the option will be exercised. If the option is out of the money (is making a loss), there is no obligation to exercise the option. The option will be allowed to lapse. Options carry less risk than forward or future contracts. However, as a result they require greater initial outlay to enter when compared to forwards and future contracts.

For example, an entity has an option to buy shares at $2 in 6 months' time. If, in 6 months, the share price is $3, the entity will exercise the option as they are buying shares at a cheap price.

If the share price in 6 months' is $1.50, the entity will allow the option to expire. They would not want to pay $2 for shares only worth $1.50.

Illustration 6 – derivative financial instrument

Entity A enters into a call option on 1 June 20X5, to purchase 10,000 $1 equity shares in another entity on 1 November 20X5 at an exercise price of $10 per share. The cost of the option is $1 per share to be acquired. A has a year end of 30 September.

By 30 September, the fair value of each option has increased to $1.30. A exercises the option on 1 November and the shares are classified as fair value through profit or loss. The share price at this date is $12.

Accounting treatment

Initial recognition

On 1 June 20X5. the cost of the option is recognised:

Debit	Call option (10,000 × $1)	$10,000
Credit	Cash	$10,000

Subsequent treatment – at year-end

On 30 September, the increase in fair value is recorded. The derivative is classified as fair value through profit or loss. At the year-end, the derivative is revalued to fair value with gains or losses recorded in profit or loss.

Debit	Call option (10,000 × ($1.30 – 1))	$3,000
Credit	Profit or loss – gain on option	$3,000

NB. The fair value of the option does not equal the actual share price. The fair value of the option is the expected gain from being in the derivative contract. It can be approximated as the actual price of the shares less the exercise price. As the option has a fair value of $1.30, the entity's share price would be in the region of $11.30 as at year-end. 10,000 shares at $11.30 are worth $113,000 but would have cost $110,000 (being exercise price $10 + the cost of option $1 × 10,000). A gain of $3,000 arises from the option as shown above.

Subsequent treatment – on exercise of the option

On 1 November, the option is exercised, the shares recognised and the call option derecognised. As the shares are financial assets at fair value through profit or loss, they are recognised at $120,000 (10,000 × the current market price of $12).

Debit	Investment in shares at fair value	$120,000
Credit	Cash (10,000 × $10)	$100,000
Credit	Call option (10,000 + 3,000 carrying amount)	$13,000
Credit	Profit or loss – further gain (β)	$7,000

The total gain recognised is $10,000 which equates to $1 per share, being the difference between the share price of $12 and the price paid of $11 ($1 for the cost of the option and $10 upon exercise). As $3,000 has already been recognised in the year ended 30 September 20X5, the remaining $7,000 is recognised upon exercise.

Test your understanding 11 (integration question)

B entered into a forward contract on 30 November 20X1 to buy platinum for $435m on 31 March 20X2. The contract was entered into on 30 November 20X1 at nil cost.

B does not plan to take delivery of the platinum but to settle the contract net in cash, i.e. B hopes to generate a profit from short term price fluctuations.

The year end is 31 December 20X1 and the price of platinum has moved to $455m at that date.

On 31 March 20X2, the value of the underlying item has changed such that the equivalent purchase of platinum would now cost $442m.

Required:

Prepare journal entries to record the above transaction.

Illustration 7 – derivative financial instrument with foreign currency

On 1 March 20X1, ABC entered into a forward foreign exchange contract to buy 5 million florins for $1 million on 31 January 20X3. ABC's reporting date is 30 June.

Relevant exchange rates were as follows:

1 March 20X1 $1 = 5 florins

30 June 20X1 $1 = 4.7 florins

30 June 20X2 $1 = 4.2 florins

Required:

Prepare relevant extracts from ABC's statement of profit or loss and other comprehensive income and statement of financial position to show how the forward foreign exchange contract is accounted for at 30 June 20X2 and 20X1.

(a)   **Extracts from financial statements**

Statement of profit or loss for year ended 30 June 20X2

	20X2 $	20X1 $
Gain on derivative **(W2)**	126,646	63,830

Statement of financial position at 30 June 20X2

	20X2 $	20X1 $
Derivative asset **(W1)**	190,476	63,830

Workings

(W1) Value of derivative

At each reporting date, derivatives are valued at fair value with gains or losses recorded in the profit or loss account.

The fair value of the derivative at certain dates can be determined by comparing the amount paid in $ for 5m Florins through being in the contract, in this case $1m, to the amount paid if ABC were NOT in the contract (translating the 5m florins using the exchange rates at the relevant date).

These calculations are given below:

	$
Value of forward contract at 1 March 20X1 (FI 5m/5) – 1m	Nil
Value of forward contract at 30 June 20X1 (FI 5m/4.7) – 1m	63,830
Value of forward contract at 30 June 20X2 (FI 5m/4.2) – 1m	190,476

(W2) Gain

As the fair value of the derivative is increasing as time progresses, a gain is recorded. The journal entries recorded at each date will record the movement in the derivatives fair value. At each date the following journal is posted:

Dr Derivative

Cr P/L

The gains recorded via this journal at each year end are calculated below:

	$
Gain for year ended 30 June 20X1	63,830
Gain for year ended 30 June 20X2 (190,476 – 63,830)	126,646

Test your understanding 12 (OTQ style)

AB entered into a forward contract on 31 January 20X1 to purchase B$1 million at a contracted rate of A$1:B$0.75 on 31 May 20X1. The contract cost was A$nil. AB prepares its financial statements to 31 March each year in A$.

At 31 March 20X1, an equivalent contract for the purchase of B$1 million could be acquired at a rate of A$1:B$0.80.

Required:

Which one of the following shows the impact of the forward contract on profit or loss in the year ended 31 March 20X1:

A   A$83,333 gain

B   A$83,333 loss

C   A$1,250,000 loss

D   A$1,333,333 gain

9 Other aspects of IFRS 9

IFRS 9 also includes details regarding the accounting of impairments of financial assets, derecognition of financial instruments and hedge accounting. However, all of these issues are out of the scope of the CIMA F2 syllabus. As a result no further content will be included on these topics.

Test your understanding 13 (further OTQs)

1   A financial instrument is any contract that gives rise to a financial _____ of one entity and a financial _____ or _____ instrument of another entity.

   Select the correct words to complete the above sentence, from the following options:

   asset, bond, equity, liability, obligation, share

2   PT issued 1 million 4% cumulative redeemable $1 preference shares on 1 January 20X1.

   Which of the following statements are TRUE in respect of the above financial instrument? Select all that apply.

   A   At the date of issue, PT would credit equity share capital with $1 million.

   B   If the preference shares were issued at a discount, the effective rate of interest would be lower than 4%.

   C   The dividends of $40,000 paid each year would be recognised in the statement of changes in equity.

   D   The preference shares would be remeasured each year at amortised cost using the effective interest rate.

3   SQ issued $2 million 5% convertible bonds on 1 January 20X1 at par value. The bond is redeemable at par after 5 years or can be converted into equity shares on the basis of 2 shares for every $1 of bond.

   The prevailing market rate at 1 January 20X1 for similar bonds without conversion rights was 10% per annum.

   Calculate the carrying amount of the liability element of the bonds at 31 December 20X1 (to the nearest $).

   $_____

4   BD entered into a forward contract on 31 August 20X1 to purchase B$3 million at a contracted rate of A$1: B$1.5 on 30 November 20X1. The contract cost was $nil. At 31 October 20X1, BD's financial year-end, an equivalent contract for the purchase of B$3 million could be acquired at a rate of A$1: B$1.7.

> **Complete the following journal entry to record the financial instrument in the financial statements of BD for the year ended 31 October 20X1 (state the amount to the nearest A$).**
>
> Dr
>
> Cr
>
> **Note:** In the assessment, you may have to choose the headings for the Dr and Cr from a selection of choices.

5 KM made an investment in a debt instrument on 1 June 20X0 at its nominal value of $2 million. The instrument carries a fixed coupon interest rate of 6% and the instrument will be redeemed at a premium on 31 May 20X4. KM's business model is to hold debt investments until their redemption date.

How should this instrument be classified in the financial statements of KM?

A Financial liability

B Fair value through profit or loss financial asset

C Amortised cost

D Fair value through other comprehensive income financial asset

6 CG acquired 20,000 equity shares in FM on 1 November 20X2 for $5 per share. The related transaction costs were $2,500. The investment was classified as fair value through other comprehensive income. At 31 December 20X2, CG's reporting date, FM's shares were trading at $6.25.

The requirement per IFRS 9 to include impairment can be ignored.

How would the gain on the investment be measured and recorded in CG's statement of profit or loss and other comprehensive income for the year ended 31 December 20X2?

A Gain of $22,500 recorded in profit or loss

B Gain of $22,500 recorded in other comprehensive income

C Gain of $25,000 recorded in profit or loss

D Gain of $25,000 recorded in other comprehensive income

7   AF acquired an equity investment on 1 January 20X1 for its fair value of $12,000. Transaction costs of $350 were also incurred. The investment was classified as FVOCI.

The fair value of the shares rose to $13,500 on 31 December 20X1, the entity's reporting date.

The amount shown within other comprehensive income relating to the investment in shares for the year ended 31 December 20X1 is:

A $13,500

B $1,850

C $1,500

D $1,150

10   Chapter summary

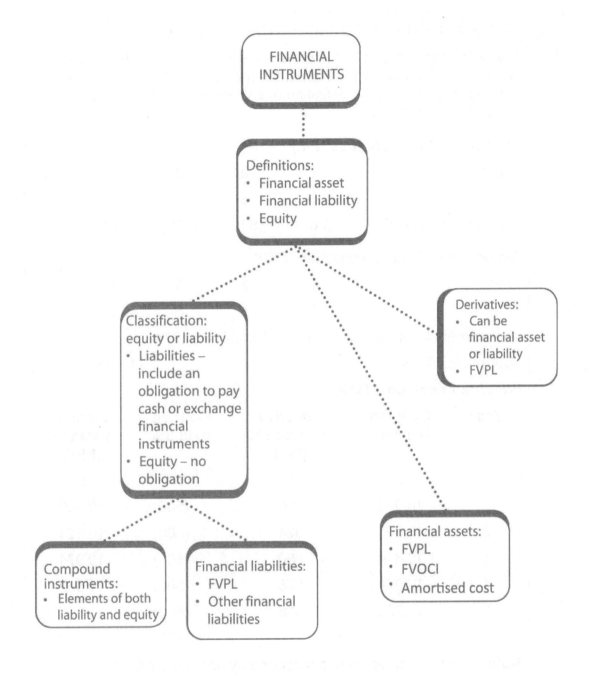

Test your understanding answers

Test your understanding 1 (integration question)

The redeemable nature of the preference shares means that there will be an obligation to transfer cash at the redemption date and therefore the instrument meets the definition of a financial liability and should be classified as such.

Statement of profit or loss (P/L)

Year	1	2	3	4	5
	$	$	$	$	$
Finance costs **(W1)**	(800)	(824)	(850)	(878)	(908)

Statement of financial position (SFP)

Year	1	2	3	4	5
	$	$	$	$	$
Non-current liabilities	10,300	10,624	10,974		
Current liabilities				11,352	0

(W1) Amortised cost table

Year	Opening balance	Effective interest 8% (P/L)	Coupon paid 5%	Closing balance (SFP)
	$	$	$	$
1	10,000	800	(500)	10,300
2	10,300	824	(500)	10,624
3	10,624	850	(500)	10,974
4	10,974	878	(500)	11,352
5	11,352	908	(500)	
			(11,760)	0

Note: Effective interest rate is multiplied by opening balance.

Note: Coupon rate is multiplied by nominal (par) value of debt i.e. $10,000.

Test your understanding 2 (integration question)

Amortised cost table

Year		Opening balance	Effective interest 8% (P/L)	Coupon paid 2%	Closing balance (SFP)
		$	$	$	$
1	**(W1)**	304,335	24,347	(7,200)	321,482
2		321,482	25,718	(7,200)	340,000
3		340,000	27,200	(7,200)	
				(360,000)	0
			77,265		

Note: Effective interest rate is multiplied by opening balance.

Note: Coupon rate is multiplied by the par value of the debt.

(W1) Net proceeds = opening balance

	$
Nominal value	360,000
Discount 14%	(50,400)
Issue costs	(5,265)
	304,335

Tutorial note – extra detail regarding effective interest rate

The total finance cost will be as follows:

		$
Redemption value (at par)		360,000
Payments	2% × 360,000 × 3 years	21,600
		381,600
Net proceeds **(W1)**		(304,335)
Total finance cost		77,265

The total finance cost will be allocated at a constant rate based upon carrying amount over the life of the instrument. The constant rate is known as the effective interest rate and is 8% for these redeemable debentures. The annual finance cost is calculated using the 8% effective interest rate as illustrated in the amortised cost table above.

As the capitalised transaction costs reduce the net proceeds of the liability, then total finance costs are increased. The transactions costs are indirectly included within total finance costs.

As a result, the effective interest rate used to spread these total finance costs over the life of the loan would have also increased (to 8% in this case). The transaction costs are spread over the life of the liability as part of the effective interest rate of 8% used to determine the finance costs each year. Effectively, the transaction costs are taken to the profit or loss as an expense over the lifetime of the loan.

Test your understanding 3 (OTQ style)

The correct answer is A = $18,966

Working

	$
Nominal value	20,000
Discount 2.5%	(500)
Cash received	19,500
Issue costs	(534)
	18,966

Test your understanding 4 (OTQ style)

Carrying amount of bonds at the end of year 1 = $131,405

Amortised cost working

Year	Opening balance	Effective interest 10% (P/L)	Coupon paid 3%	Closing balance (SFP)
	$	$	$	$
1	123,550	12,355	(4,500)	131,405

Note: Effective interest rate is multiplied by opening balance.

Note: Coupon rate is multiplied by the par value of debt.

Test your understanding 5 (integration question)

(a) **Journal entry to initially recognise convertible bonds:**

Dr Bank $36,000

Cr Financial Liability $29,614

Cr Equity (bal fig) $6,386

Year	Cash flow (W1) $	Discount factor 9%	Present value $
20X1–X3	720	2.531	1,822
20X3	36,000	0.772	27,792
			29,614

(W1) Cash flow = 2% × 36,000 = $720

(b) **Statement of profit or loss year ended 31 December 20X1**

                                               $

Finance costs **(W2)**   (2,665)

Statement of financial position at 31 December 20X1

                                               $

Equity

Equity option   6,386

Liabilities

Non-current liabilities **(W2)**   31,559

(W2) Amortised cost table

Year	Opening balance $	Effective interest 9% (P/L) $	Coupon paid 2% $	Closing balance (SFP) $
20X1	29,614	2,665	(720)	31,559

Note: Effective interest rate is multiplied by opening balance.

Note: Coupon rate is multiplied by the par value of the debt.

(c) **Journal entries required**

Dr Non-current liabilities	$6,386
Cr Equity reserve	$6,386

Being the correct treatment of the initial recognition, after splitting the liability and equity component.

Dr Finance costs (2,665 – 720)	$1,945
Cr Non-current liabilities	$1,945

Being the adjustment to finance costs to reflect the effective rate applied to the liability component.

Test your understanding 6 (OTQ style)

Journal entry to record initial recognition of convertible bonds:

	$000
Dr Bank	5,000
Cr Financial Liability	**4,735**
Cr Equity (bal fig)	**265**

Year	Cash flow (W1)	Discount factor 6%	Present value
	$		$
1–3	200,000	2.673	534,600
3	5,000,000	0.840	4,200,000
			4,734,600

(W1) Cash flow = 4% × 5,000,000 = $200,000

Test your understanding 7 (OTQ style)

Carrying amount of liability component at 31 December 20X0 = $9,322,600

Year	Opening balance	Effective interest 7% (P/L)	Coupon paid	Closing balance (SFP)
	$	$	$	$
1	9,180,000	642,600	(500,000)	9,322,600

Note: Effective interest rate is multiplied by opening balance.

Note: Coupon rate is multiplied by par value of the debt (5% × 10m).

Test your understanding 8 (OTQ style)

The correct journal entry is C:

Dr Investment $40,000

Cr Profit or loss $40,000

The investment is held for trading and should be classified as fair value through profit or loss. The transaction costs of $12,000 are expensed and the initial recognition of the investment would be $300,000. The fair value at the year-end is $340,000 ($3.40 × 100,000) and the gain in profit or loss is $40,000.

Test your understanding 9 (integration question)

Statement of profit or loss (P/L)

Year	1	2
	$	$
Finance income	600	612

Statement of financial position (SFP)

Year	1	2
	$	$
Non-current assets		
Financial assets	5,100	5,212

(W1) Amortised cost table

Year	Opening balance	Effective interest 12% (P/L)	Coupon received 10%	Closing balance (SFP)
	$	$	$	$
1	5,000	600	(500)	5,100
2	5,100	612	(500)	5,212

Note: Effective interest rate is multiplied by opening balance.

Note: Coupon rate is multiplied by par value of the investment.

Test your understanding 10 (Integration question)

(a) The business model is to hold the asset until redemption. Therefore, the debt instrument will classified to be measured at amortised cost.

The asset is initially recognised at its fair value plus transaction costs of $97,000 ($95,000 + $2,000).

Interest income will be recognised in profit or loss using the effective rate of interest.

	b/f	Interest (8%)	Receipt	c/f
	$	$	$	$
y/e 31/12/X1	97,000	7,760	(5,000)	99,760
y/e 31/12/X2	99,760	7,981	(5,000)	102,741
y/e 31/12/X3	102,741	8,219	(5,000)	105,960

In the year ended 31 December 20X1, interest income of $7,760 will be recognised in profit or loss and the asset will be held at $99,760 on the statement of financial position.

In the year ended 31 December 20X2, interest income $7,981 will be recognised in profit or loss and the asset will be held at $102,741 on the statement of financial position.

In the year ended 31 December 20X3, interest income of $8,219 will be recognised in profit or loss and $105,960 would be received to settle the asset.

(b) The bond would be classified as fair value through profit or loss.

The asset is recognised at its fair value of $95,000. The transaction costs of $2,000 would be expensed to profit or loss.

In the year ended 31/12/X1, interest income of $5,000 ($100,000 × 5%) would be recognised in profit or loss. The asset would be revalued to $110,000 with a gain of $15,000 ($110,000 – $95,000) recognised in profit or loss.

On 1/1/X2, the cash proceeds of $110,000 would be recognised and the financial asset would be derecognised.

Test your understanding 11 (integration question)

On 30 November 20X1 (contract date):

Derivative has no value. There is no cost of the contract and no movements in platinum prices that would create a gain or loss. Fair value would be zero.

On 31 December 20X1 (reporting date):

Derivative is classified as fair value through profit or loss. The derivative will be revalued to fair value at year-end with gains or losses taken to profit or loss.

Dr Derivative (financial asset)	$20m (455m-435m)
Cr P/L (gain)	$20m

On 31 March 20X2 (settlement):

The contract would again be revalued to fair value with gains or losses recorded in profit or loss.

Dr P/L (loss)	$13m (455m-442m)
Cr Derivative (financial asset)	$13m

The contract is then settled net, cash would be received and the derivative derecognised.

Dr Bank	$7m
Cr Derivative (to derecognise)	$7m

To record the settlement of the contract

Test your understanding 12 (OTQ style)

The correct answer is B = A$83,333 loss

The value of the derivative will be the difference between the value of the contract when settled compared with the cost of B$1 million being purchased at the year-end rate.

Cost of B$1 million at the contracted rate of B$0.75 = 1 m/0.75 = A$1,333,333

Cost of B$1 million at the year-end rate of B$0.80 = 1 m/0.8 = A$1,250,000

Therefore, the derivative results in a liability at the year-end date of A$83,333 (1,333,333 – 1,250,000) as the contract has unfavourable terms when compared to the year-end rate. The loss on the derivative would be charged to the statement of profit or loss in the year to 31 March 20X1. **Note:** the journal entry to record the derivative would be

Dr P/L (loss)	A$83,333
Cr Derivative liability	A$83,333

Test your understanding 13 (further OTQs)

1   A financial instrument is any contract that gives rise to a financial **asset** of one entity and a financial **liability** or **equity** instrument of another entity (IAS 32, para 11).

2   **D is the only correct statement.**

A is incorrect as the redeemable preference shares should be recognised as a liability, not equity. The need to redeem the preference shares create an obligation.

B is incorrect. A discount on issue would be an additional cost and therefore would increase the effective rate of interest rather than decrease it.

C is incorrect. As the preferences shares are considered a financial liability, the dividends paid would be expensed through profit or loss as a finance cost rather than being shown as a dividend paid in the statement of changes in equity.

3   **The carrying amount of the liability element of the bonds at 31 December 20X1 is $1,683,210 (W2).**

Year(s)	Cash flow (W1) $	Discount factor 10%	Present value $
1–5	100,000	3.791	379,100
5	2,000,000	0.621	1,242,000
			1,621,100

(W1) Cash flow = 5% × 2 million = $100,000

(W2) Amortised cost table

Year	Opening balance $	Effective interest 10% (P/L) $	Coupon paid 5% $	Closing balance (SFP) $
20X1	1,621,100	162,110	(100,000)	1,683,210

4   **Dr P/L – loss on derivative A$235,294**

Cr Derivative liability A$235,294

Cost of B$3 million at the contracted rate of B$1.5 = 3m/1.5 = A$2m

Cost of B$3 million at the year-end rate of B$1.7 = 3m/1.7 = A$1,764,706

The contracted rate has unfavourable terms compared to the year-end rate and therefore the derivative results in a liability.

5   **C is the correct answer.**

A is not correct as KM made an investment. They provided finance therefore it is a financial asset rather than liability.

B is not correct as KM intends to hold the debt until all cash flows are received. It is not holding the investment for trading purposes so FVPL is incorrect.

D is not correct as KM's business model is not to hold and sell debt financial assets.

KM intends to hold the financial asset until maturity. Amortised cost is the acceptable classification.

6   **B is the correct answer.**

A and C are not correct as gains on FVOCI investments are recognised through other comprehensive income.

D is not correct as the transaction costs are added to the asset at initial recognition.

The gain is ($6.25 × 20,000) – (($5 × 20,000) + $2,500) = $22,500.

7   **D is the correct answer**

The gain recorded in equity within the FVOCI reserves and held within other comprehensive income is calculated as $1,150 (13,500 – (12,000 + 350)).

Earnings per share

Chapter learning objectives

Lead	Component
C2: Discuss additional disclosure issues related to the group accounts	Discuss disclosure requirements relating to: (b) Earnings per share

1 Session content

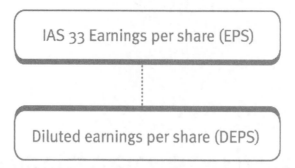

IAS 33 Earnings per share (EPS)

Diluted earnings per share (DEPS)

2 Earnings per share

NB. EPS is part of syllabus area F2C: Group accounts. However, the decision was made by the author of these materials to present EPS alongside the content from F2B: Financial reporting standards. This decision is made based upon practical experience regarding the most efficient place to position EPS in relation with the rest of the syllabus to promote ease of learning for candidates.

Earnings per share (EPS) is widely regarded as the most important indicator of a company's performance.

It is also used in the calculation of the price earnings ratio, a ratio closely monitored by analysts for listed companies. The price earnings ratio is equal to market price per share divided by earnings per share and gives an indicator of the level of confidence in the company by the market.

Consequently, EPS is the topic of its own accounting standard, IAS 33, which details rules on its calculation and presentation to ensure consistent treatment and comparability between companies.

3 Basic EPS

The basic EPS calculation is:

$$EPS = \frac{Earnings}{Number\ of\ shares}$$

This is expressed as dollars or cents per share (cents if the amount is less than $1).

- Earnings: Net profit attributable to ordinary equity shareholders of the parent entity, i.e. group profit after tax less profit attributable to non-controlling interests and irredeemable preference share dividends.

NB Profits attributable to non-controlling interest (NCI) will only be included with group financial statements. Group financial statements are covered in the 'Group accounts' section of the syllabus (Chapter 11 – 17). Chapter 12 provides further detail regarding how the NCI share of profit is determined. Group basic and diluted EPS will be calculated using the figures within the group financial statements and will be different from the EPS disclosed in the individual accounts.

- Number of shares: Weighted average number of ordinary shares on a time weighted basis.

Issue of shares at full market price

An issue at full market price brings additional resources to the entity, but the impact on earnings is only from the date of issue. Therefore the number of shares are time apportioned.

> **Illustration 1 – Issue of shares at market price**
>
> A has earnings of $300,000 during the year ended 31 December 20X6. On 1 January 20X6, A had share capital of 100,000 $1 shares. On 1 March 20X6 a further 60,000 shares were issued at $3.25 per share.
>
> **Required:**
>
> Calculate basic EPS for year ended 31 December 20X6
>
> **Solution**
>
> $$EPS = \frac{Earnings}{Number\ of\ shares}$$
>
> $$EPS = \frac{\$300,000}{(100,000 \times 2/12) + (160,000 \times 10/12)}$$
>
> $$EPS = \frac{\$300,000}{150,000}$$
>
> EPS = $2 per share

Test your understanding 1 (integration question)

A company issued 200,000 shares at market price ($3.00) on 1 July 20X8. There was no issue of shares in the year ended 31 December 20X7.

Relevant information

	20X8	20X7
Profit attributable to the ordinary shareholders for the year ending 31 December	$550,000	$460,000
Number of ordinary shares in issue at 31 December	1,000,000	800,000

Required:

Calculate the EPS for the years ended 31 December 20X7 and 20X8.

Test your understanding 2 (OTQ style)

Gerard's earnings for the year ended 31 December 20X4 are $2,208,000. On 1 January 20X4, the issued share capital of Gerard was 8,280,000 ordinary shares of $1 each. The company issued 3,312,000 shares at full market value on 30 June 20X4.

Required:

Calculate the EPS for Gerard for the year ended 31 December 20X4.

Bonus issue/Scrip issues

Bonus issues are issues of shares to current shareholders, based upon the shareholder's current shareholding, for free (no cash is raised).

Bonus issue may also be referred to as scrip issues.

A bonus issue:

- does not provide additional resources to the issuer.

- means that the shareholder owns the same proportion of the business before and after the issue.

In the calculation of EPS:

- the bonus shares are deemed to have always been in issue and therefore are reflected for the full period.

- the comparative figures are also restated to include the bonus shares.

The EPS calculation becomes:

$$EPS = \frac{Earnings}{No.\ of\ shares\ before\ bonus \times bonus\ fraction}$$

$$Bonus\ fraction = \frac{No.\ of\ shares\ after\ bonus\ issue}{No.\ of\ shares\ before\ bonus\ issue}$$

E.g. Company B holds 100,000 shares and makes a 1 for 10 bonus issue. 100,000/10 = 10,000 new shares issued.

$$Bonus\ fraction = \frac{110,000}{100,000} = \frac{11}{10}$$

- to adjust the comparative figures, multiply the previous year's basic EPS by the inverse of the bonus fraction, i.e. 100,000/110,000 or 10/11.

Illustration 2 – Bonus issue

A company makes a bonus issue of one new share for every five existing shares held on 1 July 20X8.

	20X8	20X7
Profit attributable to the ordinary shareholders for the year ending 31 December	$550,000	$460,000
Number of ordinary shares in issue at 31 December	1,200,000	1,000,000

Basic EPS for year ended 31 December 20X8 (with comparative)

Calculation of EPS in 20X8 accounts.

$$20X8\quad \frac{\$550,000}{1,200,000} = 45.8c$$

$$20X7\quad \frac{\$460,000}{1,200,000} = 38.3c$$

In the example above, the computation for the comparative has been reworked in full. However, if last year's EPS is given then calculate the comparative EPS by multiplying this by the bonus fraction inverted.

Last year's EPS = 46c ($460,000/1m)

The bonus fraction is:

$$\frac{1,200,000}{1,000,000} \quad or \quad \frac{6}{5}$$

Therefore, the comparative restated is

46c × 5/6 = 38.3c

Test your understanding 3 (integration question)

At 1 April 20X2, Dorabella had 7 million $1 ordinary shares in issue. It made a bonus issue of one share for every seven held on 31 August 20X2. Its earnings for the year were $1,150,000.

Dorabella's EPS for the year ended 31 March 20X2 was 10.7c.

Required:

Calculate the EPS for the year ending 31 March 20X3, together with the comparative EPS for 20X2 that would be presented in the 20X3 accounts.

Test your understanding 4 (OTQ style)

At 1 May 20X3, Rose had 900 million $1 ordinary shares in issue. It made a bonus issue of one share for every 9 held on 1 September 20X3. Its profit before tax for the year was $800m and the income tax expense for the year was $250m.

Required:

Calculate the basic EPS for the year ended 30 April 20X4. Give your answer in cents.

Test your understanding 5 (OTQ style)

At 1 May 20X3, Rose had 900 million $1 ordinary shares in issue. It made a bonus issue of one share for every 9 held on 1 September 20X3. Rose's EPS for the year ended 30 April 20X3 was 40.0c.

Required:

Calculate the comparative EPS that would be presented in the financial statements for the year ended 30 April 20X4.

 Rights issue

Rights issues:

- contribute additional resources; and
- are normally priced below full market price.

Therefore, they combine the characteristics of issues at full market price and bonus issues.

Determining the weighted average capital, therefore, involves two steps as follows:

1   adjust for the bonus element in the rights issue, by multiplying capital in issue before the rights issue by the following fraction:

$$\frac{\text{Actual cum rights price (CRP)}}{\text{Theoretical ex rights price (TERP)}}$$

-    The cum rights price will be given to you in the exam question. It is the share price on the last trading day before the rights issue, i.e. the price of a share 'including' the rights.

-    The theoretical ex-rights price is the theoretical share price after the rights issue has occurred. This must be calculated.

2   calculate the weighted average capital in the issue on a time apportioned basis.

Illustration 3 – Theoretical ex rights price

The theoretical ex rights price was introduced in the chapter on long term finance. Here's a reminder of how to calculate it.

C makes a 1 for 4 rights issue at $1.90 per share.

The cum rights price of C's shares is $2.00.

Calculation of the TERP

	Number of shares	×	Price	=	Value
Before rights	4	×	2.00	=	8.00
Rights issue	1	×	1.90	=	1.90
After rights		×	?		

We are looking for the theoretical ex rights price (TERP), i.e. the price of a share after the rights issue, denoted by a question mark above.

Simply calculate the total value after the issue and divide it by the total number of shares after the issue.

	Number of shares	×	Price	=	Value
Before rights	4	×	2.00	=	8.00
Rights issue	1	×	1.90	=	1.90
After rights	5	×	?		9.90

TERP = 9.90/5 = 1.98

The fraction to adjust for the bonus element is (applied only to the shares before the rights issue):

CRP/TERP = 2/1.98

Illustration 4 – Rights issue

A company issued one new share for every two existing shares held at $1.50 per share on 1 July 20X8. The pre-issue market price was $3.00 per share.

Relevant information

	20X8	20X7
Profit attributable to the ordinary shareholders for the year ending 31 December	$550,000	$460,000
Number of ordinary shares in issue at 31 December	1,200,000	800,000

Calculation of basic EPS for year ended 31 December 20X8, with comparative

20X8

$$\frac{\text{Earnings}}{\text{Weighted average number of shares (W1)}} = \frac{\$550,000}{1,080,000} = 50.9 \text{ cents}$$

20X7

The prior year EPS must be adjusted to reflect the bonus element in the rights issue.

$$\text{EPS} = 57.5c \text{ (W3)} \times \frac{\$2.50 \text{ (W2)}}{\$3.00} = 47.9 \text{ cents}$$

NB: To restate the EPS for the previous year simply multiply EPS by the inverse of the rights issue bonus fraction.

(W1) 20X8 Weighted average number of shares

The number of shares before the rights issue must be adjusted for the bonus element in the rights issue using the theoretical ex rights price.

6/12 × 800,000 × 3.00/2.50 **(W2)**	480,000
6/12 × 1,200,000	600,000
	1,080,000

(W2) Theoretical ex rights price

	2 shares @ $3.00	$6.00
	1 share @ $1.50	$1.50
	3 shares	$7.50
Theoretical ex rights price	= $7.50/3	$2.50

(W3)

20X7 EPS	=	$460,000
		800,000
	=	57.5 cents

Test your understanding 6 (integration question)

On 31 December 20X1, the issued share capital of a company consisted of 4,000,000 ordinary shares of 25c each. On 1 July 20X2 the company made a rights issue in the proportion of 1 for 4 at 50c per share when the shares were quoted at $1.15. The profit after tax for the year ended 31 December 20X2 was $425,000. The reported earnings per share for the year ended 31 December 20X1 was 8c.

Required:

Calculate the basic EPS for the year ended 31 December 20X2, together with the comparative for 20X1 that would be presented in the 20X2 financial statements.

Test your understanding 7 (OTQ style)

At 1 May 20X3, Rose had 900 million $1 ordinary shares in issue. Its earnings for the year ended 30 April 20X4 was $550m.

On 1 July 20X3, a rights issue took place of 1 share for every 4 held at $2. The market price of each share immediately before the rights issue was $2.50.

Required:

Complete the formula below to provide the bonus fraction that would be applied to the pre-issue number of shares in the calculation of the weighted average number of shares of Rose for the year ended 30 April 20X4.

$

_____

$

Test your understanding 8 (OTQ style)

At 1 January 20X3, Lily had 400 million $1 ordinary shares in issue. On 1 August 20X3, a rights issue took place of 1 share for every 5 held at $2.75. The market price of each share immediately before the rights issue was $3.25.

The theoretical ex rights price of the rights issue is $3.17.

Required:

Calculate the weighted average number of shares that would be used in the basic earnings per share calculation for the year ended 31 December 20X3. Give your answer in millions to one decimal place.

Test your understanding 9 (OTQ style)

At 1 May 20X3, Rose had 900 million $1 ordinary shares in issue. Its earnings for the year ended 30 April 20X4 were $550m and its EPS for the previous year, ended 30 April 20X3, was 40.0c.

On 1 July 20X3, a rights issue took place of 1 share for every 4 held at $2. The market price of each share immediately before the rights issue was $2.50.

Required:

Calculate the comparative basic EPS that would be reflected in the financial statements for the year ended 30 April 20X4. Give your answers in cents to 1 decimal place.

Test your understanding 10 (case style)

XYZ has made a couple of share issues over the past few years. The directors have been reviewing the calculation of the basic earnings per share and have noticed that the calculation of the weighted average number of shares is not consistent each year. The first share issue was a bonus issue to existing shareholders. The second was an issue at full market price.

Required:

Prepare a brief note to the directors explaining why a bonus issue and issue at full market price are treated differently in the calculation of basic earnings per share.

4   Diluted earnings per share (DEPS)

Introduction

Equity share capital may change in the future owing to circumstances which exist now. The provision of a diluted EPS figure attempts to alert shareholders to the potential impact of these changes on the EPS figure.

Examples of transactions that may create such circumstances are:

- convertible bonds (or convertible preference shares)

- share options (or warrants).

When the potential ordinary shares are issued the total number of shares in issue will increase and this can have a dilutive effect on EPS i.e. it may fall. It will fall where the increase in shares outweigh any increase in profits, e.g. from a reduction in finance costs once debt has been converted.

Basic principles of calculation

 To deal with potential ordinary shares, adjust basic earnings and number of shares assuming convertibles, options, etc. had converted to equity shares on the first day of the accounting period, or on the date of issue, if later.

DEPS is calculated as follows:

$$\frac{\text{Earnings + notional extra earnings}}{\text{Number of shares + notional extra shares}}$$

Importance of DEPS

The basic EPS figure could be misleading to users if, at some future time, the number of shares in issue will increase without a proportionate increase in resources.

For example, if an entity has issued bonds convertible at a later date into ordinary shares, on conversion the number of ordinary shares will rise, no fresh capital will enter the entity and earnings will therefore only rise by the savings made by no longer having to pay the post-tax amount of interest on the bonds.

Often the earnings increase is proportionately less than the increase in the shares in issue. This effect is referred to as 'dilution' and the shares to be issued are called 'dilutive potential ordinary shares'.

IAS 33 therefore requires an entity to disclose the DEPS, as well as the basic EPS, calculated using current earnings but assuming that the worst possible future dilution has already happened. Existing shareholders can look at the DEPS to see the effect on current profitability of commitments already entered into that could create an issue of ordinary shares in the future.

For the purpose of calculating DEPS, the number of ordinary shares should be the weighted average number of ordinary shares calculated as for basic EPS, plus the weighted average number of ordinary shares which would be issued on the conversion of all the dilutive potential ordinary shares into ordinary shares. Dilutive potential ordinary shares are deemed to have been converted into ordinary shares at the beginning of the period or, if later, the date of the issue of the potential ordinary shares. This means that, if the transaction causing the potential ordinary shares was issued during the year, the number of shares converted, included within DEPS, should be pro-rated based upon the fraction of the year that the transaction had been in existence.

By disclosing DEPS, as well as EPS, users of the financial statements, will have a clearer picture regarding the entity from which to make their decisions. The user has an indication as to the financial implications of potential events that may, but have not yet, occurred. Consequently, users should be better informed in their decision making.

Convertible debt

 The principles of convertible bonds and convertible preference shares are similar and will be dealt with together.

If the convertible bonds/preference shares had been converted:

* the interest/dividend would be saved therefore earnings would be higher

* the number of shares would increase.

Note: Interest on bonds is tax deductible however preference dividends do not attract tax relief. Therefore, only convertible bonds consider the tax implications within the DEPS calculation.

Note: If there is an option to convert the debt into a variable number of ordinary shares depending on when conversion takes place, the maximum possible number of additional shares is used in the calculation.

Illustration 5 – Convertible debt and DEPS

A company has the following balances:

- $500,000 in 10% cumulative irredeemable preference shares of $1

- $1,000,000 in ordinary shares of 25c = 4,000,000 shares.

Income taxes are 30%.

On 1 April 20X1, the company issued convertible bonds for cash. Assuming the conversion was fully subscribed there would be an increase of 1,550,000 ordinary shares in issue.

The liability element of the bonds is $1,250,000 and the effective interest rate is 8%, resulting in an annual gross interest charge of $100,000.

Trading results for the years ended 31 December were as follows:

	20X2 $	20X1 $
Profit before interest and tax	1,100,000	991,818
Interest on convertible bonds	(100,000)	(75,000)
Profit before tax	1,000,000	916,818
Income tax	(300,000)	(275,045)
Profit after tax	700,000	641,773

Calculation of basic and diluted EPS for years ended 31 December 20X1 and 20X2.

	20X2 $	20X1 $
Basic EPS		
Profit after tax	700,000	641,773
Less: Preference dividend (10% × $500,000)	(50,000)	(50,000)
Earnings	650,000	591,773
EPS based on 4,000,000 shares	16.25c	14.8c

DEPS

Earnings as above	650,000	591,773
Notional extra earnings:		
Interest on the convertible bonds (only 9 months in 20X1)	100,000	75,000
Less: Income tax on interest at 30%	(30,000)	(22,500)
Adjusted earnings	720,000	644,273
EPS 20X2 based on 5,550,000 shares	13.0c	
EPS 20X1 based on 5,162,500 shares		12.5c

Convertible preference shares are dealt with on the same basis, except that often they do not qualify for tax relief so there is no tax increase to be adjusted for.

As the convertible was issued after 3 months of 20X1, the DEPS for 20X1 must pro-rate the converted number of shares included in the calculation to show the proportion of the year that the convertible existed. In 20X1, only 75% of the conversion is included in the DEPS being 1,162,500 shares (9/12 x 1,550,000). Therefore, notional shares for 20X1 is 5,162,500 (4,000,000 + 1,162,500).

Test your understanding 11 (OTQ style)

A company had 8.28 million shares in issue at the start of the year and made no new issue of shares during the year ended 31 December 20X4, but on that date it had in issue convertible loan stock 20X6–20X9.

Assuming the conversion was fully subscribed there would be an increase of 2,070,000 ordinary shares in issue. The liability element of the loan stock is $2,300,000 and the effective interest rate is 10%. Assume a tax rate of 30%.

The earnings for the year were $2,208,000 giving rise to a basic earnings per share of 26.7 cents.

Required:

Calculate the fully diluted EPS for the year ended 31 December 20X4.

Test your understanding 12 (OTQ style)

On 1 January 20X1, Pillbox, a listed entity, had 10 million $1 ordinary shares in issue. The earnings for the year ended 31 December 20X1 were $5,950,000. Pillbox made no new issue of shares during the year. The basic earnings per share was 59.5 cents.

Pillbox is subject to income tax at a rate of 30%.

On 1 January 20X1, Pillbox issued convertible bonds. Assuming the conversion was fully subscribed there would be an increase of 2,340,000 ordinary shares in issue. The liability element of the bonds is $2,600,000 and the effective interest rate is 10%.

Required:

Calculate the diluted EPS for the year ended 31 December 20X1.

Options and warrants to subscribe for shares

An option or warrant gives the holder the right to buy shares at some time in the future at a predetermined price.

The cash received by the entity when the option is exercised will be less than the market price of the shares, as the option will only be exercised if the exercise price is lower than the market price. The increase in resources does not match the increase there would have been if the issue of shares were at market value. The options will therefore have a dilutive effect on EPS.

 The total number of shares issued on the exercise of the **option** or **warrant** is split into two:

- the number of shares issued if the cash received had been used to buy shares at fair value (using the average price of the shares during the period)

- the remainder, which are treated like a bonus issue (i.e. as having been issued for no consideration).

The number of shares issued for no consideration is added to the weighted average number of shares when calculating the DEPS.

These 'free' shares are equal to:

$$\text{No. of options} \times \frac{FV - EP}{FV}$$

FV = fair value of the share price

EP = exercise price of the shares

An alternative approach could be used to the above. No method is preferable and both will arrive to the same answer. The alternative is illustrated below:

Step 2: Number of shares purchased at average market value from cash raised by option   x

Step 3: Free element (for inclusion in DEPS notional shares)   x   β

                                ———

Step 1: Number of options in issue   x

Illustration 6 – Options and DEPS

On 1 January 20X7, a company has 4 million ordinary shares in issue and issues options over another million shares. The profit after tax for the year attributable to ordinary shareholders is $500,000.

During the year to 31 December 20X7, the average fair value of one ordinary share was $3 and the exercise price for the shares under option was $2.

Required:

Calculate basic EPS and DEPS for the year ended 31 December 20X7

Solution

$$\text{Basic EPS} = \frac{\$500,000}{4,000,000} = 12.5c$$

Options

	$
Earnings	500,000
Number of shares	
Basic	4,000,000
Options **(W1)**	333,333
	4,333,333

The DEPS is therefore $\dfrac{\$500,000}{4,333,333} = 11.5c$

(W1) Number of free shares issued

$$\text{Free shares} = \text{No. of options} \times \frac{FV - EP}{FV}$$

$$\text{Free shares} = 1,000,000 \times \frac{3.00 - 2.00}{3.00} = 333,333$$

Or, using the alternative approach:

Step 2: Number of shares purchased at average market value from cash raised by option ((2 × 1m)/3)	666,667
Step 3: Free element (for inclusion in DEPS notional shares)	333,333 β
	─────
Step 1: Number of options in issue	1,000,000

Test your understanding 13 (OTQ style)

A company had 8.28 million shares in issue at the start of the year. No issue of shares occurred during the year ended 31 December 20X4, but on that date there were outstanding options to purchase 920,000 ordinary $1 shares at $1.70 per share. The average fair value of ordinary shares was $1.80. Earnings for the year ended 31 December 20X4 were $2,208,000 giving rise to a basic EPS of 26.7c.

Required:

Calculate the fully DEPS for the year ended 31 December 20X4.

Test your understanding 14 (OTQ style)

On 1 January 20X1, Pillbox, a listed entity, had 10 million $1 ordinary shares in issue. The earnings for the year ended 31 December 20X1 were $5,950,000 and Pillbox made no new issue of shares during the year. The basic earnings per share for the year was 59.5c.

As at the year ended 31 December 20X1, there were outstanding options to purchase 74,000 ordinary $1 shares at $2.50 per share. The average fair value of one ordinary $1 share was $4.

Required:

Calculate the diluted EPS for the year ended 31 December 20X1.

Test your understanding 15 (further OTQs)

Questions (1) to (3) below are all based on the following scenario:

On 1 January 20X9, CSA, a listed entity, had 3,000,000 $1 ordinary shares in issue. On 1 May 20X9, CSA made a bonus issue of 1 for 3.

On 1 September 20X9, CSA issued 2,000,000 $1 ordinary shares for $3.20 each. The profit before tax of CSA for the year ended 31 December 20X9 was $1,040,000. The income tax expense for the year was $270,000.

The basic earnings per share for the year ended 31 December 20X8 was 15.4 cents.

On 1 November 20X9, CSA issued convertible loan stock. Assuming the conversion was fully subscribed there would be an increase of 2,400,000 ordinary shares in issue. The liability element of the loan stock is $4,000,000 and the effective interest rate is 7%.

CSA is subject to income tax at a rate of 30%.

Required:

1   Calculate the basic earnings per share to be reported in the financial statements of CSA for the year ended 31 December 20X9 in accordance with the requirements of IAS 33 Earnings Per Share.

2   Calculate the comparative EPS that would be presented alongside the basic EPS in the financial statements for the year ended 31 December 20X9 in accordance with the requirements of IAS 33 Earnings Per Share.

3   Calculate the diluted earnings per share for the year ended 31 December 20X9, in accordance with the requirements of IAS 33 Earnings Per Share.

The following scenario relates to question 4 only.

On 1 July 20X2 SJL, a listed entity, had 6 million $1 ordinary shares in issue. On 1 March 20X3, SJL made a rights issue of 1 for every 3 shares held at a price of $4. The market price for the shares on the last day of quotation cum rights was $5 per share. SJL's earnings for the year ended 30 June 20X3 were $4.5 million.

4   Calculate the basic earnings per share to be reported in the financial statements of SJL for the year ended 30 June 20X3, in accordance with the requirements of IAS 33 Earnings Per Share.

The following scenario relates to question 5 only.

The ordinary shareholders of DPR held options to purchase 200,000 $1 ordinary shares at $4.25 per share. The average fair value of one $1 ordinary share in the period in question was $5.15.

5   What number of shares should be added to the denominator of the diluted EPS calculation to reflect the free shares that exist within the options (to the nearest whole number of shares)?

5 Chapter summary

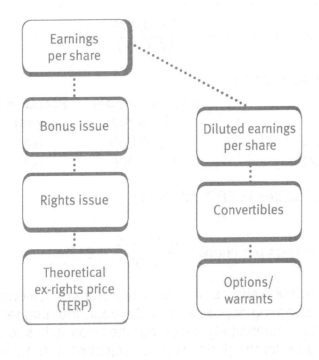

Test your understanding answers

Test your understanding 1 (integration question)

20X7   Earnings per share = $\dfrac{\$460,000}{800,000}$ = 57.5c

Issue at market price

Date	Actual number of shares	Fraction of year	Total
1 Jan 20X8	800,000	6/12	400,000
1 July 20X8	1,000,000	6/12	500,000
Number of shares in EPS calculation			900,000

20X8   Earnings per share = $\dfrac{\$550,000}{900,000}$ = 61.1c

Since the 200,000 shares have only generated additional resources towards the earning of profits for half a year, the number of new shares is adjusted proportionately. Note that the approach is to use the earnings figure for the period without adjustment, but divide by the average number of shares weighted on a time basis.

Test your understanding 2 (OTQ style)

Issue at full market price

Date	Actual number of shares	Fraction of year	Total
1 January 20X4	8,280,000	6/12	4,140,000
30 June 20X4	11,592,000 (W1)	6/12	5,796,000
Number of shares in EPS calculation			9,936,000

(W1) New number of shares

Original number	8,280,000
New issue	3,312,000
New number	11,592,000

The earnings per share for 20X4 would now be calculated as:

$$\frac{\$2,208,000}{9,936,000} = 22.2c$$

Test your understanding 3 (integration question)

The number of shares issued on 31 August 20X2 is 7,000,000 × 1/7 = 1,000,000

The EPS for 20X3 is 1,150,000/8,000,000 × 100 c = 14.4c

The bonus fraction is (7 + 1)/7 = 8/7

20X2 adjusted comparative = 10.7 × 7/8 (bonus fraction inverted) = 9.4c.

Test your understanding 4 (OTQ style)

Basic EPS = 55c

The number of shares after the issue on 1 September 20X3 is 900m × 10/9 = 1,000m

The earnings for the year ended 30 April 20X4 is $800m – $250m = $550m

Therefore, the EPS for the year ended 30 April 20X4 is $550m/1,000m = 55c

Test your understanding 5 (OTQ style)

Comparative EPS = 36.0c

The bonus fraction = 10/9 (1 new share for every 9 held).

The comparative = 40.0 × 9/10 (bonus fraction inverted) = 36.0c.

Test your understanding 6 (integration question)

20X2 EPS

$$EPS = \frac{\$425,000}{4,754,902 \ (W1)} = 8.9c \text{ per share}$$

20X1 EPS

Applying correction factor to calculate adjusted comparative figure of EPS:

$$8c \times \frac{\text{Theoretical ex rights price}}{\text{Actual cum rights price}} = 8c \times \frac{1.02 \ (W2)}{1.15} = 7.1 \text{ c per share}$$

(W1) Current year weighted average number of shares

The number of shares before the rights issue must be adjusted for the bonus element in the rights issue using the theoretical ex rights price.

6/12 × 4,000,000 × 1.15/1.02 **(W2)**	2,254,902
6/12 × 5,000,000 (*)	2,500,000
	4,754,902

(*) 4m × 5/4 = 5m

(W2) Theoretical ex rights price

			$
Prior to rights issue	4 shares	worth 4 × $1.15 =	4.60
Taking up rights	1 share	cost 50c =	0.50
	5		5.10

i.e. theoretical ex rights price of each share is $5.10 ÷ 5 = $1.02

Test your understanding 7 (OTQ style)

The fraction to apply to the pre-issue number of shares is:

$$\frac{\$2.50}{\$2.40 \text{ (W1)}}$$

(W1) Theoretical ex rights price

			$
Prior to rights issue	4 shares	worth 4 × $2.50 =	10.00
Taking up rights	1 share	cost $2.00 =	2.00
	5		12.00

i.e. theoretical ex rights price of each share is $12 ÷ 5 = $2.40

Test your understanding 8 (OTQ style)

Weighted average number of shares = 439.2 million

7/12 × 400m × 3.25/3.17	239.2m
5/12 × 480m (*)	200.0m
	439.2m

(*) 400m × 6/5 = 480m

Test your understanding 9 (OTQ style)

Comparative EPS = 38.4 cents per share

$$40c \times \frac{2.4 \text{ (W1)}}{2.5} = 38.4c \text{ per share}$$

(W1) Theoretical ex rights price

			$
Prior to rights issue	4 shares	worth 4 × $2.50 =	10.00
Taking up rights	1 share	cost $2.00 =	2.00
	5		12.00

i.e. theoretical ex rights price of each share is $12 ÷ 5 = $2.40

The rights bonus fraction to apply in the weighted average calculation for the current year is 2.50/2.40.

This is inverted and multiplied by the previous year's EPS in order to restate the comparative.

Test your understanding 10 (case style)

Note to directors

You have correctly noticed that the calculation of the weighted average number of shares for the basic earnings per share is different depending on whether a bonus issue or full market price issue has been made. The reason for this difference is explained below.

A bonus issue does not raise any new finance and therefore the profit for the year will have been generated with the same level of resources throughout the year. As the issue results in no additional resources it is treated as if it has always been in existence. For this reason, comparative figures also need to be restated.

The issue at full market price brings additional resources which will impact on profits from the date of issue. Therefore a weighted average number of shares is used to calculate EPS, so that the numerator and denominator are stated on a like for like basis.

Also, please note that the proportions held by shareholders after a bonus issues remain unaffected whilst the proportions of shares held by shareholders after a full market prices share issue may changes (as new investors may acquire the shares).

Please let me know if you have any further queries on the matter.

Test your understanding 11 (OTQ style)

Diluted EPS = 22.9 cents per share

If this loan stock was converted to shares the impact on earnings would be as follows.

	$	$
Basic earnings		2,208,000
Add notional interest saved		
($2,300,000 × 10%)	230,000	
Less tax relief foregone $230,000 × 30%	(69,000)	
		161,000
Revised earnings		2,369,000
Number of shares if loan converted		
Basic number of shares		8,280,000
Notional extra shares		2,070,000
Revised number of shares		10,350,000

$$\text{DEPS} = \frac{\$2,369,000}{10,350,000} = 22.9c$$

Test your understanding 12 (OTQ style)

Diluted EPS

Earnings (5.95m + (10% × $2.6m × 70%))	$6,132k
Shares (10m + 2.34m)	12,340k
Diluted EPS	**49.7c**

Test your understanding 13 (OTQ style)

	$
Earnings	2,208,000
Number of shares	
Basic	8,280,000
Options **(W1)**	51,111
	8,331,111

The DEPS is therefore $\dfrac{\$2,208,000}{8,331,111} = 26.5c$

(W1) Number of free shares issued

$$\text{Free shares} = \text{No. of shares under option} \times \frac{FV - EP}{FV}$$

$$\text{Free shares} = 920,000 \times \frac{1.80 - 1.70}{1.80} = 51,111$$

Tutorial note:

An alternative way of viewing the above calculation (of the free shares) is as follows:

Finance raised via exercise of options would be $1.70 × 920,000 = $1,564,000

To raise this amount of finance via a market price issue would require $1,564,000/$1.80 = 868,889 shares

Therefore, the number of free shares awarded in the option scheme = 920,000 – 868,889 = 51,111

Test your understanding 14 (OTQ style)

Diluted EPS

Earnings	$5,950k
Shares (10m + (74k × (4 − 2.50)/4))	10,028k
Diluted EPS	**59.3c**

Test your understanding 15 (further OTQs)

1 **Basic earnings per share = 16.5 cents**

Profit after tax ($1,040,000 − $270,000)		$770,000
Weighted average number of shares		
At 1 January 20X9	3,000,000	
Bonus issue	1,000,000	
Full market price issue (2,000,000 × 4/12)	666,667	
		4,666,667
Basic EPS for 20X9 $770,000/4,666,667		16.5 cents

2 **Comparative EPS (restated) = 11.6 cents**

Last year's EPS 15.4c × 3/4 bonus fraction inverted = 11.6c

3 **Diluted earnings per share = 11.4 cents**

Reported profit after tax (as in answer (1))	$770,000	
Plus post tax saving of finance costs (70% × 7% × $4m × 2/12)	$32,667	
		$802,667
Weighted average number of shares:		
As reported in answer (1)	4,666,667	
Weighted average dilution from potential share issue (2,400,000 × 2/12)	400,000	
		5,066,667
Fully diluted EPS $802,667/5,066,667		15.8 cents

4   Basic EPS = 65.4 cents

$$EPS = \frac{\$4,500,000}{6,877,193 \ (W1)} = 65.4 \text{ cents}$$

(W1) Current year weighted average number of shares

The number of shares before the rights issue must be adjusted for the bonus element in the rights issue using the theoretical ex rights price.

8/12 × 6m × 5/4.75 **(W2)**	4,210,526
4/12 × 8m	2,666,667
	6,877,193

(W2) Theoretical ex rights price

			$
Prior to rights issue	3 shares	worth 3 × $5 =	15
Taking up rights	1 share	cost $4 =	4
	4		19

Theoretical ex rights price of each share is $19 ÷ 4 = $4.75

5   Number of free shares = 34,951

Free shares = 200,000 × (5.15 – 4.25)/5.15 = 34,951

Leases

Chapter learning objectives

Lead outcome	Component outcome
B1: Explain relevant financial reporting standards for revenue, leases, financial instruments, intangible assets and provisions	Explain the financial reporting standards for: (b) Leases

1   Session content

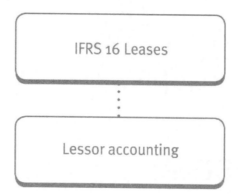

2   Introduction

An entity may need a particular asset for its operations but may not have the cash available to purchase the asset outright. As a result, the entity may enter a lease agreement whereby the entity gets to use the asset on a day to day basis but pays for the asset via periodic rental payments.

This is a common method of financing utilised by many businesses.

 Definitions

'A lease is a contract, or part of a contract, that conveys the right to use an asset (the underlying asset) for a period of time in exchange for consideration.'

The **lessor** is the **'entity that provides the right to use an underlying asset in exchange for consideration.'**

The **lessee** is the **'entity that obtains the right to use an underlying asset in exchange for consideration.'**

A **right-of-use asset 'represents the lessee's rights to use an underlying asset for the lease term.'** (IFRS 16, Appendix A).

3   Lessee accounting

 Lessee accounting is covered within F1. It is assumed knowledge at CIMA F2.

4   Lessor accounting

The **lessor** is the **'entity that provides the right to use an underlying asset in exchange for consideration.'** (IFRS 16, Appendix A).

The lessor provides the asset to the lessee and receives payments.

A lessor must classify its leases as finance or operating leases.

Finance leases and operating leases

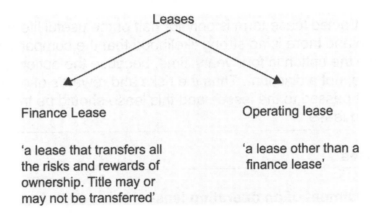

Leases

Finance Lease

'a lease that transfers all
the risks and rewards of
ownership. Title may or
may not be transferred'

Operating lease

'a lease other than a
finance lease'

Indications of a finance lease

To determine whether a lease is a finance or operating lease, the substance of
the lease agreement should be considered. According to IFRS 16 *Leases*, a
lease is probably a finance lease if one or more of the following apply:

- Ownership is transferred to the lessee at the end of the lease.

- The lessee has the option to purchase the asset for a price substantially
  below the fair value of the asset and it is reasonably certain the option will
  be exercised.

- The lease term is for the major part of the asset's useful life.

- The present value of the minimum lease payments amount to substantially
  all of the fair value of the asset.

- The leased assets are of such a specialised nature that only the lessee
  can use them without major modification.

- The lessee bears losses arising from cancelling the lease.

- Lessee has ability to continue the lease for a secondary period at a rate
  below market rent.

Illustration 1 – Classification of lease

A company has entered into a four-year lease to provide a machine to
a customer. The lease rentals of $100,000 are payable annually in
advance, with an optional secondary period of three years at rentals of
80%, 60% and 40% of the previous annual rental within the primary
period. It is agreed that these rentals represent a fair commercial rate.
The machine has a useful life of eight years and a cash value of
$600,000.

**Would this lease agreement be a finance lease or an operating
lease?**

> **Solution**
>
> The contracted lease term is only for half of the useful life of the machine and there is no strong likelihood that the company will exercise the option in four years' time, because the option is priced at fair value, not a discount. Thus the risks and rewards of ownership have not passed to the lessee and this lease should be treated as an operating lease.

Operating leases

Accounting treatment of an operating lease

- Lease receipts are shown as income in the statement of profit or loss on a straight line basis over the term of the lease, unless another systematic basis is more appropriate.

- Any difference between amounts charged and amounts paid will be recognised as accrued income or deferred income in the statement of financial position.

> **Illustration 2 – operating lease**
>
> Mosala Ltd entered into a four year operating lease on 1 January 20X1 to rent a combine harvester to Manure. Mosala provided an initial rent free period of 12 months followed by three annual payments of $2,000 in arrears on 31 December each year. The annual payments commence on 31 December 20X2.
>
> **Prepare extracts from the financial statements of Mosala Ltd for the year ended 31 December 20X2?**
>
> Total receipts = $6,000 (3 × $2,000)
>
> Rental income spread over lease term = 6,000/4 = $1,500
>
> In year 1, no cash was received creating an accrued income balance of $1,500.
>
> Dr Accrued income $1,500
>
> Cr Rental income $1,500
>
> In year 2, cash of $2,000 was received
>
> Dr Cash $2,000
>
> Cr Rental income $1,500
>
> Cr Accrued income $500

> ## Statement of profit or loss for year ended 31 December 20X2 (extract)
>
> | | $ |
> |---|---|
> | Operating lease income ($6,000/4) | 1,500 |
>
> ## Statement of financial position as at 31 December 20X2 (extract)
>
> | | $ |
> |---|---|
> | Current assets | |
> | Accrued income (1,500 – 500) | 1,000 |

> ## Test your understanding 1 (OTQ style)
>
> RLP entered into a three year operating lease on 1 May 20X2 to provide the use of an item of office equipment. It received a deposit of $750 and will receive lease payments of $500 on 30 April 20X3, 20X4 and 20X5.
>
> In the year ended 30 April 20X3, RLP has recorded all receipts related to the lease as income in the statement of profit or loss.
>
> **Calculate the income to be recognised in the statement of profit or loss for the year ended 30 April 20X3.**

Finance leases

At the inception of a lease, lessors present finance leases by derecognising the leased asset and recording a receivable for the future receipts from the lease.

Net Investment of the lease

The finance lease receivable is equal to the **net investment of the lease**.

This is calculated as the **present value** of all unreceived:

*   Fixed rental payments
*   Variable rental payments
*   Residual value guarantees (amounts the lessee guarantees that the leased asset will be worth at the end of the lease)
*   Unguaranteed residual values
*   Termination penalties

The payments are discounted at the rate implicit in the lease.

Illustration 3 – Calculating the net investment

On 31 December 20X1, Rain leases a machine to Snow on a three year finance lease and will receive $10,000 per year in arrears. Snow has guaranteed that the machine will have a market value at the end of the lease term of $2,000.

The interest rate implicit in the lease is 10%.

Required

Calculate Rain's net investment in the lease as at 31 December 20X1.

Solution

The net investment in the lease must include the present value of:

- fixed lease payment
- residual value guarantees that are expected to be paid.

Date	Description	Amount	Discount rate	Present value
20X2	Receipt	10,000	0.909	9,090
20X3	Receipt	10,000	0.826	8,260
20X4	Receipt	10,000	0.751	7,510
20X4	Guaranteed residual value	2,000	0.751	1,502
	Net investment in lease			26,362

A receivable of $26,362 is recognised. The asset leased would be derecognised and any difference taken as a gain or loss to the statement of profit or loss.

Subsequent treatment

The carrying amount of the lease receivable is:

- increased by the finance income earned
- decreased by the cash receipts.

 Test your understanding 2 (OTQ style)

Brendan Ltd leases machinery to Stirling Ltd on 1 January 20X1. The lease is for four years at an annual cost of $2,000 payable annually in arrears. The useful life of the asset is deemed to be 4 years. The normal cash price (and fair value) of the asset is $5,710, the same as its carrying amount, and there is no residual value. The present value of the minimum lease payment is $5,710. The implicit rate of interest is 15%.

Required:

What will be the total receivable shown on the SOFP and the impact to the SOPL of Brendan Ltd for the year ended 31st December 20X1?

A   Receivable $5710, P/L $857 expense

B   Receivable $5710, P/L $857 income

C   Receivable $4567, P/L $857 income

D   Receivable $4567, P/L $857 expense

Test your understanding 3 (OTQ style)

Freddy Ltd leases machinery to May Ltd on 1 January 20X1. The lease is for 4 years with an annual rental repayment of $4,000 payable in advance. The useful life of the asset is deemed to be 4 years and the present value of total lease payments equalled the carrying amount of the asset on inception. The carrying amount at inception was $13,132. The implicit rate of interest is 15%.

Required:

What will be shown on the statement of financial position and the statement of profit or loss of Freddy for the year ended 31 December 20X1?

A   Receivable $11,420, P/L income $1,713

B   Receivable $10,502, P/L income $1,370

C   Property plant and equipment $12,000, P/L expense $4,000

D   Receivable $9,132, P/L income $4,000

Test your understanding 4 (further OTQs)

1   In lessor accounting, in a _____ lease arrangement, the risks and rewards of the asset leased are transferred to the lessee, whereas in _____ lease arrangements they remain with the lessor.

    Select the correct words to complete the above sentence, from the following options:

    finance, operating

2   Milner Ltd hires out industrial machinery to customers on long-term operating leases. On 1 January 20X1, Milner entered into a 7 year lease on a transportable drilling rig. The terms of the lease are:

    • $175,000 payable on 1 January 20X1

    •   Six rentals of $70,000 payable on 1 January 20X2 – 20X7

Required:

What will be shown in Milner Ltd's SOFP and SOPL for the year ended 31 December 20X1 in relation to the lease arrangement?

A   SOFP No impact, P/L rental income $175,000

B   SOFP Deferred income $90,000, P/L rental income $85,000

C   SOFP Deferred income $85,000, P/L rental income $90,000

D   SOFP Accrual 70,000, P/L rental expense $70,000

3   Emilia leases an asset to its customer on 1 January 20X5. The lease term is 5 years. The lease payments of $10,000 are received in arrears. The economic lifetime of the asset is 8 years. The fair value of the asset was $40,000 which is equal to the present value of the lease payments. The rate implicit in the lease was 8%. Emilia prepares accounts with a year end of 31 December.

Which of the following statements are true?

A   Emilia will record a right-of-use asset and lease liability when entering the lease agreement

B   The lease receivable would have a carrying amount of $40,000 at the year end

C   Investment income of $3,200 is recorded within the statement of profit or loss

D   Emilia still records and depreciates the asset leased to the customer

4   IFRS 16 outlines the accounting treatment used by lessors.

Which of the following statements regarding lessor accounting is true?

A   As leased assets are owned by the lessor, lessors will always record the asset they are leasing to a customer within their statement of financial position

B   Operating leases require the recognition of a receivable valued at the net investment in the lease

C   if the present value of lease payments is the majority of a leased asset's fair value, this indicates a finance lease

D   Lessors will always record investment income within profit or loss regardless of the type of lease

5   **Which TWO of the following situations would normally lead to a lease being classified as a finance lease?**

   A   The lease transfers ownership of the asset to the lessee by the end of the lease term

   B   The lease term spans approximately half of the economic life of the asset

   C   The leased assets are of a specialised nature such that only the lessee can use them without major modifications being made

   D   At the inception of the lease, the present value of the lease payments is 60% of the amount the leased asset would cost to purchase

6   On 1 October 20X3, Fresco leased an item of plant under a five-year finance lease agreement to a customer. The plant had a cash purchase cost of $25 million. The agreement had an implicit finance cost of 10% per annum and required an immediate deposit of $2 million and annual rentals of $6 million paid on 30 September each year for five years.

   What would be the net investment of the lease recorded by Fresco?

   A $18,394

   B $22,176

   C $24,176

   D $25,000

5 Chapter summary

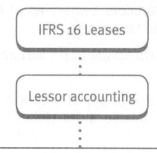

IFRS 16 Leases

Lessor accounting

Finance lease
- Derecognise asset
- Record receivable at net investment in lease
- Record interest income in profit or loss

Operating lease
- No derecognition of asset
- Record interest income in profit or loss

Test your understanding answers

Test your understanding 1 (OTQ style)

Correct rental income for statement of profit or loss in the year ended 30 April 20X3 = $750

Total lease receipts = 750 + (3 × 500) = $2,250

Length of lease = three years

Annual rental income to statement of profit or loss = $2,250/3 = $750

Test your understanding 2 (OTQ style)

C

As Brendan Ltd is leasing out the asset to Stirling Ltd, the question is set from the perspective of the lessor.

The lease term is all of the useful economic lifetime. The present value of the minimum lease payments of the lease is equal to the fair value of the asset. This indicates that the risk and rewards transfer to the lessee. The lease is a finance lease.

The asset should be derecognised and a receivable of $5,710 (the net investment in the lease) is recorded at the 1st January 20X1.

To work out the receivable outstanding at 31st December 20X1:

Year	Balance b/f ($)	Interest income @15% ($)	Receipt ($)	Carried forward ($)
1	5,710	857	(2,000)	4,567

Therefore, the year-end receivable on the SOFP = $4,567.

The SOPL includes rental **income** = $857

NB. No profit or loss would arise from the derecognition of the asset as the carrying amount is equal to the net investment in the lease.

Test your understanding 3 (OTQ style)

B

The lease term is all of the useful lifetime. The present value of the lease payments of the lease is equal to the fair value of the asset at $13,132. This indicates that the risk and rewards transfer to the lessee. The lease is a finance lease.

The asset should be derecognised (therefore, option C is incorrect) and a receivable of $9,132 (the net investment in the lease) is recorded at the 1 January 20X1.

An initial cash receipt of $4,000 was received at inception.

The net investment in the lease is calculated as lease payments not received at the commencement date. This is calculated as follows:

Date	Description	Amount	Discount rate (15%)	Present value
Yr 2-4	Receipt	4,000	2.283	9,132
	Net investment in lease			9,132

For rental receipts in advance, cash receipts are taken before interest is calculated. As a result, the receivable outstanding at 31 December 20X1 for Freddy is:

Year	Balance b/f ($)	Receipt ($)	Sub-total	Interest income @15% ($)	Carried forward ($)
1	9,132	0	9,132	1,370	10,502

Therefore, the year-end receivable on the SOFP = $10,502.

The SOPL includes **interest income** = $1,370

NB. No profit or loss would arise from the derecognition of the asset as the carrying amount is equal to the present value of total lease payments $13,132 ($9,132 + $4,000).

Test your understanding 4 (further OTQs)

1   In lessor accounting, in a **finance** lease arrangement, the risks and rewards of the asset leased are transferred to the lessee, whereas in **operating** lease arrangements they remain with the lessor.

2   **The correct answer is B**

Rental income to the SOPL will be determined by spreading the total rental receipts (including deposits and incentives) using the straight line basis.

The rental income in 31 December 20X1 is calculated as:

(175,000 + (70,000 × 6))/7 = 595,000/7 = $85,000

As cash received in 20X1 ($175,000) is higher than the rental income within the SOPL, deferred income of $90,000 ($175,000 – $85,000) will be recognised in the SOFP.

Deferred income = $90,000

Rental income = $85,000

3   The correct answer is C

Interest income of $3,200 is recorded within the statement of profit or loss

Emilia provides the customer with a lease where the risks and rewards transfer to the lessee. The lease is a finance lease. This is noted due to the present value of the minimum lease payments being equal to the fair value and the lease term being the majority of the economic lifetime of the asset.

As a result, Emilia should derecognise the asset, recording a lease receivable at the net investment in the lease and a gain or loss on disposal. Interest income will be recorded at the rate implicit in the lease. This would be recorded at $3,200 (40,000 × 8%).

Option A is incorrect as right-of-use assets and lease liabilities are recorded by the lessee, not the lessor.

Option B is incorrect as the lease receivable would have a carrying amount of $33,200. This is calculated as the initial net investment in the lease plus interest income less lease receipts (40,000 + 3,200 -10,000).

Option D is incorrect as it considers the lease as an operating lease instead of a finance lease.

4   The correct answer is D

Lessors will always record investment income within profit or loss regardless of the type of lease.

Lessors within an operating lease will record rental receipts as income within their profit or loss on a systematic basis over the life of the lease.

Lessors providing a finance lease will record investment income based on the lease receivable × implicit rate of the lease.

Option A is incorrect as assets will be derecognised from the lessor's accounts under finance lease arrangements.

Option B is incorrect as it is finance leases that record the lease receivable at the net investment in the lease, not operating lease arrangements.

Option C is incorrect as a finance lease is indicated when the present value of the minimum lease payments is substantially all the fair value of the asset, not the majority of the fair value.

5   The correct answers are A and C

The lease term needs to be the majority of the useful life, and the present value of the lease payments should be substantially all of the fair value of the asset. Therefore B and D are incorrect.

6 **The correct answer is C**

In the accounts of the lessor, a finance lease will initially derecognise the leased asset, recorded a receivable at the net investment of the lease and record a gain or loss in profit or loss.

The requirement asks for the net investment of the lease. This is the receivable initially recorded and is calculated as the present value of the fixed payments in the lease plus any guaranteed and unguaranteed residual values.

The net investment of the lease is calculated as follows:

	Receipt ($)	Discount factor	PV ($)
t_0	2,000	1	2,000
t_{1-5}	6,000	3.696	22,176
			24,176

6

Revenue from contracts with customers

Chapter learning objectives

Lead outcome	Component outcome
B1: Explain relevant financial reporting standards for revenue, leases, financial instruments, intangible assets and provisions	Explain the financial reporting standards for: (a) Revenue

1 Session content

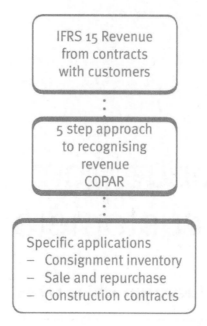

2 IFRS 15 Revenue from contracts with customers

 IFRS 15 defines revenue as **'Income arising in the course of an entity's ordinary activities'** (IFRS 15, appendix A).

Revenue does not include:

- Proceeds from sale of non-current assets

- Sales tax and other similar taxes

- Other amounts collected on behalf of others. For example, in an agency relationship, the agent would only recognise commission.

 # 3 5-step approach

IFRS 15 – Revenue recognition: A five step process

An entity recognises revenue by applying the following five steps:

1   **Identify the contract**

2   **Identify the separate performance obligations within a contract**

3   **Determine the transaction price**

4   **Allocate the transaction price to the performance obligations in the contract**

5   **Recognise revenue when (or as) a performance obligation is satisfied.**

The 5 steps can be easily remembered using the acronym, COPAR:

- **C**ontract
- **O**bligations
- **P**rice
- **A**llocate price
- **R**ecognise revenue.

The five steps will be considered in more detail in this section. However, the following illustration may help you to gain an understanding of the basic principles.

> ### Illustration 1 – The five steps
>
> On 1 December 20X1, Wade receives an order from a customer for a computer as well as 12 months of technical support. Wade delivers the computer (and transfers its legal title) to the customer on the same day.
>
> The customer paid $420 upfront. The computer sells for $300 and the technical support sells for $120. Wade's year-end is 31 December 20X1.
>
> **The 5 steps would be applied to this transaction as outlined below:**
>
> **Step 1 – Identify the contract**
>
> There is an agreement between Wade and its customer for the provision of goods and services.
>
> **Step 2 – Identify the separate performance obligations within a contract**
>
> There are two performance obligations (promises) within the contract:
>
> - The supply of a computer
> - The supply of technical support.
>
> **Step 3 – Determine the transaction price**
>
> The total transaction price is $420.
>
> **Step 4 – Allocate the transaction price to the performance obligations in the contract**
>
> Based on standalone sales prices, $300 should be allocated to the sale of the computer and $120 should be allocated to the technical support.
>
> **Step 5 – Recognise revenue when (or as) a performance obligation is satisfied**
>
> Control over the computer has been passed to the customer so the full revenue of $300 should be recognised on 1 December 20X1.
>
> The technical support is provided over a 12 month period. The performance obligation is satisfied over that 12 month period, so its revenue should be recognised over that time. In the year ended 31 December 20X1, revenue of $10 (1/12 × $120) should be recognised from the provision of technical support.

The five steps of revenue recognition will now be considered in more detail.

Step 1: Identify the contract

IFRS 15 *Revenue from contracts with customers* says that a contract is an agreement between two or more parties that creates rights and obligations. A contract does not need to be written.

An entity can only account for revenue if the contract meets the following criteria:

- the parties to the contract have approved and are committed to fulfilling the contract

- each party's rights can be identified

- the payment terms can be identified

- the contract has commercial substance, and

- it is probable that the entity will be paid.

> ### Example 1 – Identifying the contract
>
> Aluna has a year end of 31 December 20X1.
>
> On 30 September 20X1, Aluna signed a contract with a customer to provide them with an asset on 31 December 20X1. Control over the asset passed to the customer on 31 December 20X1. The customer will pay $1m on 30 June 20X2.
>
> By 31 December 20X1, as a result of changes in the economic climate, Aluna did not believe that it was probable that they would collect the consideration that Aluna was entitled to. Therefore, the contract cannot be accounted for and no revenue should be recognised.

Step 2: Identifying the separate performance obligations within a contract

Performance obligations are promises to transfer distinct goods or services to a customer.

Some contracts contain more than one performance obligation. For example:

- An entity may enter into a contract with a customer to sell a car **(one performance obligation)**, which includes one year's free servicing and maintenance **(another separate performance obligation).**

- An entity might enter into a contract with a customer to provide a course of 5 lectures **(one performance obligation)**, as well as to provide a textbook on the first day of the course **(another separate performance obligation)**.

The distinct performance obligations within a contract must be identified.

An entity must decide if the nature of a performance obligation is:

- to provide the specified goods or services itself (i.e. it is the principal), or

- to arrange for another party to provide the goods or service (i.e. it is an agent).

If an entity is an agent, then revenue is recognised based on the fee or commission to which it is entitled.

Illustration 2 – Agency sales

Rosemary's revenue includes $2 million for goods it sold acting as an agent for Elaine. Rosemary earned a commission of 20% on these sales and remitted the difference of $1.6 million (included in cost of sales) to Elaine.

Required:

How should the agency sale be treated in Rosemary's statement of profit or loss?

Solution

Rosemary should not have included $2 million in its revenue as it is acting as the agent and not the principal. Only the commission element of $400,000 ($2 million × 20%) can be recorded in revenue. The following adjustment is required:

	$
Dr Revenue	1,600,000
Cr Cost of sales	1,600,000

Step 3: Determining the transaction price

In accordance to IFRS 15 *Revenue from contracts with customers,* the transaction price is the amount of consideration an entity expects in exchange for satisfying a performance obligation.

When determining the transaction price, the following must be considered:

- variable consideration

- significant financing components

- non-cash consideration

- consideration payable to a customer.

Variable consideration

If a contract includes variable consideration (for example, a bonus based on delivery of the contract), it shall be included within **'the transaction price if it is highly probable that a significant reversal in the amount of cumulative revenue will not occur when the uncertainty is resolved'** (IFRS 15, para 56).

Illustration 3 – Variable consideration

On 1 December 20X1, Bristow provides a service to a customer for the next 12 months. The consideration is $12 million. Bristow is entitled to an extra $3 million if, after twelve months, the number of mistakes made falls below a certain threshold.

Required:

Discuss the accounting treatment of the above in Bristow's financial statements for the year ended 31 December 20X1 if:

(a) **Bristow has experience of providing identical services in the past and it is highly probable that the number of mistakes made will fall below the acceptable threshold.**

(b) **Bristow has no experience of providing this service and is unsure if the number of mistakes made will fall below the threshold.**

Solution:

The $12 million consideration is fixed. The $3 million consideration that is dependent on the number of mistakes made is variable.

Bristow must estimate the variable consideration. It could use an expected value or a most likely amount. Since there are only two outcomes, $0 or $3 million, then a most likely amount would better predict the entitled consideration.

(a) Bristow expects to hit the target. Using a most likely amount, the variable consideration would be valued at $3 million.

Bristow must then decide whether to include the estimate of variable consideration in the transaction price.

Based on past experience, it seems highly probable that a significant reversal in revenue recognised would not occur. This means that the transaction price is $15 million ($12m + $3m).

As a service, it is likely that the performance obligation would be satisfied over time. The revenue recognised in the year ended 31 December 20X1 would therefore be $1.25 million ($15m × 1/12).

> (b) Depending on the estimated likelihood of hitting the target, the variable consideration would either be estimated to be $0 or $3 million.
>
> Whatever the amount, the estimated variable consideration cannot be included in the transaction price because it is not highly probable that a significant reversal in revenue would not occur. This is because Bristow has no experience of providing this service. Therefore, the transaction price is $12 million.
>
> As a service, it is likely that the performance obligation would be satisfied over time. The revenue recognised in the year ended 31 December 20X1 would be $1 million ($12m × 1/12).

Note that if a product is sold with a right to return it (e.g. a two week returns policy) then the consideration is considered to be variable. The entity must estimate the likelihood of any returns and record revenue based upon the amounts that are highly likely not to be returned.

As a result of such arrangements, a refund liability should be recorded. The refund liability should equal the consideration received (or receivable) that the entity does not expect to be entitled to as a result of returns (and so will be refunded to the customer).

Illustration 4 – Rights to return products

Nardone enters into 50 contracts with customers. Each contract includes the sale of one product for $1,000. Cash is received upfront and control of the product transfers on delivery. Customers can return the product within 30 days to receive a full refund. Nardone can sell the returned products at a profit.

Nardone has significant experience in estimating returns for this product. It estimates that 48 products will not be returned.

Required:

How should the above transaction be accounted for?

Solution:

The fact that the customer can return the product means that the consideration is variable.

The estimated variable consideration is $48,000 (48 products × $1,000). The variable consideration should be included in the transaction price because, based on Nardone's experience, it is highly probable that a significant reversal in the cumulative amount of revenue recognised ($48,000) will not occur.

Therefore, revenue of $48,000 and a refund liability of $2,000 ($1,000 × 2 products expected to be returned) should be recognised.

> The journal entry to record the sale is:
>
> Dr Cash $50,000
>
> Cr Revenue $48,000
>
> **Cr Refund liability $2,000**

Financing

In determining the transaction price, an entity must consider if the timing of payments provides the customer or the entity with a significant financing benefit.

The existence of a financing element to the sale can be indicated by:

- a difference between the amount paid and the cash selling price
- an extended time period between the transfer of the goods or service and the payment date.

If there is a significant financing component, then the consideration receivable needs to be discounted to present value using the rate at which the customer would borrow.

Illustration 5 – discounted present value

A retailer of electrical goods offers two year 0% finance on items offered for sale at $3,000. The cash price of the goods is $2,500. The rate of interest on the retailers borrowing is 7%.

How should this transaction be recorded in the first 12 months after the sale?

As the customer will take 2 years to pay and a difference between the cash price and the repayment exists, this contract includes a significant financing element.

The discount factor for $1 receivable in two years' time with a 7% interest rate is 0.873.

The revenue from sale of the goods is the present value of the amount receivable in two years' time, i.e. $2,619 (3,000 × 0.873).

Dr Receivable	$2,619
Cr Revenue	$2,619

The discount on the receivable balance is then unwound over the two year period up to the date of receipt and the interest is recognised as finance income. Therefore, after one year the adjustment would be:

Dr Receivable	$183 (2,619 × 7%)
Cr Finance income (P/L)	$183

Note that this is in accordance with IFRS 9 *Financial Instruments*. The receivable balance is a financial asset shown at amortised cost.

Test your understanding 1 – Rudd (integration question)

Rudd enters into a contract with a customer to sell equipment on 31 December 20X1. Control of the equipment transfers to the customer on that date. The price stated in the contract is $1m and is due on 31 December 20X3.

Market rates of interest available to this particular customer are 10%.

Required:

Explain, with supporting calculations, how this transaction should be accounted for in the financial statements of Rudd for the year ended 31 December 20X1, 20X2 and 20X3.

Non-cash consideration

Customers do not always pay using cash or credit. The customer may pay using shares in their entity, share options or using other assets.

Any non-cash consideration should be valued at fair value.

Illustration 6 – Non- cash consideration

Dan sells a good to Stan. Control over the good is transferred on 1 January 20X1. The consideration received by Dan is 1,000 shares in Stan with a fair value of $4 each. By 31 December 20X1, the shares in Stan have a fair value of $5 each.

Required:

How much revenue should be recognised from this transaction in the financial statements of Dan for the year ended 31 December 20X1?

Solution:

The contract contains a single performance obligation.

Consideration for the transaction is non-cash. Non-cash consideration is measured at fair value.

Revenue should be recognised at $4,000 (1,000 shares × $4) on 1 January 20X1.

Any subsequent change in the fair value of the shares received is not recognised within revenue but instead accounted for in accordance with IFRS 9 Financial Instruments.

Consideration payable to a customer

Sometimes amounts are paid to customers as part of the contract. These payments are often an incentive to encourage completion of the sale.

If consideration is paid to a customer in exchange for a distinct good or service, then it is essentially a purchase transaction and should be accounted for in the same way as other purchases from suppliers. For example, suppliers may sell their produce to supermarkets but may also have to pay the supermarket for shelf space.

If the consideration paid to a customer is not in exchange for a distinct good or service, an entity should account for it as a reduction of the transaction price. For example, a car manufacturer sells their newest model electric cars to car dealerships but has to pay the dealer to install chargers at the dealer's premises.

Illustration 7 – Consideration payable to a customer

Golden Gate enters into a contract with a major chain of retail stores. The customer commits to buy at least $20m of products over the next 12 months. The terms of the contract require Golden Gate to pay $1m to compensate the customer for changes to its retail stores to accommodate the new products.

By the 31 December 20X1, Golden Gate has transferred products with a sales value of $4m to the customer.

Required:

How much revenue should be recognised by Golden Gate in the year ended 31 December 20X1?

Solution

The payment made to the customer is not in exchange for a distinct good or service. Therefore, the $1m paid to the customer is treated as a reduction to the transaction price.

The total transaction price is being reduced by 5% ($1m/$20m). Therefore, Golden Gate reduces the transaction price of each good by 5% as it is transferred.

By 31 December 20X1, Golden Gate should have recognised revenue of $3.8m ($4m × 95%).

Step 4: Allocate the transaction price

Contracts can include a number of performance obligations e.g. sales of products including warranty periods. Prices should be allocated to each separate performance obligation within a contract.

The total transaction price should be allocated to each performance obligation in proportion to stand-alone selling prices.

The best evidence of a stand-alone selling price is the observable selling price of a good or service sold separately.

If a stand-alone selling price is not directly observable, then the entity estimates the stand-alone selling price.

Discounts

In relation to a bundled sale, any discount should generally be allocated across each component in the transaction.

The entire discount should only be allocated to a specific individual component of the transaction if that component is regularly sold separately at a discount.

> **Test your understanding 2 – Shred (integration question)**
>
> Shred sells a machine and one year's free technical support for $100,000. It usually sells the machine for $95,000 but does not sell technical support for this machine as a stand-alone product. Other support services offered by Shred attract a mark-up of 50%. It is expected that the technical support will cost Shred $20,000.
>
> **Required:**
>
> How much of the transaction price should be allocated to the machine and to the technical support?

NB. The sale of a warranty as part of a package is treated under IFRS 15 in the same way as any bundled sale (as per the technical support in the TYU above). This is a different context to the **costs** of providing a warranty which are covered under IAS 37 Provisions, contingent liabilities and contingent assets (see Chapter 7).

Step 5: Recognise revenue

Revenue is recognised **'when (or as) the entity satisfies a performance obligation by transferring a promised good or service to a customer'** *(IFRS 15, para 31).*

At the start of a contract, for each performance obligation identified, an entity must determine whether it satisfies the performance obligation:

- at a point in time (see section 4 below), or

- over time (see section 5).

4 Satisfying a performance obligation at a point in time

The performance obligation is satisfied at a point in time when a customer obtains **control** of a promised asset.

Control of an asset refers to the ability to direct the use of, and obtain substantially all of, the remaining benefits from the asset.

Control includes the ability to prevent other entities from obtaining benefits from an asset i.e. an entity can restrict the assets use.

The following are indicators of the transfer of control:

- **'The entity has a present right to payment for the asset**
- **The customer has legal title to the asset**
- **The entity has transferred physical possession of the asset**
- **The customer has the significant risks and rewards of ownership of the asset**
- **The customer has accepted the asset.'** (IFRS 15, para 38)

Specific applications – when does control transfer?

The point at which control is transferred to a customer and revenue can be recorded can be complicated to determine. Varying terms and conditions can lead to uncertainty as to the accounting treatment of particular types of sale transactions. Directors have been known to attempt to take advantage of this uncertainty by manipulating the accounts in their favour, often leading to inappropriate revenue recognition.

The following section looks at some of these more complicated "sales" in detail and gives guidance to help determine the appropriate accounting treatments using IFRS 15.

Examples include:

- consignment inventory
- sale and repurchase arrangements.

Consignment inventory

Consignment inventory is inventory which:

- is legally owned by one party

- is held by another party, on terms which give the holder the right to sell the inventory in the normal course of business or, at the holder's option, to return it to the legal owner.

This type of arrangement is common in the motor trade.

The manufacturer sells inventory to the dealer which the dealer can then sell on to a 3rd party customer. The sale comes with an option to return the items to the manufacturer if not sold by the dealer.

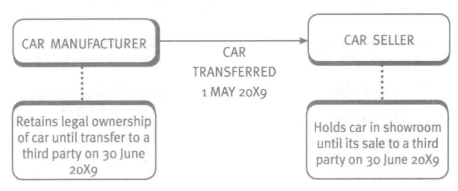

Inventory is legally owned by the manufacturer until:

- the dealer sells inventory onto a third party, or

- the dealer's right to return expires and the inventory is still not sold.

However, the inventory is physically held by the dealer.

Revenue should only be recorded if control of the asset sold transfers to the third party customer. Consignment inventory meets most of the conditions described above for recording revenue at a point in time. However, particular attention should be paid to the need for the customer to hold the **risks and rewards** of ownership.

Accounting for consignment inventory arrangements

If the risks and rewards transfer to the customer, the sale is recorded.

If the risks and rewards are not deemed to have transferred to the customer, no sale is recorded.

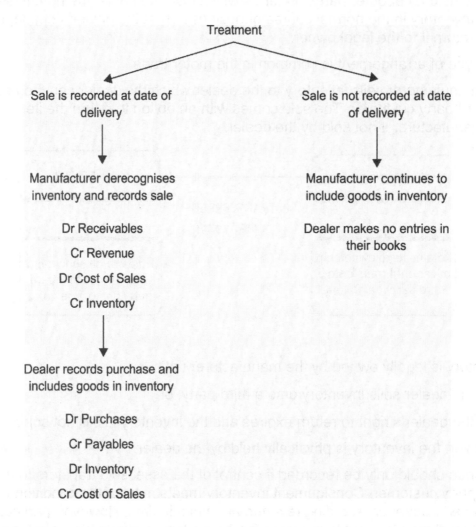

Illustration 8 – consignment inventory

Carmart, a car dealer, obtains inventory from Zippy, its manufacturer, on a consignment basis. The purchase price is set at delivery. Usually, Carmart pays Zippy for the car the day after Carmart sells to a customer. However, if the car remains unsold after six months then Carmart is obliged to purchase the car. There is no right of return. Further, Carmart is responsible for insurance and maintenance from delivery.

Required:

Describe how Zippy should account for the above scenario.

Solution:

Revenue can be recorded at a point in time if the customer obtains control of the promised asset. Indicators of a customer obtaining control include whether the customer has legal title to the asset, the customer has the significant risks and rewards of ownership of the asset and the customer has accepted delivery of the asset. It is obvious that Carmart has accepted delivery. However, whether the risks and rewards have transferred to Carmart is less clear cut.

Indicators regarding the transfer of risk and rewards to Carmart include:

- Carmart faces the risk of slow movement and obsolescence as it is obliged to purchase the car and has no right of return.

- As prices are set at delivery, Carmart is exposed to risks of damaging the car.

- Carmart insures and maintains the cars.

- Carmart faces the risk of theft.

- Carmart can sell the cars to the public.

Carmart has the risk of ownership associated with these cars. Therefore, Zippy records revenue and derecognises the cars from inventory on the date of delivery.

Test your understanding 3 (case style)

On 1 January 20X6 Gillingham, a manufacturer, entered into an agreement to provide Canterbury, a retailer, with machines for resale.

The terms of the agreement are:

- Canterbury pays the cost of insuring and maintaining the machines.

- Canterbury can also display the machines in its showrooms and use them as demonstration models.

- When a machine is sold to a customer, Canterbury pays Gillingham the factory price at the time the machine was originally delivered.

- All machines remaining unsold six months after their original delivery must be purchased by Canterbury at the factory price at the time of delivery.

- Gillingham can require Canterbury to return the machines at any time within the six-month period.

- Canterbury can return unsold machines to Gillingham at any time during the six-month period, without penalty.

At 31 December 20X6, the agreement is still in force and Canterbury holds several machines which were delivered less than six months earlier.

Required:

In relation to the above arrangement, which entity should recognise the machines as inventory for the period that they are held by Canterbury?

Sale and repurchase agreements

A sale and repurchase agreement is where an entity sells an asset but retains a right to repurchase the asset at some point in the future.

Sale and repurchase agreements are common in property developments and in maturing inventories such as whisky or cheese.

The asset has been 'legally' sold, but there is either a commitment or an option to repurchase the asset at a later date.

The point in time at which to recognise revenue depends upon whether the control has transferred to the customer.

Factors to consider when determining who has control of the asset:

- Has the entity transferred all of the risks and benefits of the asset (and therefore control)?

    e.g. can the entity still use the asset? Does the entity bear costs associated with the asset?

- Was the asset "sold" at a price different to market value?

- Is the entity obliged to repurchase the asset?

- If the entity has the option to repurchase the asset are they likely to exercise this option?

- Is the sale is to a bank or financing company?

- Is repurchase at a fixed price or market value?

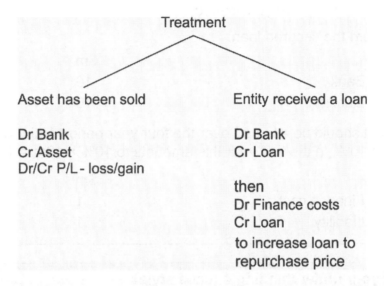

Illustration 9 – sale and repurchase

Xavier sells its head office, which cost $10 million, to Yorrick, a bank, for $10 million on 1 January. Xavier has the option to repurchase the property on 31 December, four years later, at $14.64 million. Xavier will continue to use the property as normal throughout the period and is responsible for the maintenance and insurance. The head office was valued at $18m at transfer on 1 January and is expected to rise in value throughout the four year period. The effective interest rate is 10%.

Required:

Giving reasons, show how Xavier should record the transaction described above during the first year following transfer.

Solution:

Per IFRS 15, revenue is only recorded at a point in time if control is transferred to the customer.

Factors to consider:

- The option to repurchase is likely to be exercised as the option repurchase price is lower than the actual expected value at the repurchase date.

- Xavier continues to insure and maintain the property.

- Xavier will benefit from a rising property price, as repurchase is at a fixed price rather than market value.

- Xavier continues to benefit from use of the property.

Xavier should continue to recognise the head office as an asset in the statement of financial position, as the risks and rewards of ownership remain with Xavier. No revenue is recorded on the sale. This is a secured loan with total interest of $4.64 million ($14.64 million – $10 million) over the four year period.

To record the secured loan:

		$m
Dr	Bank	10
Cr	Liability	10

Interest should be accrued over the four year period at the effective rate of 10%. In the first year this amounts to 10% × 10m = 1m.

		$m
Dr	Finance cost	1
Cr	Liability	1

Test your understanding 4 (case style)

On 1 April 20X4, Triangle sold maturing inventory that had a carrying amount of $3 million, to Factorall, a finance house, for $5 million.

Its estimated market value at this date was in excess of $5 million and is expected to be $8.5 million as at 31 March 20X8.

The inventory will not be ready for sale until 31 March 20X8 and will remain on Triangle's premises until this date.

The sale contract includes a clause allowing Triangle to repurchase the inventory at any time up to 31 March 20X8 at a price of $5 million plus interest at 10% per annum compounded from 1 April 20X4.

The proceeds of the sale have been debited to the bank and the sale (and associated profit) has been recognised in Triangle's statement of profit or loss.

Required:

(a) Discuss how the sale of inventory should be accounted for in accordance with the principles of IFRS 15 *Revenue from contracts with customers*.

(b) Prepare any accounting adjustments required to Triangle's financial statements for the year ended 31 March 20X5.

5   Satisfying a performance obligation over time

An entity satisfies a performance obligation and, correspondingly, should recognise revenue over time, if one of the following criteria is met:

- **the customer simultaneously receives and consumes the benefits provided by the entity's performance as the entity performs**
  i.e. the entity provides a service (Kaplan classroom courses, cleaning and maintenance services).

- **the entity's performance creates or enhances an asset (for example, work in progress) that the customer controls as the asset is created or enhanced**
  i.e. construction work to create a new building/structure on land owned by the customer.

- **the entity's performance does not create an asset with an alternative use to the entity and the entity has an enforceable right to payment for performance completed to date'** (IFRS 15, para 35)
  i.e. construction of highly specialised assets.

Accounting for revenue recorded over time

'For each performance obligation satisfied over time, an entity shall recognise revenue over time by measuring the progress towards complete satisfaction of that performance obligation' (IFRS 15, para 39).

Methods of measuring progress include:

- output methods (such as surveys of performance or time elapsed as a proportion of total contract price/time)

- input methods (such as costs or time elapsed incurred to date as a proportion of total expected costs/time).

As a result, revenue will be recognised based on the amount of progress made compared to the total price.

Test your understanding 5 (OTQ style)

Cleanezee Ltd provides industrial cleaning services to their clients. On 1 July 20X2, Cleanezee Ltd agreed a 12 month contract to clean a disused warehouse for Dirtee Co totalling $120,000 payable in advance.

The reporting date is 30 September 20X2.

Required:

Complete the following journal entry to record the above transaction in the financial statements for the year ended 30 September 20X2.

Dr Cash $120,000

Cr Revenue $ _____

Cr _____ $_____

Scenarios whereby performance obligations are satisfied over time could commonly involve construction companies building an asset for a customer. As long as the construction company is not able to use the asset, and has a right to payment for work to date, revenue would be recognised over time.

 In calculating the entries to be made for such contracts, the following 4-step approach can be helpful:

Step 1 – Calculate overall profit or loss

Step 2 – Determine the progress towards completion

Step 3 – Determine figures for inclusion in the statement of profit or loss

Step 4 – Determine figures for inclusion in the statement of financial position.

Step 1 – Calculate overall profit or loss

	$
Contract price	X
Less: Costs incurred to date	(X)
Less: Estimated costs to complete	(X)
Overall profit/(loss)	X/(X)

If the expected outcome is a **profit**:

- revenue and costs should be recognised according to the progress of the contract.

If the expected outcome is a **loss**:

- the whole loss should be recognised immediately creating a provision for an onerous contract as per IAS 37 (see chapter 8).

If the expected outcome or progress is **unknown** (often due to it being in the very early stages of the contract):

- revenue should be recognised only to the level of recoverable costs incurred.

This results in no profits being recorded on a contract with unknown outcomes.

Step 2 – Determining the progress of a contract

There are two acceptable methods of measuring progress towards satisfying a performance obligation:

- Input methods – commonly based on costs incurred e.g. (costs incurred to date/total costs) × 100% = % complete

- Output methods – based on performance completed, such as work certified to date e.g. (work certified/contract price) × 100% = % complete.

Step 3 – Statement of profit or loss

If profitable (from step 1)

	$
Revenue (Total price × progress %) **less** revenue recognised in previous years	X
Cost of sales (Total costs × progress %) **less** cost of sales recognised in previous years	(X)
Profit	X

If loss making (from step 1)

	$	
Revenue (Total price × progress %) **less** revenue recognised in previous years	X	
Cost of sales β	(X)	β
Total loss on contract (from step 1)	(X)	

 The balancing figure (β) is a short cut to achieve the relevant cost of sales. The cost of sales would actually be made up of the costs matching the stage of progress (% × total costs) plus an additional amount recognised as a provision for an onerous lease. The provision would ensure the entire loss on the contract is recorded immediately. However, for ease of presentation, cost of sales is reflected within these materials as a balancing figure.

Step 4 – Statement of financial position

Some contracts where performance obligations are satisfied over time will be large scale projects and can span a number of years. Billing is difficult to keep accurate as progress continues. As a result, the full amount of work performed may not have been billed or amounts in excess of the work performed may have been billed to the customer.

At the year end, this discrepancy in billing will create a **contract asset or liability**, recorded in the statement of financial position. This will be calculated as shown below:

	$
Costs to date (actual costs, not necessarily cost of sales)	X
Profit/(loss) to date	X/(X)
Less: Amount billed to date	(X)
Contract asset/(liability)	X/(X)

 These figures are **cumulative** and not annual.

Contract asset or liability

IFRS 15 is not prescriptive about the treatment of contract assets or liabilities.

As alternatives to the term 'contract asset', IFRS 15 also allows the terms receivable and work-in-progress to be used. If revenue exceeds cash received, this could be included within trade receivables. If costs to date exceed cost of sales, this could be included within inventory, as work-in-progress.

If the cash received exceeds the revenue recognised to date, there will be a contract liability (acting effectively as deferred income).

If a contract is loss making, there will be a provision recorded to recognise the full loss under the onerous contract, as per IAS 37. This can either be termed as a contract liability or a provision.

Illustration 10 – input method contract

Softfloor House Ltd specialises in the construction of trendy bars and gastro-pubs for their customers. The projects generally take a number of months to complete. The company has three contracts in progress at the year ended April 20X1. Softfloor have an enforceable right for payment for work completed to date.

	A	B	C
	$000	$000	$000
Costs incurred to date	200	90	560
Estimated costs to complete	200	110	140
Contract price	600	300	750
Progress billings	40	70	630

Softfloor calculates the percentage of completion by using the cost basis.

Required:

Calculate the effects of the above contract upon the financial statements.

Solution

These contracts lead to the creation of an asset that is controlled by the customers. As a result, the revenue from these contracts should be recorded over time. A 4-step approach is followed to determine the impact to the financial statements as follows:

Overall contract profit

	A	B	C
	$000	$000	$000
Contract price	600	300	750
Costs incurred to date	(200)	(90)	(560)
Estimated costs to complete	(200)	(110)	(140)
Gross profit	200	100	50

% of completion on cost basis

A 200/400 = 50%

B 90/200 = 45%

C 560/700 = 80%

Statement of profit or loss (extract)

	A	B	C
	$000	$000	$000
Revenue (% × contract price)	300	135	600
Costs (% × total cost)	(200)	(90)	(560)
Gross profit	100	45	40

Statement of financial position (extract)

	A	B	C
	$000	$000	$000
Costs incurred	200	90	560
Profit recognised	100	45	40
Less: progress billings	(40)	(70)	(630)
Contract assets/(liabilities)	260	65	(30)

Illustration 11 – output method contract

Hardfloor House Ltd constructs and refurbishes nightclubs on behalf of their customers. The project generally takes a number of months to complete. The company has three contracts in progress at the year ended April 20X1.

	A $000	B $000	C $000
Costs incurred to date	320	540	260
Estimated costs to complete	40	90	120
Contract price	416	684	400
Work certified to date	312	456	200
Progress billings	250	350	230

Hardfloor House Ltd calculates the percentage of completion by using the work certified basis.

Required:

Calculate the effects of the above contract upon the financial statements.

Solution

Overall contract profit

	A $000	B $000	C $000
Contract price	416	684	400
Costs incurred to date	(320)	(540)	(260)
Estimated costs to complete	(40)	(90)	(120)
Gross profit	56	54	20

% of completion on work certified basis

A   312/416 = 75%

B   456/684 = 66.67%

C   200/400 = 50%

Statement of profit or loss (extract)

	A $000	B $000	C $000
Revenue (% × contract price)	312	456	200
Costs (% × total cost)	(270)	(420)	(190)
Gross profit	42	36	10

Statement of financial position (extract)

	A	B	C
	$000	$000	$000
Costs incurred	320	540	260
Profit recognised	42	36	10
Less: progress billings	(250)	(350)	(230)
Contract asset	112	226	40

Illustration 12 – contracts spanning number of years

Continuing from the previous illustration, Hardfloor House, all three contracts were completed in the next financial period with the following cumulative results:

	A	B	C
	$000	$000	$000
Total costs incurred to date	370	640	380
Contract price	416	684	400
Progress billings	410	670	390

Required:

Calculate the effects of the above contracts upon the financial statements in the next financial period.

Solution

Statement of profit or loss (extract)

	A	B	C
	$000	$000	$000
Revenue (100% × contract price) – amounts recognised	104	228	200
Costs (100% × total cost) – amounts recognised	(100)	(220)	(190)
Gross profit	4	8	10

Statement of financial position (extract)

	A	B	C
	$000	$000	$000
Costs incurred (cumulative)	370	640	380
Profit recognised (cumulative)	46	44	20
Less: progress billings (cumulative)	(410)	(670)	(390)
Contract assets	6	14	10

Explanatory note

Contract A:

Revenue

Total contract price – revenue already recognised = $104,000 ($416,000 – $312,000)

Costs

Total cost to date – costs already recognised = $100,000 ($370,000 – $270,000)

Profits

Annual profit = $4,000 ($104,000 – $100,000)

Overall profit = $46,000 ($416,000 – $370,000)

Contract B:

Revenue

Total contract price – revenue already recognised = $228,000 ($684,000 – $456,000).

Costs

Total cost to date – costs already recognised = $220,000 ($640,000 – $420,000)

Profits

Annual profit = $8,000 ($228,000 – $220,000)

Overall profit = $44,000 ($684,000 – $640,000)

Contract C:

Revenue

Total contract price – revenue already recognised = $200,000 ($400,000 – $200,000)

Costs

Total cost to date – costs already recognised = $190,000 ($380,000 – $190,000)

Profits

Annual profit = $10,000 ($200,000 – $190,000)

Overall profit = $20,000 ($400,000 – $380,000)

Test your understanding 6 (integration question)

Hindhead Ltd constructs specialist equipment for its customers for use in the building industry. Each piece of equipment takes between one and two years to build. Hindhead has an enforceable right to payment for performance completed to date.

The entity has four contracts in process at the year-end 30 April 20X1:

	A	B	C	D
	$000	$000	$000	$000
Contract price	500	890	420	750
Work certified to date	375	534	280	–
Costs incurred to date	384	700	468	20
Estimated costs to complete	48	115	168	650
Progress billings	360	520	224	–

Required:

Prepare extracts from the financial statements for each of the four projects, assuming that revenues and profits are recognised on the work certified basis.

Test your understanding 7 (further OTQs)

1   On 1 April 20X3, LJB sold a freehold property to a finance house for $7 million. The contractual terms require LJB to repurchase the property on 31 March 20X6 for $8.8 million. LJB has the option to repurchase on 31 March 20X4 for $7.6 million or on 31 March 20X5 for $8.2 million. Prior to disposal, the carrying amount of the property was $6 million.

At 31 March 20X4, LJB decided not to take up the option to repurchase.

Which of the following statements are TRUE in respect of LJB's financial statements for the year ended 31 March 20X4? Select all that apply.

A   As the option to repurchase has not been exercised, LJB should derecognise the property and record a profit on disposal of $1 million in the statement of profit or loss.

B   LJB would recognise the property as part of its non-current assets at 31 March 20X4.

C   LJB would recognise a liability of $7 million in its statement of financial position at 31 March 20X4.

D   Finance costs of $0.6 million will be recorded in the LJB statement of profit or loss during the year ended 31 March 20X4.

2　EC signs a contract with a customer to deliver an off the shelf IT system on 1 July 20X2 and to provide support services for a three year period from that date. The total contract price is $600,000 and EC would normally sell equivalent IT systems (without the support service) for $450,000.

Calculate the amount of revenue that should be recognised in EC's statement of profit or loss in respect of the above contract in the year ended 31 December 20X2. State your answer in $.

3　The following information relates to a contract to construct an asset for a customer for which revenue should be recorded over time:

	$
Contract price	5 million
Work certified to date	2 million
Costs to date	1.8 million
Estimated costs to complete	2.2 million

What is the revenue, cost of sales and gross profit that should be recognised in accordance with IFRS 15, assuming that the entity's policy is to calculate performance obligation progress on the input (costs incurred) basis?

	Revenue	Cost of sales	Gross profit
A	$2 million	$1.8 million	$200,000
B	$2 million	$1.6 million	$400,000
C	$2.25 million	$1.8 million	$450,000
D	$2.25 million	$2 million	$250,000

4   The following information relates to a contract to construct an asset for a customer for which revenue should be recorded over time:

	$
Contract price	300,000
Work certified to date	120,000
Costs to date	150,000
Estimated costs to complete	200,000

What are the cost of sales and gross profit figures that should be recognised in accordance with IFRS 15, assuming that the entity's policy is to calculate performance obligation progress on the output (work certified) basis?

	Cost of sales	Gross profit
A	$170,000	$50,000 loss
B	$100,000	$20,000
C	$140,000	$20,000 loss
D	$70,000	$50,000

5   An internet travel agent receives $5,000 on 1 April 20X2 for arranging a holiday to Cyprus. It will pass on 90% of this amount to the holiday company, with payment due on 15 June 20X2. The customer will deal directly with the holiday company in the event of any problems.

The travel agent's financial reporting date is 31 May 20X2.

Required:

Which one of the following statements is correct in respect of the treatment of the travel agent's arrangement within their financial statements for the year ended 31 May 20X2?

A   The travel agent should recognise $5,000 as revenue immediately and should accrue for the $4,500 payment to the holiday company, recognising the expense as a cost of sale.

B   The travel agent should recognise $500 as revenue and $4,500 as deferred income.

C   The travel agent should recognise $500 as revenue and $4,500 as a payable.

D   The travel agent should not recognise any revenue. The entire $5,000 should be credited to deferred income.

6   A company is currently accounting for a contract to construct an asset controlled by the customer. The contract price is $2 million and work certified at the year-end is $1.3 million. Costs incurred to date amount to $1.4 million and it is estimated that a further $1 million will be incurred in completing this project. $1.3 million has been invoiced to the customer.

What is the amount that should be recorded in the statement of financial position for contract assets or liabilities in relation to this contract? Stage of completion is calculated on an input (costs incurred) basis.

A $nil

B $0.1m liability

C $0.3m asset

D $0.3m liability

6   Chapter summary

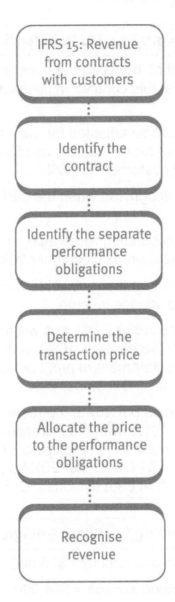

Test your understanding answers

Test your understanding 1 – Rudd (integration question)

Due to the length of time between the transfer of control of the asset and the payment date, this contract includes a significant financing component.

The consideration must be adjusted for the impact of the financing transaction. A discount rate should be used that reflects the characteristics of the customer i.e. 10%.

Revenue should be recognised when the performance obligation is satisfied.

Revenue, and a corresponding receivable, should be recognised at $826,000 ($1m × 0.826) on 31 December 20X1.

Each year, the discount on the receivable will be unwound by 10%, taking the increase to finance income.

For the year to 31 December 20X2, this will mean that the receivable increases by $82,600 ($826,000 × 10%), with $82,600 being shown as finance income in the statement of profit or loss. This would make the receivable $908,600 at 31 December 20X2.

For the year to 31 December 20X3, the receivable would increase by $90,860 ($908,600 × 10%), with the increase also being taken to finance income. This makes the receivable $1m (subject to a small rounding difference) at 31 December 20X3 equalling the cash received from the customer on that date (Dr Cash, Cr Receivable).

Test your understanding 2 – Shred (integration question)

Price allocated to sale of machine = $76,000

Price allocated to support service = $24,000

The selling price of the machine is $95,000 based on previous selling prices for the product.

There is no observable selling price for the technical support. Therefore, the stand-alone selling price needs to be estimated.

Based on the information provided regarding the cost of the technical support, the selling price can be estimated. The selling price of the service would be $30,000 ($20,000 × 150%).

The total standalone selling prices of the machine and support are $125,000 ($95,000 + $30,000). Total consideration receivable is only $100,000. The customer is receiving a discount of 20% ($25,000/$125,000) for purchasing a bundle of goods and services.

IFRS 15 says that an entity must consider whether the discount relates to the whole bundle or to a particular performance obligation. As the technical support is not normally sold separately, it cannot be deemed to be normally sold at a discount. As a result, the discount is apportioned across both performance obligations within the contract.

The transaction price allocated to the machine is $76,000 ($95,000 × 80%).

The transaction price allocated to the technical support is $24,000 ($30,000 × 80%).

The revenue will be recognised when (or as) the performance obligations are satisfied.

Test your understanding 3 (case style)

Revenue can be recorded at a point in time when control is transferred to the customer. Control transfers if the risk and rewards of ownership are held by the customer.

Factors indicating that the risks and benefits of ownership are with Canterbury:

- Canterbury pays the cost of insuring and maintaining the machines, suggesting they are exposed to the risk of theft and breakdown.

- Canterbury can display the machines and use them as demonstration vehicles, suggesting they have a certain level of control over the machines held on their premises.

- The price paid by Canterbury is determined at the time of delivery, suggesting that Canterbury will either benefit or suffer from any subsequent sale at a different price.

- Canterbury is required to purchase any machines that they have held for a six month period.

Factors indicating that the risks and benefits of ownership are with Gillingham:

- Gillingham can require Canterbury to return the machines at any time within the six-month period, suggesting that Gillingham still exercises control over the machines.

- Canterbury can return unsold machines to Gillingham at any time during the six-month period, without penalty. Therefore, they can transfer the significant risk of obsolescence back to Gillingham.

As a result, the risks and rewards do not transfer until such time as the assets are sold by Canterbury to a third party or the 6 month time period elapses (when Canterbury is forced to pay Gillingham). Revenue can only be recorded at that point in time.

Control is not transferred to Canterbury on delivery. Gillingham should record no revenue and continue to recognise the goods within its inventories.

Test your understanding 4 (case style)

(a) **Accounting treatment**

IFRS 15 does not allow revenue to be recognised until control has transferred to the buyer.

There is a clause allowing Triangle to repurchase the inventory, indicating a sale and repurchase agreement. Where there is an option to repurchase, whether control has transferred to the buyer must be considered. The likelihood of the option being exercised should be assessed.

Triangle can repurchase the inventory at $7,320,500 at 31 March 20X8, i.e. $5 million × 1.1^4 = $7,320,500. Since the market value is expected to be $8.5 million at this time, it is likely that Triangle will repurchase the inventory.

Furthermore, since the goods remain on Triangle's premises during the 4 years, Triangle is still exposed to the risks of ownership and have managerial involvement/control over the goods.

A final indicator that this is not a straightforward sale is that Triangle have received proceeds of $5 million whilst the current market value is in excess of this amount (Note however that this factor alone would not lead to the conclusion that there is not a sale, as Triangle may have chosen to sell the goods at a discount).

In conclusion, control of the asset is retained by Triangle.

Triangle should not have recorded a sale, but instead should have recorded a loan of $5 million with a finance cost of 10% per annum. The goods should remain in inventory at their cost of $3 million.

(b) **Accounting adjustments**

Journals

	$m
Dr Revenue (to reverse the sale)	5
Cr Liability	5

To correct the entries Triangle recorded in error.

	$m
Dr Closing inventory (SFP)	3
Cr Closing inventory (SP/L)	3

Reinstate the closing inventory.

	$m
Dr Finance cost	0.5
Cr Liability	0.5

Record the interest for the year at 10% × $5m = $0.5m.

Test your understanding 5 (OTQ style)

Dr Cash	$120,000
Cr Revenue	$30,000
Cr Deferred income	$90,000

The cleaning services provided sees the customer, Dirtee, receive and consume the benefits of Cleanezee's work simultaneously. As a result, revenue will be recorded over time.

The entity will use input methods for determining the performance obligation satisfied. Time elapsed would be the most appropriate method giving the information provided.

The contract is for 12 months of which 3 months of the total service has elapsed. The entity will recognise $30,000 (3/12 × $120,000) in revenue.

As cash has been received in excess of the recognised revenue, deferred income of $90,000 ($120,000 – $30,000) must also be recorded.

Test your understanding 6 (integration question)

Overall profit/loss on contract

	A $000	B $000	C $000	D $000
Contract price	500	890	420	750
Costs to date	(384)	(700)	(468)	(20)
Costs to complete	(48)	(115)	(168)	(650)
Total estimated profit	68	75	(216)	80

% completion on work certified basis

A 375/500 = 75%

B 534/890 = 60%

C 280/420 = 66.7%

D 0/750 = 0%

Statement of profit or loss and other comprehensive income

	A $000	B $000	C $000	D $000
Revenue (% × contract price or recoverable costs))	375	534	280	20
Cost of sales (% × total cost or β if loss making)	(324)	(489)	(496)β	(20)
Gross profit/loss	51	45	(216)	–

Statement of financial position (extract)

	A $000	B $000	C $000	D $000
Costs incurred	384	700	468	20
Profits/losses recognised	51	45	(216)	–
Progress billings	(360)	(520)	(224)	–
Contract assets	75	225	28	20

Project C

A loss has been made on this contract of $216,000 therefore we must recognise the whole of the loss immediately. The revenue will be calculated as normal and the cost of sales becomes the balancing figure.

Project D

Although work has been performed on this project no work has yet been certified, hence we cannot recognise a profit in the statement of profit or loss. However, we cannot ignore that costs have been incurred, hence they become the cost of sales and the revenue becomes the same amount to recognise a nil profit.

Test your understanding 7 (further OTQs)

1   **B and D are correct.**

A is not correct. Although the option to repurchase has not been exercised, there is still a requirement to repurchase at 31 March 20X6. Therefore, the risks and rewards of ownership have not transferred to the finance house.

C is not correct. The liability at the year-end would be $7.6 million as this is the repurchase price at the reporting date. The extra $0.6 million reflects interest for the year on the liability and will be recorded within the statement of profit or loss.

2   **Revenue = $475,000**

Total revenue from support services = $150,000 (600,000 – 450,000)

Annual revenue from support services = $50,000 (150,000/3 years)

Revenue to be recognised in current period = $25,000 (50,000 × 6/12 for July to Dec)

Therefore, total revenue to be recognised = $475,000 (450,000 (for IT system) + 25,000 (for service))

3   **C is the correct answer**

	$m
Total revenue	5
Costs to date	(1.8)
Costs to complete	(2.2)
Total profit	1

% completion = 1.8 million/4 million = 45%

	$m
Revenue (45% × 5)	2.25
Cost of sales (45% × 4)	(1.8)
Gross profit	0.45

4   **A is the correct answer**

	$
Total revenue	300,000
Costs to date	(150,000)
Costs to complete	(200,000)
Total loss	(50,000)

Stage of completion using work certified = 40% (120,000/300,000)

	$m
Revenue (40% × 300,000)	120,000
Cost of sales (ß)	(170,000)
Gross loss	(50,000)

NB. The cost of sales of $170,000 is actually made up the costs of sales as per the stage of completion = $140,000 (40% × (150,000 + 200,000)) + £30,000 provision as onerous contract per IAS 37. This is simplified by using a balancing figure.

5   **The correct statement is C.**

The agent will only recognise the commission element of $500 (10% × $5,000) as revenue. It is only the agent, not the principal. The 90% balance of $4,500 will be shown as a payable balance (due to the holiday company). The $4,500 is not deferred income as it will not be recognised as revenue at a later date.

6   **D $0.3m liability**

Statement of financial position (extract)

	$m
Costs to date	1.4
Recognised loss (W1)	(0.4)
Progress billings	(1.3)
Contract liability	**(0.3)**

(W1) Recognised loss

	$m
Expected outcome:	
Total revenue	2
Costs to date	(1.4)
Costs to complete	(1)
Total loss	(0.4)

The contract is loss making so the entity would record the entire loss of $0.4m immediately.

Provisions, contingent liabilities and contingent assets

Chapter learning objectives

Lead outcome	Component outcome
B1: Explain relevant financial reporting standards for revenue, leases, financial instruments, intangible assets and provisions	Explain the financial reporting standards for: (c) Provisions

1 Session content

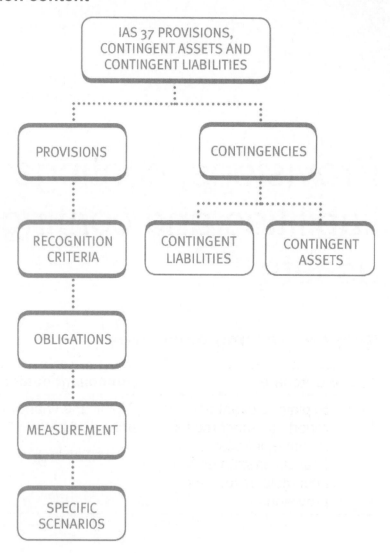

2 Introduction

The problem

Until the issue of IAS 37 *Provisions, Contingent Liabilities and Contingent Assets*, provisions was an accounting area that was open to manipulation.

- Provisions were often recognised as a result of an intention to make expenditure, rather than an obligation to do so.

- Entities would often create provisions to depress profits in good years and then reverse them at a later date when profits needed a boost (a technique known as profit smoothing).

- Several items could be aggregated into one large provision that was then reported as an exceptional item (the 'big bath provision').

- Inadequate disclosure meant that in some cases it was difficult to ascertain the significance of provisions.

As a result, IAS 37 introduced a set of criteria that must be satisfied before a provision can be recognised. The standard also requires comprehensive disclosure of any provisions that have been made so that users can understand the impact that they have had on the financial performance of the reporting entity.

3   Provisions

 A provision is **'a liability of uncertain timing or amount'** (IAS 37, para 10).

 A liability is **'a present obligation of the entity arising from past events, the settlement of which is expected to result in an outflow from the entity of resources embodying economic benefits'** (IAS 37, para 10).

 Recognition of a provision

A provision can be recognised when, and only when, all of the following conditions are met:

- **'an entity has a present obligation (legal or constructive) as a result of a past event**

- **it is probable that an outflow of resources embodying economic benefits will be required to settle the obligation, and**

- **a reliable estimate can be made of the amount of the obligation.**

If any one of these conditions is not met, no provision may be recognised' (IAS 37, para 14).

Obligations

IAS 37 says that the obligation can be:

- legal, i.e. arising from

  - a contract

  - legislation

  - other operation of law

- constructive, i.e. the entity has created a valid expectation via

  - established pattern of past practice

  - published policy or statement.

Illustration 1 – constructive obligation

A retail store has a policy of refunding purchases by dissatisfied customers, even though it is under no legal obligation to do so. Its policy of making refunds is generally known.

Should a provision be made at the year end?

- The policy is well known and creates a valid expectation.

- There is a constructive obligation.

- It is probable some refunds will be made.

- These can be measured using expected values.

Conclusion: A provision is required.

Probable outflow

The outflow of resources must be considered to be more likely than not.

Where there are a number of similar obligations, probability is assessed across the entire class of obligations rather than individually.

Illustration 2 – probable outflow

An entity sells goods with a warranty covering customers for the cost of repairs required within the first 12 months after purchase. Past experience suggests that 95% of goods sold will not require a warranty repair.

Should a provision be made for warranty repairs?

If each sale were considered individually, no provision would be made as there is only a 5% probability of the goods being returned for repair.

However, if sales are considered as a whole, there is a high likelihood of 5% being returned for repair. Therefore, a provision should be made for the expected cost of repairs to 5% of the goods sold in the last 12 months.

Reliable estimate

The standard states that situations in which a reliable estimate cannot be made should be rare.

The estimate should be:

- the best estimate of likely outflow

- a prudent estimate

- discounted when time value of money is material.

Test your understanding 1 (integration question)

An entity has a policy of only carrying out work to rectify damage caused to the environment when it is required by local law to do so. For several years the entity has been operating an oil rig that causes such damage in a country that did not have legislation in place requiring any rectification.

A new government has now been elected in that country and, at the reporting date, has just brought in legislation requiring rectification of environmental damage. The legislation will have retrospective effect.

Required:

Explain whether a provision should be recognised.

Test your understanding 2 (OTQ style question)

You are an accountant working for SZ, a manufacturer that provides warranties to its customers for all sales. Under the terms of the warranty, SZ undertakes to make good manufacturing defects that become apparent within 2 years from the date of sale. Based on past experience, it estimates that 8% of goods will be returned for repair within this 2 year period.

Which of the following statements regarding the warranty is true if IAS 37 is to be correctly applied within SZ's current year financial statements?

A   The warranty will have no impact on the accounts of SZ

B   A disclosure is included in the financial statements outlining the potential costs of the warranty

C   A provision for the warranty is recognised in the financial statements based upon 8% of the total revenue for the current period

D   A provision for the warranty is recognised of 4% of annual revenue as the total cost will be spread over the 2 year period in which the costs are expected to be incurred

4   Specific applications

The standard provides additional guidance on how to apply the rules to specific scenarios.

Future operating losses

Provisions cannot be made for future operating losses as they do not meet the definition of a liability (they are an expectation rather than an obligation).

Onerous contracts

An onerous contract is **'a contract in which the unavoidable costs of meeting the obligations under the contract exceed the economic benefits expected to be received under it'** (IAS 37, para 10).

Per IAS 37, a provision is required for the cheapest option of exiting the contract, which is the lower of:

- cost of fulfilling the contract

- any compensation/penalties payable for failing to fulfil it.

Illustration 3 – onerous contract

CEG has ten years left to run a sales contract that has recently seen costs spiral. The present value of the costs to be incurred on completion of the contract, estimated as at the reporting date, is $50,000. The cost of terminating the contract early is $55,000.

How should the above scenario be accounted for?

A provision should be made for $50,000 which is the lowest net cost of exiting the contract. In this case, the entity would see the contract out as this create the lowest costs incurred.

To record the provision:

	$000
Dr Expense (profit or loss)	50
Cr Provision	50

When the rental payments are subsequently paid, the provision for the costs of the onerous contract will reduce.

The following entry is posted:

Dr Provision

Cr Cash

Restructuring

According to IAS 37, a restructuring is a programme planned and controlled by management that materially changes the scope of business undertaken or the manner in which that business is conducted.

A provision can only be made if:

- **'the entity has a detailed formal plan, and**

- **has raised a valid expectation in those affected that it will carry out the restructuring by**

  - **starting to implement it, or**

  - **announcing it'** (IAS 37, para 72).

A provision can then only be made for costs that are:

- **'necessarily entailed by the restructuring, and**

- **not associated with the ongoing activities of the entity'** (IAS 37, para 80).

Per IAS 37, costs specifically not allowed include retraining/relocation of existing staff, marketing and investment in new systems.

Illustration 4 – restructuring

On 14 June 20X2, a decision is made by the board of directors of KCM to close down a division and a detailed plan is drawn up. At the year end of 30 June 20X2, no announcement has been made in respect of the closure and no steps have been taken to implement the decision. The expected costs of closing the division are $750,000.

Should a provision be made for the expected costs of closing the division?

No – a board decision is not sufficient to require a provision as no obligation exists.

A detailed formal plan must exist, however this alone is not sufficient to create an obligation. The plan must also have been communicated to those affected by it. A constructive obligation will arise at this point in time as management have then created a valid expectation that the plan will proceed and they are unlikely to change their mind.

Test your understanding 3 (OTQ style question)

The board of CLH agreed to close down two of its divisions, A and B, at its board meeting on 18 November 20X3. Detailed plans have been formalised for each division's closure and these were approved by the board at this meeting.

The current status of each of the closures is as follows:

Division A

Letters have been sent to customers warning them to seek an alternative source of supply and a redundancy programme was announced to all staff working in the division on 1 December.

The expected costs of closure are $2.5 million and this includes $450,000 for re-deploying staff to other divisions.

Division B

The directors want to deal with the closures one at a time. Therefore, no announcements have yet been made about the closure of division B. The directors are keen to minimise the effect that the closures will have on staff working in other divisions and have, therefore, decided to keep this closure quiet for the moment.

The expected costs of closure are $1.5 million. All staff are likely to be made redundant and therefore no re-deployment costs are included in this estimate.

Required:

Which of the following options is the most appropriate accounting treatment of the above decisions in the financial statements of CLH for the year ended 31 December 20X3?

A   Division A provides for $2,500,000. Division B provides for $1,500,000.

B   Division A provides for $2,050,000. Division B provides for $1,500,000.

C   Division A provides for $2,050,000. Division B records nothing in relation to the restructuring in its accounts.

D   Division A records nothing in relation to the restructuring in its accounts. Division B records nothing in relation to the restructuring in its accounts.

Provisions for dismantling/decommissioning costs

When a facility such as an oil well or mine is authorised by the government, the licence normally includes a legal obligation for the entity to decommission the facility at the end of its useful life. IAS 37 requires a provision to be recognised for the decommissioning costs.

The decommissioning costs form part of the cost of the asset and are capitalised and expensed over the life of the asset (as part of the depreciation charge).

The provision is only recorded once damage has been incurred to the land upon which the oil well or mine will be located. The obligation to incur the decommission costs is only created at the point damage/changes to the land occurs.

To record the provision:

Dr Asset (oil well/mine)

Cr Provision

The provision should be based on the present value of the expected decommissioning cost and therefore, in addition, a finance cost will arise each year as the discount is unwound.

To unwind the discount:

Dr Finance cost (P/L)

Cr Provision

Illustration 5 – decommissioning costs

On 1 January 20X1, KJC acquires a mine costing $5 million and, as part of the licence granted by the government for operation of the mine, it will be required to pay decommissioning costs at the end of the mine's useful life of 20 years. The present value of these decommissioning costs is $1 million and the discount rate applied is 10%.

KJC depreciate assets on a straight line basis.

Explain the effect of the above transaction on the financial statements of KJC for the year ended 31 December 20X1.

The total cost to be recognised for the mine is $6 million (the $5 million purchase price plus the $1 million decommissioning cost).

This will then be depreciated over 20 years, resulting in an annual depreciation charge of $300,000 ($6 million/20 years). Note that, by capitalising the decommissioning cost, its effect on profit is spread over the 20 year life of the mine.

The decommissioning costs are recorded by making a provision. The initial provision is based on the present value of the costs and the provision is increased each year to reflect the unwinding of the discount applied. In the year ended 31 December 20X1, this would create a finance cost of $100,000 (10% × $1 million).

> The overall effect on the financial statements for the year ended 31 December 20X1 is:
>
> **Statement of profit or loss**
>
> | | $000 |
> |---|---:|
> | Depreciation ($6 million/20 yrs) | (300) |
> | Finance cost ($1 million × 10%) | (100) |
>
> **Statement of financial position**
>
> | | $000 |
> |---|---:|
> | Non-current assets: | |
> | Mine ($6m – $300k) | 5,700 |
> | Non-current liabilities: | |
> | Provision ($1m + (10% × $1m)) | 1,100 |

5 Contingent liabilities and assets

 A contingent liability is defined as:

- **'a possible obligation that arises from past events and whose existence will be confirmed only by the occurrence or non-occurrence of one or more uncertain future events not wholly within the control of the entity, or**

- **a present obligation that arises from past events but is not recognised because:**

  - **it is not probable that an outflow of resources embodying economic benefits will be required to settle the obligation, or**

  - **the amount of the obligation cannot be measured with sufficient reliability'** (IAS 37, para 10).

Accounting for a contingent liability

According to IAS 37, a contingent liability is:

- not recognised

- disclosed in a note, unless the possibility of outflow is remote.

 A contingent asset is defined as a **'possible asset that arises from past events and whose existence will be confirmed only by the occurrence or non-occurrence of one or more uncertain future events not wholly within the control of the entity'** (IAS 37, para 10).

Accounting for a contingent asset

According to IAS 37, a contingent asset is:

- not recognised

- disclosed in a note, if an inflow is considered probable.

Disclosures required for contingent liabilities and assets

According to IAS 37, the following will be disclosed for contingent liabilities and assets:

- Description of nature of contingent liability/asset

- An estimate of its financial effect

- An indication of uncertainties relating to amount or timing of outflow/inflow

- For contingent liabilities, the possibility of any reimbursement.

Illustration 6 – contingent liabilities and assets

Entity A is suing entity B in respect of losses sustained from faulty goods supplied by entity B. Entity A's lawyers are unwilling to state the likelihood of the claim being successful.

Entity B's lawyers have told entity B to expect to have to pay damages but are unable at present to provide a reliable estimate of the amount payable.

How would each entity account for the above scenario?

Entity A has a contingent asset in the form of damages receivable. However, no disclosure would be likely at this point as contingent assets are only disclosed when they are considered probable and entity A's lawyers are unwilling to confirm this.

Entity B has a contingent liability relating to the damages payable. Entity B has a possible liability which would be treated as a contingent liability. Entity B should disclose information about the anticipated payment unless its probability is considered to be remote.

Test your understanding 4 (Case style)

BH's directors are unsure how to treat a number of potential transactions in the financial statements for the year ended 31 August 20X5. Details of these transactions are provided below:

Transaction 1

A significant amount of inventory was stolen in July 20X5 and BH has made a claim with its insurance provider to recover the value of the goods. It is hoping to receive $1.5 million from the insurer however it has not yet received confirmation that the claim has been accepted. It is keen however to recognise the $1.5 million to cancel out the effect of the stolen goods on profit for the year.

Transaction 2

A customer is suing BH for production delays caused by the theft of the inventory, as BH was unable to provide replacement goods on a timely basis. BH does not believe that it is responsible for covering the cost of the delay, however, BH's lawyers have indicated that there is a possibility, based on precedent, that the customer's claim could be successful.

Transaction 3

BH has placed an order for plant and machinery with a purchase cost of $4 million. The plant and machinery has not been delivered at the year-end, however, BH believes it should recognise a liability for the $4 million as it has signed a contract with the supplier agreeing the price.

Required:

You have been asked to draft a note, to be circulated to the board of directors, explaining how the above transactions should be reflected in the financial statements of BH for the year ended 31 August 20X5. Please note that the majority of the directors do not have a financial background and will not necessarily understand accounting terminology.

Test your understanding 5 (OTQ style question)

You work as a CIMA qualified accountant for PK, a small family business, and the Managing Director has sent you the following email:

"I've recently found out from our health and safety manager that, due to a change in legislation enacted on 30 November 20X0, we are required to fit smoke filters to our factories by 30 June 20X1. I assume this means that we will have to recognise an expense for the fitting of the filters in our financial statements for the year ended 31 December 20X0. We will not be fitting the filters until June 20X1. Please can you drop me a line and confirm whether I'm correct about this.

Many thanks, Fatima."

Required:

Which of the following will be the most appropriate response to Fatima's email?

A   Your assumptions are correct. An expense and a provision will be required to record the cost of the fitting of the filters within the financial statements for the year ended 31 December 20X0.

B   Your assumptions are incorrect. Only a disclosure of a contingent liability will be required in relation to the potential costs of the fitting of the filters within the financial statements for the year ended 31 December 20X0.

C   Your assumptions are incorrect. The costs of fitting the filters will have no impact on the financial statements of PK. Neither recognition nor disclosure of the costs is required for the year ended 31 December 20X0.

D   I am afraid I do not know the answer to your query. I will be unable to perform the adequate research required to provide you with an appropriate answer unless I am paid an off-the-books bonus in cash.

Summary

The accounting treatment can be summarised as follows:

Degree of probability of an outflow/ inflow of resources	Liability	Asset
Virtually certain	Recognise	Recognise
Probable	Make provision	Disclose by note
Possible	Disclose by note	No disclosure
Remote	No disclosure	No disclosure

Test your understanding 6 (OTQ style question)

1   HH has announced the closure of one of its divisions prior to its reporting date and is unsure which costs to include in its provision. The closure is expected to take place on 1 March 20X5 and HH's reporting date is 30 November 20X4.

Which of the costs should be recognised within a provision for closure of the division as at 30 November 20X4? Select all that apply.

A   Redundancy costs

B   Operating loss expected for period from 1 December 20X4 to 1 March 20X5

C   Legal and professional fees relating to closure

D   Staff retraining

2   KJ operates in the oil industry and causes contamination. It runs its operations in a country in which there is no environmental legislation. KJ has a widely published environmental policy in which it undertakes to clean up all contamination that it causes and it has a record of honouring this policy.

Which one of the following statements is correct?

A   KJ should not make a provision as there is no legislation requiring it to incur costs of cleaning up the contamination.

B   KJ has created a constructive obligation by publishing its environmental policy and, therefore, a provision is required.

C   KJ should make a provision for the costs of cleaning up the contamination that it is expected to cause.

D   KJ should disclose a contingent liability in case it decides to incur the clean-up costs for contamination caused.

3 **Which one of the following situations would require a provision in the financial statements of FM at its reporting date, 31 October 20X2?**

A The government introduced new laws on data protection which come into force on 1 January 20X3. FM's directors have agreed that this will require a large number of staff to be retrained and have produced a reliable estimate of the costs of this training.

B FM have a policy of making refunds to customers for any goods returned within 28 days of sale and has done so for many years. It is under no obligation to make the refunds. It anticipate that 5% of sales made in October 20X2 will be returned by 28 November 20X2.

C FM has recently purchased an item of machinery and health and safety legislation requires that a major overhaul should be carried out once every 3 years. FM have estimated the cost of the overhaul and are planning to make a provision of 1/3 of the cost to represent the asset's use to date.

D FM is being sued by a customer for faulty goods supplied. FM's lawyers have estimated that there is a 40% likelihood of the customer's claim being successful and believes that a reliable estimate can be made of the damages that would be payable.

4 LR have claimed compensation of $30,000 from another entity for breach of copyright. The solicitors of LR have advised that their claim is 80% likely to succeed.

Which one of the following is the correct treatment of the above situation in the financial statements of LR?

A An asset of $30,000 should be recognised in the financial statements.

B An asset of $24,000 should be recognised in the financial statements.

C The claim should be disclosed in a note to the financial statements.

D The financial statements should not recognise or disclose any information about the claim.

6 Chapter summary

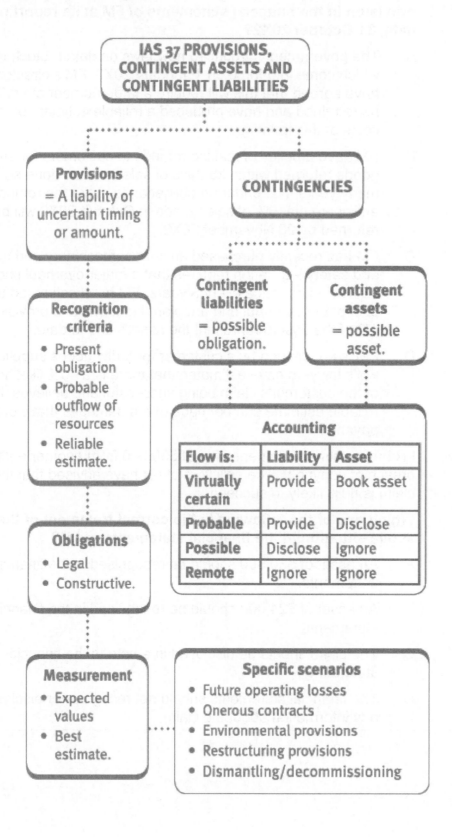

Test your understanding answers

Test your understanding 1 (integration question)

As the new legislation will have retrospective effect, there is a present obligation arising from the damage already caused by the oil rig and therefore a provision should be made, assuming that a reliable estimate can be made of the costs involved.

Test your understanding 2 (OTQ style question)

C

The accounting standard that is being applied here is IAS 37 Provisions, contingent liabilities and contingent assets. To recognise a provision, the entity will Dr P/L Cr Provision. This accounting standard lists three recognition criteria that, if satisfied, result in the recognition of a provision in the financial statements. They are:

- a present obligation is created arising from a past event

- it is considered probable that an outflow of resources will be required to satisfy the obligation

- the outflow can be reliably estimated.

In this case, there is a present obligation arising from a past event. By offering warranties, SZ have created a contractual obligation to make repairs for any sales made in the past 2 years. The sale itself is the past event giving rise to the obligation.

It must be considered probable that there will be an outflow of resources required to satisfy the obligation. The entire class of sales should be considered when assessing the probability and, from SZ's past experience, it is considered probable that 8% of the goods will require repair. Therefore, the provision is based on this amount.

The provision should be recorded based on total costs to be incurred. The provision will record the estimate for total costs in full based on the position as at the year end. The provision is recorded based on 8% of current year revenue.

Finally, a provision can only be recorded if a reliable estimate can be made of the outflow required. This shouldn't be a problem for warranty repairs as past experience can be used to calculate the average cost of a repair and we have information about the number of goods sold.

A disclosure would be required if there was a possible chance of incurring the costs. This would be disclosed as a contingent liability (see section 5 later). This is not relevant as SZ considers a probable likelihood of incurring the costs based on past experience.

To show nothing in the accounts is only relevant if the chances of incurring the costs are remote.

Test your understanding 3 (OTQ style question)

C

Division A provides for $2,050,000. Division B records nothing in relation to the restructuring in its accounts.

The accounting treatment is governed by IAS 37 Provisions, Contingent Liabilities and Contingent Assets, which states that a provision should only be made for closure of a division if there is a formal detailed plan and it has been communicated to those who will be affected by it. It also contains rules on what costs should be provided.

Division A

As notice of the closure has been sent to customers and staff involved, a valid expectation has been created that the closure of the division will go ahead. A constructive obligation exists and provision should be made for the costs of closure. Only the costs necessarily entailed by the closure should be included in the provision. The costs of redeployment ($450,000) are associated with the ongoing activities and should be excluded from the provision.

Assuming that the other closure costs meet the criteria necessary, a provision of $2,050,000 would be made in the financial statements for the year ended 31 December 20X3.

Division B

Although there is a detailed formal plan for this closure, it has not been communicated outside the board of directors and, therefore, no obligation exists at the year end. No provision should be made for the expected costs of closure of division B.

Test your understanding 4 (Case style)

Note to Directors

As requested, I've prepared this note to explain how three transactions should be reflected in the financial statements for the year ended 31 August 20X5.

Transaction 1 – $1.5 million potential receipt from insurer re theft of inventory

Unfortunately, we cannot recognise this $1.5 million in the financial statements as we are not certain that we will receive the money.

This is known in accounting terms as a contingent asset and, if we consider it probable (greater than 50% chance) that the claim will be accepted and the amount will be received then we should disclose information about it (the nature of the claim and the likely amount) in a note to the financial statements. If, however, we only consider it possible rather than probable (i.e. less than 50% chance) then no disclosure should be made at all.

The amount can only be recognised as an asset when its receipt becomes virtually certain. This would be when the insurer confirms that it will pay the money out.

Transaction 2 – customer claim re production delays

The claim by the customer is an example of a contingent liability and should be disclosed in a note to the financial statements unless its likelihood is considered 'remote'.

The delay in providing the goods to the customer gives rise to a potential obligation and the lawyer's opinion suggests that the likelihood is more than remote. We should, therefore, disclose information about the claim in a note to the financial statements.

If we actually thought that the likelihood was probable (>50% chance) and a reliable estimate could be made of the damages payable then a provision would be required and we would have to recognise the expected damages as an expense in the statement of profit or loss.

The probability is a matter of judgement and this is something that should be discussed further with the lawyers.

Transaction 3 – contract for purchase of plant and machinery

The obligation to pay $4 million does not arise until the plant and machinery has been delivered and accepted by BH. Therefore, no liability would be recognised until then.

Test your understanding 5 (OTQ style question)

C

Your assumptions are incorrect. The costs of fitting the filters will have no impact on the financial statements of PK. Neither recognition nor disclosure of the costs is required for the year ended 31 December 20X0.

To recognise a provision as per IAS 37, the following criteria must be met:

- a present obligation is created arising from a past event

- it is considered probable that an outflow of resources will be required to satisfy the obligation

- the outflow can be reliably estimated.

Although the legislation has already been enacted, the requirement to fit the smoke filters does not arise for another six months after the reporting date. As a result, as at the year end, there is no 'past event giving rise to a present obligation'.

If no obligation exists in the first place, the likelihood of the outflow of resources being probable, possible or remote is irrelevant. Therefore, PK should not create a provision and recognise an expense; neither should they disclose the costs as a contingent liability. Nothing will be recorded in the financial statements in relation to these potential costs.

It's also worth noting that, even if there was a requirement to fit the filters by the reporting date and PK had not done so, PK would still not have to make a provision for the cost of fitting the filters. There is only an obligation to incur the cost when the filters have been installed. The directors may deliberately refuse to incur the costs. However, as a result, PK would be required to make a provision for any fines or penalties arising from non-compliance with the legislation (i.e. fines incurred for not fitting the filters).

CIMA qualified accountants are required to comply with the CIMA ethical guidance and principles. To refuse to perform their duties as an accountant (for which it could be assumed a salary would be paid to the accountant) unless further compensation is paid could be an attempt to extort money from the PK business. The request to receive the bonus "off the books" and in cash could be a direct attempt to evade tax. Either way, this response would be deemed to be unethical and unprofessional. It would be wholly inappropriate to respond in such a manner.

Test your understanding 6 (OTQ style question)

1   **Costs A and C**

B is incorrect as provisions cannot be made for future operating losses.

D is incorrect as staff training relates to the ongoing activities of the business.

2   **B is the correct statement.**

A is incorrect. Although there is no legal obligation, there is a constructive obligation and, therefore, a provision is still required.

C is incorrect. A provision would be made only for contamination that had already been caused (as there must be a past event resulting in a present obligation).

D is incorrect. As KJ has created a constructive obligation, it is not considered to be contingent.

3   **B is the correct answer.**

A is incorrect. There is no obligation at the reporting date.

C is incorrect. There is no present obligation to carry out the overhaul (the entity could choose to sell the asset instead).

D is incorrect. This would be a contingent liability. It fails to meet the recognition criteria for a provision as it is not considered probable (more likely than not).

4   **C**

An asset cannot be recognised until it is virtually certain (80% would not suggest this). However, as the success of the claim is considered probable, disclosure would be made of this contingent asset.

8

Intangible assets

Chapter learning objectives

Lead outcome	Component outcome
B1: Explain relevant financial reporting standards for revenue, leases, financial instruments, intangible assets and provisions	Explain the financial reporting standards for: (e) Intangible assets

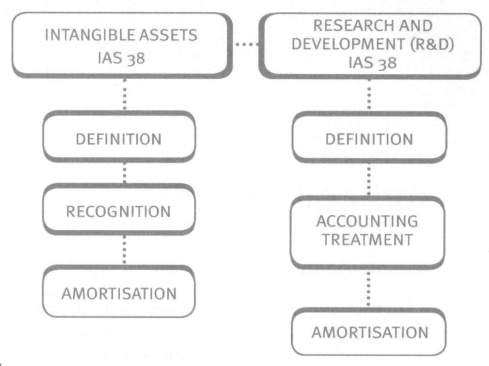

 1   IAS 38 Intangible Assets

Definition

As per IAS 38 Intangible Assets, an intangible asset is **'an identifiable non-monetary asset without physical substance** (IAS 38, para 8).

Intangible assets include items such as:

*   licences and quotas

*   intellectual property, e.g. patents and copyrights

*   brand names

*   trademarks

An asset is identifiable if it is either:

*   separable, or

*   arises from contractual or other legal rights' (IAS 38, para 12).

An asset is deemed separable if the asset can be bought or sold separately from the rest of the business.

As a result, goodwill arising from the acquisition of a business is not accounted for as an intangible asset as per IAS 38. It cannot be sold individually without disposing of the rest of the entity. Therefore, it is IFRS 3 *Business combinations,* and not IAS 38, that considers the accounting of goodwill in such circumstances. See Chapter 11 Subsidiaries (CSOFP) for more information regarding IFRS 3 and the accounting of goodwill.

The importance of intangible assets in the digital age

The landscape for business has dramatically altered within the modern era as markets have entered the digitalisation age.

Recent decades have seen rapid technological advancements, such as the invention of the internet, the development of miniaturised, portable technologies utilised by both industries and individuals alike, the exponential growth of automatisation within business, to name but a few.

In turn, the frequency of the occurrence of intangible assets within company accounts has multiplied dramatically. Decades ago, the value of tangible, physical assets dwarfed the value of Intangibles both in terms of presence on the statement of financial position and within perceived business valuations. This is no longer the case.

Technological innovation has forced most businesses to recognise the increased economic advantages created by the use of technology, whether from improved internal production processes (think automation), or from increased consumer sales via the use of websites and apps. As businesses become more technologically dependent, the level of intangibles will increase (e.g. through increased intellectual property, copyrights, licences and patents required to use the technology successfully).

Companies also need to produce products that take advantage of, or are compatible with, new technological developments. This creates increased frequency, and importance, of research and development expenditure.

Technological innovations have enabled sophisticated methods of collating, storing and using vast amounts of data by companies. This data has become incredibly valuable to companies as they can (and do) use it to their advantage. Companies like Facebook and Amazon has developed algorithms that use data to predict consumer behaviour which have greatly increased the company's value (both in terms of financial value and influence).

These examples illustrate the evolving landscape companies operate in which, consequently, has increased the relevance of intangibles to both large and small entities. Never before has it been more important that accountants understand the many accounting issues that surround intangible assets.

2   Recognition of intangible assets

To be recognised in the financial statements, an intangible asset must meet

- **'the definition of an intangible asset, and**

- **the recognition criteria'** of the framework (IAS 38, para 18)

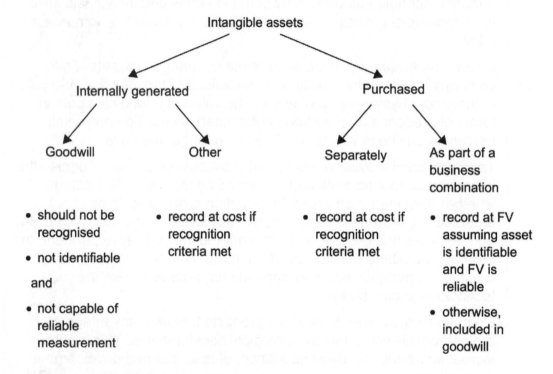

Internally-generated intangibles

Generally, internally-generated intangible assets **cannot be capitalised**, as they cannot be identified separately from the costs associated with running the business. They rarely meet the recognition criteria outlined in the framework as they are not capable of reliable measurement.

The following internally-generated intangibles can never be recognised:

- goodwill

- brands

- publishing titles

- newspaper mastheads

- customer lists

- intellectual property

This accounting treatment is controversial. Under this approach, an entity that generates significant benefits through its intellectual property or its investments in staff development (e.g. creative design industries, football clubs) will have a statement of financial position that could greatly undervalue the entity.

Brands

- The accounting treatment of brands has been a matter of controversy for some years. IAS 38 *Intangible Assets* has now ended the controversy by stating that internally-generated brands and similar assets may never be recognised.

- Expenditure on internally-generated brands cannot be distinguished from the cost of developing the business as a whole, so should be written off as incurred.

- Where a brand name is separately acquired and can be measured reliably, then it should be separately recognised as an intangible non-current asset, and accounted for in accordance with the general rules of IAS 38.

Purchased intangibles

Purchased intangibles should be **recognised at cost**, which could be cash or the fair value of shares given in exchange.

The cost should include the purchase price plus any directly attributable costs of preparing the asset for its intended use.

Recognition and measurement

Intangibles purchased separately

An intangible asset purchased separately from a business should be capitalised at cost.

Intangibles acquired within a business combination

Where an identifiable intangible asset is acquired within an acquisition of a business and it can be measured reliably on initial recognition, it should be capitalised separately from purchased goodwill. The asset's cost will be its fair value.

If the fair value of an intangible asset purchased as part of an acquisition of a business cannot be measured reliably, the intangible asset should not be recognised and will be included within goodwill.

The cost of an intangible asset

As per IAS 38 *Intangible assets*, the cost of an intangible asset comprises:

- its price to purchase, including import duties and non-refundable taxes on acquisition, after deducting trade discounts and rebates

- any directly attributable cost of preparing the asset for its intended use.

> Examples of directly attributable costs are:
>
> - costs of employee pay arising directly from bringing the asset to its working condition
>
> - professional fees.
>
> Examples of costs that are not a cost of an intangible asset are:
>
> - costs of introducing a new product or service (including costs of advertising and promotional activities)
>
> - costs of conducting business in a new location or with a new class of customer (including costs of staff training)
>
> - administration and other general overhead costs.

3   Subsequent measurement of intangible assets

To account for intangible assets as at the reporting date, there is a choice between:

- the cost model

- the revaluation model.

The cost model

- The intangible asset should be carried at cost less amortisation and any impairment losses.

- This model is more commonly used in practice.

The intangible asset is amortised over the useful life, with the annual expense being shown in the statement of profit or loss each year.

An intangible asset with a **finite useful life** must be amortised over that life, normally using the straight-line method with a zero residual value.

An intangible asset with an **indefinite useful life:**

- should not be amortised

- should be tested for impairment annually, and more often if there is an actual indication of possible impairment.

Intangible assets are regarded as having an indefinite life if there is no foreseeable limit to the period over which the asset is expected to generate net cash inflows for the entity.

Amortisation

The depreciable amount of an intangible asset should be allocated on a systematic basis over the best estimate of its useful life. Amortisation should start from the date the asset is available for use.

The useful life of an intangible asset should take account of such things as:

- the expected usage of the asset
- possible obsolescence and expected actions by competitors
- the stability of the industry
- market demand for the products and services that the asset is generating.

The method of amortising the asset should reflect the pattern in which the assets' economic benefits are expected to be consumed by the entity. If that proves difficult to determine, then the straight-line method is acceptable. The residual value of the intangible should be assumed to be zero unless there is a commitment from a third party to purchase the asset or the entity intends to sell the asset and a readily available active market exists. The annual amortisation amount will be charged to profit or loss as an expense.

The useful life and method of amortisation should be reviewed at least at each financial year-end. Changes to useful life or method of amortisation should be effective as soon as they are identified and should be accounted for as changes in accounting estimates (IAS 8 – not testable within the F2 syllabus), by adjusting the amortisation charge for the current and future periods.

The revaluation model

Intangible assets may be revalued to their fair value. The fair value should be determined by an active market.

An active market exists where all of the following conditions are met:

- items traded in the market are homogenous
- willing buyers and sellers can be found at any time
- prices are available to the public.

IAS 38 states that active markets for intangible assets are rare, and specifically prohibits the revaluation of patents, brand names, trademarks and publishing rights.

Most intangible assets have value because of their uniqueness, and are therefore, unlikely to be homogeneous. Certain licences or quotas (e.g. taxi cab licences, farm milk quotas) may fit this model and could possibly be revalued, but most other intangible assets will not.

4 Derecognition of intangible assets

An intangible asset is derecognised:

(a) on disposal; or

(b) when no future economic benefits are expected from it.

A gain or loss on disposal is recorded in profit or loss, being the difference between proceeds on disposal and carrying amount of the intangible asset. Gains or losses from disposing intangible assets are not included within revenue.

5 Research and development

Technology is rapidly playing a part in everyday life, whether in the workplace or as part of an individual's social activities. In an ever-expanding digital world, the need for entities to consider how to benefit from the use of new technology is more important than ever. Whether researching how to best gain efficiencies through use of up-to-date software and hardware, or developing new products to sell to tech-loving consumers, companies nowadays are much more dependent and influenced by technological innovation.

Research and development is not restricted to just areas of technology. The need for research and development will extend to any industry (e.g. pharmaceuticals, cosmetics, education, construction), and any aspect of a business' operations (e.g. environmental and social implications, product development, recruitment, training methods).

IAS 38 deals with the accounting of research and development costs.

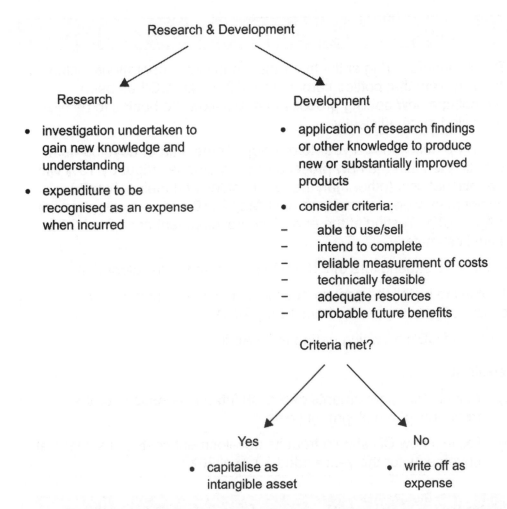

It is only expenditure incurred after the recognition criteria have been met which should be recognised as an asset. Expenditure recognised as an expense in profit or loss cannot subsequently be reinstated as an asset.

If an item of plant is used in the development process, the depreciation on the plant is added to the development costs in intangible assets during the period that the project meets the development criteria. That is because the economic benefit gained from the plant in this period is only realised when the development project is complete and production is underway.

The depreciation will eventually be taken to the statement of profit or loss as part of the amortisation of the development costs once the project is underway.

Amortisation

Development expenditure should be amortised over its useful life as soon as commercial production begins.

Illustration 1 – Research and development

CD is a manufacturing entity that runs a number of operations including a bottling plant that bottles carbonated soft drinks. CD has been developing a new bottling process that will allow the bottles to be filled and sealed more efficiently.

The new process took a year to develop. At the start of development, CD estimated that the new process would increase output by 15% with no additional cost (other than the extra bottles and their contents). Development work commenced on 1 May 20X0 and was completed on 20 April 20X1. Testing at the end of the development confirmed CD's original estimates.

CD incurred expenditure of $180,000 on the above development.

CD plans to install the new process in its bottling plant and start operating the new process from 1 May 20X1.

The end of CD's reporting period is 30 April.

Required:

(a) Explain the requirements of IAS 38 Intangible Assets for the treatment of development costs.

(b) Explain how CD should treat its development costs in its financial statements for the year ended 30 April 20X1.

Solution

(a) Development expenditure can only be regarded as an intangible if it meets the criteria of IAS 38. If the criteria are not met the cost must be written off as research costs to the statement of profit or loss.

The criteria to capitalise development costs are as follows:
- the project is expected to be profitable
- the intention to use or sell the developed item
- resources to complete the project exist
- technically feasible to complete the project
- the ability to use or sell the asset
- the expenditure can be reliably measured

Capitalised development costs are then amortised over the products' expected useful life.

(b) All of the above criteria seem to have been met by CD's new process:

– it is technically feasible, it has been tested and is about to be implemented

– it has been completed and CD intends to use it

– the new process is estimated to increase output by 15% with no additional costs other than direct material costs hence profitability

– the expenditure can be measured at $180,000

CD will treat the $180,000 development cost as an intangible non-current asset in its statement of financial position at 30 April 20X1. Amortisation will start from 1 May 20X1 when the new process starts operation.

Test your understanding 1

An entity has incurred the following expenditure during the current year:

(a) $100,000 spent on the initial design work of a new product – it is anticipated that this design will be taken forward over the next two year period to be developed and tested with a view to production in three years' time.

(b) $500,000 spent on the testing of a new production system which has been designed internally and which will be in operation during the following accounting year. This new system should reduce the costs of production by 20%.

How should each of these costs be treated in the financial statements of the entity?

Test your understanding 2

An entity has incurred the following expenditure during the current year:

(i) A brand name relating to a specific range of chocolate bars, purchased for $200,000. By the year end, a brand specialist had valued this at $250,000.

(ii) $500,000 spent on developing a new line of confectionery, including $150,000 spent on researching the product before management gave approval to fully fund the project.

(iii) Training costs for staff to use a new manufacturing process. The total training costs amounted to $100,000 and staff are expected to remain for an average of 5 years.

Explain the accounting treatment for the above issues.

Illustration 2 – Amortisation of development expenditure

Improve has deferred development expenditure of $600,000 relating to the development of New Miracle Brand X. It is expected that the demand for the product will stay at a high level for the next three years. Annual sales of 400,000, 300,000 and 200,000 units respectively are expected over this period. Brand X sells for $10.

How should the development expenditure be amortised?

Solution

There are two possibilities for writing off the development expenditure:

- Write off in equal instalments over the three-year period, i.e. $200,000 pa.

- Write off in relation to total sales expected (900,000 units).
  Year 1 (400,000/900,000) × $600,000 = $266,667
  Year 2 (300,000/900,000) × $600,000 = $200,000
  Year 3 (200,000/900,000) × $600,000 = $133,333

Case Study Questions

2015 CIMA Professional Qualification Syllabus, Case Study Exam, May 2017 – Question

You receive an email from Gillian Ashworth, the Finance Director

From: Gillian Ashworth, Finance Director

To: Finance Officer

Subject: Contract agreements and R&D expenditure

I have just come out of a meeting with Dr Robert Voss, the Research & Development Director and Roger Ashworth, the Managing Director.

We have been in negotiations with two major oil companies to open 20 hydrogen fuelling stations throughout Mayland. This is excellent news for us - at last we will start to reap the benefits of the hard work and money that has gone into developing the fuelling system. The long-term potential is excellent, hydrogen fuelled cars are the future and we are now one of the major players in that market.

Dr Voss mentioned that the profit from the contracts would initially be very low as all the research and development expenditure incurred in developing the fuelling system would be charged to profit and loss in the first year

Please send him an email explaining how we will treat the expenditure on the new product in the financial statements under IAS 38 Intangible Assets.

Regards

Gillian Ashworth
Finance Director
Ashworth Lea

 Case Study Suggested Answer

2015 CIMA Professional Qualification Syllabus, Case Study Exam, May 2017 – Suggested Answer

EMAIL TO DR VOSS

Accounting for R&D Expenditure

The accounting for R&D is dealt with under IAS 38, *Intangible Assets*.

Research expenditure

Research is investigation undertaken to gain new scientific or technical knowledge and understanding. According to IAS38, research expenditure must be written off as an expense. The expenditure that we incurred in researching the technology for the fuelling system has therefore already been written off to the statement of profit or loss

Development expenditure

Development is the application of research findings or other knowledge to plan or design for the production of new or substantially improved processes, products or services before the start of commercial production. IAS38 allows for development expenditure to be capitalised provided it meets certain criteria:

- The technical feasibility of completing the intangible asset (so that it will be available for use or sale): we have already completed the development of the fuelling system and are about to sell it.

- Intention to complete and use or sell the asset: we have already opened our first fuelling station and are in negotiations with major oil companies to open more stations in the future.

- Ability to use or sell the asset: the opening of the fuelling station confirms the ability to use the asset and we have established that there is a market for the product.

- Existence of a market or, if to be used internally, the usefulness of the asset: we have already established that there is a market for the product.

- Availability of adequate technical, financial, and other resources to complete the asset: the asset has already been completed.

- The cost of the asset can be measured reliably: the costs relating to the new product have been separately recorded.

Once we recognised that the project to develop the fuelling system met the criteria above, the development expenditure was capitalised and is shown in our statement of financial position as an intangible asset.

Treatment of capitalised development expenditure

The development expenditure that has already been capitalised will be amortised, in accordance with the accruals concept, over its finite life. Amortisation will begin in this financial year as the asset is now available for use.

© Copyright CIMA – 2015 CIMA Professional Qualification Case Study Exam May 2017

Test your understanding 3

1   Cowper plc has spent $20,000 researching new cleaning chemicals in the year ended 31 December 20X0. They have also spent $40,000 developing a new cleaning product which will not go into commercial production until next year. The development project meets the criteria laid down in IAS 38 *Intangible Assets*.

   How should these costs be treated in the financial statements of Cowper plc for the year ended 31 December 20X0?

   A $60,000 should be capitalised as an intangible asset on the statement of financial position.

   B $40,000 should be capitalised as an intangible asset with subsequent amortisation taken to profit or loss. $20,000 should be expensed as research costs in the statement of profit or loss.

   C $40,000 should be capitalised as an intangible asset and should not be amortised. $20,000 should be expensed as research costs in the statement of profit or loss.

   D $60,000 should be expensed as research costs in the statement of profit or loss

2   Thom Co is an entity that holds a number of intangible assets. Thom Co's finance director is unsure of their accounting treatment.

   Which TWO of the following items should Thom Co capitalise as intangible assets?

   A   a purchased brand name –'Yorke'

   B   purchased staff training courses

   C   Thom Co's internally generated brand

   D   licences and quotas

3   Sam Co has provided the following information as at 31 December 20X6:

   (i)   Project A – $50,000 has been spent on market research regarding potential product options during the year.

   (ii) Project B – $80,000 had been spent on this project in the previous year and $20,000 this year. The project was capitalised in the previous year. During 20X6, it was decided to abandon this project as it would not operate profitably.

   (iii) Project C – $100,000 was spent developing a prototype product. The expenditure meets the criteria of IAS 38 and is to be capitalised.

   Which of the following adjustments will be made in the financial statements as at 31 December 20X6?

   A   Reduce profit by $70,000 and increase non-current assets by $100,000

   B   Reduce profit by $150,000 and increase non-current assets by $20,000

   C   Reduce profit by $130,000 and increase non-current assets by $180,000

   D   Reduce profit by $150,000 and increase non-current assets by $100,000

4   **Which of the following statements concerning the accounting treatment of research and development expenditure are NOT true, according to IAS 38 *Intangible Assets*?**

   A   Research is original and planned investigation undertaken with the prospect of gaining new knowledge and understanding.

   B   Development is the application of research findings.

   C   Depreciation of plant used specifically on developing a new product can be capitalised as part of development costs.

   D   Research expenditure, once treated as an expense, can be reinstated as an asset once development conditions are met.

5   Sharrakazam is a console games developer who offers access to their games via monthly subscriptions paid by their customers.

Which of the following should be included in a company's statement of financial position as an intangible asset under IAS 38 *Intangible Assets*?

A   Internally developed software that manages customer access to the subscription services

B   Internally generated goodwill created from the success of Sharrakazam's latest released game – FIFO 2019

C   Intellectual property created by Sharrakazam's games writing staff

D   Payments made on the successful registration of a copyright for Sharrakazam's newest in-development game – GTA (Great Tax Accountant) XX.

6   During the year to 31 December 20X8, X Co incurred $200,000 development costs for a new product. In addition, X Co spent $60,000 on 1 January 20X8 on machinery specifically used to help develop the new product and $40,000 on building the new product's brand identity. Commercial production of the new product is expected to start during 20X9.

The machinery is expected to last 4 years with no residual value.

What amount should be capitalised within intangible assets during the year ended 31 December 20X8?

$ _____

7   **Which TWO of the following criteria must be met before development expenditure is capitalised according to IAS 38 *Intangible Assets*?**

A   The project is deemed to be technically feasible

B   Future revenue must be received from the project

C   The ability to use or sell the item in development is held by the entity

D   Performance obligations within the contract can be identified

8   **For each issue, identify the correct accounting treatment in Madeira's financial statements:**

	Capitalise as intangible	Expense
$400,000 developing a new process which will bring in no revenue but is expected to bring significant cost savings		
$400,000 developing a new product. During development a competitor launched a rival product and now Madeira is hesitant to commit further funds to the process		
$400,000 spent on marketing a new product which has led to increased sales of $800,000		
$400,000 spent on designing a new corporate logo for the business		

6 Summary diagram

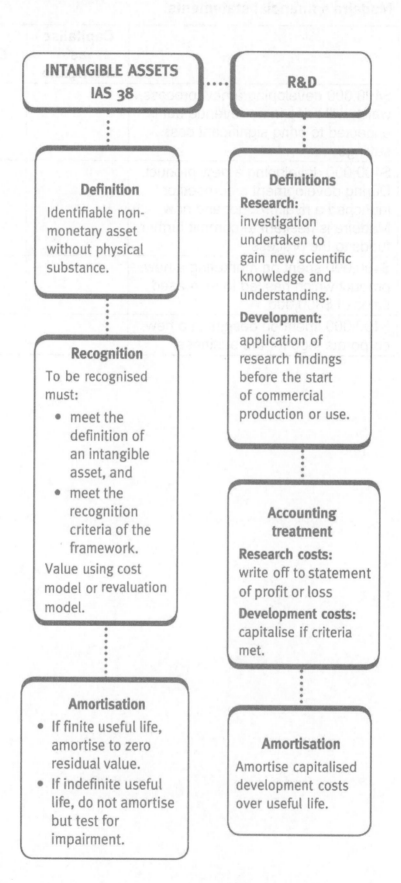

INTANGIBLE ASSETS
IAS 38

R&D

Definition
Identifiable non-monetary asset without physical substance.

Definitions
Research: investigation undertaken to gain new scientific knowledge and understanding.

Development: application of research findings before the start of commercial production or use.

Recognition
To be recognised must:
- meet the definition of an intangible asset, and
- meet the recognition criteria of the framework.

Value using cost model or revaluation model.

Accounting treatment
Research costs: write off to statement of profit or loss
Development costs: capitalise if criteria met.

Amortisation
- If finite useful life, amortise to zero residual value.
- If indefinite useful life, do not amortise but test for impairment.

Amortisation
Amortise capitalised development costs over useful life.

Test your understanding answers

Test your understanding 1 – R and D

(a)　These costs are research costs as they are only in the early design stage and must be written off to the statement of profit or loss for the period.

(b)　These appear to be development costs that meet the capitalisation criteria, i.e. expect to complete, will produce economic benefits, etc. Therefore these costs should be capitalised as an intangible asset on the SOFP. Amortisation will not begin until production starts.

Test your understanding 2

(i)　The brand name is a purchased intangible asset, so can be capitalised at the cost of $200,000.

Intangible assets can only be revalued if an active market exists. This is unlikely here, as the brand name will not be a homogeneous item. Therefore, the item should be held under the cost model.

The brand should be written off over its expected useful life. If this has an indefinite useful life then no amortisation is charged. However, if the asset was deemed to have an indefinite life, an annual impairment review would be required.

(ii)　The $500,000 relates to research and development. Of the total, $150,000 should be expensed to the statement of profit or loss, as management had not displayed either the intention to complete, or the release of the resources to complete.

Therefore $350,000 can be capitalised as an intangible asset as development costs.

(iii)　The training costs must be expensed in the statement of profit or loss. The movement of staff cannot be controlled, and therefore there is no way of restricting the economic benefits. If the staff leave, the company receives no benefit.

Test your understanding 3

1   **C is the correct answer**

$20,000 is research and should be written off as incurred. $40,000 should be capitalised as a development asset, but is not amortised until commercial production begins.

2   **A and D are the correct answers**

Training expenditure cannot be capitalised as Thom Co cannot control the future economic benefits arising from training their staff. This is because the staff members may leave Thom Co and find employment elsewhere.

Internally generated brands cannot be capitalised.

3   **B is the correct answer**

The expenditure in relation to projects A and B should be expensed as research costs during the year. $70,000 will be expenses ($50,000 + $20,000).

The costs capitalised in the previous year for project B would be expensed during 20X6 as the project would fail to meet the criteria for treatment as development costs per IAS 38. This would increase expenses by $80,000 and reduce non-current assets by $80,000.

Project C should be capitalised as development costs and will increase the value of non-current assets by $100,000.

Overall, $150,000 is expensed ($50,000 + $20,000 + $80,000) and non-current assets have increased by $20,000 ($100,000 − $80,000).

4   **D is the correct answer**

Development costs can only be capitalised if they met the capitalisation criteria. The previously expensed research did not meet the criteria at the point of incurring the costs and so should never be capitalised.

5   **D is the correct answer**

Internally generated intangible assets cannot be recognised. Options A-C describe internally generated intangible assets.

6   **$215,000**

The development costs of $200,000 can be capitalised, as can the depreciation on the asset while the project is being developed. The asset is used for a year on the project, so the depreciation for the first year ($60,000/4 years = $15,000) can be added to intangible assets. The $40,000 is expenditure contributing towards an internally generated brand and cannot be capitalised.

7   **A and C are the correct answers**

Future economic benefits must be received from the project not future revenue. Benefits may arise in the form of cost savings as well as revenue.

The identification of performance obligations is a factor to consider when recognising revenue under IFRS 15.

8

	Capitalise as intangible	Expense
$400,000 developing a new process which will bring in no revenue but is expected to bring significant cost savings	✓	
$400,000 developing a new product. During development a competitor launched a rival product and now Madeira is hesitant to commit further funds to the process		✓
$400,000 spent on marketing a new product which has led to increased sales of $800,000		✓
$400,000 spent on designing a new corporate logo for the business		✓

Income Taxes

Chapter learning objectives

Lead	Component
B1: Explain relevant financial reporting standards	Explain the financial reporting standards for: (f) Income taxes

1 Session content

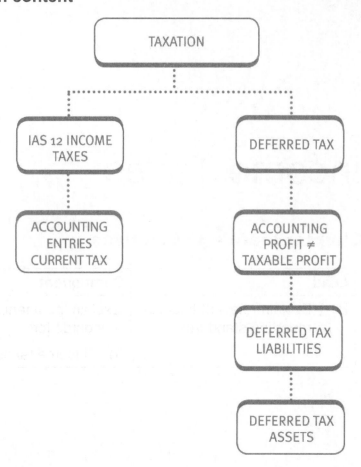

2 IAS 12 Income taxes

IAS 12 *Income taxes* covers the general principles of accounting for tax.

The income tax expense in the statement of profit or loss typically consists of three elements:

- current tax expense for the year
- under or over provisions in relation to the tax expense of the previous period
- deferred tax.

Current tax

Current tax is the estimated amount of tax payable on the taxable profits of the enterprise for the period.

Taxable profits are the profits on which tax is payable, calculated in accordance with the rules of local tax authorities.

At the end of every accounting period, the entity will estimate the amount of tax payable in respect of the period. This estimate is normally recorded as a period end adjustment by making the following double entry:

Dr Income tax expense (SPL)

Cr Income tax liability (SFP – current liability)

Under and over provisions

Income tax for the period is accrued in one financial period and then settled in the next. The amount settled often differs from the amount accrued in the previous year's financial statements. The difference between the amount accrued (in the previous year) and the amount settled (in the current year) is recorded in the current year's income tax expense as an under or over provision relating to the prior period.

Amount settled > amount previously recognised => under-provision. This creates an additional tax expense (debit).

Amount settled < amount previously recognised => over-provision. This creates a reduction in tax expense (credit).

Example 1

Simple has estimated its income tax liability for the year ended 31 December 20X4 at $180,000. In the previous year the income tax liability had been estimated as $150,000.

Required:

Calculate the tax charge that will be recognised in the statement of profit or loss for the year ended 31 December 20X4 if the amount that was actually agreed and settled with the tax authorities in respect of 20X3 was:

(a) $165,000

(b) $140,000

State what the income tax liability would be at 31 December 20X4 in each of the above circumstances.

Example 1 answer

(a) **Under provision**

Statement of profit or loss charge:

	$
Current tax expense for year	180,000
Add: under-provision relating to prior year (165,000 – 150,000)	15,000
Income tax expense	195,000

(b) **Over provision**

Statement of profit or loss charge:

	$
Current tax expense for year	180,000
Less: over-provision relating to prior year (150,000 – 140,000)	(10,000)
Income tax expense	170,000

In both situations, the income tax liability at 31 December 20X4 would be $180,000 (reflecting the current year's liability only).

By making an adjustment to the income tax expense to reflect the under/over provision, any remaining tax liability balance relating to the previous period has been written off through profit or loss.

3 Deferred tax

Deferred tax is:

- the estimated **future** tax consequences of transactions and events recognised in the financial statements of the **current** and **previous** periods.

Deferred tax does not represent the tax payable to the tax authorities.

Deferred tax is a basis of allocating tax charges to particular accounting periods. It is an application of the accruals concept and aims to eliminate a mismatch between:

- **accounting profit**, the profit before tax figure in the statement of profit or loss, and

- **taxable profit**, the figure on which the tax authorities base their tax calculations.

The differences between accounting profit and taxable profit can be caused by:

- permanent differences (e.g. expenses not allowed for tax purposes)

- temporary differences (e.g. expenses allowed for tax purposes but in a later accounting period).

Only temporary differences are taken into account when calculating deferred tax.

 Temporary differences are differences between the carrying amount of an asset or liability in the statement of financial position and its tax base (i.e. the amount attributed to it for tax purposes).

Examples of temporary differences include:

- certain types of income and expenditure that are taxed on a cash, rather than an accruals basis, e.g. certain provisions

- the difference between the depreciation charged on a non-current asset and the actual tax allowances given (see the expandable text below for an example of this scenario).

 The accounting problem

One important reason why deferred tax should be recognised is that profit for tax purposes may differ from the profit shown by the financial statements. Such a difference may be caused by permanent or temporary differences.

For example, if expenses in the statement of profit or loss are not allowed for tax purposes (fines & penalties are included in the accounts but no tax relief is granted in tax computations), a **permanent difference** arises. Permanent differences do not cause any deferred tax implications. There is no need for any accounting adjustments resulting from permanent differences.

A **temporary difference** arises when an expense is allowed for both tax and accounting purposes, but the timing of the allowance differs. For example, if relief for capital expenditure is given at a faster rate for tax purposes than the depreciation in the financial statements, the tax charge will be lower in the first years than it would have been based on the accounting profit, but in subsequent years the tax charge will be higher.

It is important to remember that **only temporary differences give rise to deferred tax**.

For example, an item of plant and machinery is purchased by U in 20X0 for $300,000. The asset's estimated useful life is 6 years, following which it will have no residual value. Plant and machinery is depreciated on a straight-line basis.

Tax depreciation for this item is given at 25% on the straight-line basis for the first 4 years.

Let us first calculate the figures that would appear in the financial statements over the six-year life of the asset:

Financial statements	20X0 $000	20X1 $000	20X2 $000	20X3 $000	20X4 $000	20X5 $000
Opening carrying amount	300	250	200	150	100	50
Accounting depreciation charge	50	50	50	50	50	50
Closing carrying amount	250	200	150	100	50	0

Depreciation is charged at $50,000 per annum ($300,000/6 years).

Now let us look at how this asset would be treated for tax purposes:

Tax computation	20X0 $000	20X1 $000	20X2 $000	20X3 $000	20X4 $000	20X5 $000
Opening carrying amount	300	225	150	75	0	0
Tax depreciation	75	75	75	75	–	–
Tax base	225	150	75	0	0	0

We can see from comparing the above two tables that the carrying amount of the asset per the accounts differs from the tax base. The annual reduction in the carrying amount applied by the entity (that is, accounting depreciation) differs from the reduction applied in the tax computation. By the end of the asset's useful life, the two have caught up, as they both show the asset with a carrying amount of 0, but the different treatment over 6 years creates the need for deferred tax.

The deferred tax adjustments attempt to smooth out the tax charge in the P/L for the impacts of the temporary differences. For example, in 20X0, the tax profits will be $25,000 lower than accounting profits. The tax charge will be lower than expected based on accounting profits. A deferred tax adjustment will be posted to bring the recorded tax charge in the financial statements in line with what would be expected as per the accounting profits. In this case, an extra deferred tax expense would be required to show the impact of the temporary difference. This would be added to current tax expenses and the tax expense is increased.

This is an application of the matching concept. The accounting of the tax implications are being matched to the accounting treatment of the transaction causing the tax (in this case, the depreciation charge).

4 Accounting for deferred tax

Deferred tax is accounted for using a statement of financial position approach as follows:

1   Establish the temporary difference at the year-end = carrying amount of net assets less the tax base.

2   Deferred tax balance (for SFP) = temporary difference × tax rate

Note that this could be a liability or asset, depending on whether the future tax consequence would increase or decrease the tax payable.

–   It will be a deferred tax liability if the carrying amount of net assets is greater than the tax base. This is the situation where there are taxable temporary differences.

–   It would be a deferred tax asset if the carrying amount of net assets was lower than the tax base. In this situation there would be deductible temporary differences.

3   Record the journal entry with the increase/decrease in deferred tax balance in year.

The cumulative deferred tax balance in the statement of financial position would be presented as a **non-current** item.

The movement in the deferred tax balance is usually recognised as an adjustment to the income tax expense in the statement of profit or loss. However, according to IAS 12 *Income taxes*, if it relates to an item that has been recognised in other comprehensive income then the deferred tax impact should also be recognised in other comprehensive income. This is covered in more detail later in the chapter.

Illustration 1 – Deferred tax accounting

Messy Ltd has purchased an asset for $300 and this will be depreciated over three years on a straight line basis.

The tax depreciation will be $140 in year 1, $110 in year 2 and $50 in year 3.

The current tax rate is 30%.

Required:

Prepare the journal entries required to record the deferred tax on the above asset for years 1, 2 and 3.

Solution

Year	SFP carrying amount	Tax base	Temporary difference	Deferred tax balance (Difference × 30%)
	$	$	$	$
1	300	300		
	(100)	(140)		
	200	160	40	12
2	(100)	(110)		
	100	50	50	15
3	(100)	(50)		
	0	0	0	0

The temporary difference at the tax rate (30%) represents the total deferred tax liability required in the statement of financial position. The difference is a taxable temporary difference because the accounting depreciation is less than the tax depreciation, i.e. the carrying amount in the SFP is greater than the tax base.

The movement in the deferred tax balance represents the increase/ (decrease) in the deferred tax liability required for the year. These are the entries to be made to the statement of profit or loss.

Statement of profit or loss	Year 1	Year 2	Year 3
Income tax expense/(credit)	12	3	(15)
Statement of financial position			
Non-current liabilities			
Deferred tax	12	15	0

Journal entries

Year 1

Dr Income tax expense (SPL)	$12
Cr Deferred tax liability (SFP)	$12

Year 2

Dr Income tax expense (SPL)	$3
Cr Deferred tax liability (SFP)	$3

Year 3

Dr Deferred tax liability (SFP)	$15
Cr Income tax expense (SPL)	$15

Illustration 2 – Deferred tax accounting

An entity, Dive, provides the following information regarding its assets and liabilities as at 31 December 20X1.

	Carrying amount	Tax base	Temporary difference
Assets			
A machine cost $100,000. Depreciation of $18,000 has been charged to date. Tax allowances of $30,000 have been claimed.			
Accrued interest receivable in the statement of financial position is $1,000. The interest will be taxed when received.			
Trade receivables have a carrying amount of $10,000. The revenue has already been included in taxable profit.			
Inventory has been written down by $500 to $4,500 in the financial statements. The reduction is ignored for tax purposes until the inventory is sold.			

Liabilities			
Current liabilities include accrued expenses of $1,000. This is deductible for tax on a cash paid basis.			
Accrued expenses have a carrying amount of $5,000. The related expense has been deducted for tax purposes.			

Required:

Complete the table with carrying amount, tax base and temporary difference for each of the assets and liabilities and calculate Dive's deferred tax balance as at 31 December 20X1. The applicable tax rate is 30%.

Solution:

	Carrying amount	Tax base	Temp. difference
	$	$	$
Non-current asset	82,000	70,000	12,000
Interest receivable	1,000	Nil	1,000
Receivables	10,000	10,000	Nil
Inventory	4,500	5,000	(500)
Accrual (cash basis for tax)	(1,000)	Nil	(1,000)
Accrual (already had tax relief)	(5,000)	(5,000)	Nil

The net temporary difference as at the reporting date is as follows:

	$
Non-current assets	12,000
Interest receivables	1,000
Receivables	–
Inventory	(500)
Accrual (cash basis for tax)	(1,000)
Accrual (already had tax relief)	–
	11,500

There will be a deferred tax liability because the carrying amount of the net assets and liabilities exceeds their net tax base. The deferred tax liability is calculated by applying the relevant tax rate to the temporary difference.

The deferred tax liability is therefore $3,450 ($11,500 × 30%).

Assuming that there is no opening deferred tax liability, the following accounting entry is required:

Dr Tax expense (P/L) $3,450

Cr Deferred tax liability (SFP) $3,450

Test your understanding 1 (integration question)

Aquarius Ltd's draft financial statements for the year ended 31 December 20X9 show a profit before tax of $170,000. At 31 December 20X9, there are cumulative taxable temporary differences of $50,000, i.e. the carrying amount of the net assets is higher than the tax base by this amount. Current tax for the year at 30% has been estimated at $33,000.

For the year ended 31 December 20X8, the financial statements had a profit before tax of $145,000. At 31 December 20X8, the cumulative taxable temporary differences were $40,000 and current tax for the year at 30% was $30,000.

Required:

For the years ended 31 December 20X8 and 31 December 20X9:

(a)   Prepare the journal entry to record deferred tax

(b)   Prepare extracts from the statement of profit or loss and the statement of financial position showing how the current and deferred tax would be reflected.

Test your understanding 2 (integration question)

Parker Ltd's statement of financial position includes a number of assets and liabilities that give rise to temporary differences as follows at the current reporting date:

	Carrying amount	Tax base
	$000	$000
Property, plant and equipment (1)	26,500	18,000
Financial assets (2)	1,020	1,000
Trade receivables (3)	5,700	6,500
Warranty provision (4)	(1,200)	0
Long-term borrowings (2)	(22,200)	(19,500)

1   Property, plant and equipment is depreciated in the financial statements on a straight line basis over the assets' useful lives. Tax depreciation is 30% on a reducing balance basis.

2   The financial asset and long-term borrowings are measured using the amortised cost method in the financial statements. Tax is payable/receivable on interest and any redemption premium on a cash received/paid basis and, therefore, a temporary difference arises.

3   Trade receivables have a gross receivables balance of $6.5 million however Parker Limited has created a specific allowance against $800,000 which is four months old at the reporting date. Bad debts only become tax deductible after 12 months.

4   Parker Limited offers one year warranties on its products. Warranty costs are tax deductible when warranty repairs are incurred.

The corporate income tax rate is 25%.

Required:

Calculate the deferred tax balance on the above assets and liabilities at the reporting date, clearly stating for each item whether the deferred tax balance would be an asset or liability.

5 Deferred tax on losses

In accordance with IAS 12 *Income taxes*, **a deferred tax asset** is recognised on unutilised losses carried forward (as there will be a future tax benefit when the losses are offset against future profits).

However, the asset can only be recognised to the extent that it is probable that future taxable profits will be available against which the losses can be utilised.

Test your understanding 3 (OTQ style)
Simpson Limited has only been trading for two years and has not yet made a profit. It has losses available for carry forward of $75,000. It expects to make profits of $25,000 per annum for the next two years but is not in a position to estimate profits beyond this.
The current corporate income tax rate is 30%.
Required:
Prepare the journal entry to record the deferred tax arising on the losses.

6 Deferred tax impact in OCI

Any deferred tax charge/credit that relates to an item that has been recognised in other comprehensive income should also be recognised in other comprehensive income.

The most common example of this relates to the revaluation of non-current assets:

- When an asset is revalued upwards, it increases the carrying amount of the asset but it does not affect the tax base.

- The cumulative temporary difference increases and this gives rise to an additional deferred tax liability.

- The revaluation surplus is recognised in other comprehensive income.

- Therefore, the movement in the deferred tax liability that relates to the revaluation surplus should also be recognised in other comprehensive income.

Test your understanding 4 (integration question)

On 1 January 20X8, Simone Limited decided to revalue its land for the first time. The land was originally purchased 6 years ago for $65,000 and it was revalued to its current market value of $80,000 on 1 January 20X8.

The difference between the carrying amount of Simone's net assets and the (lower) tax base at 31 December 20X8 was $27,000. These temporary differences included the impact of the revaluation described above. Any other temporary differences were caused by accelerated capital allowances on other non-current assets.

The opening deferred tax liability at 1 January 20X8 was $2,600 and Simone's tax rate was 25%.

Required:

Prepare the journal entry required to record the movement in deferred tax in the year ended 31 December 20X8 in the financial statements of Simone Limited.

Test your understanding 5 (further OTQs)

1   Tamsin plc's accounting records show the following:

Income tax payable for the year	$60,000
Opening deferred tax liability	$3,200
Closing deferred tax liability	$2,600

Calculate the income tax expense that would be recognised in Tamsin plc's statement of profit or loss for the year.

2   On 1 January 20X1, Pegasus plc acquired motor vehicles at a cost of $100,000. The carrying amount of the motor vehicles at 31 December 20X2 was $60,000 and the tax base was $56,250. The corporate income tax rate was 30%.

Calculate the deferred tax liability at 31 December 20X2.

3   A piece of machinery cost $500. Tax depreciation to date has amounted to $220 and depreciation charged in the financial statements to date is $100. The rate of income tax is 30%.

Which one of the following statements is TRUE?

A   The tax base of the asset is $400

B   The cumulative temporary difference is $220

C   The asset gives rise to a deferred tax liability of $36

D   The expense relating to deferred tax recorded in the profit or loss totalled $120

4   ST has unused tax losses of $150,000 at its reporting date, 31 December 20X3. It estimates that it will make profits of $120,000 over the next five years but cannot be certain of profitability beyond five years' time.

The corporate income tax rate is 25%.

Calculate the deferred tax asset that should be recognised in ST's statement of financial position at 31 December 20X3 in respect of the losses.

5   In the statement of financial position of XY at 31 March 20X9, there is a warranty provision of $350,000. The balance on the provision at the end of the previous year was $275,000. Warranty costs are deducted for tax purposes on a cash paid basis.

The corporate income tax rate is 20%.

Calculate the charge or credit that would appear in the statement of profit or loss of XY for the year ended 31 March

20X9 in respect of the deferred tax arising on the above warranty provision. State your answer in $ and clearly state whether the amount would be a debit or credit in the statement of profit or loss.

6   AB made an investment of $250,000 in equity shares in another entity on 1 June 20X3. It classified the investment as fair value through other comprehensive income (FVOCI) and the fair value of the investment at 31 October 20X3, the reporting date, was $280,000.

AB will pay tax on the shares when they are sold. The tax base of the shares is therefore $250,000 (their original cost).

The corporate income tax rate is 25%.

Complete the journal entry below to record the deferred tax arising on the FVOCI investment in the financial statements of AB for the year ended 31 October 20X3.

Dr

Cr

Note: in the assessment, you would choose the headings for the Dr and Cr from a selection of choices.

7   WS revalued its property, plant and equipment upwards by $100,000 for the first time on 31 December 20X3, its reporting date. Prior to the revaluation, the carrying amount of the property, plant and equipment was $850,000 and the tax base was $625,000.

WS's tax rate is 25%. Its deferred tax liability brought forward in respect of the property, plant and equipment was $62,000.

Which one of the following statements is TRUE in respect of deferred tax on the above property, plant and equipment?

A   The deferred tax liability at 31 December 20X3 is $56,250

B   A temporary difference of $100,000 is used to calculate the deferred tax implications

C   An increase in the deferred tax asset of $19,250 is recorded

D   There is a deferred tax charge reflected through other comprehensive income in the year ended 31 December 20X3 of $25,000

7   Chapter summary

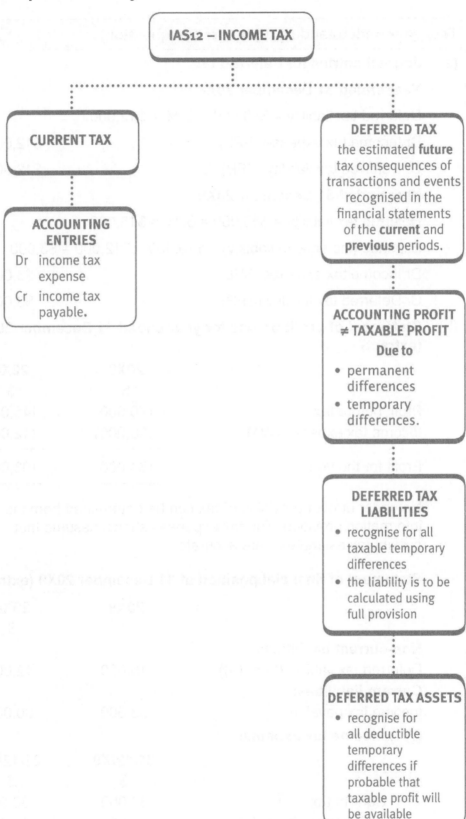

Test your understanding answers

Test your understanding 1 (integration question)

(a) **Journal entries for deferred tax**

Year ended 31 December 20X8

Deferred tax liability = $40,000 × 30% = $12,000

Dr Income tax expense (SPL)	$12,000
Cr Deferred tax liability (SFP)	$12,000

Year ended 31 December 20X9

Deferred tax liability = $50,000 × 30% = $15,000

Expense (increase in liability) = $15,000 – $12,000 = $3,000

Dr Income tax expense (SPL)	$3,000
Cr Deferred tax liability (SFP)	$3,000

(b) **Statement of profit or loss for year ended 31 December 20X9 (extract)**

	20X9 $	20X8 $
Profit before tax	170,000	145,000
Income tax expense **(W1)**	(36,000)	(42,000)
Profit for the year	134,000	103,000

No under or over provision of tax can be determined from the information provided. The tax expenses shown assume that current tax estimates were accurate.

Statement of financial position at 31 December 20X9 (extract)

	20X9 $	20X8 $
Non-current liabilities:		
Deferred tax liability (from (a))	15,000	12,000
Current liabilities:		
Income tax payable	33,000	30,000

(W1) Income tax expense

	31/12/X9 $	31/12/X8 $
Current tax	33,000	30,000
Deferred tax (from (a))	3,000	12,000
	36,000	42,000

Test your understanding 2 (integration question)

	Temporary difference	Deferred tax balance (25%)	Deferred tax liability /asset
	$000	$000	
Property, plant and equipment	8,500	2,125	liability
Financial assets	20	5	liability
Trade receivables	(800)	(200)	asset
Warranty provision	(1,200)	(300)	asset
Long-term borrowings	(2,700)	(675)	asset

Test your understanding 3 (OTQ style)

Dr Deferred tax asset (SFP)	$15,000
Cr Statement of profit or loss (SPL)	$15,000

The temporary difference is $75,000 (the value of the losses available for carry forward). However, a deferred tax asset can only be recognised to the extent it is probable that these losses can be utilised and, based on current estimates, the recoverability is only $50,000 (2 × $25,000 profit).

Therefore a deferred tax asset of only $50,000 × 30% = $15,000 can be recognised.

Test your understanding 4 (integration question)

Journal entry for deferred tax

Deferred tax liability c/f = $27,000 × 25% = $6,750.

Amount relating to revaluation surplus on land = ($80,000 – $65,000) × 25% = $3,750.

Increase in deferred tax liability to be recorded = $6,750 – $2,600 = $4,150.

Of which, $3,750 should be charged to revaluation reserve and the remainder charged to profit or loss.

Dr Income tax expense (SPL)	$400
Dr Revaluation reserve (SFP)	$3,750
Cr Deferred tax liability (SFP)	$4,150

The impact to revaluation reserve during the year would be noted as part of the movements in other comprehensive income within the SOPLOCI.

Test your understanding 5 (further OTQs)

1   **Income tax expense = $59,400**

	$
Current tax expense	60,000
Decrease in deferred tax liability (3,200 – 2,600)	(600)
	59,400

2   **Deferred tax liability at 31 December 20X2 = $1,125**

Temporary difference = 60,000 – 56,250 = 3,750

Deferred tax liability = 30% × 3,750 = 1,125

3   **C is true**

The tax base of the asset = $500 – $220 = $280

The cumulative temporary difference = $400 (CV) – $280 = $120

This results in a deferred tax liability of $120 × 30% = $36

4   **Deferred tax asset = $30,000**

	$
Losses – capped to the extent they are recoverable	120,000
Tax rate	× 25%
	30,000

5   **Impact in statement of profit or loss = $15,000 credit**

	$
Deferred tax asset at year end (20% × 350,000)	70,000
Deferred tax asset at start of year (20% × 275,000)	55,000
Increase in deferred tax asset	15,000

6   **Dr FVOCI reserve $7,500**

Cr Deferred tax liability $7,500

Temporary difference =$30,000 ($280,000 less $250,000)

Deferred tax liability = $7,500 ($30,000 × 25%)

The gain on the financial asset is recorded in FVOCI reserve, therefore the tax effect should also be recorded in FVOCI reserve. The annual movement in the FVOCI reserve will be detailed as part of OCI within SOPLOCI.

7   The correct statement is D

Deferred tax liability at 31 December 20X3

	$
Carrying amount of PPE (850,000 + 100,000)	950,000
Tax base	(625,000)
Temporary difference	325,000
Tax rate	× 25%
Deferred tax liability	81,250

Therefore, A and B are incorrect.

The deferred tax liability has increased by $19,250, not a deferred tax asset. C is incorrect.

Deferred tax reflected in OCI

	$
Revaluation surplus	100,000
Tax rate	× 25%
	25,000

Deferred tax impact in profit or loss

	$
Liability at year end	81,250
Less liability at start of year	(62,000)
Total increase in deferred tax liability	19,250
Less: reflected in OCI	(25,000)
Credit to SPL	(5,750)

Foreign currency transactions

Chapter learning objectives

Lead outcome	Component outcome
B1: Explain relevant financial reporting standards	Explain the financial reporting standards for:
	(g) Effects of changes in foreign currency rates

1 Session content

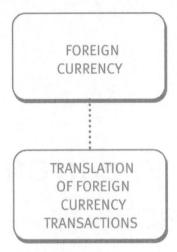

2 IAS® 21 *The effects of changes in foreign exchange rates*

IAS 21 deals with:

- the definition of functional and presentation currencies

- accounting for individual transactions in a foreign currency

These two areas are considered as part of the 'Financial reporting standards' syllabus area. Only this content is covered within this chapter.

- translating the financial statements of a foreign subsidiary.

This area is considered part of the 'Group accounts' section of the syllabus. This content is dealt with separately in Chapter 16.

3 Functional and presentation currencies

 The **functional currency** is **'the currency of the primary economic environment in which the entity operates'** (IAS 21, para 8). In most cases this will be the local currency.

An entity should consider the following when determining its functional currency:

- **'The currency that mainly influences sales prices for goods and services**

- **The currency of the country whose competitive forces and regulations mainly determine the sales prices of goods and services**

- **The currency that mainly influences labour, material and other costs of providing goods and services'** (IAS 21, para 9)

'The following factors may also be considered:

- The currency in which funding from issuing debt and equity is generated

- The currency in which receipts from operating activities are usually retained' (IAS 21, para 10).

The entity maintains its day-to-day financial records in its functional currency.

 The **presentation currency** is the currency in which the entity presents its financial statements. This can be different from the functional currency, particularly if the entity in question is a foreign owned subsidiary. It may have to present its financial statements in the currency of its parent, even though that is different to its own functional currency.

Illustration 1

Chive is an entity located in a country whose currency is dollars ($).

Seventy per cent of Chive's sales are denominated in dollars and 30% of them are denominated in sterling (£). Chive does not convert receipts from customers into other currencies. Chive buys most of its inventories, and pays for a large proportion of operating costs, in sterling.

Chive has two bank loans outstanding. Both of these loans are denominated in dollars.

Required:

What is the functional currency of Chive?

Solution:

Firstly, the primary indicators of functional currency should be applied. Most of Chive's sales are denominated in dollars and so this would suggest that the dollar is its functional currency. However, since a lot of the costs of the business are denominated in sterling, it could be argued that its functional currency is sterling.

Since the primary indicators of functional currency are not clear cut, it is important to look at the secondary indicators. Receipts are retained in both dollars and sterling. However, funding is generated in the form of dollar loans, which further suggests that the dollar might be Chive's functional currency.

All things considered, it would seem that the functional currency of Chive is dollars. This means that any business transactions that are denominated in sterling must be translated into dollars in order to record them.

4 Translation of foreign currency transactions

Where an entity enters into a transaction denominated in a currency other than its functional currency, that transaction must be translated into the functional currency before it is recorded.

> ### Foreign currency transactions
>
> Whenever a business enters into a contract where the consideration is expressed in a foreign currency, it is necessary to translate that foreign currency amount into the functional currency for inclusion in its own accounts. Examples include:
>
> - imports of raw materials
>
> - exports of finished goods
>
> - importation of foreign manufactured non-current assets
>
> - investments in foreign securities
>
> - raising an overseas loan.

Initial recognition

- The transaction will initially be recorded by applying the spot exchange rate, i.e. the exchange rate at the date of the transaction.

Exam questions will always give relevant exchange rates within the content.

Subsequent measurement – settled transactions

When cash settlement occurs, for example payment by a receivable, the settled amount should be translated using the spot exchange rate on the settlement date.

If this amount differs from that recorded when the transaction occurred, there will be an exchange difference which is taken to the statement of profit or loss in the period in which it arises.

> ### Example 1
>
> An entity based in the US sells goods to the UK for £200,000 on 28 February 20X3 when the exchange rate was £0.55: $1.
>
> The customer pays in April 20X3 when the rate was £0.60:$1.
>
> The functional currency of the entity is the $.
>
> **Required:**
>
> How does the US entity account for the transaction in its financial statements for the year ended 31 July 20X3?

Example 1 answer

On the sale:

Translate the sale at the spot rate prevailing on the transaction date.

£200,000/0.55 = $363,636

		$
Dr	Receivables	363,636
Cr	Sales	363,636

When the cash is received:

Dollar value of cash received = $333,333 (£200,000/0.60)

Loss on transaction $30,303 (363,636 – 333,333)

		$
Dr	Bank	333,333
Dr	P/L (loss)	30,303
Cr	Receivables	363,636

Test your understanding 1

On 1 April 20X8, Collins Co buys goods from an overseas supplier, who uses Kromits (Kr) as its functional currency. Collins Co uses the dollar ($) as its functional currency. The goods are priced at Kr54,000. Payment is made 2 months later on 31 May 20X8.

The prevailing exchange rates are:

1 April 20X8 Kr1.80 : $1

31 May 20X8 Kr1.75 : $1

Required:

Record the journal entries for these transactions.

Subsequent measurement – unsettled transactions

The treatment of any outstanding foreign currency balances remaining in the statement of financial position at the year-end will depend on whether they are classified as monetary or non-monetary.

Monetary items	Non-monetary items
Currency held and assets or liabilities to be received or paid in currency.	Other items in the statement of financial position.
E.g. cash, receivables, payables, loans	E.g. non-current assets, inventory, investments
Treatment:	*Treatment:*
Retranslate using the closing rate (year-end exchange rate)	Do not translate i.e. leave at historic rate

Any exchange difference arising on the retranslation of monetary items must be taken to the statement of profit or loss in the period in which it arises.

Example 2

A US entity sells apples to an entity based in Moldovia where the currency is the Moldovian pound (Mol). The apples were sold on 1 October 20X1 for Mol 200,000 and were paid for in February 20X2.

The rate on 1 October 20X1 is US $1: Mol 1.55.

The rate on 31 December 20X1 (the reporting date) is US $1: Mol 1.34.

The functional currency of the entity is the $.

Required:

How does the US entity account for the transaction in its financial statements for the year ended 31 December 20X1?

Example 2 answer

On the sale:

Translate the sale at the spot rate prevailing on the transaction date.

Mol 200,000/1.55 = $129,032

		$
Dr	Receivables	129,032
Cr	Sales	129,032

At the reporting date:

The receivables balance is a monetary item and must be retranslated using the closing rate.

Mol 200,000/1.34 = $149,254

Gain = $20,222 (149,254 – 129,032)

		$
Dr	Receivables	20,222
Cr	P/L (gain)	20,222

Test your understanding 2

On 1 April 20X8, Collins Co buys goods from an overseas supplier, who uses Kromits (Kr) as its functional currency. Collins Co uses the dollar ($) as its functional currency. The goods are priced at Kr54,000. Payment is still outstanding at the reporting date of 30 June 20X8.

The prevailing exchange rates are:

1 April 20X8 Kr1.80 : $1

30 June 20X8 Kr1.70 : $1

Required:

Record the journal entries for these transactions.

Test your understanding 3

ABC Co has a year end of 31 December 20X1 and uses the dollar ($) as its functional currency.

On 25 October 20X1, ABC Co buys goods from a Swedish supplier for Swedish Krona (SWK) 286,000.

Rates of exchange:

25 October 20X1 $1 = SWK 11.16

16 November 20X1 $1 = SWK 10.87

31 December 20X1 $1 = SWK 11.02

Required:

Show the accounting treatment for the above transactions if:

(a)   A payment of SWK286,000 is made on 16 November 20X1.

(b)   The amount owed remains outstanding at the year-end date.

Test your understanding 4 (Foreign transaction OTQ style)

Data for Questions 1 to 3

An entity based in the US, with a functional currency of USD ($), sold goods overseas for Kr200,000 on 28 March 20X3 when the exchange rate was Kr0.65:$1.

The customer paid in April 20X3 when the rate was Kr0.70:$1.

The exchange rate at the year ended 30 June 20X3 was Kr0.75:$1.

1   **Prepare the journal entries to record the sale of the goods by the US entity.**

2   **Show the journal entries to record the payment in April 20X3.**

3   **If the amount was outstanding at the year-end, what would the gain or loss in the statement of profit or loss be?**

$ _____

4   An entity based in the US purchased goods for Kr350,000 on 28 March 20X3 when the exchange rate was Kr3.5: $1.

The exchange rate at the year ended 30 June 20X3 was Kr2.5:$1.

If the goods were unsold at the year-end, what should be the value of inventory within the statement of financial position as at the year ended 30 June 20X3?

$ _____

5   An entity, with a functional currency of $, bought land on credit for Kr100,000 when the exchange rate was 1Kr/$0.85. At the year-end, the entity had not paid its supplier. The exchange rate at the year-end was 1Kr/$0.92.

Which of the following amounts would be recorded in the financial statements at the year-end?

A	Property, plant and equipment	$92,000
B	Other comprehensive income	$8,951
C	Foreign exchange loss	$7,000
D	Trade payable	$85,000

5   Chapter summary

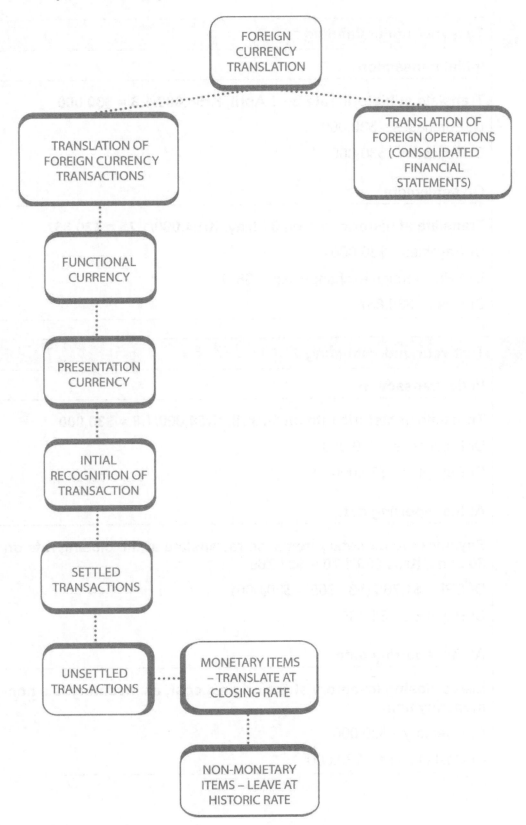

Test your understanding answers

Test your understanding 1

Initial transaction

Translate at historic rate on 1 April, Kr54,000/1.8 = $30,000

Dr Purchases $30,000

Cr Payables $30,000

On settlement

Translate at historic rate on 31 May, Kr54,000/1.75 = $30,857

Dr Payables $30,000

Dr SPL – foreign exchange loss $857

Cr Cash $30,857

Test your understanding 2

Initial transaction

Translate at historic rate on 1 April, Kr54,000/1.8 = $30,000

Dr Purchases $30,000

Cr Payables $30,000

At the reporting date

Payables are monetary items, so retranslate at the closing rate on 30 June, Kr54,000/1.70 = $31,765

Dr SPL $1,765 ($31,765 – $30,000)

Cr Payables $1,765

At the reporting date

Leave closing inventory at the original cost, as inventory is a non-monetary item

Dr Inventory $30,000

Cr Cost of sales $30,000

Test your understanding 3

(a) **Original transaction**

25 October 20X1 Value = 286,000/11.16 = $25,627

Dr Purchases $25,627

Cr Payables $25,627

16 November 20X1 Payment 286,000/10.87 = $26,311

Dr Payables $25,627

Dr SPL   **$684 (Balancing figure, 26,311 – 25,627)**

Cr Cash $26,311

(b) If **the amount remains outstanding:**

31 December 20X1 Retranslate payable 286,000/11.02 = $25,953

Dr SPL   **$326 (25,953 – 25,627)**

Cr Payables $326

Note: The inventory would not be restated and would remain at the original transaction price of $25,627.

Test your understanding 4 (Foreign transaction OTQ style)

1   **On the sale:**

Translate the sale at the spot rate prevailing on the transaction date.

Kr200,000/0.65 = $307,692

	$
Dr Receivables	307,692
Cr Revenue	307,692

2   **Loss on translation = $307,692 – $285,714 = $21,978**

The journal entries would be as follows:

Dr SPL (Balancing figure)	$21,978
Dr Bank (Kr200,000/0.70)	$285,714
Cr Receivables (Original amount)	$307,692

3   **$41,025. The monetary item must be retranslated at the rate of exchange existing at the reporting date:**

Dollar value at the reporting date = Kr200,000/0.75 = $266,667

This results in a reduction in the receivables (and therefore a foreign exchange loss) of $41,025 ($307,692 – 266,667).

For tutorial purposes the journal entry would be as follows:

Dr SPL	$41,025
Cr Receivables	$41,025

4   **$100,000**

The transactions would be recorded as follows:

28 March 20X3

Translate the purchase at the historic rate (the rate prevailing on the transaction date).

Kr350,000/3.5 = $100,000

Dr Purchases $100,000

Cr Payables $100,000

30 June 20X3

Inventory would remain unchanged at the reporting date as it is a non- monetary item (so remains at historic rate).

5   **C**

At acquisition:

Kr100,000 × 0.85 = $85,000

Dr Non-current asset	$85,000
Cr Payables	$85,000

The land is a non-monetary asset and remains at $85,000 at the year end.

Payables, as a monetary item, must be retranslated at the closing rate Kr100,000 × 0.92 = $92,000

This results in an increase in the payables.

Loss on translation = $7,000 ($92,000 – $85,000)

Dr P/L (loss)	$7,000
Cr Payables	$7,000

Group accounts – Subsidiaries (CSOFP)

Chapter learning objectives

Lead outcome	Component outcome
B2: Explain relevant financial reporting standards for group accounts	(a) Explain the financial reporting standards for the key areas of group accounts
C1: Prepare group accounts based on IFRS	Prepare the following based on financial reporting standards: (a) Consolidated statement of financial position

1 Session content

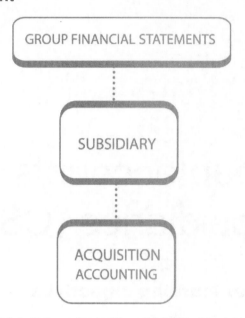

GROUP FINANCIAL STATEMENTS

SUBSIDIARY

ACQUISITION ACCOUNTING

2 Introduction

As a company grows, opportunities may present themselves to expand further by acquiring other entities. The motives to acquire another company are manyfold:

- to reduce competition in the market place

- to diversify into new markets (whether industry markets or geographical markets)

- to bring expertise in-house (e.g. retailers bringing manufacturing in-house)

- to benefit from synergies arising from the acquisition.

In certain circumstances, the entity may be required to produce a further set of financial statements which incorporate all the members of a group of companies.

The individual financial statements of the members of the group are still required to be prepared as well as the group financial statements.

This chapter investigates the circumstances which create the need for group financial statements and the processes involved in their preparation.

3   What is a group?

IFRS 10 – Consolidated financial statements

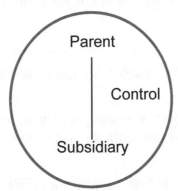

A group will exist where one company (the parent) controls another company (the subsidiary).

IFRS 10 *Consolidated Financial Statements* sets out the definition of control and gives guidance on how to identify whether control exists.

In accordance with IFRS 10, **'an investor controls an investee if and only if the investor has all of the following elements:**

- **power over the investee (see definition of power below)**

- **exposure, or rights, to variable returns from its involvement with the investee, and**

- **the ability to use its power over the investee to affect the amount of the investor's returns'** (IFRS 10, para 7).

Power is defined as **"existing rights that give the current ability to direct the relevant activities"** (IFRS 10, para 10), i.e. the activities that significantly affect the investee's returns.

Power is generally considered to have been achieved when an investor owns >50% of the voting rights in an entity. Voting rights are typically acquired through the purchase of ordinary shares in the acquired entity.

However, the definition of power is more wide ranging than simple consideration of the percentage shareholding.

 Example of control

JO owns 49% of the ordinary share capital HN. The remaining 51% of the shares in HN are held by numerous investors with very small shareholdings (no greater than 5%). JO has the right to appoint the majority of the board of directors and ensures that its representatives attend and vote at HN's meetings.

JO, despite not having greater than 50% of HN, would be deemed to control HN. JO has the ability to use its voting rights to direct the strategic decisions of HN which would affect profitability and, consequently, variable returns.

Consolidated financial statements should be prepared when the parent has control over one or more subsidiaries (for examination purposes, control is usually established based on ownership of more than 50% of the voting rights). The method of consolidation applied is known as **acquisition accounting**.

Acquisition accounting

In accordance with IFRS 10 *Consolidated financial statements*, the following rules are applied:

- The parent and subsidiary's assets, liabilities, income and expenses are combined in full. This represents the 100% control that the parent has over the subsidiary.

- Goodwill is recognised in accordance with IFRS 3 (revised) *Business Combinations.*

- The share capital of the group is the share capital of the parent only.

- Intra-group balances and transactions are eliminated in full (including the PUP adjustment (covered later in this chapter)).

- Uniform accounting policies must be used.

- Non-controlling interests are presented within equity, separately from the equity of the owners of the parent. Profit and total comprehensive income are attributed to the owners of the parent and to the non-controlling interests.

Exemption from group accounts

A parent need not present consolidated financial statements if it meets all of the following conditions:

- **'it is a wholly owned subsidiary or a partially-owned subsidiary and its owners, including those not otherwise entitled to vote, have been informed about, and do not object to, the parent not presenting consolidated financial statements**

- **its debt or equity instruments are not traded in a public market**

- **it did not file its financial statements with a securities commission or other regulatory organisation for the purpose of issuing any class of instruments in a public market**

- **its ultimate parent produces consolidated financial statements available for public use that comply with IFRS standards'** (IFRS 10, para 4).

4   Standard consolidation workings

For the consolidated statement of financial position

Note: the workings have been numbered for referencing purposes. In the assessment, you would only need to produce the workings required to answer the particular question.

(W1) Group structure

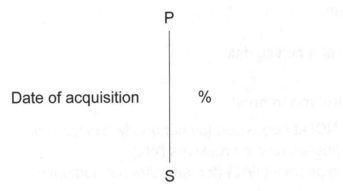

	Acquisition date	Reporting date
(W2) Net assets of subsidiary		
Share capital	X	X
Retained earnings	X	X
Other reserves	X	X
Fair value adjustments	X	X
PUP adjustment (if sub is seller)	–	(X)
	X	X

Difference = post-acquisition reserves

(W3) Goodwill

Fair value of P's investment in S	X
Value of NCI at acquisition (using fair value or proportionate share of net assets method)	X
Less: subsidiary's net assets at acquisition **(W2)**	(X)
Goodwill at acquisition	X
Impairment	(X)
Goodwill at reporting date	X

(W4) Non-controlling interest

Value of NCI at acquisition (as per goodwill calculation)	X
NCI% × post-acquisition reserves **(W2)**	X
NCI% × impairment **(W3)** (for fair value method only)	(X)
NCI at reporting date	X

(W5) Consolidated reserves

	Retained earnings	Other reserves
Parent's reserves	X	X
PUP adjustment (if parent is seller)	(X)	–
Sub: P% × post-acquisition reserves **(W2)**	X	X
Impairment (P% only when using fair value method)	(X)	–
	X	X

5 Non-controlling interest and goodwill

By definition, a subsidiary is an entity that is controlled by another entity – the parent. Control is normally achieved by the parent owning a majority i.e. more than 50% of the equity shares of the subsidiary.

Non-controlling interest (NCI) shareholders own the shares in the subsidiary that are not owned by the parent entity.

NCI shareholders are considered to be shareholders of the group and, thus their ownership interest in the subsidiary is reflected within equity.

When calculating goodwill at acquisition the value of the NCIs is added to the value of the parent's investment in the subsidiary. Consequently, the value of the subsidiary as a whole (100%) is compared against all of its net assets.

IFRS 3 *Business Combinations* allows two methods to be used to value the NCI at the date of acquisition:

- Fair value

- Proportionate share of net assets method.

IFRS 3 permits groups to choose how to value NCI on an acquisition by acquisition basis. In other words, it is possible for a group to apply the fair value method for some subsidiaries and the proportionate share of net assets method for other subsidiaries.

Fair value method

The fair value of the non-controlling interest may be calculated using the market value of the subsidiary's shares at the date of acquisition. Other valuation techniques will be applied if the subsidiary's shares are not traded in an active market. In the assessment, you will be told the fair value of the NCI or will be given the subsidiary's share price in order to be able to calculate NCI at acquisition.

Proportionate share of net assets method

Under this method, the NCI is measured by calculating the share of the fair value of the subsidiary's net assets at acquisition.

 Illustration 1 – Goodwill

Sherriff purchased 60% of Nottingham's 3,000 shares on 1 January 20X9. Sherriff paid $5,500 cash for their investment. At 1 January 20X9, the value of Nottingham's net assets was $5,000. Nottingham's share price at this date was $2.25.

Required:

Calculate the goodwill arising on the acquisition of Nottingham, valuing the NCI:

(a)   Using the fair value method

(b)   Using the proportionate share of net assets method.

Solution

Goodwill

	Fair value method	Proportionate share of net assets method
	$	$
Fair value of P's investment	5,500	5,500
Value of NCI at acquisition **(W1/W2)**	2,700	2,000
Less: value of S's net assets	(5,000)	(5,000)
Goodwill at acquisition	3,200	2,500

(W1) NCI holding – fair value method

The subsidiary's share price is provided and this is used to value the NCI's 40% holding in Nottingham.

The NCI owns:

40% × 3,000 shares = 1,200 shares

The fair value of this shareholding is:

1,200 × $2.25 = $2,700

(W2) NCI holding – proportionate share of net assets method

The NCI's 40% holding is valued by taking this proportion of the subsidiary's net assets at acquisition of $5,000.

40% × $5,000 = $2,000

Goodwill and NCI

Prior to a revision to IFRS 3 in 2008, it was only permitted to recognise the NCI using the proportionate share of net assets method. This method resulted in only the goodwill attributable to the parent shareholders being recognised in the consolidated accounts. Using the information from illustration 1, the calculation of goodwill under this method is as follows

	$
Fair value of P's investment	5,500
P% × sub's net assets at acquisition (60% × 5,000)	(3,000)
Goodwill at acquisition	2,500

Above, the parent's share (60%) has been deducted from the fair value of the parent's holding. This achieves the same answer for goodwill as adding in the NCI's share (40%) of the subsidiary's net assets and then subtracting 100% of these net assets. This method illustrates more clearly that valuing the NCI at the proportionate share of net assets is the equivalent to recording only the parent's share of goodwill.

However, the proportionate method was considered inconsistent with the treatment of the other assets of the subsidiary. Since the group controls the assets of the subsidiary, they are fully consolidated in the group accounts, i.e. 100% is added in line by line. Goodwill is an asset of the subsidiary in exactly the same way that property, inventory etc., are assets of the subsidiary. It stands to reason that, if property and inventory are consolidated in full, goodwill should be treated in the same way.

Therefore, when IFRS 3 was revised in 2008, the option of valuing the NCI at fair value was introduced. This recognises that the value of the NCI should also include the goodwill attributable to their holding. An alternative presentation of the FV goodwill calculation can be used in which the presence of the NCI share of goodwill is more transparent. Using the information from illustration 1, the calculation would be:

	$000	$000
Fair value of P's investment	5,500	
P% × sub's net assets at acquisition (60% × 5,000)	(3,000)	
Goodwill attributable to P shareholders		2,500
Fair value of NCI	2,700	
NCI% × sub's net assets at acquisition (40% × 5,000)	(2,000)	
		700
Goodwill at acquisition		3,200

In this alternative FV method calculation, the subsidiary's net assets have simply been deducted in two separate stages rather than on a single line as per the answer to illustration 1.

These alternative calculations for goodwill will achieve the same correct answers, but for assessment purposes, it is recommended that you use the format applied in the illustration's solution. The alternatives are only provided here to enable a deeper understanding of the calculations. The pro-formas used in the solution will be the default presentations in assessments and going forward in this material.

It is worth noting that the fair value of the NCI is not normally proportionate to the fair value of the parent's holding. This is because the parent's holding provides control of the subsidiary. The value of a controlling investment will include a premium for obtaining control.

Using illustration 1, the parent's holding of 60% is 1.5 times that of the NCI's 40% holding. However, the fair value (the cost) of the parent's holding of $5,500 is more than 1.5 times that of the fair value of the NCI's holding of $2,700.

Test your understanding 1 (Integrated question)

Wellington purchased 80% of the equity share capital of Boot for $1,200,000 on 1 April 20X8. Boot's share capital is made up of 200,000 $1 shares and it had retained earnings of $800,000 at the date of acquisition. The fair value of the NCI at 1 April 20X8 was $250,000.

Required:

Calculate the goodwill arising on the acquisition of Boot, valuing the NCI:

(a) Using the fair value method

(b) Using the proportionate share of net assets method.

Test your understanding 2 (Integrated question)

Ruby purchased 75% of the equity share capital of Sapphire for $2,500,000 on 1 April 20X8. Sapphire's share capital is made up of 500,000 $1 shares and it had retained earnings of $1,500,000 at the date of acquisition. The fair value of the NCI at 1 April 20X8 should be calculated by reference to the subsidiary's share price. The market value of a Sapphire share at 1 April 20X8 was $6.

Required:

Calculate the goodwill arising on the acquisition of Sapphire, valuing the NCI:

(a) Using the fair value method

(b) Using the proportionate share of net assets method.

6 Impairment of goodwill

IFRS 3 requires that goodwill is tested at each reporting date for impairment. This means that goodwill is reviewed to ensure that its value is not overstated in the consolidated statement of financial position.

If an impairment loss exists, goodwill is written down and the loss is charged as an expense in the consolidated statement of profit or loss.

This charge against profits will result in a reduction in the equity section of the consolidated statement of financial position (CSFP). How the impairment loss is charged against equity will depend on the method adopted for valuing the NCI.

Fair value method

As discussed in the expandable text 'Goodwill and NCI', valuing the NCI at fair value is equivalent to recognising goodwill in full, i.e. goodwill attributable to both the parent and NCI shareholders is recognised.

Consequently, any impairment loss is charged to both the parent and NCI shareholders in the equity section of the CSFP in accordance with their percentage holdings.

To record the impairment loss:

- Reduce goodwill by the full amount of the impairment loss (Cr).

- Reduce NCI balance held in equity by the NCI% of the impairment loss (Dr).

- Reduce consolidated retained earnings by the P% of the impairment loss (Dr).

Proportionate share of net assets method

As discussed in the expandable text above, valuing the NCI at the proportion of the subsidiary's net assets is equivalent to recognising only the goodwill attributable to the parent shareholders.

Consequently, any impairment loss is only charged to the parent shareholders in the equity section of the CSFP.

To record the impairment loss:

- Reduce goodwill by the amount of the impairment loss (Cr).

- Reduce consolidated retained earnings by the amount of the impairment loss (Dr).

 The chapters on group financial statements use the preparation of full group accounts to illustrate the topic and improve understanding of the concepts covered. However, in the exam, candidates will never have to produce the full set of group accounts. Exam questions will require calculations of figures from the group accounts or preparation of extracts from the group accounts.

Illustration 2

P acquired 75% of the equity share capital of S on 1 April 20X2, paying $900,000 in cash. At this date, the retained earnings of S were $300,000. Below are the statements of financial position of P and S as at 31 March 20X4:

	P	S
	$000	$000
Non-current assets	1,650	750
Investment in S	900	–
Current assets	450	650
	3,000	1,400

Equity		
Share capital	1,500	500
Retained earnings	900	400
Non-current liabilities	100	50
Current liabilities	500	450
	3,000	1,400

It is group elect to value the NCI at fair value at the date of acquisition. The fair value of the NCI in S at 1 April 20X2 was $275,000.

As at 31 March 20X4, goodwill was impaired by $60,000.

Required:

(a) Prepare a consolidated statement of financial position as at 31 March 20X4.

(b) Show how the CSFP would change if the proportionate share of net assets method were used to value the NCI at acquisition instead.

Illustration 2 answer

(W1) Group structure

P

75% 1 April 20X2, it is 2 years since acquisition

S

(W2) Net assets of subsidiary

	Acquisition date	Reporting date
Share capital	500	500
Retained earnings	300	400
	800	900

100 = post acquisition reserves

The post-acquisition reserves belong to the shareholders of the subsidiary and are allocated accordingly in the NCI and consolidated reserves workings, i.e. 75% to the parent and 25% to the NCI (see W4 and W5 in this example).

(W3) Goodwill

	$000
Fair value of P's investment	900
Fair value of NCI at acquisition	275
Less: sub's net assets at acquisition **(W2)**	(800)
Goodwill at acquisition	375
Impairment	(60)
Goodwill at reporting date	315

(W4) Non-controlling interest equity

	$000
Value of NCI at acquisition **(W3)**	275
NCI% × post acquisition reserves (25% × 100 **(W2)**)	25
NCI% × impairment (25% × 60 **(W3)**)	(15)
	285

The NCI is measured at its fair value of $275,000 at the date of acquisition, as given in the question. Since acquisition the subsidiary has made gains of $100,000, as shown in (W2). The NCI shareholders are entitled to 25% of these gains. Thus, their holding has increased in value by $25,000.

The NCI holding has been valued at acquisition under the fair value method. The NCI shareholders are charged with their share of the impairment loss arising on goodwill (25% × $60,000). This reduces their share of the group's equity to $285,000 at the reporting date.

(W5) Consolidated reserves

	Retained earnings
Parent's reserves	900
Sub (75% × 100 **(W2)**)	75
Impairment (75% × 60 **(W3)**)	(45)
	930

The only reserve in this question is retained earnings. The retained earnings figure in the CSFP represents those belonging to the parent shareholders. This is made up of the parent entity's retained earnings plus their share (75%) of the subsidiary's post acquisition profits less their share of any impairment losses on goodwill. Since the NCI has been valued using the fair value method, the parent shareholders are charged with their 75% share of the impairment loss.

Now that we have completed the workings, the CSFP can be completed. Remember that:

- Parent and subsidiary's assets and liabilities are combined in full.

- Consolidated share capital is parent share capital only.

- The investment in S included in P's individual statement of financial position is replaced with goodwill.

- The NCI is part of group equity and should be shown accordingly.

Consolidated statement of financial position as at 31 March 20X4

		$000
Non-current assets	(1,650 + 750)	2,400
Goodwill **(W3)**		315
Current assets	(450 + 650)	1,100
		3,815
Equity		
Share capital		1,500
Retained earnings **(W5)**		930
		2,430
Non-controlling interest **(W4)**		285
Total equity		2,715
Non-current liabilities	(100 + 50)	150
Current liabilities	(500 + 450)	950
		3,815

It is worth noting that the net assets of the group at the reporting date are $2,715,000 ($3,815,000 - $150,000 - $950,000).

This represents the net assets that are under the control of the group.

The net assets are owned by the shareholders of the group. This is reflected within the equity section of the CSFP. A group is owned by two sets of shareholders – the parent shareholders and the NCI shareholders. The parent's share of equity is $2,430,000 whilst the NCI's share is $285,000.

(b) If the proportionate share of net assets method were used, this would change the goodwill & NCI calculations. Since goodwill is impaired this method would also change retained earnings as the parent shareholders would now suffer the full amount of the impairment loss.

Note: It is being assumed that the question would still state that the impairment loss arising on goodwill is $60,000. In reality, if goodwill were being measured using the proportionate share of net assets method, this would result in a different impairment loss compared to that arising under the fair value method.

(W3), (W4), (W5) and the CSFP would become:

(W3) Goodwill

	$000
Fair value of P's investment	900
Value of NCI at proportionate share of net assets	200
(25% × 800 **(W2)**)	
Less: sub's net assets at acquisition **(W2)**	(800)
Goodwill at acquisition	300
Impairment	(60)
Goodwill at reporting date	240

(W4) Non-controlling interest equity

	$000
Value of NCI at acquisition **(W3)**	200
NCI% × post acquisition reserves	
(25% × 100 **(W2)**)	25
	225

(W5) Consolidated reserves

	Retained earnings
Parent's reserves	900
Sub (75% × 100 **(W2)**)	75
Impairment **(W3)**	(60)
	915

Consolidated statement of financial position as at 31 March 20X4

		$000
Non-current assets	(1,650 + 750)	2,400
Goodwill **(W3)**		240
Current assets	(450 + 650)	1,100
		3,740
Equity		
Share capital		1,500
Retained earnings **(W5)**		915
		2,415
Non-controlling interest **(W4)**		225
		2,640
Non-current liabilities	(100 + 50)	150
Current liabilities	(500 + 450)	950
		3,740

Test your understanding 3 (Integrated question)

P acquired 75% of the 5 million issued ordinary shares of S on 1 April 20X5, paying $6.5m in cash. At this date, the retained earnings of S were $2.5m.

The retained earnings reported in the financial statements of P and S as at 31 March 20X8 are $10.8 million and $4.5 million respectively.

The group elect to measure non-controlling interest at fair value at the date of acquisition. The fair value of the non-controlling interest was $2 million on 1 April 20X5.

An impairment review performed on 31 March 20X8 indicated that goodwill on the acquisition of S had been impaired by 20%.

Required:

1   Calculate the amounts that will appear in the consolidated statement of financial position of the P group as at 31 March 20X8 for:

(a)   Goodwill

(b)   Consolidated retained earnings

(c)   Non-controlling interest.

> 2   Re-calculate the above amounts as if the group elected to measure non-controlling interest at the proportionate share of net assets at the date of acquisition.

7   Mid-year acquisitions and the consolidated statement of financial position

The consolidated statement of financial position (CSFP) reflects the position at the reporting date. Therefore, assets and liabilities on the face of the CSFP should never be time apportioned.

However, in order to calculate the reserves at acquisition (for the net assets working), it may be required to time apportion results. Depending on the information provided, you will be required to either:

- Subtract the profits for the post-acquisition portion of the year from the closing reserves balance, or

- Add the profits for the pre-acquisition portion of the year to the opening reserves balance.

Illustration 3 – Mid-year acquisition in CSFP

An entity is acquired on 1 March 20X9. Its profits for the year ended 31 December 20X9 are $12,000 and its retained earnings at the reporting date are $55,000.

Retained earnings at acquisition will be $45,000 ($55,000 – (10/12 × $12,000).

8   Intra-group balances

The members of a group will commonly buy and sell to each other. In fact, the frequency of trade between entities is likely to increase once they become members of the same group. The parent and subsidiary will record the effects of these transactions in their individual accounts.

However, Intra-group balances and transactions must be **eliminated** from the consolidated accounts in full. The group is treated as a single entity and, therefore, cannot record trading with, or amounts owed to/from itself.

- Intra-group sales on credit will create payables and receivables owing to/from group entities. These amounts outstanding are known as intra-group balances. Intra-group balances are eliminated from the consolidated statement of financial position.

- Any profit still held within the group's assets from intra-group trading should also be eliminated (the provision for unrealised profit (PUP) adjustment).

Intra-group balances – in transit items

When eliminating intra-group receivables and payables, the account balances may disagree. This is most likely to be due to cash in transit or goods in transit. The in-transit items must be recorded as if they were received before cancellation can occur.

Cash in transit

In this situation, cash has been sent by one group entity, but has not been received by the other group entity as at the year end. The outstanding amounts would disagree as outstanding receivables would be overstated. The cash in transit is treated as if it has been received by the year-end.

The following adjustment will be required within the CSOFP to eliminate the intra-group balances:

  Dr Bank (with the amount in transit i.e. the difference)

  Dr Payables (with the lower amount)

  Cr Receivables (with the higher amount)

Goods in transit

In this situation, goods have been sent by one group entity, but have not been received by the other. This would lead to the outstanding payables amounts being understated. The in-transit inventory will need to be recorded as if it had been received by the year-end to enable cancellation of the outstanding amounts.

The following adjustment will be required:

  Dr Inventory (with the amount in transit i.e. the difference)

  Dr Payables (with the lower amount)

  Cr Receivables (with the higher amount)

Illustration 4

Extracts from the statements of financial position of P and its subsidiary S at 31 December 20X8 are as follows:

	P	S
	$000	$000
Current assets		
Inventory	750	140
Receivables	650	95
Cash	400	85
Current liabilities		
Payables	900	200

P acquired 100% of S five years ago.

P and S traded with each other and, at the reporting date, P owed S $25,000. This balance is stated after P had recorded that they had sent a cheque for $5,000 to S shortly before the year-end which S had not received by the reporting date.

Required:

What balances would be shown in P's consolidated statement of financial position at 31 December 20X8 for each category of current asset and current liabilities?

Illustration 4 answer

Extracts from P's consolidated statement of financial position at 31 December 20X8

		$000
Current assets		
Inventory	(750 + 140)	890
Receivables	(650 + 95 – 30 **(W1)**)	715
Cash	(400 + 85 + 5)	490
Current liabilities		
Payables	(900 + 200 – 25)	1,075

(W1) Intra-group balances

The question states that P owes S $25,000. P has an outstanding payable from S. This is to be eliminated by reducing payables.

The question states that there is cash in transit at the reporting date of $5,000. This needs to be recorded by increasing cash.

The intercompany receivable that needs to be eliminated is calculated as a balancing figure:

		$000
Dr Payables	↓	25
Dr Cash	↑	5
Cr Receivables	↓	30

Provision for unrealised profit (PUP) in inventory

P and S may sell goods to each other, resulting in a profit being recorded in the selling entity's financial statements. If these goods are still held by the purchasing entity at the year-end, the goods have not been sold outside of the group. The profit is unrealised from the group's perspective and should be removed.

The adjustment is also required to ensure that inventory is stated at the cost to the group. Inventory would need to be recorded at the cost incurred when the goods were first acquired by the group, not the cost to the purchasing entity after the intra-group transfer.

The PUP adjustment is equal to the profit on inventory still held in group at the year-end.

In the consolidated statement of financial position, deduct from:

- **Net assets at reporting date column** (in net assets working) **if S** sells the goods or **consolidated reserves if P sells the goods** – thereby removing the profit from the appropriate entity's retained earnings figure.

- Inventory on the face of the CSFP.

The 'PUP' adjustment

Parent sells to subsidiary

P sells goods to S for $400 at cost plus 25%. All goods remain in the inventory of S at the end of the year.

Profit made on the sale $\dfrac{25}{125} \times 400 = 80$.

Individual financial statements

P records profit	80
S records inventory	400

Group financial statements should show:

Profit	0
Inventory	320

PUP adjustment in CSFP

Dr Group retained earnings	↓	80
Cr Group inventory (CSFP)	↓	80

The group profit figure for the parent will be reduced as it is the parent that recorded the profit in this case.

It is important to note that the adjustment takes place in the group accounts only. The individual accounts are correct as they stand and will not be adjusted as a result.

Subsidiary sells to parent

PUP adjustment in CSFP

Dr Sub's net assets at reporting date	↓	80
Cr Group inventory (CSFP)	↓	80

The subsidiary's profit will be reduced as it is the subsidiary that recorded the profit in this case. The reduction in the subsidiary's profits needs to be shared between the parent and NCI shareholders in the NCI reserve & consolidated reserves workings. By adjusting for the PUP in the net assets working, this split will automatically occur between the two reserves. S's profits are shared between the parent and the non-controlling interest shareholders.

Cost structures

The method an entity uses to ensure a selling price is set that will make a profit is called its cost structure. This will be needed to determine the value of PUP adjustments. The cost structure of the intra-group sale may be given in one of two ways.

Mark up on cost (Cost plus)

A mark-up on cost starts with the cost per unit and adds a % profit to determine the profitable selling price charged.

For example, if goods are sold for $440 and there is a 25% mark up on cost, you need to calculate the profit included within the $440.

	%	$	
Revenue	125	440	
Cost of sales	100		
Gross profit	25	88	= 440 × 25/125

The PUP is $88.

Gross profit margin

The gross profit margin gives the profit as a percentage of revenue. Using the same figures as above but with a gross profit margin of 25%, the profit can be determined as follows:

	%	$	
Revenue	100	440	
Cost of sales	75		
Gross profit	25	110	= 440 × 25/100

The PUP is $110.

Illustration 5

The following summarised statements of financial position are provided for P and S as at 30 June 20X8:

	P	S
	$000	$000
Non-current assets	8,000	5,000
Investment in S	7,000	–
Current assets		
Inventory	1,600	850
Receivables	1,350	950
Cash and cash equivalents	850	400
	18,800	7,200
Equity		
Share capital $1	10,000	4,000
Share premium	2,000	500
Retained earnings	5,050	1,400
Current liabilities		
Payables	1,750	1,300
	18,800	7,200

P acquired 90% of S two years ago for $7,000,000 when the balance on the retained earnings of S was $800,000. The group elect to value NCI at fair value at acquisition and the fair value of the NCI was $650,000 at this date.

S sells goods to P at a profit margin of 20%. As a result, P's records showed a payable due to S of $50,000 at the reporting date. However this disagreed to S's receivables balance of $60,000 due to cash in transit.

At the reporting date, P held $100,000 of goods in inventory that had been purchased from S.

There has been no impairment of goodwill.

Required:

Prepare the consolidated statement of financial position at 30 June 20X8.

 Illustration 5 answer

Consolidated statement of financial position as at 30 June 20X8

		$000
Non-current assets	(8,000 + 5,000)	13,000
Goodwill	**(W3)**	2,350
Current assets		
Inventory	(1,600 + 850 – 20 **(W7)**)	2,430
Receivables	(1,350 + 950 – 60)	2,240
Cash and cash equivalents	(850 + 400 + 10 **(W6)**)	1,260
		21,280
Equity		
Share capital		10,000
Share premium		2,000
Retained earnings	**(W5)**	5,572
Non-controlling interests	**(W4)**	708
		18,280
Current liabilities		
Payables	(1,750 + 1,300 – 50)	3,000
		21,280

Note: The intra-group balances are adjusted for on the face of the consolidated statement of financial position. The PUP adjustment, calculated in W7, should be deducted from the carrying amount of inventory at the reporting date.

(W1) Group structure

P

90% 2 years since acquisition

S

(W2) Net assets of subsidiary

	Acquisition	Reporting date
	$000	$000
Share capital	4,000	4,000
Share premium	500	500
Retained earnings	800	1,400
PUP **(W7)**	–	(20)
	5,300	5,880

580
Post acq'n profit

Note: As the subsidiary sold to the parent, it is their retained earnings that must be reduced. Therefore, the PUP adjustment is reflected at the reporting date in (W2) above.

(W3) Goodwill

	$000
Fair value of P's investment	7,000
Value of NCI at acquisition (at fair value)	650
Fair value of sub's net assets at acquisition **(W2)**	(5,300)
Goodwill at acquisition	2,350
Impairment	–
Goodwill at reporting date	2,350

(W4) Non-controlling interest

	$000
Value of NCI at acquisition **(W3)**	650
NCI% × post acquisition reserves (10% × 580 **(W2)**)	58
	708

(W5) Reserves

	Retained earnings
	$000
Parent's reserves	5,050
Sub (90% × 580 **(W2)**)	522
	5,572

(W6) Intra-group balances

		$000
Dr Payables	↓	50
Dr Cash	↑	10
Cr Receivables	↓	60

(W7) PUP

Profit in inventory = $20,000 (20% × $100,000)

Test your understanding 4 (Integrated question)

The following summarised statements of financial position are provided for P and S as at 30 June 20X8:

	P	S
	$000	$000
Non-current assets	14,200	10,200
Investment in S	14,500	–
Current assets		
Inventory	5,750	3,400
Receivables	4,250	2,950
Cash and cash equivalents	2,500	1,450
	41,200	18,000
Equity		
Share capital $1	20,000	5,000
Retained earnings	12,600	7,900
Current liabilities		
Payables	8,600	5,100
	41,200	18,000

P acquired 80% of S three years ago for $14,500,000 when the balance on the retained earnings of S was $5,800,000. The group elect to value NCI at acquisition at the proportionate share of the net assets.

P sells goods to S. As a result, S's records showed a payable due to P of $550,000 at the reporting date. However, this disagreed to P's receivables balance of $750,000 due to cash in transit.

During the current year, P had sold $1,500,000 (selling price) of goods to S of which one third is held in S's inventory at the year end. The selling price was based on a mark-up of 25%.

An impairment loss of $1,000,000 should be charged against goodwill at the reporting date.

Required:

(a) Calculate the P group balances as at 30 June 20X8 for:

(i) Goodwill

(ii) Consolidated retained earnings

(iii) Non-controlling interest.

(b) Recalculate the following amounts at 30 June 20X8 to reflect what they would have been if S had sold the goods to P.

(i) Consolidated retained earnings

(ii) Non-controlling interests.

9   Goodwill – further detail and fair values

The calculation of goodwill is governed by IFRS 3 *Business Combinations.*

Goodwill is a residual amount calculated by comparing, at acquisition, the value of the subsidiary as a whole and the fair value of its identifiable net assets at this time. A residual amount may exist as a result of the subsidiary's:

*   positive reputation

*   loyal customer base

*   staff expertise.

Goodwill is capitalised as an intangible asset on the consolidated statement of financial position (CSFP). It is subject to an annual impairment review to ensure its value is not overstated on the CSFP.

Goodwill is calculated as:

Fair value of consideration transferred (by parent)	X
NCI at acquisition (at fair value or proportionate share of net assets)	X
Fair value of sub's net assets at acquisition	(X)
	___
Goodwill at acquisition	X
Impairment	(X)
	___
Goodwill at reporting date	X
	___

Negative goodwill

Occasionally, the consideration paid for the subsidiary may be less than the fair value of the identifiable net assets at acquisition. This may arise when the previous shareholders have been forced to sell the subsidiary and so are selling their holding at a bargain price.

This situation gives rise to 'negative goodwill' at acquisition and represents a credit balance. It is viewed as a gain on a 'bargain purchase' (essentially a discount received) and is credited directly to profits and so to the group's retained earnings.

As illustrated in the pro-forma calculation above, the elements of goodwill at acquisition are based on fair values (at the date of acquisition of the subsidiary).

Definition of fair value

 Fair value is defined in IFRS® 13 *Fair Value Measurement* as **'the price that would be received to sell an asset or paid to transfer a liability in an orderly transaction between market participants at the measurement date'** (IFRS 13, para 9).

We have already seen the two acceptable methods for measuring the non-controlling interest at the acquisition date. The next two sections look at the rules for measuring the fair value of the consideration transferred by the parent upon acquiring the subsidiary, and the fair value of the net assets of the subsidiary at the date of acquisition.

Fair value of parent's consideration

The value of the consideration paid by the parent for its holding in the subsidiary can comprise of a number of elements and, according to IFRS 3 *Business combinations*, each must be measured at its fair value at the date of acquisition. The parent should already have reflected this amount in its individual statement of financial position.

The types of consideration that may be included are:

- Cash (FV = amount paid)

- Shares issued by the parent (FV = market price of shares issued as at the acquisition date)

- Deferred consideration (FV = present value of amounts paid)

- Contingent consideration (FV = probability weighted present value).

Exclusions from consideration

The following should never be recognised as part of consideration paid:

- Legal and professional fees (and other directly attributable costs of acquisition)

- Provisions for future losses in subsidiary acquired.

Directly attributable costs of acquisition are expensed to the parent's statement of profit or loss. This is because they are not part of what the parent gives in return for the shareholding in the subsidiary and, resultantly, are not included in the consideration paid to acquire the shares.

Provisions for future losses or expenses are not part of the value of the parent's holding in the subsidiary. They are not included in the consideration paid. However, future losses may be recorded in the parent's individual financial statements as a provision (an outstanding, uncertain liability), if it is in accordance with IAS 37 *Provisions, Contingent Liabilities and Contingent Assets'* recognition criteria.

Deferred consideration

This is consideration, normally cash, which will be paid in the future.

It is measured at its present value at acquisition for inclusion within the goodwill calculation. The future cash flow paid is discounted at interest rates available to the parent for similar borrowings.

It is recorded in the parent's individual financial statements by:

> Dr Investments
>
> Cr Deferred consideration liability.

Every year after acquisition, the liability will need to be increased to reflect unwinding the discount. The increase in the liability is charged as a finance cost. Therefore, the entry recorded in the parent's individual financial statements is:

> Dr Finance cost (and so reduces the parent's retained earnings)
>
> Cr Deferred consideration liability.

Contingent consideration

Contingent consideration is consideration that may be paid in the future if certain future events occur or conditions are met. For example, cash may be paid in the future if certain profit targets are met.

According to IFRS 3, contingent consideration is measured at its **fair value** at the date of acquisition, to be consistent with how other forms of consideration are measured. This will typically be based on a probability weighted present value.

Adjustments to the value of contingent consideration arising from events after the acquisition date, e.g. a profit target not being met, are normally charged/credited to profits, not the cost of investment.

Illustration 6 – Fair value of consideration paid

Malawi has acquired 80% of the shares in Blantyre. The consideration consisted of:

1. Cash paid $25,460.
2. Malawi issued 10,000 shares to the shareholders of Blantyre, each with a nominal value of $1 and a market value of $4.
3. Cash of $20,000 to be paid one year after the date of acquisition.
4. Cash of $100,000 may be paid one year after the date of acquisition if Blantyre achieves a certain profit target. It is thought that there is only a 40% chance that this target will be successfully achieved. The fair value of this consideration is valued at $36,360.
5. Legal fees associated with the acquisition amounted to $15,000.

A discount rate of 10% should be used.

Required:

Calculate the fair value of Malawi's consideration paid for Blantyre to be used in the goodwill calculation.

Solution

Fair value of parent's consideration

	$
Cash	25,460
Shares (10,000 × $4)	40,000
Deferred consideration ($20,000 × 0.909)	18,180
Contingent consideration	36,360
Total FV of consideration paid by the parent	120,000

The cash payment of $20,000 in one year's time is deferred consideration as it is guaranteed that it will be paid. The future cash flow of $20,000 is discounted back to present value by applying the discount factor using an interest rate of 10% in 1 years' time (as obtained from discount tables).

The cash payment in one year's time of $100,000 dependent on Blantrye achieving a profit target is contingent consideration. This will be valued at its fair value. The question states that the fair value is $36,360.

NB. The fair value would be typically given in an assessment question. For reference, a common method used in practice is a probability weighted present value of the expected value. The expected value is $40,000 (40% × $100,000). This takes into account the expected probability of the profit target being achieved. This is discounted to present value by applying the appropriate discount factor using an interest rate of 10% in 1 years' time to give $36,360 (40,000 × 0.909).

The legal and professional fees are not included in the calculation of goodwill. They should be expensed to the statement of profit or loss.

Test your understanding 5 (Integrated question)

Duck has invested in 60% of Wicket's 10,000 $1 equity shares. Duck paid $5,000 cash consideration and issued 2 shares for every 3 shares acquired. At the date of acquisition, the market value of a Duck share was $2.25.

Duck agreed to pay $3,000 cash 2 years after acquisition. A further $1,000 in cash will be paid 3 years after acquisition if Wicket achieves a certain profit target. The fair value of this contingent consideration was deemed to be $700.

The group elect to measure NCI at fair value at the date of acquisition.

The fair value of the NCI at acquisition was $10,000 and the fair value of Wicket's net assets was $15,000.

Legal and professional fees incurred in relation to the acquisition were $2,000.

Assume a discount rate of 10%.

Required:

Calculate the goodwill arising on the acquisition of Wicket.

Test your understanding 6 (OTQ style)

Kane acquired 75% of Aaron's $1 equity shares on 1 January 20X3. Kane paid $1,000,000 at the date of acquisition and agreed to pay a further $2,500,000 2 years after acquisition.

Legal and professional fees of $150,000 were paid in respect of the acquisition.

Assume a discount rate of 8%.

Required:

Calculate the fair value of the consideration that would be recognised in the calculation of goodwill on acquisition of Aaron.

Fair value of subsidiary's net assets

According to IFRS 3 *Business combinations*, at acquisition, the subsidiary's net assets must be measured at fair value for inclusion within the consolidated financial statements.

The group must recognise the fair value of the **identifiable** assets and liabilities of the subsidiary acquired.

- According to IAS 38 *Intangible assets*, and IFRS 3 *Business combinations,* an asset is identifiable if it either:
  - is capable of being separated (sold separately, regardless of whether the subsidiary actually intends to sell it), or
  - arises from contractual or other legal rights.

- An asset or liability may only be recognised if it meets the definition of an asset or liability as at the acquisition date.
  - For example, costs relating to restructuring the subsidiary that will arise after acquisition do not meet the definition of a liability as at the date of acquisition and are not included in the consolidation.

The requirement to include the subsidiary's net assets at fair value within the group accounts creates differences between the accounting of transactions in the individual accounts. For instance:

- **Intangible assets**

  Certain internally generated intangible assets, such as brand names, patents and client lists, are not recognised in the subsidiary's individual financial statements as per IAS 38 *Intangible assets* but may be recognised on consolidation.

  These intangibles are no longer internally generated as the parent has acquired them as part of the acquisition of the subsidiary. They are identifiable and should be included in the consolidated financial statements at their fair value.

- **Contingent liabilities**

  By definition, contingent liabilities are not recognised in the subsidiary's individual financial statements (they are disclosed by note in accordance with IAS 37 *Provisions, contingent liabilities and contingent assets*).

  On consolidation, however, a contingent liability will be recognised as a liability if its fair value can be measured reliably. On assessing the value of the target subsidiary, the parent will acknowledge the potential cost of taking on responsibility for the contingent liability. In the group accounts, the contingent liability will be recognised at its fair value even if it is not probable.

These differences create the need for **fair value adjustments** within the group accounts. It is important to note that fair value adjustments are just recorded in group accounts. No adjustments are included in the individual accounts of the subsidiary.

Measuring fair value

IFRS 3 provides the following guidance on measuring the fair value of certain assets/liabilities:

Item	Valuation
Property, plant and equipment	Market value. If there is no evidence of market value, depreciated replacement cost should be used.
Intangible assets	Market value. If none exists, use an amount that reflects what the acquirer would have paid otherwise.
Inventories	(i) Finished goods should be valued at selling prices less the sum of disposal costs and a reasonable profit allowance. (ii) Work in progress should be valued at ultimate selling price less the sum of completion costs, disposal costs and a reasonable profit allowance. (iii) Raw materials should be valued at current replacement costs.
Receivables, payables and loans	Present value of future cash flows expected to be received or paid. Discounting is unlikely to be necessary for short-term receivables or payables.

Illustration 7 – Fair value of net assets

Brussels acquired 100% of the share capital of Madrid paying consideration of $8 million.

At acquisition, the statement of financial position of Madrid showed equity share capital of $3m and retained earnings of $3.25m. Included in this total is:

- Freehold land with a carrying amount of $400,000 but a market value of $950,000.

- Machinery with a carrying amount of $1.2m. No reliable market value exists for these items. They would cost $1.5m to replace as new. The machinery has an expected life of 10 years and Madrid's machines are 4 years old.

- The fair value of all other assets and liabilities is approximately equal to carrying amount.

Madrid's brand name was internally generated and so is not recognised in their statement of financial position. However, valuation experts have estimated its fair value to be $500,000.

The directors of Brussels intend to close down one of the divisions of Madrid and wish to provide for operating losses up to the date of closure which are forecast as $729,000.

An investment in plant and machinery will be required to bring the remaining production line of Madrid up to date. This will amount to $405,000 in the next 12 months.

Required:

Calculate the goodwill arising on the acquisition of Madrid.

Illustration 7 answer

The fair value of the subsidiary's net assets is used in the calculation of goodwill. Start by setting up a net assets working and filling in the subsidiary's share capital and retained earnings at acquisition – this gives us the carrying amount of the net assets at acquisition. Note that since the question only requires the calculation of goodwill, only the net assets at acquisition are required.

Net assets of subsidiary

	Acquisition $000
Share capital	3,000
Retained earnings	3,250
Carrying amount of NA at acquisition	6,250

Now consider the adjustments required to adjust the net assets from their carrying amounts to their fair values.

Land – this requires an upwards adjustment of $550,000 (fair value of $950,000 less carrying amount value of $400,000).

Machinery – the fair value is not given and so needs to be calculated. It will be measured as the depreciated replacement cost. Madrid's machines have an expected life of 10 years and are 4 years old. Therefore, their remaining life is 6 years.

Depreciated replacement cost = 6/10 × $1,500,000 = $900,000

Since their carrying amount is $1.2m and their fair value is $0.9m, a downwards fair value adjustment of $300,000 is required.

Brand – an upwards adjustment of $500,000 is required as its carrying amount is currently zero but its fair value is $500,000. Note that the brand can be recognised on consolidation as the fact that it has a fair value indicates it is separable.

The provision for future operating losses does not represent a liability at acquisition since there is no past event giving rise to an obligation. Similarly, the future investment in machinery does not represent assets that exist at acquisition and so cannot be recognised.

Now process these adjustments to complete the net assets working:

Net assets of subsidiary

	Acquisition $000
Share capital	3,000
Retained earnings	3,250
Fair value adjustments	
Land	550
Machinery	(300)
Brand	500
Fair value of sub's net assets	7,000

Now the goodwill calculation can be completed. Note that there is no NCI as the parent has acquired 100% of the subsidiary.

Goodwill

	$000
Fair value of P's investment	8,000
Fair value of sub's net assets at acquisition (working)	(7,000)
Goodwill on acquisition	1,000

Recording fair value adjustments

The fair value of the subsidiary's net assets at acquisition represents the 'cost' of the net assets to the group at the date of acquisition. Recording fair value adjustments is in accordance with the historical cost concept.

It also ensures an accurate measurement of goodwill. Assuming the fair value of the subsidiary's net assets is higher than their carrying amount, goodwill would be overstated if the fair value adjustments were not recognised.

To record fair value adjustments in the CSFP

- Adjust the net assets working at acquisition and the reporting date as appropriate:
    - The fair value adjustment arises at acquisition so there should always be an adjustment to the net assets at the date of acquisition.
    - The net assets at the reporting date should also be adjusted unless told that the assets/liabilities to which the adjustment relates are no longer held by the group as at the year-end.
- Reflect the reporting date adjustment on the face of the CSFP.

Impact on post-acquisition depreciation

Fair value adjustments often involve adjustments to non-current asset values which, consequently, involve an adjustment to depreciation.

Depreciation must be based on the carrying amount of the related non-current asset in the group accounts. Therefore, if the group non-current asset values are adjusted at acquisition then a group depreciation adjustment must be made in the post-acquisition period.

To record depreciation arising from a fair value adjustment in the CSFP:

- Adjust net assets working in the reporting date column to reflect the cumulative impact upon depreciation caused by the fair value adjustment.

- Reflect the adjustment on the face of CSFP by reducing the carrying amount of the fair valued asset.

- The extra depreciation will reduce the post-acquisition profits of the subsidiary included in consolidated reserves and NCI calculations.

Illustration 8

The following summarised statements of financial position are provided for King and Lear as at 31 December 20X7:

	King $000	Lear $000
Non-current assets	1,300	1,200
Investment in Lear	1,900	–
Current assets	200	450
	3,400	1,650
Equity		
Share capital ($1)	2,000	750
Retained earnings	1,250	300
Current liabilities	150	600
	3,400	1,650

King purchased 80% of Lear's equity shares on 1 January 20X5 for $1.9m when Lear's retained earnings were $100,000.

The group elect to measure the non-controlling interests at fair value at acquisition and the fair value of the non-controlling interests in Lear on 1 January 20X5 was $400,000. At this date, Lear's non-current assets had a fair value of $1m and the assets had a remaining useful economic life of 5 years. Their carrying amount at the date of acquisition was $850,000.

As at 31 December 20X7, an impairment loss of $50,000 has arisen on goodwill.

Required:

(a) Prepare the consolidated statement of financial position at 31 December 20X7.

Illustration 8 answer

(a) **Consolidated statement of financial position as at 31 December 20X7**

		$000
Non-current assets	(1,300 + 1,200 + 150 – 90)	2,560
Goodwill	**(W3)**	1,250
Current assets	(200 + 450)	650
		4,460
Equity		
Share capital		2,000
Retained earnings	**(W5)**	1,298
Non-controlling interests	**(W4)**	412
		3,710
Current liabilities	(150 + 600)	750
		4,460

Note: The carrying amount of non-current assets is adjusted to reflect the fair value adjustment and subsequent depreciation.

(W1) Group structure

King

80% 1 Jan 20X5

3 years since acquisition

Lear

(W2) Net assets of subsidiary

	Acquisition	Reporting date
	$000	$000
Share capital	750	750
Retained earnings	100	300
Fair value adjustment (1,000 – 850)	150	150
Depreciation adj (150 × 3/5)	–	(90)
	1,000	1,110

110 Post acquisition profit

Note: The fair value adjustment is made at acquisition and at the reporting date along with any additional depreciation that will have been charged (on the fair value uplift) in the post-acquisition period.

(W3) Goodwill

	$000
Fair value of P's investment	1,900
Value of NCI at acquisition (fair value)	400
Fair value of sub's net assets at acquisition **(W2)**	(1,000)
Goodwill at acquisition	1,300
Impairment	(50)
Goodwill at reporting date	1,250

(W4) Non-controlling interests

	$000
Value of NCI at acquisition	400
NCI% × post acquisition reserves (20% × 110 **(W2)**)	22
NCI% × impairment (20% × 50)	(10)
	412

(W5) Consolidated retained earnings

	$000
Parent's reserves	1,250
Sub (80% × 110 **(W2)**)	88
Impairment (80% × 50)	(40)
	————
	1,298
	————

Information for TYUs 7 to 9

BN acquired 75% of the 1 million issued $1 ordinary shares of AB on 1 January 20X0 for $1,850,000 when AB's retained earnings were $885,000.

The carrying amount of AB's net assets was considered to be the same as their fair value at the date of acquisition with the exception of AB's property, plant and equipment. The carrying amount of these assets was $945,000 and their market value was $1,100,000. The property, plant and equipment of AB had an estimated useful life of 5 years from the date of acquisition. BN depreciates all assets on a straight line basis.

AB sold goods to BN with a sales value of $400,000 during the year ended 31 December 20X1. All of these goods remain in BN's inventories at the year end. AB makes a 20% gross profit margin on all sales.

The retained earnings reported in the financial statements of BN and AB, as at 31 December 20X1, are $4,200,000 and $1,300,000 respectively.

The group elect to measure non-controlling interest at fair value at the date of acquisition. The fair value of the non-controlling interest was $570,000 on 1 January 20X0.

An impairment review performed on 31 December 20X1 indicated that goodwill on the acquisition of AB had been impaired by 20%. No impairment was recognised in the year ended 31 December 20X0.

Test your understanding 7 (OTQ style)

Required

Calculate the carrying amount of goodwill that will appear in the consolidated statement of financial position of the BN group at 31 December 20X1.

Test your understanding 8 (OTQ style)

Required

Calculate the balance on consolidated retained earnings at 31 December 20X1.

Test your understanding 9 (OTQ style)

Required

Which three of the following statements are true in respect of BN's non-controlling interest?

A   The non-controlling is included as a separate part of equity on the face of the consolidated statement of financial position

B   The non-controlling interest is a credit balance and should be presented within non-current liabilities

C   The non-controlling interest should be debited with its share (25%) of the post-acquisition reserves of AB

D   The non-controlling interest is adjusted to reflect its share of the goodwill impairment

E   Upon acquisition of AB, BN will initially credit the NCI with its fair value of $570,000

F   The unrealised profit adjustment results in an increase in the NCI figure

10   Treatment of investment as FVOCI

In the parent's individual financial statements, an investment in a subsidiary could be classified as fair value through other comprehensive income (FVOCI), in accordance with IFRS 9 *Financial instruments* (see Financial Instruments chapter).

This means that the investment will have been remeasured to fair value since the date of acquisition, with any gains or losses arising being taken to other comprehensive income (reserves in the CSFP).

Upon consolidation, these gains or losses are effectively intra-group gains. They should be reversed out so that the investment is restated to its fair value at **the date of acquisition** (for inclusion in the goodwill calculation as part of the consideration paid at acquisition). A journal of Dr Other components of equity (FVOCI reserve) Cr Investment in S will be posted to reverse any gain (with the opposite effect if a loss is reversed.

Illustration 9 – Reversal of FVOCI gains/losses

Root acquired 80% of the share capital of Warner on 1 January 20X2 for $750,000. The investment in Warner was classified as FVOCI in the books of Root and is held at fair value. The gains earned to date are included in other components of equity of Root. The fair value of the investment at 31 December 20X4, the reporting date, is $1,150,000. The gain on the financial asset is not a real gain to the group. No financial asset is recorded in the group accounts, only Root's individual company financial statements.

The amount to be eliminated from Root's SFP upon consolidation is the fair value at the reporting date of $1,150,000.

The amount to be included as the consideration paid in the goodwill calculation is the fair value at the date of acquisition, i.e. $750,000.

The gain of $400,000 (1,150,000 – 750,000) that has been recorded in other components of equity since the date of acquisition must be reversed out upon consolidation. Dr Other components of equity 400 Cr Investment 400.

Test your understanding 10 (further OTQs)

1   P owns 75% of S. S sells goods to P for $5,200 with a margin of 20%. 40% of these goods have subsequently been sold on by P to external parties by the reporting date.

Which one of the following adjustments would P make in relation to the above goods when preparing the consolidated statement of financial position?

A   Dr Consolidated retained earnings $520, Cr Inventory $520

B   Dr Consolidated retained earnings $390, Dr NCI $130, Cr Inventory $520

C   Dr Consolidated retained earnings $624, Cr Inventory $624

D   Dr Consolidated retained earnings $468, Dr NCI $156, Cr Inventory $624

2   Paul acquired a 100% investment in Simon on 1 July 20X2. The consideration consisted of:

–   the transfer of 200,000 shares in Paul with a nominal value of $1 each and a market price on the date of acquisition of $4.25 each

– $250,000 cash paid on 1 July 20X2

– $1,000,000 cash, payable on 1 July 20X4 (a discount rate of 8% should be used to value the liability).

Calculate the value of the consideration that Paul should use when calculating goodwill arising on the acquisition of Simon.

3   K acquired 60% of the ordinary share capital of S on 1 May 20X7 for $140,000. The investment was classified as FVOCI with any associated gains or losses recorded within other components of equity in K's individual financial statements. The investment is recorded at its fair value of $162,000 as at 30 November 20X7.

At 30 November 20X7, the other components of equity balance in the individual statements of financial position of K and S was $28,000 and $10,000 respectively. At the date of acquisition, S did not have any other components of equity in its statement of financial position.

Calculate the other components of equity balance that would appear in the consolidated statement of financial position of the K group as at 30 November 20X7.

The following scenario relates to questions (4) and (5).

Aston acquired 85% of Martin's 250,000 $1 ordinary shares on 1 January 20X4 for $480,000 when the retained earnings of Martin were $90,000. At the date of acquisition, the fair value of Martin's property, plant and equipment was $50,000 higher than its carrying amount. It was estimated to have a remaining useful life of ten years at this date.

At 31 December 20X7, the carrying amount of property, plant and equipment in the individual statements of financial position of Aston and Martin was $800,000 and $390,000 respectively.

The group elect to measure NCI at fair value at acquisition and the fair value of the NCI in Martin on 1 January 20X4 was $70,000.

4   **Calculate goodwill arising on the acquisition of Martin.**

5   **Calculate the carrying amount of property, plant and equipment that would appear in the consolidated statement of financial position of the Aston group as at 31 December 20X7.**

6   RW acquired 65% of the equity share capital of SR on 1 April 20X6 for $950,000 when the carrying amount of SR's net assets was $450,000. The group elect to measure non-controlling interest at fair value. The fair value of the NCI in SR at 1 April 20X6 was $350,000.

The only fair value adjustment made was to increase property, plant and equipment by $75,000. The remaining useful life of these assets at acquisition was 5 years.

The net assets reported in the financial statements of SR at 31 March 20X8 are $650,000.

Calculate the non-controlling interest figure shown in the RW group consolidated statement of financial position as at 31 March 20X8.

7   Bombay owns 80% of Mumbai. During the current year, Bombay has sold $1,500,000 goods to Mumbai at a mark-up of 20%. 80% of these goods have been sold on by Mumbai.

Which one of the following statements is true regarding the effects of the provision for unrealised profit within the consolidated statement of financial position of Bombay group?

A   Group inventory will need to be increased by $200,000

B   Non-controlling interest will take a 20% share of any provision for unrealised profit

C   Group retained earnings is debited with $50,000

D   Goodwill will be increased

8   **The definition of control as per IFRS 10 *Consolidated financial statements* includes which of the following:**

A   The parent must own over 50% of the ordinary share capital of the subsidiary

B   The investor has power over the investee

C   The target company must be a listed entity

D   The investor appoints greater than 50% of the board of directors

9   Michelle owns 65% of Barack. Michelle sells goods to Barack during the year. All of these goods are sold on by Barack.

Which one of the following statements regarding the consolidation of the Michelle Group is true?

A   Outstanding receivables owed to Barack and payables owed by Michelle are removed

B   100% of the ordinary share capital of Michelle and Barack are added

C   Unrealised profits will require adjustment due to the intra-group trading

D   An uplift in the fair value of Barack's net assets on acquisition will cause goodwill to reduce

11   Chapter summary

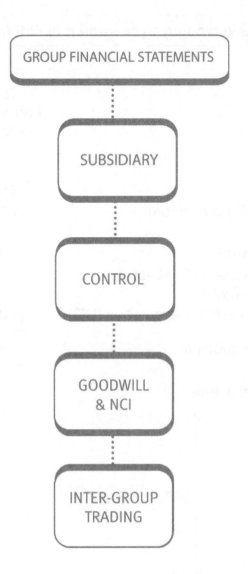

Test your understanding answers

Test your understanding 1 (Integrated question)

Goodwill

	(a) Fair value method	(b) Proportionate share of net assets method
	$000	$000
Fair value of P's investment	1,200	1,200
NCI:		
Fair value (given)	250	
Proportionate share of net assets (20% × 1,000 **(W2)**)		200
Less: S's net assets at acquisition **(W2)**	(1,000)	(1,000)
Goodwill at acquisition	450	400

(W1) Group structure

P

80% 1 April 20X8

S

(W2) Net assets of subsidiary

	Acquisition
	$000
Share capital	200
Retained earnings	800
	1,000

Test your understanding 2 (Integrated question)

Goodwill

	(a) **Fair value method**	(b) **Proportionate share of net assets method**
	$000	$000
Fair value of P's investment	2,500	2,500
NCI:		
Fair value (25% × 500 × $6)	750	
Proportionate share of net assets (25% × 2,000 **(W2)**)		500
Less: S's net assets at acquisition **(W2)**	(2,000)	(2,000)
Goodwill at acquisition	1,250	1,000

(W1) Group structure

P

|
75% 1 April 20X8
|

S

(W2) Net assets of subsidiary

	Acquisition
	$000
Share capital	500
Retained earnings	1,500
	2,000

Test your understanding 3 (Integrated question)

(a) Goodwill

	(1) Fair value method	(2) Proportionate share of net assets method
	$000	$000
Fair value of P's investment	6,500	6,500
Value of NCI at acquisition		
– at fair value	2,000	
– at proportionate share of net assets (25% × 7,500 **(W1)**)		1,875
Less: sub's net assets at acquisition **(W1)**	(7,500)	(7,500)
Goodwill at acquisition	1,000	875
Impairment (20% × goodwill at acquisition)	(200)	(175)
Goodwill at reporting date	800	700

(b) Consolidated retained earnings

	(1) Fair value method	(2) Proportionate share of net assets method
	$000	$000
Parent's reserves	10,800	10,800
Sub (75% × 2,000 **(W1)**)	1,500	1,500
Impairment loss		
– FV method (75% × 200 (part a))	(150)	
– Proportionate share of net assets method (part a)		(175)
	12,150	12,125

(c) Non-controlling interest

	(1) Fair value method	(2) Proportionate share of net assets method
	$000	$000
Value of NCI at acquisition	2,000	1,875
NCI% × post acquisition reserves (25% × 2,000 **(W1)**)	500	500
NCI% × impairment (25% × 200 (part a))	(50)	–
	2,450	2,375

(W1) Net assets of subsidiary

	Acquisition		Reporting date
	$000		$000
Share capital	5,000		5,000
Retained earnings	2,500		4,500
	7,500		9,500

2,000 post-acq'n profit

Test your understanding 4 (Integrated question)

(a) (i) Goodwill

	$000
Fair value of P's investment	14,500
Value of NCI at acquisition (20% × 10,800 **(W2)**)	2,160
Less: sub's net assets at acquisition **(W2)**	(10,800)
Goodwill at acquisition	5,860
Impairment	(1,000)
Goodwill at reporting date	4,860

(ii) **Consolidated retained earnings**

	Retained earnings $000
Parent's reserves	12,600
Sub (80% × 2,100 **(W2)**)	1,680
Impairment	(1,000)
PUP **(W4)**	(100)
	13,180

(iii) **Non-controlling interest**

	$000
Value of NCI at acquisition	2,160
NCI% × post-acquisition reserves (20% × 2,100 **(W2)**)	420
	2,580

(W1) Group structure

P
|
80% 3 years since acquisition
|
S

(W2) Net assets of subsidiary

	Acquisition	Reporting date
	$000	$000
Share capital	5,000	5,000
Retained earnings	5,800	7,900
	10,800	12,900

2,100 Post-acquisition profit

(W3) Intra-group balances

		$000
Dr Payables	↓	550
Dr Cash	↑	200
Cr Receivables	↓	750

This adjustment does not affect the answers to this question. The impacts are all shown directly within the CSFP.

(W4) PUP

Profit on sale = 25/125 × $1,500,000 = $300,000

Profit in inventory = 1/3 × $300,000 = $100,000

(b) Revised amounts, S selling to P

(i) Consolidated retained earnings

	Retained earnings $000
Parent's reserves	12,600
Sub (80% × 2,000 **(W2)**)	1,600
Impairment	(1,000)
	13,200

(ii) Non-controlling interest

	$000
Value of NCI at acquisition	2,160
NCI% × post-acquisition reserves (20% × 2,000 **(W2)**)	400
	2,560

The impact on the reserves of the seller being S rather than P is a reduction of $20,000 in NCI and an increase of $20,000 in group reserves. 20% of the PUP adjustment has been re-allocated against the NCI.

(W2) Net assets of subsidiary

The PUP adjustment would be deducted in W2 rather than W5, resulting in a reduction in S's post-acquisition profits of 2,000.

	Acquisition $000	Reporting date $000
Share capital	5,000	5,000
Retained earnings	5,800	7,900
PUP **(W7)**		(100)
	10,800	12,800

2,000 Post-acquisition profit

Test your understanding 5 (integration question)

Goodwill

	$
Fair value of consideration transferred by P	
Cash	5,000
Shares (60% × 10,000 × 2/3 × $2.25)	9,000
Deferred consideration ($3,000 × 0.826)	2,478
Contingent consideration	700
	17,178
Value of NCI at acquisition (at fair value)	10,000
Fair value of sub's net assets at acquisition	(15,000)
Goodwill on acquisition	12,178
Impairment	–
Goodwill at reporting date (in CSFP)	12,178

Note: The legal and professional fees are not included in the calculation of goodwill. They should be expensed to the statement of profit or loss.

Test your understanding 6 (OTQ style)

Fair value of consideration = $3,142,500

	$
Cash	1,000,000
Deferred consideration ($2.5 million × 0.857)	2,142,500
	3,142,500

Note: The legal and professional fees are not included in the calculation of goodwill. They should be expensed to the statement of profit or loss.

Test your understanding 7 (OTQ style)

Goodwill = $304,000

	$	$
Consideration transferred		1,850,000
Non-controlling interest at fair value		570,000
Net assets at the date of acquisition:		
Carrying amount $(1,000,000 + 885,000)	1,885,000	
Fair value increase $(1,100,000 – 945,000)	155,000	
		(2,040,000)
Goodwill on acquisition		380,000
Impairment 20% in 20X1		(76,000)
Goodwill as at 31 December 20X1		304,000

Tutorial note:

The net assets at acquisition have been incorporated into the above calculation. You can alternatively use a net assets table to calculate the amount of $2,040,000 shown above. See the solution to TYU 5 for this alternative working. Note that you would only need the acquisition column for the calculation of goodwill.

Test your understanding 8 (OTQ style)

Consolidated retained earnings

	BN $
As reported in SFP	4,200,000
Group share of AB ($273,000 (W1) × 75%)	204,750
Impairment of goodwill (76 × 75%)	(57,000)
	4,347,750

As goodwill is calculated using the FV method, the impairment charge (as taken from TYU 7 answer above) will be split between the parent and NCI shareholders, using their relevant shareholding percentages. The parent's shares will reduce the group retained earnings as shown.

(W1) Net assets of subsidiary

The post-acquisition profits can be determined via a net assets table as below:

	Acquisition	Reporting date
	$000	$000
Share capital	1,000	1,000
Retained earnings	885	1,300
Fair value adjustment (1,100 – 945)	155	155
Depreciation adj (155 × 1/5 × 2 yrs)	–	(62)
PUP adj (400 × 20%)		(80)
Goodwill impairment		
	2,040	2,313

273 post-acquisition reserves

Test your understanding 9 (OTQ style)

The correct statements are A, D and E.

B is incorrect, as NCI is part of equity rather than liabilities.

C is incorrect, as the NCI would be **credited** with its share of the post-acquisition reserves (not debited).

F is incorrect, as the unrealised profit would result in a **reduction** (not increase) in the NCI.

Test your understanding 10 (further OTQs)

1   **D** is the correct answer.

PUP adjustment = $624 ($5,200 × 20% × 60%). This is deducted from inventory.

The adjustment is split between NCI and parent shareholders as S, the subsidiary, was the seller.

$468 (75% × $624) is deducted from consolidated retained earnings.

$156 (25% × $624) is deducted from NCI.

2   **Value of consideration = $1,957,000**

	$000
Shares (200,000 × $4.25)	850
Cash	250
Deferred consideration ($1,000,000 × 0.857)	857
	1,957

3   **Other components of equity = $12,000**

	$
K's other components of equity	28,000
K's share of S's post-acquisition movement in other components of equity (60% × 10k)	6,000
Reversal of FVOCI gains from investment in subsidiary (162k – 140k)	(22,000)
	12,000

4   **Goodwill = $160,000**

	$	$
Consideration transferred		480,000
Non-controlling interest at fair value		70,000
Net assets at the date of acquisition:		
Share capital	250,000	
Retained earnings	90,000	
Fair value increase	50,000	
		(390,000)
Goodwill on acquisition		160,000

5   Property, plant and equipment = $1,220,000

	$
Aston	800,000
Martin	390,000
Fair value increase at acquisition	50,000
Fair value depreciation (50,000 × 4/10)	(20,000)
Goodwill on acquisition	1,220,000

6   Non-controlling interest equity = $409,500

	$
Value of NCI at acquisition	350,000
NCI share of S's post-acquisition net assets (35% × (650k – 450k))	70,000
NCI share of FV depreciation (35% × (75k × 2/5))	(10,500)
	409,500

An alternative approach would be to use a net assets working to calculate the adjusted post-acquisition reserves of the subsidiary as shown below:

Net assets of subsidiary

	Acquisition	Reporting date
	$000	$000
Carrying amount	450	650
Fair value adjustments:		
Property, plant and equipment	75	75
Depreciation on PPE adj (75 × 2/5)	–	(30)
	525	695

170 Post acquisition reserves

Non-controlling interest

	$
Value of NCI at acquisition	350,000
Share of S's post-acquisition net assets (35% × 170k)	59,500
	409,500

7   C

The intra-group trading between Bombay and Mumbai will cause an unrealised profit within the group accounts. This results from the good sold by Bombay to Mumbai still being held by Mumbai.

The required adjustment would reduce group inventory and retained earnings by $50,000.

The PUP adjustment is calculated as follows:

	$	%
Sales	1,500,000	120
COS	1,250,000	100
	250,000	20
20% left in group		
Provision for unrealised profit	50,000	

A share of the PUP is only allocated to non-controlling interest if the subsidiary sells to the parent. Bombay is the parent so NCI does not take a share.

Goodwill is unaffected by PUP adjustments.

8   B

IFRS 10 states that 'an investor controls an investee if and only if the investor has all of the following elements:

*   power over the investee

*   exposure, or rights, to variable returns from its involvement with the investee, and

*   the ability to use its power over the investee to affect the amount of the investor's returns.

Representing >50% of the board of directors and >50% of the ordinary share capital are indicators of power but do not form part of the definition of control.

9   D

Fair value adjustments uplifts will increase the net assets of the subsidiary at acquisition, consequently reducing goodwill.

The outstanding receivables would have been owed to Michelle and the payable owed by Barack. This is because Michelle sells to Barack. Option A describes the position as if Barack had sold to Michelle.

Only 100% of Michelle's (the parent) share capital would be included in the group accounts. Option B is incorrect.

Unrealised profit would not arise in these group accounts. All of the goods sold through intra-group trade have been sold outside of the group by the year-end. Option C is incorrect.

Group accounts – Subsidiaries (CSPLOCI)

Chapter learning objectives

Lead outcome	Component outcome
B2: Explain relevant financial reporting standards for group accounts	(a) Explain the financial reporting standards for the key areas of group accounts.
C1: Prepare group accounts based on IFRS	Prepare the following based on financial reporting standards: (b) Consolidated statement of profit or loss and other comprehensive income

1 Session content

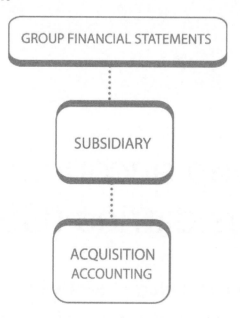

2 Consolidated statement of profit or loss and other comprehensive income

The principles of consolidation as per IFRS 10 *Consolidated financial statements* are continued within the statement of profit or loss and other comprehensive income (CSPLOCI).

A statement of profit or loss and other comprehensive income reflects the income and expenses generated by the net assets shown on the statement of financial position. It incorporates two separate statements: the statement of profit or loss and the statement of other comprehensive income.

Since the group controls the net assets of the subsidiary, the income and expenses of the subsidiary should be fully included in the consolidated statement of comprehensive income i.e. add across 100% of the parent plus 100% of the subsidiary.

Pro-forma for the CSPLOCI

Consolidated statement of profit or loss and other comprehensive income for the year ended.....

	$
Revenue (100% P + 100% S)	X
Cost of sales (100% P + 100% S)	(X)
Gross profit	X
Operating expenses (100% P + 100% S)	(X)
Profit from operations	X
Investment income (100% P + 100% S)	X
Profit before tax	X
Income tax expense (100% P + 100% S)	(X)
Profit for the year	X
Other comprehensive income (100% P + 100% S)	X
Total comprehensive income	X

Profit attributable to:

Parent shareholders (balancing figure)	X
Non-controlling interests (W)	X
	X

Total comprehensive income attributable to:

Parent shareholders (balancing figure)	X
Non-controlling interests (W)	X
	X

Consolidation adjustments and the consolidated statement of profit or loss and other comprehensive income (CSOPLOCI)

Mid-year acquisitions

If the subsidiary was acquired mid-year then only the post-acquisition results should be consolidated. Unless told otherwise, it is normal to assume that results accrue evenly over the period and, therefore, the results of the subsidiary should be time apportioned so that only the post-acquisition results are consolidated.

Intra-group investment income

Dividends paid by the subsidiary to the parent should be eliminated upon consolidation from the parent's investment income.

Non-controlling interests

According to IFRS 10 *Consolidated financial statements*, the profit for the year and the total comprehensive income for the year are analysed between the amounts attributable to the owners of the parent and the amounts attributable to the non-controlling interest. This analysis is presented at the bottom of the consolidated statement of profit or loss and it is common for the NCI figures to be calculated (working shown below) with the amounts attributable to the owners of the parent then being computed as a balancing figure.

Goodwill impairment

If the fair value method has been used to value the non-controlling interests at acquisition, the NCI share of profit will be adjusted to reflect their share of any goodwill impairment loss.

Where the proportionate share of net assets method is used, all of the goodwill impairment is allocated to the parent (as previously discussed) and therefore no adjustment is made to the NCI figure.

Standard consolidation workings

Non-controlling interest share of profit/TCI

The share of profit and total comprehensive income that belongs to the NCI is to be calculated as follows:

	$	$
Sub's profit for the year per S's SOPLOCI (time apportioned if mid-year acquisition)	X	
FV depreciation adjustment	(X)	
PUP – if S is seller	(X)	
Impairment expense (fair value method only)	(X)	
Adjusted profit	X	
NCI share of profits × NCI%		X
Sub's other comprehensive income per S's SOPLOCI (time apportioned if mid-year acquisition)	X	
Adjusted TCI	X	
NCI share of total comprehensive income × NCI%		X

There are various adjustments that may have to be made to the subsidiary's profit when calculating the NCI's share.

Illustration 1

On 1 July 20X9, Zebedee acquired 75% of the equity shares of Xavier.

The following statements of profit or loss and other comprehensive income have been produced by Zebedee and Xavier for the year ended 31 December 20X9.

	Zebedee	Xavier
	$000	$000
Revenue	1,260	520
Cost of sales	(420)	(210)
Gross profit	840	310
Operating expenses	(300)	(150)
Profit from operations	540	160
Investment income	36	–
Profit before tax	576	160
Income tax expense	(130)	(26)
Profit for the year	446	134
Other comprehensive income	100	50
Total comprehensive income	546	184

1   At 31 December 20X9, goodwill arising on consolidation was reviewed for impairment. An impairment loss of $15,000 had arisen which should be charged to operating expenses. It is group policy to measure NCI at fair value at the date of acquisition.

2   Xavier paid a dividend of $32,000 on 30 November 20X9.

Required:

Prepare the consolidated statement of profit or loss and other comprehensive income for the Zebedee group for the year ended 31 December 20X9.

Illustration 1 answer

Look out for mid-year acquisitions as the results of the subsidiary may need to be time apportioned. In this scenario, only 6 months of the subsidiary's results should be consolidated as the subsidiary was acquired half way through the year.

Zebedee

Consolidated statement of profit or loss and other comprehensive income for the year ended 31 December 20X9

	$000
Revenue (1,260 + (520 × 6/12))	1,520
Cost of sales (420 + (210 × 6/12))	(525)
Gross profit	995
Operating expenses (300 + (150 × 6/12) + 15 impairment)	(390)
Profit from operations	605
Investment income (36 – 24 **(W1)**)	12
Profit before tax	617
Income tax expense (130 + (26 × 6/12))	(143)
Profit for the year	474
Other comprehensive income (100 + (50 × 6/12))	125
Total comprehensive income	599
Profit attributable to:	
Parent shareholders (balancing figure)	461
Non-controlling interests **(W2)**	13
	474
Total comprehensive income attributable to:	
Parent shareholders (balancing figure)	580
Non-controlling interests **(W2)**	19
	599

Workings

(W1) Intra-group dividend/investment income

Sub paid $32,000

Parent received $24,000 (75% × 32,000)

Always look out for intra-group dividends in CSOPLOCI questions. Any dividend paid by the subsidiary will have partly been received by the parent (depending on their percentage holding) and this needs to be eliminated from investment income upon consolidation.

(W2) NCI share of profit and total comprehensive income

	$000	$000
Sub's profit (134 × 6/12)	67	
Impairment expense	(15)	
	52	
NCI share of profits × 25%		13
Sub's OCI (50 × 6/12)	25	
	77	
NCI share of total comprehensive income × 25%		19

For each consolidation adjustment, consider whether it affects the non-controlling interest. Here, there is goodwill impairment and, as the NCI is measured at fair value, the NCI's portion of the impairment charge should be allocated against the NCI profit.

By deducting the impairment expense from the subsidiary's profit prior to applying the NCI%, the NCI's share of the impairment charge is allocated to the NCI figure.

Test your understanding 1

Given below are the statements of profit or loss and other comprehensive income for Paris and its subsidiary, London, for the year ended 31 December 20X5.

	Paris	London
	$000	$000
Revenue	3,200	2,560
Cost of sales	(1,200)	(1,080)
Gross profit	2,000	1,480
Operating expenses	(560)	(400)
Profit from operations	1,440	1,080
Investment income	160	–
Profit before tax	1,600	1,080
Income tax expense	(400)	(480)
Profit for the year	1,200	600
Other comprehensive income	300	100
Total comprehensive income	1,500	700

Paris acquired 80% of London's equity shares on 1 October 20X5.

1   Goodwill was calculated valuing the NCI at fair value at the date of acquisition. At 31 December 20X5, it was determined that goodwill arising on the acquisition had been impaired by $30,000. Impairments are charged to operating expenses.

2   London paid a dividend of $150,000 on 15 December 20X5.

Required:

Prepare a consolidated statement of profit or loss and other comprehensive income for the year ended 31 December 20X5.

3 Intra-group balances

Intra-group balances and transactions must be eliminated in full, as the group is treated as a single entity and, therefore, cannot trade with or owe money to itself.

- Intra-group transactions are eliminated from the consolidated statement of profit or loss and other comprehensive income.

- Any profit still held within the group's assets from intra-group trading should also be eliminated (the provision for unrealised profit (PUP) adjustment).

Provision for unrealised profit (PUP) in inventory

P and S may sell goods to each other, resulting in a profit being recorded in the selling entity's financial statements. If these goods are still held by the purchasing entity at the year-end, the goods have not been sold outside of the group. The profit is unrealised from the group's perspective and should be removed.

The adjustment is also required to ensure that inventory is stated at the cost to the group. This would be the cost when the goods were first acquired by the group, not the cost to the purchasing entity after the intra-group transfer.

PUP adjustment = profit on inventory still held in group at year end.

In the consolidated statement of profit or loss:

- Add to cost of sales (to reflect reduction in closing inventory and profit)

- If S is the seller, adjust the NCI to reflect their share of the PUP adjustment.

NB. The total intragroup revenue and cost of sales will also be removed from the consolidated SPL as a separate adjustment to the PUP.

The 'PUP' adjustment

Parent sells to subsidiary

P sells goods to S for $400 at cost plus 25%. All of these goods remain in the inventory of S at the end of the year.

Profit made on the sale $\dfrac{25}{125} \times 400 = \$80$.

PUP adjustment in CSOPLOCI

The PUP adjustment of $80 is always added to cost of sales, regardless of which entity made the profit.

The NCI share of profit would be adjusted for the PUP adjustment only if the subsidiary was the seller.

Cost structures

The cost structure of the intra-group sale may be given to you in one of two ways.

Mark-up on cost (Cost plus)

If, for example, goods are sold for $440 and there is a 25% mark up on cost, the profit included within the $440 is calculated as follows:

	%	$	
Revenue	125	440	
Cost of sales	100		
Gross profit	25	88	= 440 × 25/125

The PUP is $88.

Gross profit margin

The gross profit margin gives the profit as a percentage of revenue. Using the same figures as above but with a gross profit margin of 25% the PUP would be calculated as:

	%	$	
Revenue	100	440	
Cost of sales	75		
Gross profit	25	110	= 440 × 25/100

The PUP is $110.

Test your understanding 2

Below are the statements of profit or loss for Rome and its subsidiary, Madrid, for the year ended 30 June 20X9.

	Rome	Madrid
	$000	$000
Revenue	10,350	8,400
Cost of sales	(6,200)	(5,150)
Gross profit	4,150	3,250
Operating expenses	(2,450)	(1,600)
Profit before tax	1,700	1,650
Income tax expense	(550)	(450)
Profit for the year	1,150	1,200

1   Rome acquired 60% of Madrid's equity shares on 1 July 20X7 paying $6 million. At this date, the value of Madrid's net assets was $5 million. It is Rome's group policy to value NCI at acquisition using the proportionate share of net assets method. As at 30 June 20X9, it was determined that goodwill on acquisition had been impaired by 20%. No impairment loss had arisen previously.

2   During the year ended 30 June 20X9, Rome sold $1 million of goods to Madrid at a margin of 30%. Half of these goods remained in the inventory of Madrid at the reporting date.

Required:

(a)   Prepare a consolidated statement of profit or loss for the Rome Group for the year ended 30 June 20X9.

(b)   Assume now that Madrid had sold the goods to Rome instead (all other details remain the same). Prepare the analysis of profit attributable to parent shareholders and NCI for the year ended 30 June 20X9 in this situation.

4   Fair value adjustments and the CSPLOCI

Impact on post-acquisition depreciation

Fair value adjustments often involve adjustments to non-current asset values which, consequently, involve an adjustment to depreciation.

Depreciation in the group accounts must be based on the carrying amount of the related non-current asset in the group accounts. Therefore, if the non-current asset values are adjusted at acquisition then a depreciation adjustment must be made in the post-acquisition period.

To record depreciation adjustments in the CSOPLOCI:

- An adjustment should be made to reflect the impact of the fair value adjustment on the current year's depreciation charge.

- As this depreciation charge relates to the subsidiary's assets, the adjustment should be reflected in the calculation of profit attributable to the NCI.

Illustration 2

King purchased 80% of Lear's equity shares on 1 January 20X5 for $1.9m when Lear's retained earnings were $100,000.

It is group policy to measure the non-controlling interests at fair value at acquisition. The fair value of the non-controlling interests in Lear on 1 January 20X5 was $400,000. At this date Lear's non-current assets had a fair value of $1m and the assets had a remaining useful economic life of 5 years. Their carrying amount at the date of acquisition was $850,000.

As at 31 December 20X7, an impairment loss of $50,000 has arisen on goodwill.

Required:

Explain the impact that the fair value adjustment would have on the consolidated statement of comprehensive income for the year ended 31 December 20X7.

Illustration 2 answer

Impact in consolidated statement of profit or loss and other comprehensive income

The fair value adjustment of $150,000 results in an additional depreciation charge of $30,000 ($150,000/5) each year in the consolidated financial statements.

This adjustment should be added to the relevant expense category and would also be deducted from the subsidiary's profit when calculating the profit attributable to the NCI.

Test your understanding 3

P acquired 75% of the equity shares of S on 1 December 20X8. Below are their statements of profit or loss and other comprehensive income for the year ended 31 March 20X9:

	P $	S $
Revenue	300,000	216,000
Cost of sales and operating expenses	(215,000)	(153,000)
Profit from operations	85,000	63,000
Finance costs	(16,000)	(9,000)
Profit before tax	69,000	54,000
Taxation	(21,600)	(16,200)
Profit for the year	47,400	37,800
Other comprehensive income	25,000	3,000
Total comprehensive income	72,400	40,800

1   In the post-acquisition period, P sold $50,000 of goods to S at a margin of 20%. S held $10,000 of these goods in inventory at the year end.

2   A fair value adjustment of $150,000 was recorded at acquisition to increase the value of S's property, plant & equipment. These assets have a remaining useful economic life of 5 years at acquisition. Depreciation is charged to operating costs.

3   Goodwill was reviewed for impairment at the year end. It was determined that an impairment loss of $3,000 had arisen which is to be charged to operating expenses. It is group policy to measure NCI at the proportionate share of net assets at acquisition.

Required:

Prepare the consolidated statement of profit or loss and other comprehensive income for the year ended 31 March 20X9.

Test your understanding 4

On 1 July 20X4, Tudor purchased 80% of the shares in Windsor. The summarised draft statements of profit or loss and other comprehensive income for the year ended 31 March 20X5 are as follows:

	Tudor	Windsor
	$000	$000
Revenue	60,000	24,000
Cost of sales	(42,000)	(20,000)
Gross profit	18,000	4,000
Operating expenses	(6,000)	(200)
Profit from operations	12,000	3,800
Investment income	75	–
Finance costs	–	(200)
Profit before tax	12,075	3,600
Taxation	(3,000)	(600)
Profit for the year	9,075	3,000
Other comprehensive income	1,500	500
Total comprehensive income	10,575	3,500

1 The fair values of Windsor's assets at the date of acquisition were equal to their carrying amounts with the exception of plant, which was stated in the books at $2 million but had a fair value of $5.2 million. The remaining useful life of the plant in question was four years at the date of acquisition. Depreciation is charged to cost of sales and is time apportioned on a monthly basis.

2 In the post-acquisition period, Tudor sold goods to Windsor for $12 million with a margin of 25%. By the year end, Windsor had sold $10 million of these goods (at cost to Windsor) to third parties.

3 Tudor invested $1 million in Windsor's 10% loan notes on 1 July 20X4.

4 At 31 March 20X5, it was determined that an impairment loss of $100,000 had arisen in respect of goodwill. It is group policy to measure NCI at fair value. Impairment losses should be charged to operating expenses.

Required:

Prepare the consolidated statement of profit or loss and other comprehensive income for the Tudor Group for the year ended 31 March 20X5.

Test your understanding 5 (further OTQs)

1   P acquired 80% of the equity shares of S two years ago. At the date of acquisition, the fair value of S's net assets was the same as the carrying amount with the exception of property, plant and equipment, whose fair value was higher. Property, plant and equipment had an estimated useful life of 5 years from the date of acquisition.

P purchased goods from S during the year and 50% of the items remain in P's inventories at the year end. S earns a 20% mark-up on all sales.

Goodwill impairment arose in the current year. It is group policy to measure NCI at the proportionate share of net assets.

S paid a dividend of $200,000 two months before the year end.

Which of the following adjustments would be taken into account when calculating the profit attributable to the non-controlling interest in the consolidated statement of profit or loss of the P group for the year ended 31 August 20X6? Select all that apply.

A   Provision for unrealised profit

B   Depreciation arising from the fair value adjustment

C   Goodwill impairment

D   Elimination of intra-group dividends received

Data for Questions (2) to (4)

Hard acquired 75% of the ordinary share capital of Work on 1 April 20X8. The summarised statement of profit or loss for the year-ended 31 March 20X9 is as follows:

	Hard $m	Work $m
Revenue	120	48
Cost of sales	(84)	(40)
Gross profit	36	8
Distribution costs	(5)	(0.1)
Administration expenses	(7)	(0.3)
Profit from operations	24	7.6
Investment income	0.15	–
Finance costs	–	(0.4)
Profit before tax	24.15	7.2
Tax	(6)	(1.2)
Profit for the year	18.15	6

During the year, Work sold goods too Hard for $24m, which had originally cost $18m. By the year-end, Hard had sold $20m (quoted at cost to Hard) of these goods to third parties.

Goodwill impairment of $600,000 needs to be recorded for the current year and treated as an administration expense.

NCI is calculated using the fair value method.

2   **The PUP adjustment for the year-ended 31 March 20X9 is:**

    A $1m

    B $2m

    C $5m

    D $6m

3   **What is the amount of profit attributable to the NCI for the year-ended 31 March 20X9?**

    A $1.1m

    B $1.5m

    C $1.25m

    D $1.35m

4   **What is the total amount for revenue and cost of sales to be shown in the consolidated statement of profit or loss for the year-ended 31 March 20X9?**

	Revenue	Cost of sales
A	$144m	$100m
B	$168m	$124m
C	$192m	$148m
D	$144m	$101m

5   Dredd Group owns 70% of the shares of Judge and has done for many years. Judge pays dividends of $100,000 during the year.

    Resulting from the information described above, which one of the following statements accurately describes the effects of any adjustments upon consolidation of Judge within the Dredd Group statement of profit or loss and other comprehensive income?

    A   Dividend paid is reduced by $30,000

    B   Profit before tax would remain unaffected

    C   Revenue is reduced by $100,000

    D   Dividend income is reduced by $70,000

6   Darth acquires 65% of the ordinary share capital of Obi on 1 April 20X8. Darth sells goods to Obi after that date for $1,000,000.

Revenue for the year ended 31 December 20X8 of Darth and Obi is $15m and $8m respectively.

What is the revenue figure shown in the CSOPL of Darth Group for the year ended 31 December 20X8?

A $20m

B $21m

C $22m

D $23m

5 Chapter summary

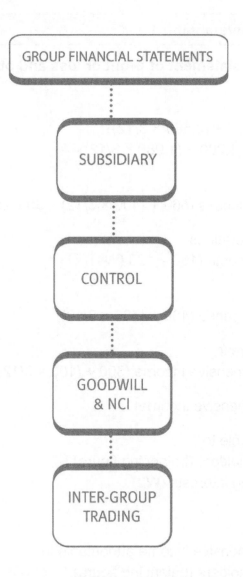

Test your understanding answers

Test your understanding 1

Consolidated statement of profit or loss and other comprehensive income

	$000
Revenue (3,200 + (2,560 × 3/12))	3,840
Cost of sales (1,200 + (1,080 × 3/12))	(1,470)
Gross profit	2,370
Operating expenses (560 + (400 × 3/12) + 30 imp)	(690)
Profit from operations	1,680
Investment income (160 – 120 **(W1)**)	40
Profit before tax	1,720
Income tax expense (400 + (480 × 3/12))	(520)
Profit for the year	1,200
Other comprehensive income (300 + (100 × 3/12))	325
Total comprehensive income	1,525
Profit attributable to:	
Parent shareholders (balancing figure)	1,176
Non-controlling interests **(W2)**	24
	1,200
Total comprehensive income attributable to:	
Parent shareholders (balancing figure)	1,496
Non-controlling interests **(W2)**	29
	1,525

Workings

(W1) Intercompany dividend

Sub paid $150,000

Parent received = $120,000 (80% × $150,000)

(W2) NCI share of profit and total comprehensive income (TCI)

	$000	$000
Sub's profit (600 × 3/12)	150	
Impairment expense	(30)	
	120	
NCI share of profit × 20%		24
Sub's OCI (100 × 3/12)	25	
	145	
NCI share of TCI × 20%		29

Test your understanding 2

(a) Consolidated statement of profit or loss

	$000
Revenue (10,350 + 8,400 – 1,000 **(W2)**)	17,750
Cost of sales (6,200 + 5,150 – 1,000 **(W2)** + 150 **(W2)**)	(10,500)
Gross profit	7,250
Operating expenses (2,450 + 1,600 + 600 **(W1)**)	(4,650)
Profit before tax	2,600
Income tax expense (550 + 450)	(1,000)
Profit for the year	1,600
Profit attributable to:	
Parent shareholders (balancing figure)	1,120
Non-controlling interests (1,200 × 40%)	480
	1,600

NB. Impairment is not deducted in the NCI working as the NCI has been valued using the proportionate method. The PUP adjustment is also not deducted, as the parent made the profit.

Workings

(W1) Goodwill and impairment

	$000
Fair value of P's investment	6,000
NCI at proportionate share of net assets (40% × 5,000)	2,000
Fair value of sub's net assets at acquisition	(5,000)
Goodwill at acquisition	3,000
Impairment (20% × 3,000)	600

(W2) Intercompany sales and PUP

Intercompany sales of $1,000,000 to be eliminated by reducing both revenue and cost of sales.

PUP adjustment to increase cost of sales:

Goods in inventory = $500,000 (1/2 × $1,000,000)

Profit in inventory = $150,000 (30% × $500,000)

(b) Analysis of profit attributable to parent shareholders and NCI

Profit attributable to:

Parent shareholders (balancing figure)	1,180
Non-controlling interests ((1,200 – 150) × 40%)	420
	1,600

As the subsidiary made the unrealised profit, the PUP adjustment is deducted from the subsidiary's profit prior to applying the NCI%.

Test your understanding 3 (integration question)

Consolidated statement of profit or loss and other comprehensive income for the year ended 31 March 20X9

	$
Revenue (300,000 + (4/12 × 216,000) – 50,000 **(W2)**)	322,000
Cost of sales and operating expenses (215,000 + (4/12 × 153,000) – 50,000 **(W2)** + 2,000 **(W2)** + 10,000 **(W3)** + 3,000 imp)	(231,000)
Profit from operations	91,000
Finance costs (16,000 + (4/12 × 9,000))	(19,000)
Profit before tax	72,000
Taxation (21,600 + (4/12 × 16,200))	(27,000)
Profit for the year	45,000
Other comprehensive income (25,000 + (4/12 × 3,000))	26,000
Total comprehensive income	71,000
Profit attributable to:	
Parent shareholders (balancing figure)	44,350
Non-controlling interests **(W4)**	650
	45,000

Total comprehensive income attributable to:	
Parent shareholders (balancing figure)	70,100
Non-controlling interests **(W4)**	900
	71,000

Workings

(W1) Group structure

P

75% | 1 December 20X8

4 months since acquisition

S

(W2) Intercompany sales and PUP

Intercompany sales of $50,000 to be eliminated by reducing both revenue and cost of sales.

PUP adjustment to increase cost of sales:

Profit in inventory = $2,000 (20% × $10,000)

(W3) Depreciation adjustment

Fair value adjustment = $150,000

Depreciation adjustment = $10,000 (1/5 × 4/12 × $150,000)

(W4) NCI share of profit and total comprehensive income

	$	$
Sub's profit for the year (4/12 × 37,800)	12,600	
Depreciation adjustment **(W3)**	(10,000)	
	2,600	
NCI share of profits × 25%		650
Sub's other comprehensive income (4/12 × 3,000)	1,000	
	3,600	
NCI share of total comprehensive income × 25%		900

Test your understanding 4 (integration question)

Consolidated statement of profit or loss and other comprehensive income for the year ended 31 March 20X5

	$000
Revenue (60,000 + (9/12 × 24,000) − 12,000 **(W2)**)	66,000
Cost of sales (42,000 + (9/12 × 20,000) − 12,000 **(W2)** + 500 **(W2)** + 600 **(W3)**)	(46,100)
Gross profit	19,900
Operating expenses (6,000 + (9/12 × 200) + 100 imp)	(6,250)
Profit from operations	13,650
Investment income (75 − 75 **(W4)**)	–
Finance costs ((9/12 × 200) − 75 **(W4)**)	(75)
Profit before tax	13,575
Taxation (3,000 + (9/12 × 600))	(3,450)
Profit for the year	10,125
Other comprehensive income (1,500 + (9/12 × 500))	1,875
Total comprehensive income	12,000
Profit attributable to:	
Parent shareholders (balancing figure)	9,815
Non-controlling interests **(W5)**	310
	10,125
Total comprehensive income attributable to:	
Parent shareholders (balancing figure)	11,615
Non-controlling interests **(W5)**	385
	12,000

Workings

(W1) Group structure

Tudor

80% | 1 July 20X4

9 months since acquisition

Windsor

(W2) Intercompany sales and PUP

Intercompany sales of $12,000,000 to be eliminated by reducing both revenue and cost of sales.

PUP adjustment to increase cost of sales:

Goods in inventory = $2,000,000 (12m – 10m)

Profit in inventory = $500,000 (25% × $2,000,000)

(W3) Depreciation adjustment

Fair value adjustment = $3.2m ($5.2m – $2m)

Depreciation adjustment = $600,000 (1/4 × 9/12 × $3.2m)

(W4) Intercompany interest

Windsor paid interest to Tudor = $75,000 (10% × $1 m × 9/12)

(W5) NCI share of profit and total comprehensive income

	$000	$000
Sub's profit for the year (9/12 × 3,000)	2,250	
Depreciation adjustment **(W3)**	(600)	
Impairment (fair value method)	(100)	
	1,550	
NCI share of profits × 20%		310
Sub's other comprehensive income (9/12 × 500)	375	
	1,925	
NCI share of total comprehensive income × 20%		385

Test your understanding 5 (further OTQs)

1   **Adjustments would be made for A and B.**

C would not be adjusted as NCI is measured using the proportionate share of net assets and therefore all goodwill impairment should be charged to the parent shareholders.

D is not adjusted as it is eliminated from the parent's investment income and has no impact on the subsidiary's profit.

2   **A $1m**

Hard has acquired 75% of Work at the start for the current period. Work is a subsidiary of Hard.

Work sells goods to Hard during the year at a profit of $6m ($24m – $18m). Some of the goods still remain within the group (Hard has not sold them on). This will create a provision for unrealised profit (PUP) adjustment.

The value of this PUP is $1m (6m × 4/24). Profits will be reduced through an increase in group cost of sales.

As the subsidiary sold to the parent, the NCI will take a share of this PUP adjustment.

3   **A $1.1m**

NCI share of profit is calculated as follows:

	$m
Sub's PAT	6
PUP (S sells to P)	(1)
Impairment (FV method)	(0.6)
	4.4
25% NCI share	**1.1**

4   **D**

Group revenue is $144m (120m + 48m – 24m (Intergroup sales)).

Groups cost of sales $101m (84m + 40m + 1m (PUP) – 24m (Intergroup sale)).

5   D

Any dividend paid by a subsidiary will be recorded as dividend income by the parent within the parent's SOPLOCI. The share of the subsidiary's dividend paid received by the parents is eliminated upon consolidation. An adjustment of $70,000 will be required removing the dividend income received from the subsidiary, Judge. This is likely to be removed from investment income.

Option D is correct.

Dividends paid are accounted for in retained earnings (held on the CSOFP and the statement of changes in equity, not the CSOPL). Revenue is unaffected by the subsidiary's dividend. Profit before tax is reduced due to the required reduction in investment income.

6   A

Revenue = $20m

Darth has only controlled Obi for 9 months of the year as Obi was acquired on 1 April (after 3 months). Consolidation will only include 9 months of Obi's revenue.

Any revenue from intra-group trading must be removed upon consolidation.

Group revenue = 100% P + 100% of S – intra-group revenue = 15m + (8m × 9/12) - $1m = $20m.

Group accounts – Associates and Joint arrangements

Chapter learning objectives

Lead outcome	Component outcome
B2: Explain relevant financial reporting standards for group accounts	(a) Explain the financial reporting standards for the key areas of group accounts.
C1: Prepare group accounts based on IFRS	Prepare the following based on financial reporting standards: (a) Consolidated statement of financial position (b) Consolidated statement of profit or loss and other comprehensive income

1 Session content

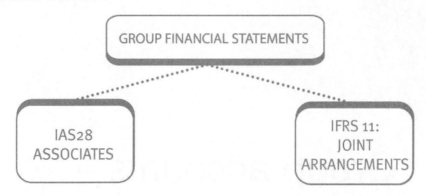

2 Introduction

A group will always include one entity over which the parent has control (the subsidiary).The group could also include further investments in other entities which, whilst not creating control in the entity, still provide the parent with a greater level of impact upon the investee than shareholdings classified as financial assets.

In this chapter, we will consider the impact to the group accounts of investments in:

*   Associates (IAS 28 *Associates*)

*   Jointly controlled entities (IFRS 11 *Joint arrangements*)

These investments are designated their own elevated status within the group accounts and have specific accounting standards outlining their accounting treatments. It is important to understand the theoretical concepts behind their accounting treatments as well as the quantifiable treatment of each within the group financial statements.

3 Investments in Associates

'An **associate** is **'an entity over which the investor has significant influence'** (IAS 28, para 3) and which is neither a subsidiary nor a joint venture of the investor.

Associates – further detail

Significant influence is defined as **'the power to participate in the financial and operating policy decisions of the investee but not control or joint control of those policies'** (IAS 28, para 3).

'A holding of 20% or more of the voting power is presumed to give significant influence unless it can be clearly demonstrated that this is not the case. At the same time, a holding of less than 20% is assumed not to give significant influence unless such influence can be clearly demonstrated'.

> IAS 28 explains that an investor probably has significant influence if:
>
> - **'It is represented on the board of directors.**
> - **It participates in policy-making processes, including decisions about dividends or other distributions.**
> - **There are material transactions between the investor and investee.**
> - **There is interchange of managerial personnel.**
> - **There is provision of essential technical information'** (IAS 28, para 6).

Associates are accounted for using **equity accounting** in accordance with IAS 28.

They are not consolidated as the parent does not have control.

Consolidated statement of financial position

The CSFP will include a single line within non-current assets called 'Investment in associate' calculated as:

Investment in associate

	$
Cost of investment	X
Add: share of post-acquisition reserves	X
Less: impairment losses	(X)
Less: PUP (if A has inventory – see later)	(X)
	X

The share of post-acquisition reserves, impairment losses and PUP would also be recorded in consolidated retained earnings.

Consolidated statement of profit or loss and other comprehensive income

The CSOPLOCI will include a single line before profit before tax called 'Share of profit of associate' calculated as:

Share of associate's profit for the year	X
Less: impairment loss	(X)
Less: PUP (if A is seller – see later)	(X)
	X

If the associate has other comprehensive income, the investor's share will also be recorded in the other comprehensive income section of CSOPLOCI.

Exemptions to equity accounting

The equity method of accounting is normally used to account for associates and joint ventures in the consolidated financial statements.

The equity method should not be used if:

*   the investment is classified as held for sale in accordance with IFRS 5, or

*   the parent is exempted from having to prepare consolidated accounts on the grounds that it is itself a wholly, or partially, owned subsidiary of another company (IFRS 10).

4 Consolidation adjustments

Adjustments required

Inter-group transactions & balances

Inter-group transactions (receivables, payables, sales and purchases) between the group (whether with the parent or subsidiary) and the associate are not eliminated within the CSOPLOCI or CSFP. This is because the associate is outside of the group. The transactions/balances are with a third party to the group and so may be reported within the group financial statements. The associate is not 100% consolidated therefore no elimination of inter group transactions is needed.

However, **unrealised profit** on transactions **must be eliminated** on consolidation as the group takes a share of the transaction.

Provisions for unrealised profit (PUP)

IAS 28 requires unrealised profits on transactions between the group and the associate to be eliminated. Only the investor's share of the profit is removed since the group financial statements only reflect the investor's share of the associate profits in the first place.

Associates PUP adjustment = **P% × profit in inventory**

Parent sells to associate

In the CSFP:

*   Reduce consolidated retained earnings (Dr)

*   Reduce investment in associate (Cr)

When the parent sells to the associate, the profit must be eliminated from the investment in the associate because the inventory is in the books of the associate. The associates' inventory is not consolidated so we cannot remove the profit from the inventory line on the CSFP.

In the CSOPLOCI:

- Increase cost of sales

Associate sells to parent

In the CSFP:

- Reduce consolidated retained earnings (Dr)

- Reduce inventory (Cr)

When the associate sells to the parent, the profit must be eliminated from the inventory. The parents' inventory is consolidated which includes the inventory purchased from the associate. The profit is removed from the inventory line on the CSFP.

In the CSOPLOCI:

- Reduce share of profit of associate

Associate PUP with parent the seller

P owns 40% of the equity shares of A.

P has sold $200,000 of goods to A at a mark-up on cost of 25%.

At the reporting date, 60% of these items remain in A's inventory.

The intercompany sale of $200,000 is not eliminated in the consolidated financial statements. However. a PUP adjustment is calculated as:

Goods in inventory	60% × $200,000 = $120,000
Profit in inventory	25/125 × $120,000 = $24,000
PUP	40% × $24,000 = $9,600

The adjustment will be:

Dr Cost of sales	$9,600
Cr Investment in associate	$9,600

In the CSPLOCI, cost of sales will increase.

In the CSFP, retained earnings will be reduced as profits have reduced. The investment in associate will also be reduced.

The associate is holding the inventory, but the associate's inventory is not consolidated on the inventory line in the CSFP and so it is not appropriate to reduce inventory.

PUP with associate the seller

Using the same information as above but with the associate selling to the parent, the adjustment will now be:

Dr Income from associate $9,600

Cr Inventory $9,600

In the CSOPLOCI, share of profit of associate will reduce.

In the CSFP, retained earnings will need to be reduced to reflect the reduction in the share of associate's profits caused by the PUP. Inventory will also be reduced as it is the parent company holding the inventory.

Illustration 1

Below are the statements of financial position of three entities as at 31 December 20X9.

	Tom $000	James $000	Emily $000
Non-current assets			
Property, plant & equipment	959	980	840
Investments: 630,000 shares in James	805	–	–
168,000 shares in Emily	224	–	–
	1,988	980	840
Current assets			
Inventory	380	640	190
Receivables	190	310	100
Cash and cash equivalents	35	58	46
TOTAL ASSETS	2,593	1,988	1,176
Equity			
Share capital ($1 shares)	1,120	840	560
Retained earnings	1,232	602	448
	2,352	1,442	1,008
Current liabilities			
Trade payables	150	480	136
Taxation	91	66	32
TOTAL EQUITY & LIABILITIES	2,593	1,988	1,176

Additional information:

1 Tom acquired its shares in James on 1 January 20X9, when James had retained earnings of $160,000. NCIs are to be valued at their fair value at the date of acquisition. The fair value of the NCI holding in James at 1 January 20X9 was $250,000.

2 Tom acquired its shares in Emily on 1 January 20X9 when Emily had retained earnings of $140,000.

3 An impairment test at the year-end shows that the goodwill for James remains unimpaired but that the investment in Emily is impaired by $2,000

Required:

Prepare the consolidated statement of financial position for the year ended 31 December 20X9.

 Illustration 1 answer

Consolidated statement of financial position as at 31 December 20X9

	$000
Non-current assets	
Goodwill **(W3)**	55
Property, plant & equipment (959 + 980)	1,939
Investment in associate **(W6)**	314.4
	2,308.4
Current assets	
Inventory (380 + 640)	1,020
Receivables (190 + 310)	500
Cash and cash equivalents (35 + 58)	93
TOTAL ASSETS	3,921.4
Equity	
Share capital ($1 shares)	1,120
Retained earnings **(W5)**	1,653.9
	2,773.9
Non-controlling interest **(W4)**	360.5
	3,134.4
Current liabilities	
Trade payables (150 + 480)	630
Taxation (91 + 66)	157
TOTAL EQUITY & LIABILITIES	3,921.4

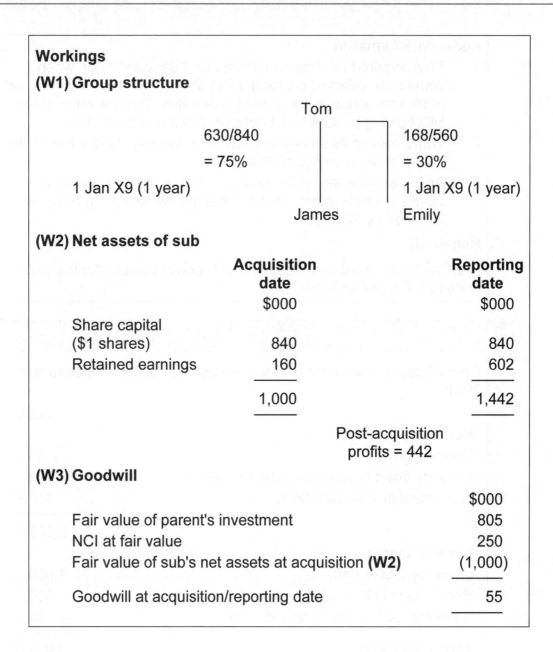

Workings

(W1) Group structure

Tom

630/840 = 75%   168/560 = 30%

1 Jan X9 (1 year)   1 Jan X9 (1 year)

James   Emily

(W2) Net assets of sub

	Acquisition date $000	Reporting date $000
Share capital ($1 shares)	840	840
Retained earnings	160	602
	1,000	1,442

Post-acquisition profits = 442

(W3) Goodwill

	$000
Fair value of parent's investment	805
NCI at fair value	250
Fair value of sub's net assets at acquisition **(W2)**	(1,000)
Goodwill at acquisition/reporting date	55

(W4) Non-controlling interests

	$000
NCI at acquisition at fair value **(W3)**	250
NCI% of post-acquisition reserves (25% × 442 **(W2)**)	110.5
	360.5

(W5) Group retained earnings

	$000
P's retained earnings	1,232
S: 75% of post-acquisition profits	
(75% × 442 **(W2)**)	331.5
A: 30% of post-acquisition profits **(W6)**	92.4
A: impairment **(W6)**	(2)
	1,653.9

(W6) Investment in associate

	$000
Cost of investment	224
P% × post acquisition profits (30% × (448 – 140))	92.4
Less: impairment	(2)
	314.4

In the question, the investment in Emily is included in Tom's SFP at its cost of $224,000. The investment was made at the start of the year.

This becomes the starting point for equity accounting i.e. the starting point for the calculation of investment in associate.

At acquisition, the retained earnings of Emily were $140,000 and at the reporting date they are $448,000. Therefore, the post-acquisition reserves of Emily are $308,000 of which 30% belong to Tom i.e. $92,400. This increases both the value of investment in associate and retained earnings.

At the reporting date, the investment is impaired by $2,000. This is a reduction in the value of the Investment. It is also an expense and so reduces retained earnings.

Test your understanding 1 (Integrated question)

P acquired 80% of the 1 million issued $1 ordinary shares of S on 1 October 20X3 for $1.5 million. S's retained earnings were $350,000 at this date.

P acquired 30% of the 500,000 issued $1 ordinary shares of A on 1 October 20X7 for $300,000 when A's retained earnings were $360,000.

The retained earnings reported in the financial statements of P, S and A as at 30 September 20X8 were $2 million, $750,000 and $400,000 respectively.

An impairment review performed on 30 September 20X8 indicated that there was no impairment to the goodwill arising on the acquisition of S, however the investment in A was impaired by $5,000.

Required:

Calculate the amounts that would appear in the consolidated statement of financial position for the P group as at 30 September 20X8 for:

(a)   Investment in associate

(b)   Consolidated retained earnings.

5   IFRS 11 Joint Arrangements

IFRS 11 *Joint Arrangements* defines two types of arrangement in which there is joint control – a joint venture and a joint operation – and sets out the accounting treatment of each.

 A **joint arrangement** is **'an arrangement of which two or more parties have joint control'** (IFRS 11, para 4).

Joint control is **'the contractually agreed sharing of control of an arrangement, which exists only when decisions about the relevant activities require the unanimous consent of the parties sharing control'** (IFRS 11, para 7).

 A **joint venture** is a **'joint arrangement whereby the parties that have joint control of the arrangement have rights to the net assets of the arrangement'** (IFRS 11, para 16).

Accounting treatment

Joint ventures are accounted for using the equity method of accounting in accordance with IAS 28 Investments in Associates and Joint Ventures.

Therefore, a joint venture is accounted for in the same way as an associate.

Illustration 2

Below is the consolidated statement of financial position of the BeerCan group as at 31 December 20X9.

	BeerCan $000
Non-current assets	
Goodwill	94
Property, plant & equipment	1,695
Investments	1,500
	3,289
Current assets	545
TOTAL ASSETS	3,834
Equity	
Share capital ($1 shares)	1,008
Retained earnings	2,609
	3,617
Current liabilities	217
TOTAL EQUITY & LIABILITIES	3,834

Additional information:

1   BeerCan acquired 40% of the ordinary shares in IPunkA, an independent brewery, for $1,500,000 on 1 January 20X9, when IPunkA had retained earnings of $144,000. BeerCan has a formal, legally binding agreement with DeceasedHorseClub (DHC), who also own 40% of IPunkA, which confirms that BeerCan and DHC have joint control of IPunkA. This agreement came into force on 1 January 20X9.

2   IPunkA's retained earnings as at 31 December 20X9 was $300,000.

3   An impairment test at the year-end shows the investment in IPunkA is impaired by $1,800.

4   The directors of BeerCan are unsure as to how to treat the investment in IPunkA. In the financial statements provided, the directors included the original investment at cost under non-current assets.

Required:

Prepare the BeerCan consolidated statement of financial position for the year ended 31 December 20X9.

Solution

Adjusted consolidated statement of financial position of the BeerCan group as at 31 December 20X9.

	BeerCan $000
Non-current assets	
Goodwill	94
Property, plant & equipment	1,695
Investments in joint venture	1,560.6
	3,349.6
Current assets	545
TOTAL ASSETS	3,894.6
Equity	
Share capital ($1 shares)	1,008
Retained earnings (2,609 + 62.4 – 1.8)	2,669.6
	3,677.6
Current liabilities	217
TOTAL EQUITY & LIABILITIES	3,894.6

The investment in IPunkA is a joint venture. The BeerCan and DHC combined shareholding creates a controlling interest (40% + 40% = 80%) and a formal, legally binding agreement exists creating joint control. As BeerCan has joint control over a separate entity, IPunkA will be treated as a joint venture by BeerCan.

Joint ventures are consolidated using equity accounting. No line by line consolidation of the joint venture (IPunkA) or cancelation of intra-group transactions arises.

A non-current asset investment is presented on the consolidated statement of financial position (see Working 1) using equity accounting. The cost will be increased by BeerCan's share of the post-acquisition movement in net assets of IPunkA. The impairment will reduce profits (via retained earnings) and the investment in the joint venture.

BeerCan's share of post-acquisition movement in profits and the impairment will affect group retained earnings.

NB. BeerCan's share of profit less the impairment expense would be included in a separate line within the consolidated statement of profit or loss before group profit before tax.

Working 1 Investment in joint venture

	$000
Cost of investment	1,500
P% of JV post-acquisition movement in net assets	62.4
40% × (300,000 − 144,000)	
Impairment	(1.8)
	─────
	1,560.6

Joint operations

A **joint operation** is a **'joint arrangement whereby the parties that have joint control of the arrangement have rights to the assets, and obligations for the liabilities, relating to the arrangement'** (IFRS 11, para 15).

A joint operation will exist where the arrangement is not structured through a separate vehicle. Jointly controlled operations commonly take the form of projects where the operators contribute their assets and resources to the operational activities of the jointly controlled operation. No separate entity is formed.

A joint operator would account for its share of the assets, liabilities, revenues and expenses (including those held and incurred jointly) relating to its involvement with the joint operation in accordance with the relevant IFRSs.

Test your understanding 2 (OTQ question)

Which one of the following statements is true?

A   A joint venture shows the joint venturer's share of assets, liabilities and profits within the group accounts on a line by line basis

B   100% of the assets and liabilities of a joint operation are included within the group statement of financial position

C   A joint venture will include the joint venturer's share of profits for a period in a separate line within the consolidated statement of profit or loss

D   If joint control of a legal entity exists, then the entity is classified as a joint operation within group accounts

6   IAS 27 Separate Financial Statements

IAS 27 *Separate financial statements* outlines how parent companies should account for their investments in subsidiaries, associates and joint ventures within the individual financial statements of the parent.

The standard states that, when an entity prepares separate financial statements from the group, investments in subsidiaries, associates, and jointly controlled entities are accounted for either:

- at cost, or

- in accordance with IFRS 9 *Financial Instruments*, or

- using the equity method as described in IAS 28 *Investments in Associates*.

Test your understanding 3 (further OTQs)

1   A joint _____ is where the parties that have joint control of the arrangement have rights to the net assets of the arrangement.

A joint _____ is where the parties that have joint control of the arrangement have rights to the assets, and obligations for the liabilities, relating to the arrangement.

Select the correct words to complete the above sentence, from the following options:

arrangement, control, operation, venture

2   The P group (comprising P and its subsidiaries) acquired 30% of the equity share capital of A on 1 October 20X6, paying $750,000 in cash. This enabled P to exercise significant influence over the operating and financial policies of A. The balance on A's retained earnings at this date was $1,500,000.

During the current year, A sold goods to P for $800,000 at a margin of 25%. P still held one quarter of the goods in inventory at 30 September 20X8.

At 30 September 20X8, an impairment review was carried out and it was determined that the investment in A was impaired by $35,000.

A's retained earnings at 30 September 20X8 was $2,500,000.

Calculate the amount that would appear for the investment in A within the consolidated statement of financial position of the P group as at 30 September 20X8.

3   The P group (comprising P and its subsidiaries) acquired 30% of the equity share capital of A on 1 October 20X6, enabling P to exercise significant influence over the operating and financial policies of A.

A made a profit for the year ended 30 June 20X7 of $600,000. Profits are deemed to accrue evenly over the year.

Between 1 October 20X6 and the reporting date, A sold goods to P for $600,000 at a margin of 20%. P still held one quarter of these goods in inventory at 30 June 20X7.

At 30 June 20X7, an impairment review was carried out and it was determined that the investment in A was impaired by $20,000.

Calculate the share of A's profits that would appear in the consolidated statement of profit or loss of the P group for the year ended 30 June 20X7.

4   **Which of the following are likely to be accounted for as an associate in the consolidated financial statements of TN?**

(i)   A 25% shareholding in ZT. TN can appoint a director to the board. There are 4 directors on the board in total, and none have control.

(ii)   A 25% shareholding in ZU. ZU is 70% owned by a company called TU.

(iii)   A 25% shareholding in ZV. TN also has an arrangement with other shareholders allowing TN access to 55% of the voting rights in ZV.

A   (i) only

B   (i) and (ii)

C   (ii) and (iii)

D   All three

5   B bought 30% of A on 1 July 20X4. A's statement of profit or loss for the year shows a profit of $400,000. A paid a dividend to B of $50,000 on 1 December. At the year end, the investment in A was judged to have been impaired by $10,000.

What will be shown under 'Share of profit from associate' in the consolidated statement or profit or loss for the year ended 31 December 20X4?

A   Nil

B $50,000

C $60,000

D $110,000

6   **Which TWO of the following issues would require adjustment in a consolidated statement of financial position?**

A   A balance owed from the parent to the associate

B   Cash in transit from the associate to the parent

C   Unrealised profit relating to goods sold from the associate to the parent

D   The value of the associate is impaired at the end of the year

7   P acquired 75% of the equity share capital of S several years ago when S's retained earnings were $3,250,000. Goodwill arising on the acquisition was $2,000,000 and this was considered to have been impaired by 20% by 30 September 20X7. It is group policy to measure NCI at fair value at the date of acquisition.

P acquired 25% of the equity share capital of V on 1 October 20X6 in a contractual arrangement that will give P joint control over V. V's retained earnings at the date of acquisition were $925,000.

The retained earnings reported in the financial statements of P, S and V as at 30 September 20X7 are $1,570,000, $5,250,000 and $1,165,000 respectively.

Calculate the consolidated retained earnings of the P group as at 30 September 20X7.

7 Chapter summary

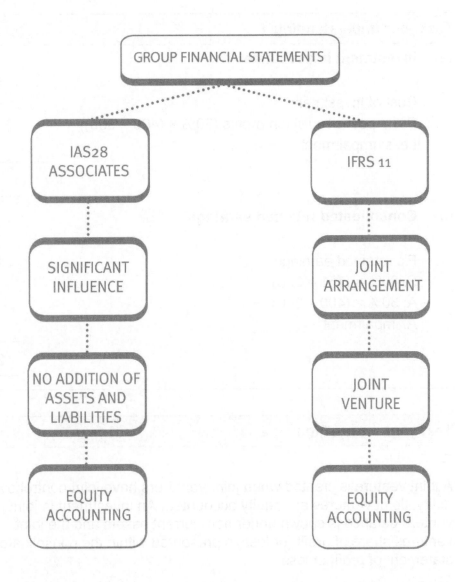

Test your understanding answers

Test your understanding 1

(a) Investment in associate

	$000
Cost of investment	300
P% × post-acquisition profits (30% × (400 – 360))	12
Less: impairment	(5)
	307

(b) Consolidated retained earnings

	$000
P's retained earnings	2,000
S: 80% × (750 – 350)	320
A: 30% × (400 – 360)	12
A: impairment	(5)
	2,327

Test your understanding 2

C

A joint venture is created when joint venturers have joint control over an entity. Joint ventures are equity accounted. An investment in joint venture balance is shown under non-current assets and the joint ventures share of profit (or loss) s presented within the consolidated statement of profit or loss.

Jointly operations are projects operated under joint control between two or more entities. Joint operations will be accounted by adding the agreed share of the assets, liabilities, income and expenses created by the operation.

Option A is incorrect as joint ventures are equity accounted so no addition of the share of assets and liabilities will occur.

Option B is incorrect as joint operations include a specific % of the assets and liabilities, income and expenses of the jointly controlled operation, not 100%.

Option D describes a joint venture not a joint operation.

Test your understanding 3 (further OTQs)

1   A joint **venture** is where the parties that have joint control of the arrangement have rights to the net assets of the arrangement.

A joint **operation** is where the parties that have joint control of the arrangement have rights to the assets, and obligations for the liabilities, relating to the arrangement.

2   **Investment in associate (A) = $1,015,000**

	$
Cost of investment	750,000
Share of post-acquisition profits (30% × (2,500–1,500))	300,000
Less: impairment	(35,000)
	1,015,000

The unrealised profit is not deducted from the investment in associate as the inventory is held by the parent at the year-end (it would be deducted from group inventory instead).

3   **Share of associate profit = $106,000**

	$
Profit of A in the post-acquisition period (600,000 × 9/12)	450,000
Unrealised profit (600,000 × 20% × 1/4)	(30,000)
	420,000
P group share	× 30%
	126,000
Less: impairment	(20,000)
	106,000

4   **A**

Item (ii) is likely to be regarded as a financial asset, as TN has no significant influence. Item (iii) is likely to be classed as a subsidiary, as TN are able to exercise control.

5   B

Share of profit of associate = $50,000

(30% ×($400,000 × 6/12) – $10,000)

The dividend would not have been in A's statement of profit or loss (they are paid out of retained earnings), so no adjustment for this would be made to the associate's share of profit.

The share of associates' profit needs to be time-apportioned for the six months of ownership, with the $10,000 impairment then deducted.

6   C and D

Inter-group balances between the parent and associate are not adjusted, whether there are items in transit or not. Unrealised profits and impairments are items that must be adjusted in the consolidated statement of financial position.

7   Consolidated retained earnings = $2,830,000

	$000
P's retained earnings	1,570
Share of S's post-acquisition retained earnings (75% × (5,250k – 3,250k))	1,500
Share of goodwill impairment (75% × 20% × 2,000k)	(300)
Share of V's post-acquisition retained earnings (25% × (1,165k – 925k))	60
	2,830

Consolidated statement of changes in equity

Chapter learning objectives

Lead outcome	Component outcome
B2: Explain relevant financial reporting standards for group accounts	(a) Explain the financial reporting standards for the key areas of group accounts.
C1: Prepare group accounts based on IFRS	Prepare the following based on financial reporting standards: (c) Consolidated statement of changes in equity

1 Session content

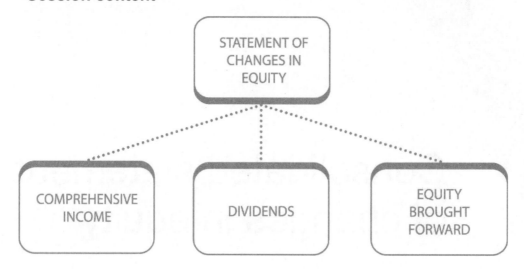

2 Consolidated statement of changes in equity – the basics

The statement of changes in equity explains the movement in the equity section of the statement of financial position from the previous reporting date to the current reporting date.

From a group perspective, equity belongs partly to the parent shareholders and partly to the NCI shareholders. A consolidated statement of changes in equity (CSOCE) will therefore be made up of two columns reflecting:

- the changes in equity attributable to parent shareholders, made up of share capital, share premium, retained earnings and any other reserves

- the changes in equity attributable to NCI shareholders.

NB. In practice the CSOCE will have a total column. This is not included in the examples within this chapter.

The basic CSOCE pro-forma is as follows:

	Parent shareholders	NCI shareholders
	$000	$000
Equity brought forward (b/f)	X	X
Comprehensive income	X	X
Dividends		
P's dividend	(X)	
NCI% × S's dividend		(X)
Equity carried forward (c/f)	X	X

Equity b/f

Parent shareholders

This is made up of the share capital, share premium, retained earnings and any other reserves as reported in last year's CSFP.

Share capital and share premium is that of the parent company only. The retained earnings and other reserves are consolidated and will need to be calculated using a working (the group reserves working).

Therefore, the same format can be used to calculate consolidated equity b/f (attributable to the parent shareholders) as for group reserves, but starting with the parent's equity rather than just the parent's reserves. This will include the parent's share capital and premium. Remember, the calculation is for the position at the start of the year so only use the subsidiary's post-acquisition reserves up to the b/f date.

NCI shareholders

This is the NCI figure that would have been reflected in last year's CSFP and can be calculated using the typical NCI working. Remember to use only post-acquisition reserves up to the b/f date.

Comprehensive income

These figures come from the foot of the consolidated statement of profit or loss and other comprehensive income (CSPLOCI) where the total comprehensive income of the group is split between the parent and NCI shareholders.

Dividends

The CSOCE reflects the dividends which are being paid outside of the group, i.e. the parent company's dividend and the share of the subsidiary's dividend paid to non-controlling interest shareholders.

Note that the share of the subsidiary's dividend paid to the parent company will have been eliminated in the group accounts as it is an intra-group transaction.

Equity c/f

Parent shareholders

Similar to the balances b/f, the equity c/f figures can be calculated using a working similar to group reserves but remembering to include the parent's share capital and share premium balances as well as their retained earnings/other reserves. The working will start with the parent's equity c/f (rather than just its reserves).

When including the subsidiary, post-acquisition reserves up to the c/f date (i.e. reporting date) will be used.

NCI shareholders

This is the NCI figure as shown in the CSFP using the standard NCI reserve working.

Illustration 1

The following are the statements of changes in equity for Fulham and Putney for the year ended 31 March 20X7:

	Fulham	Putney
	$	$
Equity b/f	132,500	60,000
Comprehensive income	85,500	21,000
Dividends	(10,000)	(6,000)
Equity c/f	208,000	75,000

Fulham acquired 80% of Putney's equity shares on 1 April 20X4 when Putney's net assets had a fair value of $35,000. No fair value adjustments were required at acquisition. It is Fulham's group policy to record NCIs at fair value at acquisition. The NCI holding in Putney had a fair value of $7,500 at the date of acquisition.

Required

Prepare the consolidated statement of changes in equity for the year ended 31 March 20X7.

 Illustration 1 answer

Consolidated statement of changes in equity for the Fulham group for the year ended 31 March 20X7

	Parent shareholders	NCI shareholders
	$	$
Equity b/f	152,500	12,500
Comprehensive income	97,500	4,200
Dividends		
P's dividend	(10,000)	
NCI% × S's dividend		(1,200)
Equity c/f	240,000	15,500

Workings

Equity attributable to parent shareholders b/f and c/f

Equity b/f and c/f attributable to the parent shareholders can be calculated using the format of the group reserves working but starting with the parent's equity rather than simply the parent's reserves. This ensures that other elements of equity such as share capital and share premium are also included:

	B/f	C/f (i.e. reporting date)
	$	$
Parent's equity	132,500	208,000
Sub: P% × post acquisition reserves		
(80% × (60,000 – 35,000))	20,000	
(80% × (75,000 – 35,000))		32,000
	152,500	240,000

The post-acquisition reserves are calculated by comparing the net assets at the start/end of the year (depending on whether calculating equity b/f or c/f) and their value at the date of acquisition. It is important to remember that net assets equal equity – so the net assets figures at the start and end of the year can be picked up from the individual entity SOCEs provided in the question.

NCI b/f and c/f

The NCI share of equity c/f is the NCI figure that would be presented on the face of the consolidated statement of financial position. To calculate the b/f figure produce a similar NCI working but based on opening rather than closing figures where necessary.

	B/f	C/f (i.e. reporting date)
	$	$
Fair value of NCI at acqn	7,500	7,500
NCI% × post-acquisition reserves		
(20% × (60,000 – 35,000))	5,000	
(20% × (75,000 – 35,000))		8,000
	12,500	15,500

Total comprehensive income figures

The foot of the consolidated statement of profit or loss and other comprehensive income should now be replicated in order to calculate the split of total comprehensive income between the parent and NCI shareholders. It is important to remember that the total comprehensive income of the group will be 100% of the parent plus 100% of the subsidiary (subject to time apportionment) plus/minus any consolidation adjustments.

Since the subsidiary has paid a dividend, the intra-group element of this will have been eliminated on consolidation.

	$
P and S comprehensive income (85,500 + 21,000)	106,500
Less elimination of inter-co dividend (80% × 6,000)	(4,800)
	101,700
Total comprehensive income attributable to:	
Parent shareholders (balancing figure)	97,500
Non-controlling interests (20% × 21,000)	4,200
	101,700

Rather than calculating the comprehensive income attributable to P's shareholders as a balancing figure, an alternative working is as follows:

	$
P comprehensive income	85,500
Less elimination of inter-co dividend (80% × 6,000)	(4,800)
Ps share of sub comprehensive income (80% × 21,000)	16,800
	97,500

Finally, the dividend figures can be calculated on the face of the CSOCE pro-forma.

Test your understanding 1 (integration question)

The following are the statements of changes in equity for Islington and Southwark for the year ended 31 March 20X7:

	Islington	Southwark
	$	$
Equity b/f	210,000	125,000
Comprehensive income	50,000	35,000
Dividends	(15,000)	(10,000)
Equity c/f	245,000	150,000

Islington acquired 75% of Southwark's equity shares on 1 April 20X4 when Southwark's net assets had a fair value of $80,000. No fair value adjustments were required at acquisition. It is Islington's group policy to record NCIs at fair value at acquisition. The NCI holding in Southwark had a fair value of $25,000 at the date of acquisition.

Required

Prepare the consolidated statement of changes in equity for the year ended 31 March 20X7.

Data for test your understandings 2 and 3

The following information is relevant for the next 2 TYU's.

On 1 January 20X5, Thunder acquired 80% of the equity share capital of Lightning when the net assets of Lightning were $65,000.

The following are the statements of changes in equity for the year ended 31 December 20X6:

	Thunder	Lightning
	$	$
Equity b/f	156,000	80,000
Comprehensive income	24,000	13,800
Dividends	(10,000)	(1,000)
Equity c/f	170,000	92,800

1   At the date of acquisition, the fair value of Lightning's net assets was deemed to equal their book value.

2   Thunder's group policy is to record the NCI at fair value at acquisition. The fair value of the NCI holding in Lightning was $23,000 at acquisition.

3   Both Thunder and Lightning paid their dividends on 30 June 20X6.

Test your understanding 2 (OTQ)

Required:

What will be the figures shown for total comprehensive income relating to Parent shareholders and NCIs within the consolidated statement of changes in equity for Thunder Group?

	Parent shareholders	**NCI shareholders**
A	$34,240	$2,760
B	$35,040	$2,760
C	$37,000	$2,560
D	$37,800	$2,760

Test your understanding 3 (OTQ)

Required:

What will be the dividends paid to Parent shareholders and NCIs within the consolidated statement of changes in equity for Thunder Group?

	Parent shareholders	**NCI shareholders**
A	$10,000	$100
B	$10,000	$200
C	$10,000	$1,000
D	$10,800	$200

Test your understanding 4 (OTQ style)

1   WM owns 75% of the equity share capital of MY. The equity attributable to the non-controlling interest at 31 December 20X3 was $650,000. The total comprehensive income of MY for the year ended 31 December 20X4 was $300,000. Dividends were paid by both group entities during 20X4. The dividends paid by MY were $60,000.

   Calculate the closing equity attributable to the NCI in the consolidated statement of changes in equity at 31 December 20X4.

2   There are a number of transactions/classes of transactions that you would expect to see on the face of the consolidated statement of changes in equity.

   For each of the headings below, identify whether they would appear on the face of the consolidated statement of changes in equity and, if so, which column(s) they would affect (by placing X(s) in the relevant boxes).

		Equity attributable to:	
	Not in CSOCE	Parent	NCI
Comprehensive income for year			
Dividends paid to parent shareholders			
Finance costs			
Dividends paid to NCI			
Gain on FVPL financial asset			
Dividend paid by associate			

3   **The following data relates to scenarios 3,4 and 5**

HN owned 80% of the $100,000 equity share capital of AE at 31 March 20X0 when the retained earnings were $250,000.

The statements of changes in equity for each entity as at the 31 March 20X2 are shown below:

Statement of changes in equity for the year ended 31 March 20X2:

	HN	AE
	$000	$000
Equity b/f	2,500	450
Comprehensive income	1,250	216
Dividends paid on 1 Jan 20X2	(100)	(25)

Required:

What will be the parent's share of total comprehensive income shown within the consolidated statement of changes in equity for the year ended 31 March 20X2? Answers are presented in $000s.

A   1,403

B   1,423

C   1,441

D   1,466

4   **Required:**

What is the parent's dividend paid within the consolidated statement of changes in equity for the year ended 31 March 20X2? Answers are presented in $000s.

A   20

B   25

C   80

D   100

5   **Required:**

Calculate the parent's equity brought forward included in the consolidated statement of changes in equity for the year ended 31 March 20X2?

The information below relates to questions (6) and (7).

CR acquired 70% of the equity share capital of TM on 1 January 20X1 when TM's net assets had a carrying amount of $3,125,000. At the date of acquisition, an adjustment of $625,000 was made to increase TM's plant and equipment to fair value. The plant and equipment had a remaining life of 10 years at this time. No other fair value adjustments were considered necessary.

It is group policy to measure the non-controlling interest at fair value at the date of acquisition and the fair value of the non-controlling interest in TM on 1 January 20X1 was $1,500,000.

Goodwill has been tested for impairment and none has arisen since acquisition.

The individual statements of changes in equity of CR and TM for the year ended 31 December 20X4 are:

	CR	TM
	$000	$000
Equity b/f	14,500	6,600
Comprehensive income	2,750	1,500
Dividends paid on 1 Jan 20X4	(200)	(100)
Equity c/f	17,050	8,000

6 **Calculate the brought forward equity attributable to the parent shareholders in the consolidated statement of changes in equity for the year ended 31 December 20X4).**

7 **Which one of the following statements is INCORRECT in respect of the consolidated statement of changes in equity for the year ended 31 December 20X4?**

 A   The statement will show the full dividend paid by the parent and the NCI share of the dividend paid by the subsidiary.

 B   The closing balance in the parent shareholders' column will agree to the consolidated retained earnings balance in the consolidated statement of financial position.

 C   The closing balance in the NCI column will agree to the NCI equity balance in the consolidated statement of financial position.

 D   100% of the parent's comprehensive income is reflected in the comprehensive income for the year attributable to the parent shareholders and the subsidiary's comprehensive income is split between parent shareholders and NCI.

3 Chapter summary

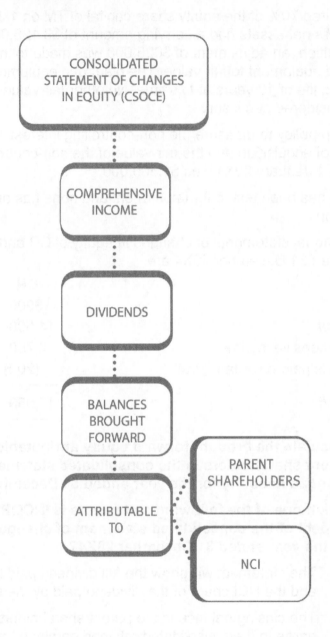

Test your understanding answers

Test your understanding 1 (integration question)

Consolidated statement of changes in equity for the year ended 31 March 20X7

	Parent shareholders $	NCI shareholders $
Equity b/f **(W4/W3)**	243,750	36,250
Comprehensive income **(W5)**	68,750	8,750
Dividends		
P's dividend	(15,000)	
NCI% × S's dividend (25% × 10,000)		(2,500)
Equity c/f **(W4/W3)**	297,500	42,500

Workings

(W1) Group structure

Islington

75% | 1 April 20X4 i.e. 3 years since acquisition

Southwark

(W2) Net assets of subsidiary

	Acq $	B/f $	C/f (i.e. reporting date) $
Net assets = equity	80,000	125,000	150,000
		Post-acquisition reserves = 45,000	Post-acquisition reserves = 70,000

(W3) NCI share of equity

	B/f	C/f (i.e. reporting date)
	$	$
NCI at acqn at fair value	25,000	25,000
NCI% × post acquisition reserves		
(25% × 45,000 **(W2)**)	11,250	
(25% × 70,000 **(W2)**)		17,500
	36,250	42,500

(W4) Parent's share of equity

	B/f	C/f (i.e. reporting date)
	$	$
Parent's equity	210,000	245,000
Sub: P% × post acquisition reserves		
(75% × 45,000 **(W2)**)	33,750	
(75% × 70,000 **(W2)**)		52,500
	243,750	297,500

(W5) Comprehensive income

	$
P comprehensive income	50,000
Less elimination of inter-co dividend	
(75% × 10,000)	(7,500)
P share of sub comprehensive income	
(75% × 35,000)	26,250
	68,750
Non-controlling interests (25% × 35,000)	8,750

Tutorial note:

The comprehensive income working above can alternatively be set out as follows:

(W5) Comprehensive income

	$
P and S comprehensive income (50,000 + 35,000)	85,000
Less elimination of inter-co dividend (75% × 10,000)	(7,500)
	77,500
Total comprehensive income attributable to:	
Parent shareholders (balancing figure)	68,750
Non-controlling interests (25% × 35,000)	8,750
	77,500

Test your understanding 2 (OTQ)

Correct answer A

	Parent shareholders $	NCI shareholders $
Total comprehensive income	34,240 **(W3)**	2,760 **(W2)**

Workings

(W1) Group structure

Thunder

80%
NCI 20%

1 January 20X5 (2 years ago)

Lightning

(W2) NCI share of S's total comprehensive income (TCI)

		$
NCI share of S's TCI	13,800 × 20%	2,760

(W3) Parent share of total comprehensive income

	$
Parent comprehensive income	24,000
Less inter-co dividend received (80% × 1,000)	(800)
Parent share of subsidiary comp income (13,800 – 2,760 **(W2)**) or ((80% × (13,800))	11,040
	34,240

Test your understanding 3 (OTQ)

Correct answer B

	Parent shareholders $	NCI shareholders $
Dividends		
100% P's dividend	(10,000)	
NCI% × S's dividend (20% × 1,000)		(200)

Dividends were paid by Lightning on 30 June 20X6. 20% of those dividends were paid to NCIs. The rest were received by Thunder (the parent) and are cancelled as intragroup transactions.

Test your understanding 4 (OTQ style)

1   **Closing balance on equity attributable to NCI at 31 December 20X4 = $710,000**

	$000
NCI equity b/f at 1 January 20X4	650
Comprehensive income (25% × 300)	75
Dividends paid (25% × 60)	(15)
	710

2

	Not in CSOCE	Equity attributable to: Parent	NCI
Comprehensive income for year		x	x
Dividends paid to parent shareholders		x	
Finance costs	x		
Dividends paid to NCI			x
Gain on FVPL financial asset	x		
Dividend paid by associate	x		

Finance costs and gains on FVPL financial assets are recorded within the statement of profit or loss. Their respective impacts would be included within comprehensive income for the year but will not be shown separately within the CSOCE.

Associate dividends paid do not impact the CSOCE. The investment in associate and the group investment income within the statement of profit or loss are adjusted as an inter-company transaction for the share received by the parent.

3   A 1,403

Total comprehensive income for group

	$000
Parent's comprehensive income	1,250
Parent's share of subsidiary's comprehensive income	173
(80% × 216k)	
less Parent's share of sub's dividends paid	(20)
(80% × 25k)	
	1,403

4   D 100

The amount shown as dividend paid within the consolidated statement of changes in equity consists of the parent's (HN's) dividend paid only. This was $100,000.

5   Equity attributable to parent shareholders b/f (in $000s) = 2,580

	$000
Parent's equity b/f	2,500
Sub: P% × post acquisition reserves b/f	80
(80% × (450 – (100 + 250)))	
	2,580

6   Equity attributable to parent shareholders b/f = $16,801,250

	$
Parent's equity b/f	14,500,000
Sub: P% × post acquisition reserves b/f	
(70% × 3,287,500 (see below))	2,301,250
	16,801,250

Net assets of subsidiary

	Acq $000	B/f $000
Net assets = equity	3,125	6,600
Fair value adjustment	625	625
Depreciation adjustment		
(625 × 3/10)		(187.5)
	3,750	7,037.5

Post-acquisition reserves = 3,287.5

7   **The incorrect statement is B.**

The closing balance in the parent shareholders' column represents **equity** attributable to the parent shareholders. This includes consolidated retained earnings but also the parent's share capital, share premium and the parent's share of any other reserves.

Consolidated statement of cash flows

Chapter learning objectives

Lead outcome	Component outcome
B2: Explain relevant financial reporting standards for group accounts	(a) Explain the financial reporting standards for the key areas of group accounts
C1: Group accounts based on IFRS	Prepare the following based on financial reporting standards: (d) Consolidated statement of cash flows

1 Session content

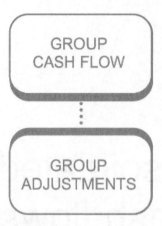

- Acquisition of subsidiary
- Associates
- Non-controlling interests

2 Objective of statements of cash flows

- IAS 7 *Statement of cash flows* provides guidance on the preparation of a statement of cash flows.

- The objective of a statement of cash flows is to provide information on an entity's changes in cash and cash equivalents during the period.

- The statement of financial position and statement of profit or loss and other comprehensive income (SOPLOCI) are prepared on an accruals basis and do not show how the business has generated and used cash in the accounting period.

- The SOPLOCI shows profits on an accruals basis even if the company is suffering severe cash flow problems.

- Statements of cash flows enable users of the financial statements to assess the **liquidity, solvency** and **financial adaptability** of a business.

 Definitions:

- **'Cash consists of cash in hand and deposits repayable upon demand, less overdrafts. This includes cash held in a foreign currency.**

- **Cash equivalents are short-term, highly liquid investments that are readily convertible into known amounts of cash and are subject to an insignificant risk of changes in value.**

- **Cash flows are inflows and outflows of cash and cash equivalents'** (IAS 7, para 6).

3 Classification of cash flows

IAS 7 *Statement of cash flows* does not prescribe a specific format for the statement of cash flows, although it requires that cash flows are classified under three headings:

- **cash flows from operating activities**, defined as the entity's principal revenue earning activities and other activities that do not fall under the next two headings

- **cash flows from investing activities**, defined as the acquisition and disposal of long-term assets and other investments (excluding cash equivalents)

- **cash flows from financing activities**, defined as activities that change the size and composition of the entity's equity and borrowings.

Classification of cash flows

Cash flows from operating activities

There are two methods of calculating the cash from operations.

- The **direct method** shows operating cash receipts and payments. This includes cash receipts from customers, cash payments to suppliers and cash payments to and on behalf of employees. The Examiner has indicated that the direct method will not be examined and is not considered further within this text.

- The **indirect method** uses a working that reconciles profits to cash flows from operating activities. The working starts with profit before tax and adjusts it for non-cash charges and credits, to reconcile it to the net cash flow from operating activities.

IAS 7 permits either method.

Under the **indirect method** adjustments are needed for a number of items, the most frequently occurring of which are:

- depreciation, amortisation and impairment
- profit or loss on disposal of non-current assets
- change in inventory
- change in receivables
- change in payables.

These adjustments are required to bring profits in line with operating cash flows.

Cash flows from investing activities

Cash flows to appear under this heading include:

- cash paid for property, plant and equipment and other non-current assets
- cash received on the sale of property, plant and equipment and other non-current assets
- cash paid for investments in or loans to other entities (excluding movements on loans from financial institutions, which are shown under financing)
- cash received for the sale of investments or the repayment of loans to other entities (again excluding loans from financial institutions).

Cash flows from financing activities

Financing cash flows mainly comprise receipts or repayments of principal from or to external providers of finance.

Financing **cash inflows** include:

- receipts from issuing shares or other equity instruments
- receipts from issuing debentures, loan notes, bonds and from other long-term and short-term borrowings (other than overdrafts, which are normally included in cash and cash equivalents).

Financing **cash outflows** include:

- repayments of amounts borrowed (other than overdrafts)
- the capital element of lease rental payments
- payments to reacquire or redeem the entity's shares.

Interest and dividends

There are divergent and strongly held views about how interest and dividend cash flows should be classified. Some regard them as part of operating activities, because they are as much part of the day to day activities as receipts from customers, payments to suppliers and payments to staff. Others regard them as part of financing activities, the heading under which the instruments giving rise to the payments and receipts are classified. Still others believe they are part of investing activities, because this is what the long-term finance raised in this way is used for.

IAS 7 allows interest and dividends, whether received or paid, to be classified under any of the three headings, provided the classification is consistent from period to period.

The practice adopted in this exam is to classify:

- interest received as a cash flow from investing activities
- interest paid as a cash flow from operating activities
- dividends received as a cash flow from investing activities
- dividends paid as a cash flow from financing activities.

4 Pro-forma statement of cash flows

Group statement of cash flows

	$	$
Cash flows from operating activities		
Group profit before tax	X	
Adjustments for:		
Finance costs	X	
Investment income	(X)	
Share of associate's profit	(X)	
Depreciation	X	
Amortisation	X	
Impairment of goodwill	X	
Profit/loss on sale of property, plant and equipment	(X)/X	
	X	
(Increase)/decrease in inventory	(X)/X	
(Increase)/decrease in receivables	(X)/X	
Increase/(decrease) in payables	X/(X)	
Cash generated from operations	X	
Interest paid	(X)	
Tax paid	(X)	
Net cash from operating activities		X

Cash flows from investing activities

Sale proceeds on disposal of property, plant and equipment	X
Purchases of property, plant and equipment	(X)
Investment income received	X
Dividends received from associate	X
Acquisition of subsidiary, net of cash balances	(X)/X

Net cash used in investing activities	X

Cash flows from financing activities

Loans – issue/repayment	X/(X)
Share issues	X
Dividends paid to NCI	(X)
Dividends paid to parent shareholders	(X)

Net cash used in financing activities	X

Increase/decrease in cash and cash equivalents	X/(X)
Opening cash and cash equivalents	X

Closing cash and cash equivalents	X

 ## 5 The consolidated statement of cash flows

Single entity statements of cash flows have already been assessed in F1.

In the F2 assessment, questions are more likely to focus on the group aspects of a consolidated statement of cash flows. The pro-forma of the consolidated statement of cash flows is exactly the same as the pro-forma for the single entity cash flow but with some extra complications resulting from group issues.

A typical question will ask you to calculate a cash-flow figure/adjustment that would be presented on the statement of cash flows. You may also be tested on which section of the statement a particular figure would appear under and, therefore, you should have good knowledge of the pro-forma statement itself (shown above).

A balancing figure approach is typically used to calculate a cash flow figure/adjustment. By plotting the movements in the statement of financial position balance from the beginning to the end of a period, the cash flow/adjustment is derived as the missing figure.

NB. In the exercises in this chapter, workings have been shown using both columnar formats and T account formats. It is important that you choose the method that works best for you – use the one that most helps you get to the right answer!

In a consolidated statement of cash flows, there are specific issues that will arise that would not have been considered within single entity cash flows. Examples include:

- Dividends paid to non-controlling interests (financing cash outflow)

- Dividends received from the associate (investing cash inflow)

- Cash flows related to the acquisition of a subsidiary during the year (cash received/paid net of the sub's cash balance)

If there has been an acquisition of a subsidiary during the year, its impact will need to be considered when using workings to calculate other cash flows.

Dividends paid to non-controlling interests

- When a subsidiary has paid a dividend, only the share paid to the non-controlling interest is reflected in the consolidated financial statements (the share paid to the parent is eliminated as an intra-group transaction).

- The dividends paid to the non-controlling interests should be disclosed separately from the dividends paid to the parent shareholders in the statement of cash flows.

- To calculate the amount paid, reconcile the non-controlling interest in the statement of financial position from the opening to the closing balance.

Illustration 1 – Dividend paid to NCI

The following information has been extracted from the consolidated financial statements of WG for the years ended 31 December:

	20X7	20X6
	$000	$000
NCI in consolidated SFP	780	690
NCI's total comprehensive income in CSOPLOCI	120	230

Required:

What is the dividend paid to non-controlling interests in the year 20X7?

Solution

Steps:

1   Set up a working (column or T account style).

2   Insert the opening and closing balances and the NCI share of total comprehensive income (TCI) for the year.

3   The balancing figure is the cash paid to the NCI.

Non-controlling interests

	$000
Bal b/f	690
Comprehensive income attributable to the NCI	120
	810
Dividends paid (balance)	(30)
Bal c/f	780

or

Non-controlling interests

	$000		$000
Dividends paid (bal fig)	30	Balance b/f	690
Balance c/f	780	Share of TCI in year	120
	810		810

Watch out for an acquisition of a subsidiary in the year. This will affect the NCI and will need to be included in the working, showing the value of NCI that has been acquired in the period as a credit. Consideration will need to be made of the method of valuing NCI (proportionate or fair value).

Note that, where the column format is produced, the result is the NCI column from the consolidated statement of changes in equity.

Information for TYUs 1 and 2

Extracts from Group A's consolidated financial statements for the year ended 31 December 20X1 are shown below.

Extract from consolidated statement of financial position as at 31 December:

	20X1	20X0
	$000	$000
Retained earnings	4,325	1,625
Non-controlling interests	580	440

Extract from consolidated statement of profit or loss and other comprehensive income for year ended 31 December 20X1:

	$000
Profit attributable to:	
Equity shareholders of the parent	3,200
Non-controlling interest	300
	3,500
Total comprehensive income attributable to:	
Equity shareholders of the parent	3,800
Non-controlling interest	500
	4,300

Test your understanding 1 (OTQ style)

Required:

Using the information above, calculate the dividends paid to the non-controlling interest of Group A for the year ended 31 December 20X1.

Test your understanding 2 (OTQ style)

Required:

Using the information above, calculate the dividends paid to the parent shareholders of Group A for the year ended 31 December 20X1.

Dividends received from associates

- Associates generate cash flows into the group to the extent that dividends are received out of the profits of the associate.

- Such dividends received from associates should be disclosed separately in the statement of cash flows.

- To calculate the amount received, reconcile the investment in associate in the statement of financial position from the opening to the closing balance.

- The share of profit/loss of the associate is a non-cash item included within profit and therefore will be an adjustment in the operating activities section of the statement of cash flows.

- If other comprehensive income includes any share of OCI of the associate then this should be taken into account when calculating the cash flow, but should not be adjusted for within operating activities as it is not part of profit.

Illustration 2 – Dividend received from associates

The following information has been extracted from the consolidated financial statements of H for the year ended 31 December 20X1:

Consolidated statement of profit or loss and other comprehensive income

	$000
Profit from operations	734
Share of profit of associate	48
Profit before tax	782
Income tax expense	(304)
Profit for the period	478

Other comprehensive income:

Share of other comprehensive income of associate	12

Group statement of financial position

	20X1	20X0
	$000	$000
Investment in associate	466	456

Required:

Show the figures relevant to the associate to be included in the group statement of cash flows for the year ended 31 December 20X1.

Solution

When dealing with the dividend from the associate, the process is the same as already seen with the non-controlling interest.

Set up a working (column or T-account format) and bring in all the balances that relate to the associate. When balancing the account, the balancing figure will be the cash received from the associate.

(W1) Dividend received from associate

	$000
Bal b/f	456
Share of profit of associate	48
Share of OCI of associate	12
	516
Less Bal c/f	(466)
Dividend received from associate	50

(W1) Dividend received from associate

or

Associate

	$000		$000
		Dividend received	
Balance b/f	456	(bal fig)	50
Profit of associate	48		
OCI of associate	12	Balance c/f	466
	516		516

Extracts from statement of cash flows for the year ended 31 December 20X1

	$000
Cash flows from operating activities	
Profit before tax	782
Adjustment for:	
Share of profit of associate	(48)
Investing activities	
Dividend received from associate **(W1)**	50

Test your understanding 3 (OTQ style)

Group B's statement of profit or loss and other comprehensive income reports 'Share of associate's profit' of $750,000 and 'Share of associate's other comprehensive income' of $25,000. The opening and closing statements of financial position show:

	Closing	Opening
	$000	$000
Investment in associate	500	200

Required:

Calculate the dividends received from associate that would appear within cash flows from investing activities in the consolidated statements of cash flows of Group B.

Acquisition of subsidiaries

Standard accounting practice

- On the acquisition of a subsidiary during the financial year, the group cash flow statement should include the acquired subsidiary's cash flows arising from the date control is achieved.

- Cash payments to acquire subsidiaries must be reported separately in the statement of cash flows under investing activities.

Acquisitions

- In the statement of cash flows, the actual cash flow arising for the purchase is recorded and presented within cash flows from investing activities. The cash outflow is presented net of any cash balances purchased with the subsidiary.

Illustration 3 – Mid-year acquisitions

Jordan buys 70% of the equity shares of Pippen for $500,000 in cash. At the acquisition date, Pippen had cash and cash equivalents of $35,000.

Required:

Show how this acquisition would be presented within the consolidated statement of cash flows for Jordan.

Solution:

Although Jordan paid $500,000 for the shares, Jordan also gained control of Pippen's cash for $35,000. In the consolidated statement of cash flows, the cash flows from investing activities section would present the cash paid on acquisition net of the cash received from Pippen, as follows:

	$000
Cash flows from investing activities	
Acquisition of a subsidiary (500,000 – 35,000)	(465)

- All assets and liabilities acquired must be included in any workings to calculate the cash movement for an item during the year. As the subsidiary's net assets would have been 100% consolidated within the CSOFP, the impact of the acquisition must be considered in any workings used to calculate cash flows. This applies to all assets (including goodwill) and liabilities acquired and also to the NCI reconciliation (to calculate dividends paid to NCI).

Illustration 4 – Mid-year acquisitions

The extracts of an entity's statement of financial position is shown below:

	20X8	20X7
	$	$
Inventory	74,666	53,019

During the year, a subsidiary was acquired. At the date of acquisition, the subsidiary had an inventory balance of $9,384.

Required:

Calculate the movement on inventory included in the cash generated from operations section of the statement of cash flows.

Solution

At the beginning of the year, the inventory balance of $53,019 **does not** include the inventory of the subsidiary.

At the end of the year, the inventory balance of $74,666 **does** include the inventory of the newly acquired subsidiary.

In order to calculate the correct cash movement, the acquired inventory must be excluded as it is dealt with in the cash paid to acquire the subsidiary. The comparison of the opening and closing inventory figures is then calculated on the same basis.

The movement on inventory is a $12,263 ((74,666 – 9,384) – 53,019) increase. This is shown as a negative adjustment in cash flows from operating activities.

Illustration 5

The following are extracts from a group's consolidated financial statements.

	Closing balance	Opening balance
	$000	$000
Group statement of financial position extracts		
Receivables	500	400
Loans	300	600

During the accounting period, a subsidiary was acquired. Extracts from the subsidiary's individual statements of financial position at the acquisition date are as follows:

	$000
Receivables	70
Loans	80

Required:

Demonstrate how the above transactions would be reflected in the consolidated statement of cash flows.

Solution

Consolidated statement of cash flows (extracts)

	$000
Cash flows from operating activities	
Adjustments for:	
Increase in receivables **(W1)**	(30)
Cash flows from financing activities	
Repayment of loans **(W2)**	(380)

(W1) Receivables

	$000
Opening balance	400
Acquisition of subsidiary	70
	470
Increase in receivables	30
Closing balance	500

(W2) Loans

	$000
Opening balance	600
Acquisition of subsidiary	80
	680
Therefore redemption/cash paid (bal figure)	(380)
Closing balance	300

Test your understanding 4 (OTQ style)

Group P's opening and closing statements of financial position show the following:

	Closing	Opening
	$000	$000
Non-current assets (NBV)	500	150

During the year, the group acquired a 75% shareholding in a subsidiary which held non-current assets of $200,000 at the acquisition date.

Depreciation of $50,000 was charged during the period.

No disposals of non-current assets occurred during the year.

Required:

How much cash was spent on non-current assets in the year?

Test your understanding 5

Group R's opening and closing statements of financial position show the following:

	Closing	Opening
	$000	$000
Inventory	100	200
Receivables	300	200
Payables	500	200

During the period, the group acquired a subsidiary with the following working capital at acquisition:

	$000
Inventory	50
Receivables	200
Payables	40

Required:

Prepare the extracts required for the movements in working capital that should be shown in the operating activities section of the statement of cash flows?

Test your understanding 6

The group financial statements of Linford are given below:

Consolidated statement of profit or loss and other comprehensive income for the year ended 30 September 20X9

	$m
Revenue	600
Cost of sales	(300)
Gross profit	300
Operating expenses	(150)
Finance costs	(44)
Share of associate profit	17
Profit before tax	123
Taxation	(35)
	88
Other comprehensive income:	
Gain on revaluation of PPE	15
	103
Profit attributable to:	
Parent shareholders	78
Non-controlling interests	10
	88
Total comprehensive income attributable to:	
Parent shareholders	91
Non-controlling interests	12
	103

Consolidated statements of financial position as at

	30 Sept 20X9		30 Sept 20X8	
	$m	$m	$m	$m
Non-current assets				
Goodwill	25		19	
Property, plant and equipment	240		280	
Investments in associates	80	345	70	369
Current assets				
Inventory	105		90	
Receivables	120		100	
Cash and cash equivalents	30		75	
		255		265
		600		634
Share capital		100		100
Retained earnings		194		142
Revaluation reserve		103		90
Non-controlling interest		72		40
		469		372
Non-current liabilities				
12% loan stock		–		90
Deferred taxation	30		24	
		30		114
Current liabilities				
Trade payables	65		55	
Taxation	10		8	
Overdraft	26		85	
		101		148
		600		634

Notes to the accounts

1   **Acquisition of subsidiary**

During the year ended 30 September 20X9, Linford purchased 80% of the issued equity share capital of Christie for $100m, payable in cash. The net assets of Christie at the date of acquisition were assessed as having fair values as follows:

	$m
PPE	60
Inventory	30
Receivables	25
Bank and cash	10
Trade payables	(15)
Taxation	(5)
	105

It is group policy to measure NCI at the proportionate share of the fair value of net assets at acquisition.

2   **Goodwill**

Goodwill suffered an impairment during the year.

3   **Property, plant and equipment**

The only disposal in the year was of land with a carrying amount of $90m. The profit on disposal of $10m is included within operating expenses. Depreciation of $58m was charged on PPE in the year.

Required:

Prepare the consolidated statement of cash flows for Linford group for the year ended 30 September 20X9.

Test your understanding 7 (further OTQs)

1   **Which three of the following items would be included in the 'cash flows from investing activities' section of the consolidated statement of cash flows?**

A   Cash paid on acquisition of a subsidiary, net of cash acquired

B   Goodwill on acquisition of a subsidiary

C   Gain on disposal of property, plant and equipment

D   Investment income received

E   Dividends received from associate

F   Share of associate profit

2   FG's consolidated statement of financial position shows receivables of $6,500,000 at 31 May 20X2 and $5,300,000 at 31 May 20X1. FG acquired 80% of the share capital of AB on 1 January 20X2, when AB had a receivables balance of $2,200,000.

Calculate the movement in receivables shown within the operating activities section of FG's consolidated statement of cash flows for the year ended 31 May 20X2. Clearly state whether the amount should be added to or deducted from profit.

3   SB's consolidated statement of financial position shows an investment in associate of $3,200,000 at 30 November 20X4 and $1,200,000 at 30 November 20X3. SB's share of associate's profit for the year ended 30 November 20X4 was $2,300,000 and its share of associate's other comprehensive income was $150,000.

There were no acquisitions or disposals of associates in the year ended 30 November 20X4.

SB group's consolidated statement of cash flows for the year ended 30 November 20X4 would include dividends received from associates of:

A $300,000

B $450,000

C $2,000,000

D $4,450,000

4   Which one of the following statements is INCORRECT in respect of the preparation of the consolidated statement of cash flows?

   A   Dividends from associates are a cash inflow within investing activities.

   B   Dividends to non-controlling interest are a cash inflow within financing activities.

   C   A gain on disposal of property, plant and equipment should be deducted from profit in the cash flow from operating activities section as it is a non-cash item included within profit.

   D   Goodwill impairment should be added back to profit in the cash flow from operating activities section as it is a non-cash item included within profit.

5   The carrying amount of property, plant and equipment (PPE) in XY's consolidated statement of financial position was $10,000,000 at 31 March 20X2 and $9,500,000 at 31 March 20X1. There were no disposals or revaluations of PPE in the year. Depreciation of $1,000,000 was charged to profit in the year ended 31 March 20X2. XY purchased 80% of the shares in ABC on 31 October 20X1. The PPE in ABC at the date of acquisition was $1,100,000.

   Calculate the cash outflow for the purchase of PPE presented in the consolidated statement of cash flows of the XY group for the year ended 31 March 20X2.

6   Chapter summary

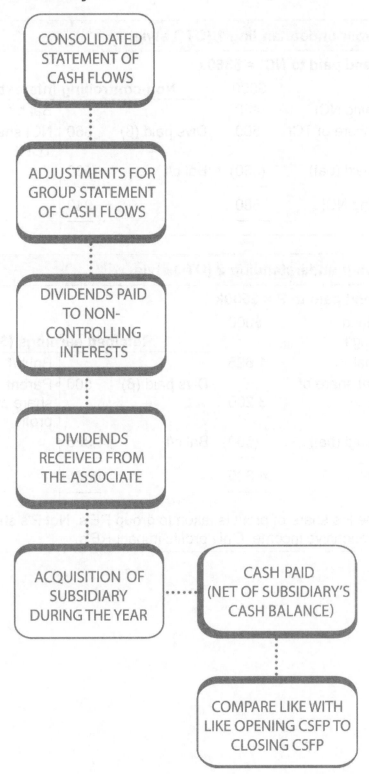

Test your understanding answers

Test your understanding 1 (OTQ style)

Dividend paid to NCI = $360k

	$000	Non-controlling interests ($000)			
Opening NCI	440			Bal b/f	440
NCI share of TCI	500	Divs paid (β)	360	NCI share of TCI	500
Divi paid (bal)	(360)	Bal c/f	580		
Closing NCI	580		940		940

Test your understanding 2 (OTQ style)

Dividend paid to P = $500k

Retained earnings	$000	Retained earnings ($000)			
Op. bal	1,625			Bal b/f	1,625
Parent share of profit	3,200	Divs paid (β)	500	Parent share of profit	3,200
Divi paid (bal)	(500)	Bal c/f	4,325		
Cl. bal	4,325		4,825		4,825

NB The P's share of profit is taken to group RE's. Not P's share of total comprehensive income. Only profits impact RE's.

Test your understanding 3 (OTQ style)

Dividend received from associate = $475k

	$000	Investment in Associate ($000)			
Opening investment in associate	200	Bal b/f	200		
Share of profits	750	Share of profits	750	Divis received (β)	475
Share of OCI	25	Share of OCI	25		
Dividend received from assoc (bal)	(475)			Bal c/f	500
Closing investment in associate	500		975		975

Test your understanding 4 (OTQ style)

Cash spent on NCAs = $200k

	$000	Non-current assets ($000)			
Opening NBV	150	Bal b/f	150	Depreciation	50
Depreciation	(50)	New sub	200		
New sub	200	Additions – cash (β)	200		
				Bal c/f	500
Additions – cash (β)	200				
			550		550
Closing NBV	500				

Test your understanding 5 (integration question)

Extracts to be included within cash generated from operations (in $000s)

Decrease in inventory	**150**
Decrease in receivables	**100**
Increase in payables	**260**

	$000	**Inventory ($000)**			
Opening inventory	200	Bal b/f	200		
New sub	50	New sub	50		
				Decrease (β)	150
Decrease (β)	(150)			Bal c/f	100
Closing inventory	100		250		250

	$000	**Receivables ($000)**			
Opening rec'bles	200	Bal b/f	200		
New sub	200	New sub	200		
				Decrease (β)	100
Decrease (β)	(100)			Bal c/f	300
Closing rec'bles	300		400		400

	$000	**Payables ($000)**			
Opening payables	200			Bal b/f	200
New sub	40			New sub	40
Increase (β)	260				
		Bal c/f	500	Increase (β)	260
Closing payables	500				
			500		500

Test your understanding 6 (integration question)

Group statement of cash flows for Linford for year ending 30 September 20X9

Cash flows from operating activities	$m	$m
Group profit before tax	123	
Adjustments for:		
Depreciation	58	
Goodwill impairment **(W1)**	10	
Profit on sale of property	(10)	
Share of associate's profit	(17)	
Finance costs	44	
	208	
Decrease in inventory ((105 – 90) – 30)	15	
Decrease in receivables ((120 – 100) – 25)	5	
Decrease in payables ((65 – 55) – 15)	(5)	
Cash generated from operations	223	
Finance costs paid	(44)	
Tax paid **(W3)**	(32)	
Net cash from operating activities		147
Cash flows from investing activities		
Proceeds on disposal of property (90 + 10)	100	
Purchase of property, plant and equipment **(W2)**	(33)	
Dividends received from associate **(W6)**	7	
Acquisition of sub, net of cash balances (100 – 10)	(90)	
Net cash used in investing activities		(16)
Cash flows from financing activities		
Repayment of loan – 12% loan stock	(90)	
Dividends paid to NCI **(W5)**	(1)	
Dividends paid to parent shareholders **(W4)**	(26)	(117)
Increase in cash and cash equivalents		14
Brought forward cash and cash equivalents (75 – 85)		(10)
Carried forward cash and cash equivalents (30 – 26)		4

Workings

(W1) Goodwill

	$m
Bal b/f	19
Acquisition of sub (below)	16
	35
Impairment (balance)	(10)
Bal c/f	25

Or

Goodwill

B/f	19	**Impairment (balance)**	10
Acquisition of subsidiary (below)	16	C/f	25
	35		35

Goodwill of acquired sub:

	$m
Fair value of P's investment	100
NCI at proportion of net assets (20% × 105)	21
Fair value of sub's net assets at acquisition	(105)
Goodwill at acquisition	16

(W2) PPE

	$m
Bal b/f	280
Revaluation	15
New subsidiary	60
Depreciation	(58)
Disposal	(90)
	207
Cash paid for new assets (balance)	33
Bal c/f	240

Or

PPE

B/f	280	Depreciation	58
Revaluation	15	Disposal	90
New sub	60	C/f	240
Bank (balance)	**33**		
	388		388

(W3) Taxation

	$m
Bal b/f (8 + 24)	32
SP/L charge	35
New subsidiary	5
	72
Cash paid (balance)	(32)
Bal c/f (10 + 30)	40

Or

Taxation

Bal c/f (10 + 30)	40	Bal b/f (8 + 24)	32
		SP/L charge	35
		New sub	5
Bank (balance)	**32**		
	72		72

(W4) Dividends paid to parent shareholders

	$m
Bal b/f (on retained earnings)	142
Profit for the period (attributable to parent)	78
	220
Cash paid (balance)	(26)
Bal c/f	194

Or

Retained earnings

C/f	194	B/f	142
		Profit	78
Divis paid (balance)	**26**		
	220		220

(W5) Non-controlling interests

	$m
Bal b/f	40
NCI share of total comprehensive income per CSOPLOCI	12
New subsidiary (105 × 20%)	21
	73
Dividends paid (balance)	(1)
Bal c/f	72

Or

Non-controlling interests

C/f	72	B/f	40
		Comp income	12
Bank (balance)	1	New sub (105 × 20%)	21
	73		73

(W6) Investment in associate

	$m
Bal b/f	70
Share of profits	17
	87
Cash received (balance)	(7)
Bal c/f	80

Or

Investment in associate

B/f	70	C/f	80
Share of profit	17	**Bank (balance)**	7
	87		87

Test your understanding 7 (further OTQs)

1   **Items A, D and E**

B is not a cash flow and will not appear anywhere in the consolidated statement of cash flows.

C and F would be adjustments to profit reflected in the cash flows from operating activities section of the statement.

2   **Movement in receivables = $1,000,000 addition**

i.e. positive adjustment in operating activities section

	$000
Bal b/f	5,300
Acquisition of subsidiary	2,200
	7,500
Decrease (balance)	(1,000)
Bal c/f	6,500

3   **B Dividends received from associate = $450,000**

Positive figure in investing activities section

	$000
Bal b/f	1,200
Profit from associate	2,300
OCI from associate	150
	3,650
Dividends received (balance)	(450)
Bal c/f	3,200

Or

Associate ($000)

Bal b/f	1,200		
Profit from associate	2,300		
OCI from associate	150	Dividends received – balance	**450**
		Bal c/f	3,200
	3,650		3,650

4   **B is incorrect**

NCI dividends are a cash outflow, not inflow.

5   **Cash outflow from purchase of PPE = $400,000**

	$000
Bal b/f	9,500
Depreciation	(1,000)
Held on acquisition of ABC	1,100
	9,600
Cash paid (bal fig)	400
Bal c/f	10,000

Foreign subsidiaries

Chapter learning objectives

Lead outcome	Component outcome
C1: Prepare group accounts based on IFRS	Prepare the following based on financial reporting standards:
	(a-d) Statement of financial position, statement of profit or loss and other comprehensive income, statement of changes in equity, and statement of cash flows

1 Session content

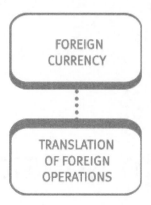

2 IAS® 21 *The effects of changes in foreign exchange rates*

IAS 21 deals with:

- the definition of functional and presentation currencies

- accounting for individual transactions in a foreign currency

These two areas are considered as part of the 'Financial reporting standards' syllabus area. These topics are covered in detail within Chapter 10.

- translating the financial statements of a foreign operation.

This area is considered part of the 'Group accounts' section of the syllabus. Only this content is covered within this chapter.

3 Groups containing foreign subsidiaries

Within an increasingly global economy, groups including acquisitions and mergers of companies based overseas are common place.

If a parent is to acquire control of a subsidiary that uses a different functional currency from the parent, complications regarding the consolidation arise.

The two main complications are:

- the translation of the foreign currency subsidiary into the parent's functional currency

- the resulting calculation and recognition of foreign currency exchange gains or losses

4   Translating the financial statements of a foreign subsidiary

If the functional currency of a subsidiary is different to that of the parent entity, it will be necessary to translate the subsidiary's financial statements into the parent's presentation currency prior to consolidation.

If the parent prepares accounts in $ and acquires a subsidiary with accounts prepared in €, translation of the subsidiary's financial statements into $ must occur before consolidation commences.

This is done using the 'closing rate' method and the following exchange rates should be used in the translation:

Statement of profit or loss and other comprehensive income

Income and expenses – average rate for the year.

Statement of financial position

- Assets and liabilities – closing rate (the rate at the reporting date)

- Goodwill of subsidiary – closing rate.

 5   Exchange gains or losses on translation

Exchange differences arise upon translation of the subsidiary and can be separated into two main components:

- **Exchange difference on net assets** – The subsidiary's closing net assets will have been translated at closing rate (described above).

   Closing net assets should be equal to opening net assets plus total comprehensive income.

   Opening net assets are initially translated at the opening rate (last years' closing rate) and the comprehensive income for the year (i.e. movement on net assets) will have been translated at average rate (as described above). This would create a difference between closing net assets and opening net assets plus total comprehensive income. This difference is caused by fluctuations in exchange rates (the variations between opening, closing and average rates). This difference is the foreign currency exchange gain or loss from translating net assets.

- **Exchange difference on goodwill** – Foreign subsidiary goodwill is calculated in the currency used by the subsidiary. The year-end goodwill is translated at closing rate (as described above).

   Goodwill at the year-end should equal goodwill brought forward less annual impairment

411

Goodwill brought forward would have been translated at the current year's opening rate (the previous year's closing rate), any impairment in the year will be translated at average rate in the statement of profit or loss. If exchange rates have fluctuated during the year, a difference will arise between goodwill at the year-end compared to goodwill brought forward less annual impairment. This difference is the annual exchange gain or loss from translating the goodwill.

The sum of exchange differences on net assets and the annual exchange difference on goodwill is recognised **within other comprehensive income.**

The exchange difference on net assets is always split between parent and NCI based on the group shareholdings.

The treatment of the goodwill exchange difference depends upon the method used for valuing the NCI – fair value method or proportionate method. If the fair method is used, a portion of the exchange difference is allocated to parent and the NCI. Otherwise, if the proportionate method is used, the exchange difference is allocated only to the parent.

To calculate the annual exchange differences, the following pro-formas can be used.

Exchange difference on net assets for the year

	A$
Closing net assets at closing rate	X
Less opening net assets at opening rate	(X)
Less comprehensive income for the year at average rate	(X)
Exchange gain/(loss)	X/(X)

Exchange difference on goodwill for the year

	A$
Closing goodwill at closing rate	X
Less opening goodwill at opening rate	(X)
Add back impairment for the year at relevant rate	X
(question should provide guidance on the rate used to translate impairment)	
	X/(X)
Exchange gain/(loss)	

Treatment in the consolidated statement of financial position

The group share of these foreign exchange differences would be held in a separate reserve within equity in the statement of financial position. This reserve would show the total exchange gains or losses arising since acquisition.

Illustration 1 – Exchange difference on translation of subsidiary

To help understand the exchange difference, consider the following scenario.

A subsidiary, whose functional currency is the Dit (D), prepares its financial statements for the year ended 31 December 20X1 and the movement on net assets is as follows:

	D000
Opening net assets at 1 January 20X1	15,000
Comprehensive income for the year ended 31 December 20X1	1,750
Closing net assets at 31 December 20X1	16,750

The parent's presentation currency is the dollar ($) and exchange rates were as follows:

At 1 January 20X1	5 Dits = $1
At 31 December 20X1	7 Dits = $1
Average rate for the year ended 31 December 20X1	6.2 Dits = $1

Required:

Calculate the foreign currency gain or loss on translation of the subsidiary's net assets for the year ended 31 December 20X1

Solution:

The brought forward net assets were translated at this year's opening rate (last year's closing rate). The comprehensive income has been translated at average rate for the year. The closing net assets have been translated at this year's closing rate for inclusion in the consolidated statement of financial position.

This gives rise to the following exchange difference:

	D000	Exchange rate	$000
Closing net assets at closing rate	16,750	7	2,393
Less opening net assets at opening rate	(15,000)	5	(3,000)
Less comprehensive income for the year at average rate	(1,750)	6.2	(282)
Exchange difference arising on translation of subsidiary			(889)

This loss is presented in group other comprehensive income (in the CSOPOCI) and reserves (in the CSOFP). The loss is allocated between the parent shareholders and the non-controlling interests based on their respective shareholdings.

Another way of presenting this calculation is:

	D000	Exchange rate	$000
Opening net assets	15,000	5	3,000
Comprehensive income	1,750	6.2	282
Exchange difference (bal)			(889)
Closing net assets	16,750	7	2,393

NB. A further exchange difference then arises upon consolidation as goodwill is recognised at the closing rate in the consolidated statement of financial position each year and, therefore, is re-translated from opening to closing rate.

Example 1

This example walks you through the entire process of preparing a set of consolidated financial statements with a foreign subsidiary. Note that you will not be asked to do this in full in your assessment, but understanding the process will help you to answer any questions that arise.

P acquired 75% of the share capital of S on 1 January 20X5 for 500,000Fr, when the retained earnings of S were 120,000Fr. The functional currency of S is Fr. The functional currency and presentation currency of P is $.

Statements of financial position at 31 December 20X6

	P $000	S Fr000
Non-current assets	1,250	850
Investment in S	100	–
Current assets	325	150
	1,675	1,000
Share capital	700	250
Reserves	675	350
Liabilities	300	400
	1,675	1,000

Statements of profit or loss and other comprehensive income for

	P	S
	$000	Fr000
Revenue	600	150
Expenses	(475)	(90)
Profit for the year	125	60
Other comprehensive income	–	–
Total comprehensive income	125	60

the year ended 31 December 20X6 (summarised)

Exchange rates:

1 January 20X5	$1 = 5.0Fr
31 December 20X5	$1 = 4.2Fr
31 December 20X6	$1 = 4.5Fr
Average for the year ended 31 December 20X5	$1 = 4.6Fr
Average for the year ended 31 December 20X6	$1 = 4.4Fr

P has a policy of measuring NCI at acquisition at fair value. The fair value of the NCI holding in S at acquisition was 160,000Fr. The goodwill has been impaired by 10% in the year ended 31 December 20X5 and a further 10% of its carrying amount in the current year. The impairment each year has been translated at the average rate for the year.

Required:

Prepare the consolidated statement of financial position and consolidated statement of profit or loss and other comprehensive income for the year ended 31 December 20X6.

Note: Work to the nearest $1,000.

Example 1 answer (the basics)

P Group consolidated statement of financial position at 31 December 20X6

	$000
Goodwill **(W3)**	52
Non-current assets (1,250 + 189 **(W1)**)	1,439
Current assets (325 + 33 **(W1)**)	358
	1,849
Share capital	700
Reserves **(W5)**	715
Non-controlling interests **(W4)**	45
Payables (300 + 89 **(W1)**)	389
	1,849

Workings:

Translation of sub's financial statements

A good starting point is to translate the basic financial statements of the subsidiary so that the figures are in the presentation currency of the parent ready for adding across on the face of the main statements.

(W1) Translation of S's statement of financial position at 31 December 20X6

Using closing rate of 4.5	$000
Non-current assets (850/4.5)	189
Current assets (150/4.5)	33
Liabilities (400/4.5)	89

Translation of S's statement of profit or loss and other comprehensive income for the year ended 31 December 20X6

Using average rate of 4.4	$000
Revenue (150/4.4)	34
Expenses (90/4.4)	(20)
Profit/TCI for year (60/4.4)	14

To complete the consolidated statement of financial position the usual workings should then be prepared: net assets, goodwill, NCI reserve and group (consolidated) reserves.

When preparing the net assets working, translate the net assets at acquisition using the acquisition rate and the net assets at the reporting date using the closing rate.

The difference between the two will reflect the translated post-acquisition reserves (for inclusion in both the NCI reserve and group reserve workings). This figure includes both the movement in post-acquisition reserves and the cumulative exchange difference to date on the net assets of the subsidiary. The detailed answer that follows this solution demonstrates this point.

(W2) Net assets of subsidiary

	Acquisition date	Reporting date
	Fr000	Fr000
Share capital	250	250
Reserves	120	350
	370	600
Translation rate	Acquisition rate = 5	Closing rate = 4.5
Translated net assets ($000)	74	133

Post-acquisition reserves = 59 ($000)

Goodwill

When calculating goodwill, start in the **functional currency of the subsidiary and then translate** into the presentation currency of the parent using three different rates: acquisition rate, opening rate and closing rate.

The difference between opening and closing rate will be part of the exchange difference to be recognised within other comprehensive income for the year.

The difference between acquisition and closing rate will be part of the foreign currency translation reserve that has arisen since the subsidiary was acquired and should be included in the group reserves working.

(W3) Goodwill

	Fr000
Fair value of P's investment	500
NCI at fair value	160
Fair value of sub's net assets at acquisition **(W2)**	(370)
Goodwill at acquisition	290
Impairment year ended 31 Dec 20X5 (10% × 290)	(29)
Gross goodwill at 31 December 20X5	261
Impairment year ended 31 Dec 20X6 (10% × 261)	(26)
Goodwill at reporting date	235

Translation of goodwill:

	$000
At acquisition date (290/5)	58
Less impairment in y/e 31 Dec 05 at average rate (29/4.6)	(6)
Exchange difference y/e 31 Dec 05 (balancing figure)	10
At 31 Dec 05 (261/4.2)	62
Less impairment in y/e 31 Dec 06 at average rate (26/4.4)	(6)
Exchange difference y/e 31 Dec 06 (balancing figure)	(4)
At 31 Dec 06 (235/4.5)	52

NCI

When preparing the non-controlling interests working, remember that this is a reserve and builds up over time.

- The value at acquisition should be translated at the acquisition rate.

- The post-acquisition reserves have already been translated in the net assets working.

- Any impairment will also have been translated in the goodwill working.

- Remember to include the NCI's share of any cumulative exchange difference on goodwill if NCI is measured using the fair value method at acquisition. This exchange difference has already been calculated in the goodwill working.

(W4) Non-controlling interests in the CSFP

	$000
NCI at acquisition (160/5)	32
NCI% × post acquisition reserves (25% × 59 **(W2)**)	15
NCI% × cumulative impairment loss (25% × (6 + 6 **(W3)**))	(3)
NCI% × cumulative exchange difference on goodwill (25% × (10 − 4) **(W3)**)	1
	45

Group reserves

The group reserves working then follows on from the NCI reserve as usual. The first figure to include is the parent's reserves (already in the parent's presentation currency). The group reserves then include the remaining (parent's) share of the figures partly included in the NCI reserve working.

(W5) Group reserves

	$000
P	675
S: (75% × 59)	44
Impairment (75% × (6 + 6))	(9)
Exchange difference on goodwill (75% × (10 − 4))	5
	715

Finally, to complete the consolidated statement of profit or loss and other comprehensive income for the year, we need to calculate the current year exchange difference on net assets.

(W6) Exchange difference for the year

	$000
Closing net assets at closing rate **(W2)**	133
Less opening net assets at opening rate (600 − 60)/4.2	(129)
Less comprehensive income for the year at average rate **(W1)**	(14)
Exchange difference on net assets for the year	(10)
Current year exchange difference on goodwill **(W3)**	(4)
Total exchange difference for the year	(14)

The exchange difference on net assets is split between parent and NCI based on the percentage holdings.

As the NCI has been measured using the fair value method, the exchange difference on goodwill should also be allocated between parent and NCI.

Statement of profit or loss and other comprehensive income

We can now complete the consolidated statement of profit or loss and other comprehensive income, including the above exchange difference for the year within other comprehensive income.

P Group consolidated statement of profit or loss and other comprehensive income for the year ended 31 December 20X6

	$000
Revenue (600 + 34 **(W1)**)	634
Expenses (475 + 20 **(W1)** + 6 impairment **(W3)**)	(501)
Profit for the year	133
Other comprehensive income	
Items that may be reclassified subsequently to profit or loss:	
Foreign exchange difference **(W6)**	(14)
Total comprehensive income	119
Profit for the year attributable to:	
Parent shareholders (balance)	131
Non-controlling interest (25% × (14 **(W1)** – 6 **(W3)**))	2
	133

	$000
Total comprehensive income attributable to:	
Non-controlling interest (2 (above) – (25% × 14 **(W6)**))	(2)
Parent shareholders (balance)	121
	119

Example 1 answer (detailed)

In the net assets working (W2), the movement in post-acquisition reserves each year can be analysed further. This will enable accurate calculation of the foreign currency translation reserve shown in the CSOFP.

To analyse the movement, firstly calculate the comprehensive income of the subsidiary for the year ended 31 December 20X5:

Movement on net assets of subsidiary

	Fr000
Net assets at acquisition (1 Jan X5)	370
Comprehensive income for y/e 31 Dec X5 (bal fig)	170
Comprehensive income for y/e 31 Dec X6 (S's SCI)	60
Net assets at 31 Dec X6	600

Now consider the movements each year, including the exchange difference that arises when the closing net assets are translated at closing rate for the consolidated statement of financial position.

Movement on post-acquisition reserves

	$000
Net assets at acquisition (1 Jan X5) at acquisition rate (370/5)	74
Comprehensive income for y/e 31 Dec X5 at average rate (170/4.6)	37
Exchange difference for y/e 31 Dec X5 (bal fig)	18
Net assets at 31 Dec X5 at closing rate (370 + 170)/4.2	129
Comprehensive income for y/e 31 Dec X6 at average rate (60/4.4)	14
Exchange difference for y/e 31 Dec X6 (bal fig)	(10)
Net assets at 31 Dec X6 at closing rate (600/4.5)	133

Therefore the post-acquisition reserves of 59 ($000) shown in W2 is:

	$000
Movement in post-acquisition reserves (37 + 14)	51
Foreign exchange differences (18 – 10)	8
	59

In the basic approach above, a combined reserves working was presented in working 5. However, in practice all the exchange differences arising on translation of the subsidiary are held in a separate foreign currency translation reserve. The retained earnings reserve and foreign currency reserve in the above example would therefore be:

(W5a) Group retained earnings

	$000
P	675
S: 75% × 51 (movement on reserves excl. exchange diffs)	38
Impairment (75% × (6 + 6) **(W3)**)	(9)
	704

(W5b)Group foreign currency translation reserve

	$000
Exchange differences on net assets of subsidiary since acquisition (75% × 8)	6
Exchange difference on goodwill since acquisition (75% × (10 – 4))	5
	11

Group retained earnings plus foreign currency translation reserve = 715 (704 + 11) as shown in W5 using the combined approach.

Test your understanding 1 (Further practice integration question)

Paul is an entity whose functional and presentational currency is the dollar ($). On 1 January 20X7, Paul acquired 80% of the share capital of Simon, an entity whose functional currency is the Franc. Simon's reserves at this date showed a balance of Fr4,000. Paul paid Fr21,000 for the investment in Simon.

Below are the financial statements of Paul and Simon for the year ended 31 December 20X8.

Statements of financial position at 31 December 20X8

	Paul $	Simon Fr
Non-current assets	60,000	25,000
Investment in Simon	4,200	
Current assets	35,800	15,000
	100,000	40,000
Equity		
Share capital	50,000	15,000
Reserves	20,000	14,000
	70,000	29,000
Current liabilities	30,000	11,000
	100,000	40,000

Statements of profit or loss and other comprehensive income for the year ended 31 December 20X8

	Paul $	Simon Fr
Revenue	25,000	10,000
Operating expenses	(10,000)	(4,000)
Profit from operations	15,000	6,000
Finance costs	(5,000)	(1,500)
Profit before tax	10,000	4,500
Tax	(3,000)	(1,000)
Profit for the year	7,000	3,500
Other comprehensive income	–	–
Total comprehensive income	7,000	3,500

Exchanges rates have been as follows:

	Fr: $1
1 January 20X7	5
31 December 20X7	3
31 December 20X8	2
Average for the year ended 31 December 20X8	2.5

It is Paul's policy to measure NCI at fair value at the date of acquisition and the fair value of the non-controlling interest in Simon was deemed to be Fr4,500 at this date. Goodwill had been reviewed for impairment as at 31 December 20X7 but none had arisen. At 31 December 20X8, it was determined that goodwill should be impaired by Fr1,000.

Required:

Prepare the consolidated statement of financial position and the consolidated statement of profit or loss and other comprehensive income for the year ended 31 December 20X8.

Fair value adjustments in a foreign subsidiary

To deal with fair value adjustments in a foreign subsidiary, apply the following rules:

- On the face of the consolidated statement of financial position, translate the fair value adjustment using the closing rate

- In the statement of profit or loss, translate any fair value depreciation adjustment relating to the current year using the average rate.

The impact of the fair value adjustment would then need to be carefully considered when calculating the exchange difference for the year on the net assets:

- The profit for the year should be adjusted for the current year fair value depreciation

- The opening and closing net assets should be adjusted for the fair value adjustment less accumulated depreciation at that point in time.

Example 4 below demonstrates how the fair value adjustment would affect the exchange difference calculation.

Example 2

In Example 1, P acquired 75% of the share capital of S on 1 January 20X5 for Fr 500,000, when the reserves of S were Fr 120,000. S's total share capital was Fr 250,000 and the reserves at the current reporting date of 31 December 20X6 were Fr 350,000. The fair value of the NCI at the date of acquisition was Fr 160,000 and it was group policy to measure NCI at fair value at acquisition.

S's total comprehensive income for the year ended 31 December 20X6 was Fr 60,000.

Relevant exchange rates were as follows:

1 January 20X5 $1 = 5Fr

31 December 20X5 $1 = 4.2Fr

31 December 20X6 $1 = 4.5Fr

Average for the year ended 31 December 20X5 $1 = 4.6Fr

Average for the year ended 31 December 20X6 $1 = 4.4Fr

Let's now assume that, at the date of acquisition, the fair value of S's net assets equalled carrying amount with the exception of an item of plant whose fair value exceeded carrying amount by Fr 200,000. The plant had a remaining useful life at the date of acquisition of 10 years.

The carrying amounts of property, plant and equipment of P and S at 31 December 20X6 were $1,250,000 and Fr 850,000 respectively.

In a change to the scenario in Example 1, let's also assume that goodwill has not been impaired.

Required:

Calculate the following amounts that would appear in the consolidated financial statements of the P group for the year ended 31 December 20X6 (work to the nearest $):

1   Carrying amount of property, plant and equipment at 31 December 20X6

2   Total exchange difference arising on translation of S that would be recognised in other comprehensive income for the year.

Example 2 answer

Requirement 1 answer

Carrying amount of property, plant and equipment at 31 December 20X6 = $1,474,000

	$000
PPE	
(1,250 + 224 **(W1)**)	1,474

Requirement 1 technique

In Example 1, the first step was to translate the financial statements of S. If there is a fair value adjustment then this can be built into this translation.

(W1) Translation of S's net assets at 31 December 20X6

Using closing rate of 4.5	$000
Non-current assets (850 + 200 FV – 40 dep)/4.5	224
(Note: FV depreciation = 200 × 2/10)	

To answer the first requirement, add the translated non-current assets of S to the parent's property, plant and equipment.

Requirement 2 answer

Total exchange difference for year = $12,000 loss

Exchange difference in OCI:

	$000
Exchange loss on goodwill **(W2)**	(1)
Exchange loss on net assets **(W3)**	(11)
Total exchange loss for the year	(12)

Requirement 2 technique

To calculate the exchange difference for the year, perform the goodwill calculation and consider the movement on net assets for the year.

(W2) Goodwill

	Fr000
Fair value of Ps investment	500
NCI at fair value	160
Fair value of sub's net assets at acquisition	
(250 + 120 + 200 FV)	(570)
Goodwill at acquisition and reporting date	
(no impairment)	90

Translation of goodwill:

	$000
At acquisition date (90/5)	18
Exchange difference y/e 31 Dec 05 (balancing figure)	3
At 31 Dec 05 (90/4.2)	21
Exchange difference y/e 31 Dec 06 (balancing figure)	(1)
At 31 Dec 06 (90/4.5)	20

The fair value adjustments are then built into the calculation of the foreign currency gain or loss from translation of S's net assets. The fair value adjustment less cumulative depreciation is added to the closing net assets and the current year fair value depreciation is deducted from S's total comprehensive income for the year.

(W3) Net assets

	Fr000	Rate	$000
Opening net assets (Closing less CI for year)	720	4.2	171
Comprehensive income for year (60 – 20 FV dep'n)	40	4.4	9
Exchange difference (bal fig)			(11)
Closing net assets (250 + 350 + 200 – 40)	760	4.5	169
(SC + reserves + FV adjustment)			

Requirement 2 can now be answered.

6 Foreign subsidiaries: key examinable issues

Assessment questions are likely to focus on the calculation and accounting treatment of the exchange differences. Candidates are also commonly tested on the impact of translation on individual figures from the consolidated statement of profit or loss and other comprehensive income and statement of financial position.

The key things to remember are:

- Profit or loss and other comprehensive income items are translated at **average rate** each year.

- Assets and liabilities are translated at **closing rate** each year.

- Exchange differences arising on the retranslation of the subsidiary (on net assets and goodwill) are recognised **within other comprehensive income**.

- The exchange difference on net assets is attributed between parent shareholders and NCI based on their percentage holdings.

- The exchange difference on goodwill will be attributed as follows:

  - All to parent shareholders, if NCI is measured using proportion of net assets method

  - Between parent shareholders and NCI (based on their percentage holdings) if the NCI is measured using the fair value method

  - Note that this is consistent with the treatment of goodwill impairment.

Test your understanding 2 (OTQ style)

Upper acquired 85% of the equity shares of Lower, an entity whose functional and presentation currency is the Dinar (D), on 1 January 20X1 for cash consideration of D750,000. The carrying amount of the net assets of Lower at the date of acquisition were D500,000 and this equated to fair value with the exception of an item of plant whose fair value was D120,000 higher than carrying amount. The asset had a remaining useful life of 5 years at the date of acquisition and depreciation is charged on a straight line basis.

It is group policy to measure non-controlling interest at fair value at the date of acquisition and the fair value of the non-controlling interest in Lower on 1 January 20X1 was D150,000.

At the 31 December 20X4, the carrying amounts of Upper's and Lower's property, plant and equipment were $950,000 and D440,000 respectively. The carrying amount of Lower's net assets at 31 December 20X4 was D620,000 and its total comprehensive income for the year ended 31 December 20X4 was D75,000.

Goodwill is tested for impairment annually but none was considered to have arisen as at 31 December 20X4.

The Upper group's presentation currency is the $.

Relevant exchange rates are:

Date	D to $1
1 January 20X1	7.8
31 December 20X3	9.0
31 December 20X4	8.2
Average rate for year ended 31 December 20X4	8.6

Required:

Calculate the property, plant and equipment figure of the Upper group for the year ended 31 December 20X4.

State your answer to the nearest $.

Test your understanding 3 (Data set OTQ style)

Required:

Using the information from the previous TYU for Upper group, calculate the goodwill of Lower as shown within the Upper group consolidated statement of financial position as at 31st December 20X4.

State your answer to the nearest $.

Test your understanding 4 (Data set OTQ style)

Required:

Using the information from the previous TYUs for Upper group, calculate the total exchange difference arising on the translation of Lower that would be presented in other comprehensive income for the year ended 31st December 20X4.

State your answer to the nearest $.

Test your understanding 5 (Data set OTQ style)

HB presents its consolidated financial statements in $. HB has one subsidiary FA which uses £ as its functional currency. FA is not wholly owned. FA was acquired on 1 January 20X1 at a cost of £3,800,000. The fair value of the net assets of FA at the acquisition date was £2,000,000. The goodwill of FA has been calculated using the FV method. The FV of non-controlling interest as at the acquisition date was £400,000. There has been no impairment of FA's goodwill.

Relevant exchange rates are

1 Jan 20X1 $1/£2.0

31 Dec 20X1 $1 /£2.5

Average rate for the year ended 31 Dec 20X1 $1/£2.25

31 Dec 20X2 $1/£1.5

Average rate for the year ended 31 Dec 20X2 $1/£1.75

Required:

What is the value of goodwill of FA as shown on the consolidated statement of financial position for the year ended 31 Dec 20X2 (to the nearest $)?

A   880,000

B   977,778

C   1,100,000

D   1,466,667

Test your understanding 6 (Data set OTQ style)

Required:

Using the information from the previous TYU for the HB group, what is the annual foreign currency gain or loss on translation of goodwill recorded in other comprehensive income for the year ended 31 Dec 20X2? Figures in brackets denote a loss.

A   ($366,667)

B $366,667

C   ($586,667)

D $586,667

Test your understanding 7 (Data set OTQ style)

Required:

Using the information from the previous TYU for the HB group, which one of the following statements is incorrect?

A   The annual foreign currency gain or loss on the translation of FA's net assets should be shown in other comprehensive income

B   FA's functional currency is £'s therefore FA's head office is based in a country which uses £'s

C   FA's NCI's will be allocated a share of the annual foreign currency gain or loss from translating FA's goodwill

D   FA's statement of financial position is translated at the closing rate and the consolidated statement of profit or loss is translated using the average rate

Test your understanding 8 (Foreign consolidation OTQ style)

1   IAS 21 provides guidance on how to account for foreign currency transactions and subsidiaries.

Which of the following statements are TRUE? Select all that apply.

A   The functional currency is the currency in which an entity must present its financial statements.

B   Subsidiaries must present their financial statements in the presentation currency of their parent.

C   When determining functional currency, entities should select the currency in which the majority of its purchases are made.

D   When translating a foreign subsidiary, the exchange difference should be recognised as other comprehensive income.

E   The presentation currency is decided by the directors.

2   P owns 80% of the equity share capital of its foreign subsidiary F. F prepares financial statements in groats. Both entities have a reporting date of 31 March. At 1 April 20X3, the net assets of F were 20 million groats. The total comprehensive income of F for the year ended 31 March 20X4 was 2,200,000 groats. F does not pay dividends and goodwill was fully written off prior to 31 March 20X3. The presentation currency of P is the dollar, $.

Relevant exchange rates are:

Date	Groats to $1
31 March 20X3	2.5
31 March 20X4	2.0
Average rate for year ended 31 March 20X4	2.2

Calculate the group exchange gain or loss arising from translating the foreign subsidiary F for the year ended 31 March 20X4 (state your answer to the nearest $).

3   North acquired 75% of the equity shares of South on 1 October 20X1 for Fr180,000. The carrying amount of the net assets of South at the date of acquisition was Fr98,000 and this was considered to be the same as fair value.

It is group policy to measure non-controlling interest at fair value at the date of acquisition and the fair value of the non-controlling interest in South on 1 October 20X1 was Fr45,000.

Goodwill is tested for impairment annually. There was no impairment in the year ended 30 September 20X2, however goodwill was considered to have been impaired by 20% in the year ended 30 September 20X3. The impairment was translated at average rate for inclusion in the statement of consolidated profit or loss.

The North group's presentation currency is the $.

Exchange rates are:

Date	Fr to $1
1 October 20X1	3.0
30 September 20X2	2.7
30 September 20X3	2.4
Average rate for year ended 30 September 20X3	2.5

Calculate the exchange gain or loss on the translation of goodwill in the year ended 30 September 20X3 that would be recognised in other comprehensive income. Give your answer to the nearest $.

4   **Complete the sentences below by placing one of the options in each of the spaces (you may need to use the same option more than once).**

When a foreign operation is included in a consolidated set of financial statements, the assets and liabilities of the operation will be translated at _____ rate in the statement of financial position and the income and expenses will be translated at _____ rate in the consolidated statement of profit or loss and other comprehensive income.

An exchange difference arises on net assets and goodwill and this should be recognised each year in the statement of _____.

The exchange difference is calculated by translating the opening position at the _____ rate, the closing position at the _____ rate and any movements in the year (typically) at the _____ rate.

Options:

acquisition; average; closing; opening; other comprehensive income; profit or loss

5   Yorkshire holds an 80% holding in Humber, an overseas entity. The Yorkshire group's presentation currency is $ and Humber's functional currency is the Groat (Gr). The carrying amount of property, plant and equipment (PPE) in Yorkshire's statement of financial position at the reporting date is $1,700,000. Humber's PPE at the same date has a carrying amount of Gr 800,000.

Yorkshire acquired Humber 3 years ago and, at the date of acquisition, the fair value of Humber's PPE exceeded carrying amount by Gr 250,000. The PPE had a remaining useful life at this date of 10 years.

Humber is the only subsidiary in the Yorkshire group.

Exchange rates are:

Date	Gr to $1
Acquisition (3 years ago)	7.5
Reporting date	6.2
Average rate for year	6.4

Calculate the carrying amount of property, plant and equipment of the Yorkshire Group at the reporting date. Give your answer to the nearest $.

7 Chapter summary

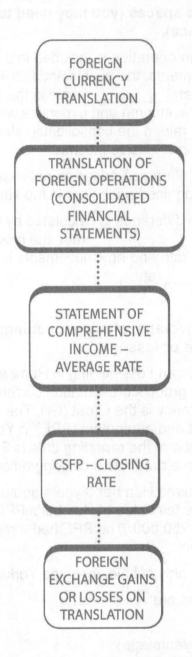

FOREIGN
CURRENCY
TRANSLATION

TRANSLATION OF
FOREIGN OPERATIONS
(CONSOLIDATED
FINANCIAL
STATEMENTS)

STATEMENT OF
COMPREHENSIVE
INCOME –
AVERAGE RATE

CSFP – CLOSING
RATE

FOREIGN
EXCHANGE GAINS
OR LOSSES ON
TRANSLATION

Test your understanding answers

 Test your understanding 1 (Further practice integration question)

Consolidated statement of financial position at 31 December 20X8

	$
Goodwill **(W3)**	2,750
Non-current assets (60,000 + (25,000/2))	72,500
Current assets (35,800 + (15,000/2))	43,300
	118,550
Equity	
Share capital	50,000
Reserves **(W5)**	29,720
	79,720
Non-controlling interests **(W4)**	3,330
Current liabilities (30,000 + (11,000/2))	35,500
	118,550

Consolidated statement of profit or loss and other comprehensive income for the year ended 31 December 20X8

	$
Revenue (25,000 + (10,000/2.5))	29,000
Operating expenses (10,000 + (4,000/2.5) + 400 **(W3)**)	(12,000)
Profit from operations	17,000
Finance costs (5,000 + (1,500/2.5))	(5,600)
Profit before tax	11,400
Tax (3,000 + (1,000/2.5))	(3,400)
Profit for the year	8,000

Other comprehensive income

Items that may be reclassified subsequently to profit or loss:

Foreign exchange gains **(W7)**	5,583
Total comprehensive income	13,583

Profit attributable to:

Parent shareholders (balance)	7,800
NCI shareholders **(W6)**	200
	8,000

Total comprehensive income attributable to:

Parent shareholders (balance)	12,266
NCI shareholders (200 + (5,583 **(W7)** × 20%)	1,317
	13,583

Workings

(W1) Group structure

Paul

80% | 2 years ago

Simon

(W2) Net assets of subsidiary

	Acquisition date	Reporting date
	Fr	Fr
Share capital	15,000	15,000
Retained earnings	4,000	14,000
	19,000	29,000
Translation	Acq'n rate = 5	Closing rate = 2
Translated net asset ($000)	3,800	14,500
Post-acq'n reserves (incl. exchange diff)	10,700	

(W3) Goodwill

	Fr
Fair value of P's investment	21,000
NCI at fair value	4,500
Fair value of sub's net assets at acquisition **(W2)**	(19,000)
Goodwill at acquisition/start of the year	6,500
Impairment	(1,000)
Goodwill at reporting date	5,500

Translation of goodwill:

	$
At acquisition (6,500/5)	1,300
Exchange difference prior to current year (bal fig)	867
Opening goodwill at opening rate (6,500/3)	2,167
Impairment in current year at average rate (1,000/2.5)	(400)
Exchange difference current year (bal fig)	983
Goodwill at reporting date (5,500/2)	2,750

(W4) Non-controlling interests

	$
NCI at acquisition (4,500/5)	900
NCI% × post acquisition reserves (20% × 10,700 **(W2)**)	2,140
NCI% × impairment (20% × 400)	(80)
NCI% × exchange diff on goodwill (20% × (867 + 983) **(W3)**)	370
	3,330

(W5) Reserves

	$
Paul	20,000
Simon: (80% × 10,700 **(W2)**)	8,560
Impairment (80% × 400)	(320)
Exchange difference on goodwill (80% × (867 + 983) **(W3)**)	1,480
	29,720

(W6) NCI share of profits

	Fr
S's profit for the year	3,500
Impairment (fair value method)	(1,000)
NCI share of profits (Fr)	2,500
× 20%	500
Translated at average rate (500 @ 2.5)	$200

(W7) Foreign exchange difference for OCI

	$
Closing net assets at closing rate **(W2)**	14,500
Less opening net assets at opening rate (29,000 – 3,500)/3	(8,500)
Less comprehensive income for the year at average rate (3,500/2.5)	(1,400)
Exchange difference on net assets	4,600
Exchange difference on goodwill **(W3)**	983
Total exchange difference for the year	5,583

Test your understanding 2 (OTQ style)

Property, plant and equipment

	$
Upper	950,000
Lower (440,000 + 120,000(FV) – 96,000 (below))/8.2	56,585
Carrying amount of consolidated PPE	1,006,585

Working – FV depreciation

	D
FV depreciation (120,000 × 4/5)	96,000

Test your understanding 3 (OTQ style)

Goodwill as at 31 December 20X4 = $34,146.

Goodwill

	D
Fair value of Upper's investment	750,000
NCI at fair value at acquisition	150,000
Fair value of Lower's net assets at acquisition (500,000 + 120,000)	(620,000)
Goodwill at acquisition and reporting date (no impairment)	280,000

Translated at the closing rate of 8.2D/$1 = 280,000/8.2 = $34,146

Test your understanding 4 (OTQ style)

Total exchange difference for year (for OCI)

	$
Exchange difference on net assets **(W1)**	6,718
Exchange difference on goodwill **(W2)**	3,035
Total exchange gain for the year	9,753

(W1) Net assets

	D	Rate	$
Closing net assets (620,000 + 120,000 – 96,000) (Net assets + FV adj – FV dep of 120 × 4/5)	644,000	8.2	78,537
Less Opening net assets (Closing less CI for year)	593,000	9.0	(65,889)
Comprehensive income for year (75,000 – 24,000 FV dep)	51,000	8.6	(5,930)
Exchange difference (bal fig)			6,718

(W2) Goodwill translation

	$
At closing rate (280,000/8.2)	34,146
At opening rate (280,000/9.0)	31,111
Exchange gain for year	3,035

Test your understanding 5 (OTQ style)

D $1,466,667

	£
Cost of investment	3,800,000
NCI at acquisition	400,000
All FA's net assets ay acquisition	(2,000,000)
	2,200,000

FA's goodwill will be translated at the closing rate for inclusion within the consolidated statement of financial position of HB group as at the year ended 31 Dec 20X2. The closing rate is $1/£1.5.

Goodwill = $1,466,667 (2,200,000/1.5)

Test your understanding 6 (OTQ style)

D $586,667

Annual forex gain from translating FA's goodwill

		$
Goodwill at closing rate	£2,200,000/1.5	1,466,667
Goodwill at opening rate	£2,200,000/2.5	(880,000)
		586,667

Test your understanding 7 (OTQ style)

B – FA's functional currency is £'s therefore FA's head office is based in a country which uses £'s

The location of an entity's head office is not a factor in determining the functional currency of an entity. Factors that are considered when determining functional currency are:

- The currency that mainly influences sales prices for goods and services

- The currency of the country whose competitive forces and regulations mainly determine the sales prices of goods and services

- The currency that mainly influences labour, material and other costs of providing goods and services.

NB. FA's goodwill has been calculated using the fair value method. Therefore, any share of the gain or loss on translation will be allocated between the parent and the NCI.

If the goodwill was calculated using the proportionate method, the exchange gain or loss relates to the parent only. There is no need to allocate any to NCI's.

Test your understanding 8 (Foreign consolidation OTQ style)

1   **D and E are the true statements.**

A is incorrect. An entity can choose a presentation currency that differs to its functional currency.

B is incorrect. Subsidiaries may choose to present their financial statements in the presentation currency of the parent (and may be under pressure to do so) but there is no regulatory requirement to do so.

C is incorrect. When determining functional currency, the currency that mainly influences sales prices and the currency that mainly influences labour, material and other costs should be considered. Costs are not given preference over sales prices.

2   **Exchange difference = $2,100,000**

	$000
Closing net assets at closing rate (20m + 2.2m)/2.0	11,100
Less opening net assets at opening rate 20m/2.5	(8,000)
Less comprehensive income for the year at average rate 2.2m/2.2	(1,000)
Exchange difference on net assets	2,100
No exchange difference on goodwill as fully written off	–
Total exchange difference for the year	2,100

3   **Exchange gain on goodwill for year ended 30 September 20X3 = $5,456**

	Fr
Fair value of parent's investment	180,000
NCI at fair value at acquisition	45,000
Less fair value of net assets at acquisition	(98,000)
Goodwill at acquisition/start of the year	127,000
Impairment (20% × 127,000)	(25,400)
Goodwill at reporting date	101,600

Translation of goodwill:	$
Opening goodwill at opening rate (127,000/2.7)	47,037
Impairment in current year at average rate (25,400/2.5)	(10,160)
Exchange difference current year (bal fig)	5,456
Goodwill at reporting date (101,600/2.4)	42,333

4   When a foreign operation is included in a consolidated set of financial statements, the assets and liabilities of the operation will be translated at **closing** rate in the statement of financial position and the income and expenses will be translated at **average** rate in the consolidated statement of profit or loss and other comprehensive income.

An exchange difference arises on net assets and goodwill and this should be recognised each year in the statement of **other comprehensive income**.

The exchange difference is calculated by translating the opening position at the **opening** rate, the closing position at the **closing** rate and any movements in the year (typically) at the **average** rate.

5   **Property, plant and equipment = $1,857,258**

Property, plant and equipment

	$
Yorkshire	1,700,000
Humber (800,000 + 250,000 (FV) – 75,000 (below))/6.2	157,258
Carrying amount of consolidated PPE	1,857,258

Working – FV depreciation

	Gr
FV depreciation (250,000 × 3/10)	75,000

Related party disclosures

Chapter learning objectives

Lead outcome	Component outcome
C2: Discuss additional disclosure issues related to the group accounts	Discuss disclosure requirements related to: (a) Transactions between related parties

1   Session content

DEFINITION OF A
RELATED PARTY

THE NEED FOR
DISCLOSURE OF
RELATED PARTIES

DISCLOSURE
OF RELATED
PARTIES

2   Introduction

Related party relationships are a normal feature of business.

The existence of a related party relationship and transactions with related parties may affect the profit or loss of an entity. It is important for users to be aware of related parties and any transactions that have occurred in the period.

3   IAS 24 Related Party Disclosures

 A related party is **'a person or entity that is related to the entity that is preparing its financial statements (the reporting entity)'** (IAS 24, para 9).

A relationship typically exists if control, joint control, common control or significant influence exists between the party and the reporting entity.

Typical related parties are:

*   Key management personnel

*   Close family members of key management personnel

*   Entities that are members of the same group (including parent, subsidiaries, associates and joint ventures).

Note however that the following are normally considered **not** to be related parties:

- **'two entities simply because they have a director/member of key management personnel in common**

- **two joint venturers simply because they share joint control of a joint venture**

- **providers of finance**

- **key customers and suppliers'** (IAS 24, para11).

Key management personnel

 Key management personnel are **'those persons having authority and responsibility for planning, directing and controlling the activities of the entity, directly or indirectly, including any director (whether executive or otherwise) of that entity'** (IAS 24, para 9).

Close family members

 'Close members of the family of a person are those family members who may be expected to influence, or be influenced by, that person in their dealings with the entity.

They would include:

- **children**

- **spouse or domestic partner**

- **children, and other dependents, of spouse or domestic partner'** (IAS 24, para 9).

 Related parties – the detail

'A person or close member of that person's family is related to a reporting entity if that person:

- **has control or joint control over the reporting entity**

- **has significant influence over the reporting entity**

- **is a member of the key management personnel of the reporting entity or of a parent of the reporting entity'** (IAS 24, para 9).

'An entity is related to a reporting entity if any of the following conditions applies:

- **The entity and the reporting entity are members of the same group**

- **One entity is an associate or joint venture of the other entity**

- Both entities are joint ventures of the same third party
- One entity is a joint venture of a third entity and the other entity is an associate of the third entity
- The entity is a post-employment benefit plan for the benefit of employees of either the reporting entity or an entity related to the reporting entity
- The entity is controlled or jointly controlled by a person identified as a related party to the reporting entity
- A person identified as a related party of the reporting entity has significant influence over the entity or is a member of the key management personnel of the entity' (IAS 24, para 9)

Related parties – exclusions from definition

'In the context of this standard, the following are not necessarily related parties:

(a) two entities simply because they have a director or other member of key management personnel in common, notwithstanding the above definition of 'related party'

(b) two venturers simply because they share joint control over a joint venture

(c) providers of finance

(d) trade unions

(e) public utilities

(f) government departments and agencies, simply by virtue of their normal dealings with an entity (even though they may affect the freedom of action of an entity or participate in its decision-making process)

(g) a customer, supplier, franchisor, distributor or general agent with whom an entity transacts a significant volume of business, merely by virtue of the resulting economic dependence' (IAS 24, para 11).

4   Disclosure requirements

 A related party transaction is **'a transfer of resources, services or obligations between a reporting entity and a related party, regardless of whether a price is charged'** (IAS 24, para 9).

'Where there have been transactions between the entity and a related party, the entity is required to disclose:

- **The nature of the related party relationship**

- **The nature of the transaction**

- **The amount of the transaction**

- **Any outstanding balance relating to the transaction**

- **Any provisions for doubtful debts remaining to the amount of any outstanding balance'** (IAS 24, para 18).

 Disclosure requirements

The standard concerns the disclosure of related party transactions in order to make readers of financial statements aware of the position and to ensure that the financial statements show a true and fair view.

If there have been transactions between related parties, an entity shall disclose the nature of the related party relationship as well as information about the transactions and outstanding balances necessary for an understanding of the potential effect of the relationship on the financial statements.

In certain circumstances, the existence of a related party should be disclosed, regardless of whether or not there have been any transactions.

Disclosures that related party transactions were made on terms equivalent to those that prevail in arm's length transactions are made only if such terms can be substantiated.

'At a minimum, disclosures shall include:

- **the amount of the transactions**

- **the amount of outstanding balances: their terms and conditions, including whether they are secured, and the nature of the consideration to be provided in settlement and details of any guarantees given or received**

- **provisions for doubtful debts related to the amount of outstanding balances**

- **the expense recognised during the period in respect of bad or doubtful debts due from related parties'** (IAS 24, para 18).

In addition, IAS 24 requires an entity to disclose **'key management personnel compensation in total and for each of the following categories:**

- **short-term employee benefits**
- **post-employment benefits**
- **other long-term benefits**
- **termination benefits**
- **equity compensation benefits'** (IAS 24, para 17).

Examples of related parties

Examples of related party transactions would be:

- **'Purchases/sales of goods (even if no price is charged)**
- **Purchases/sales of property or other assets**
- **Rendering/receipt of services**
- **Leasing arrangements**
- **Management contracts**
- **Finance arrangements, e.g. loan guarantee'** (IAS 24, para 21).

Example 1

You decide to set up a business in an office block offering training facilities. Your brother is the owner of the building and, in order to help you start your business, he agrees to give you your office with no charge for a four-year period.

After three successful years of business, your student numbers have doubled and you decide to take early retirement and sell your business.

Your business is put up for sale.

Explain what information should be disclosed in the accounts regarding this transaction and why it is important to do this.

Example 1 answer

You must disclose:

- the nature of the related party transaction, i.e. rental of premises

- the related party, i.e. your brother owns the building

- the amount of the transaction, i.e. the fact that you have use of the premises rent free and how much rent you are saving (based on the 'market rate' for the rental of these premises).

This information is important for a prospective buyer of the business because they will need to be aware of these facts when they look at the profits for the business. If you did not disclose this matter, the prospective buyer would think they could make similar profits if they purchased the business. Although the profit figures are correct, they are distorted by the fact that the new owners would incur a rent charge for that building, hence the profits would reduce, assuming all things remain the same.

Test your understanding 1 (case style)

CB is an entity specialising in importing a wide range of non-food items and selling them to retailers. George is CB's founder and chief executive. He owns 40% of CB's equity shares:

- CB's largest customer, XC accounts for 35% of CB's revenue. XC has just completed negotiations with CB for a special 5% discount on all sales.

- During the accounting period, George purchased a property from CB for $500,000. CB had previously declared the property surplus to its requirements and had valued it at $750,000.

- George's daughter, Mariana, is a director in a financial institution, FC. During the accounting period, FC advanced $2 million to CB as an unsecured loan at a favourable rate of interest.

Required:

You are an accountant working for CB and you have been asked by the Financial Director to prepare a briefing note, to be presented at the next Board of Directors meeting, explaining the extent to which the above transactions should be classified and disclosed in CB's financial statements in accordance with IAS 24 *Related Party Disclosures*.

The Finance Director tells you that the Board are not interested in the generic rules of IAS 24. They just want to know about any disclosure requirements for the specific transactions mentioned above.

He also let you know that George is particularly keen to avoid disclosing his purchase of the property and believes he shouldn't have to as the property is not required by the business anymore. He is happy however for the bank loan to be disclosed as he believes shareholders will be pleased that a favourable rate of interest has been achieved.

Test your understanding 2 (OTQ style questions)

1   **Which of the following would be regarded as a related party of entity RP?**

    Select all that apply.

    C, a key customer of RP

    P, the direct parent entity of RP

    UP, the parent of P and the ultimate parent of the group in which RP is consolidated

    Mr D, a director of P

    Mrs D, the wife of Mr D, a director of P

    O, an entity that is not part of the UP group but of which Mr D is also a director

2   **Which of the following are not related parties of the reporting entity RP in accordance with IAS 24?**

    Select all that apply.

    S, who supplies approximately 75% of the goods purchased by RP

    V, a joint venture in which RP can exercise joint control

    J, the other party that shares joint control of V with RP

    MS, a member of key management personnel of RP

    MS2, an entity in which MS is also a member of key management personnel

    B, the main finance provider of RP

5   Chapter summary

IAS24 Related party disclosures

The need for disclosure of related parties
• Users need to be aware of related party relationships
  – Users need to know which transactions have not
    been made at arm's length

Disclosure of related parties
• Parent/subsidiary relationships
• Disclosure of transactions and balances
• Key management compensation

Test your understanding answers

Test your understanding 1 (case style)

Briefing note on compliance with IAS 24 Related Party Disclosures

As requested, I've explained the requirements of IAS 24 with respect to each of the transactions identified.

Discount awarded to largest customer

According to IAS 24, a customer with whom an entity transacts a significant volume of business is not a related party merely by virtue of the resulting economic dependence. Therefore, XC is not a related party and the negotiated discount does not need to be disclosed.

Purchase of property

A party is related to an entity if it has an interest that gives it significant influence over the entity. A party is also related to an entity if he/she is a member of the key management personnel of the entity.

George satisfies both of these definitions. His 40% holding demonstrates the ability to exert significant influence and his chief executive role clearly makes him a member of key management personnel.

Therefore, the sale of the property for $500,000 must be disclosed as a related party transaction and its valuation should also be disclosed so that users of the financial statements can understand the impact that the transaction has on the financial statements.

Even if the transaction was at market value, it should still be disclosed. There is no option to avoid disclosure in these circumstances.

Bank loan with favourable interest rate

Providers of finance are not related parties simply because of their normal dealings with the entity. However, if a party is a close member of the family of any individual categorised as a related party, they are also a related party. As Mariana is George's daughter and George is a related party, Mariana is also a related party. The loan from FC will need to be disclosed along with the details of Mariana and his involvement in the arrangements.

Test your understanding 2 (OTQ style questions)

1   **The related parties of RP are: P, UP, Mr D and Mrs D**

Key customers (C) and an entity that shares a director in common (O) are specified by IAS 24 as not being related parties.

All of the other parties above are mentioned in the definition of a related party.

2   **The parties that are not related to RP are: S, J, MS2 and B**

Key suppliers (S), joint venturers who share control of a joint venture (J), an entity that has a member of key management personnel in common (MS2) and providers of finance (B) are specified by IAS 24 as not being related parties.

Joint ventures (V) and a person who has control or significant influence over the entity (MS) are included in the definition of a related party.

Integrated reporting

Chapter learning objectives

Lead outcome	Component outcome
D1: Discuss the Integrated Reporting <IR> Framework	(a) Describe the role of the International Integrated Reporting Council (IIRC)
	(b) Explain integrated thinking
	(c) Discuss the international <IR> framework
D2: Explain the Six Capitals of integrated reporting	Explain the measurement and disclosure issues of:
	(a) Financial Capital
	(b) Manufactured Capital
	(c) Intellectual Capital
	(d) Human Capital
	(e) Social and Relationship Capital
	(f) Natural Capital

1 Overview of chapter

2 Financial and non-financial reporting

This chapter covers syllabus area F2D Integrated reporting. This makes up 10% of the syllabus. Integrated reporting was covered briefly within F1 and will be significantly expanded upon at strategic level within F3.

Financial reporting

According to the International Accounting Standards Board's (IASB's) conceptual framework, the objective of financial reporting is to **'provide information about the reporting entity that is useful to existing and potential investors, lenders and other creditors in making decisions about providing resources to the entity' (Framework, para 1.2)**

Financial statements provide historic financial information, but they do not provide a full picture of a business' operations, performance and value.

Non-financial reporting

To help users make decisions, it may be helpful to provide information relating to other aspects of an entity's performance found outside of the scope of the traditional financial statements, such as:

- how the business is managed;
- its future prospects;

- the entity's policy on the environment;

- its attitude towards social responsibility etc.

There has been increasing pressure for entities to provide important non-financial information in their annual reports. It can be argued that the disclosure of non-financial data can be just as, if not even more, valuable to users' decision making than the financially driven focus of the accounts.

Following the onset of the banking crisis in 2007, created by an apparent dependence on short term financial factors rather than focussing on benefits formed from other forms of capital over longer timescales, it was felt that a paradigm shift in reporting priorities was required.

Financial statements have traditionally only reported the financial capitals of companies in detail, and have not presented detailed information on the non-financial capital base.

This type of corporate reporting no longer fully reflects the needs of users of accounting information in the 21st century.

The International Integrated Reporting Council (IIRC) has produced a revolutionary framework known as the Integrated Reporting framework (<IR> framework). The <IR> approach proposes a fundamental change to the way that entities are managed and report to stakeholders.

3 Introduction to integrated reporting <IR>

What is integrated reporting?

Integrated reporting is the process of producing an integrated report.

An integrated report should be a single document which is the organisation's primary report – in most jurisdictions, the equivalent of the Annual Report.

Typically, the integrated report will be prepared on an annual basis. Integrated reporting is mostly voluntary but certain jurisdictions have made integrated reports mandatory (e.g. South Africa, Brazil).

The primary purpose of an integrated report is to explain to providers of financial capital how an entity creates value over time.

Integrated reporting <IR> demonstrates the linkages between an organisation's strategy, governance and financial performance and the social, environmental and economic context within which the entity operates.

By reinforcing these connections, integrated reporting can help business to take more sustainable decisions and enable investors and other stakeholders to understand how an organisation is really performing.

It is important to note that the integrated report does not replace need to produce the financial statements but discloses further detail alongside the annual report.

Integrated thinking

Integrated thinking is defined within the <IR> framework as **'the active consideration by an organisation of the relationships between its various operating and functional units and the capitals that the organisation uses or affects.'** <IR> framework IIRC.

At the heart of <IR> is the growing realisation that a wide range of factors determine the value of an organisation – some of these are financial or tangible in nature and are easy to account for in financial statements (e.g. property, cash), while many, such as intellectual capital, competition and energy security, are not. The consideration of how both the financial and non-financial factors contribute to an entity's value is called integrated thinking.

Historically, significant emphasis has been placed on monitoring and assessing the financial value of businesses. Directors and shareholders use the financial statements to assess the entity's financial value. For example, financial capital (cash) can be invested in property, plant and equipment to improve efficiency and bottom line profitability.

Integrated thinking promotes the realisation that not all value held by the entity is created via such financially driven investment. Value is also created through staff well-being and motivation, through the intellectual property and skills of the entity's staff, from the natural surroundings and resources (land, water, minerals) within the proximity of the entity, from the reputation of the entity with stakeholders and the wider community and not just from making profits.

<IR> is needed by business and investors. Businesses need a reporting environment that is conducive to understanding and articulating their strategy, which helps to drive performance internally and attract financial capital for investment. Investors need to understand how the strategy being pursued creates value over time.

Each element of an Integrated Report should provide insights into an organisation's current and future performance.

Test your understanding 1 (OTQ style)

Which of the following best describes an example of 'integrated thinking'?

A   The annual preparation of the financial statements

B   Directors investing in on-site crèche and leisure facilities for use by staff

C   A strategic focus on improving financial performance through cost cutting of all unnecessary costs such as staff entertainment, charitable donations and local sponsorship

D   Overstating profits to ensure profit targets are met guaranteeing board bonus payments

4   International Integrated Reporting Council (IIRC)

Background

The International Integrated Reporting Council (IIRC) was formed in August 2010 and aims to establish integrated reporting as the norm within mainstream business practice.

The IIRC aims to create a globally accepted framework (<IR> framework) for a process that results in communications by an organisation about value creation over time.

The IIRC brings together a cross section of representatives from corporate, investment, accounting, securities, regulatory, academic and standard-setting sectors as well as civil society. This coalition is promoting the communication of value creation across industries as the next step in reporting for business.

The mission of the IIRC

The IIRC's mission is **to create the globally accepted International <IR> Framework** that elicits from organisations material information about their strategy, governance, performance and prospects in a clear, concise and comparable format.

The International <IR> Framework will underpin and accelerate the evolution of corporate reporting, reflecting developments in financial, governance, management commentary and sustainability reporting.

The IIRC will seek to secure the adoption of <IR> by report preparers and gain the recognition of standard setters and investors.

Objective of the IIRC

At the time of its formation, the IIRC's stated objective was to develop an internationally accepted integrated reporting framework by 2014 to create the foundations for a new reporting model to enable organisations to provide concise communications of how they create value over time.

After a consultation process, the IIRC published the first version of its 'International Integrated Reporting Framework' in December 2013.

Test your understanding 2 (OTQ style)

The role of the International Integrated Reporting Council is to:

A   enforce the adoption of integrated reporting by all companies by 2021

B   create the Integrated Reporting Framework from which the preparation of integrated reports will be based

C   approve, authorise and audit integrated reports prepared by all entities

D   develop ethical guidelines for accountants

5   The <IR> Framework

The <IR> Framework is intended as guidance for all businesses producing integrated reports.

The contents of the <IR> Framework can be accessed via the following link https://integratedreporting.org/resource/international-ir-framework/.

Its executive summary states 'It is anticipated that, over time, <IR> will become the corporate reporting norm. No longer will an organisation produce numerous, disconnected and static communications. **This will be delivered by the process of integrated thinking**, and the application of principles such as connectivity of information'.

The objective of the <IR> framework

- to establish guiding principles and content elements that govern the overall content of an integrated report

- to explain the fundamental concepts that underpin integrated reports.

The concept of integrated thinking

Integrated Reporting (<IR>) is seen by the IIRC as the basis for a fundamental change in the way in which entities are managed and report to stakeholders.

A stated aim of <IR> is to support integrated thinking and decision-making.

Integrated thinking is described in the <IR> Framework as **'the active consideration by an organisation of the relationships between its various operating and functional units and the capitals that the organisation uses or affects'.**

Purpose and objectives of integrated reporting

The <IR> Framework sets out the **purpose** of an integrated report as follows:

'The primary purpose of an integrated report is to explain to providers of financial capital how an entity creates value over time. An integrated report benefits all stakeholders interested in an entity's ability to create value over time, including employees, customers, suppliers, business partners, local communities, legislators, regulators, and policy-makers.'

The **objectives** for integrated reporting include:

- To improve the quality of information available to providers of financial capital to enable a more efficient and productive allocation of capital

- To provide a more cohesive and efficient approach to corporate reporting that draws on different reporting strands and communicates the full range of factors that materially affect the ability of an organisation to create value over time

- To enhance accountability and stewardship for the broad base of capitals (financial, manufactured, intellectual, human, social and relationship, and natural) and promote understanding of their interdependencies

- To support integrated thinking, decision-making and actions that focus on the creation of value over the short, medium and long term.

Fundamental concepts for <IR>

There are three fundamental concepts underpinning integrated reporting:

1   Value creation for the organisation and for others

Value created by an organisation over time manifests itself in increases, decreases or transformations of the capitals (see 3 below) caused by the organisation's business activities and outputs.

An organisation's activities, its interactions and relationships, its outputs and the outcomes for the various capitals it uses and affects, influence its ability to continue to draw on these capitals in a continuous cycle.

2   The value creation process

At the core of the value creation process is an entity's business model, which draws on various capitals and inputs, and by using the entity's business activities, creates outputs (products, services, by-products, waste) and outcomes (internal and external consequences for the capitals).

 Tutorial Note

An understanding of the way which the <IR> framework considers the two concepts above is not required in CIMA F2. Value creation is covered in more detail within P2 and business models contributing to value is considered within E2. The concepts will be explored further within strategic level. At this stage, candidates only need an awareness that the concepts exist.

 3   The capitals

The capitals are the resources and the relationships used and affected by the organisation.

They are identified in the <IR> Framework as:

- financial

- manufactured

- intellectual

- human

- social and relationship, and

- natural capital.

These categories of capital are not required to be adopted in preparing an entity's integrated report, and an integrated report may not cover all capitals – the focus is on capitals that are relevant to the entity.

The stock and flow of capitals

The capitals are stocks of value that are increased, decreased or transformed through the activities and outputs of the organisation. For example, an organisation's financial capital is increased when it makes a profit, and the quality of its human capital is improved when employees become better trained.

The overall stock of capitals is not fixed over time. There is a constant flow between and within the capitals as they are increased, decreased or transformed. For example, when an organisation improves its human capital through employee training, the related training costs reduce its financial capital. The effect is that financial capital has been transformed into human capital. Although this example is simple and presented only from the organisation's perspective, it demonstrates the continuous interaction and transformation between the capitals, albeit with varying rates and outcomes.

Many activities cause increases, decreases or transformations that are far more complex than the above example and involve a broader mix of capitals or of components within a capital (e.g. the use of water to grow crops that are fed to farm animals, all of which are components of natural capital).

Categories and descriptions of the capitals

For the purpose of the <IR> Framework, the capitals are categorised and described as follows:

- **Financial capital** – The pool of funds that is:
  - available to an organisation for use in the production of goods or the provision of services
  - obtained through financing, such as debt, equity or grants, or generated through operations or investments.

- **Manufactured capital** – Manufactured physical objects (as distinct from natural physical objects) that are available to an organisation for use in the production of goods or the provision of services, including:
  - buildings
  - equipment
  - infrastructure (such as roads, ports, bridges, and waste and water treatment plants)

  The objects contribute to the production process rather than being the actual output.

  Manufactured capital is often created by other organisations, but includes assets manufactured by the reporting organisation for sale or when they are retained for its own use.

- **Intellectual capital** – Organisational, knowledge-based intangibles, including:

  - intellectual property, such as patents, copyrights, software, rights and licences

  - 'organisational capital' such as tacit knowledge, systems, procedures and protocols

- **Human capital** – People's competencies, capabilities and experience, and their motivations to innovate, including their:

  - alignment with and support for an organisation's governance framework, risk management approach, and ethical values

  - ability to understand, develop and implement an organisation's strategy

  - loyalties and motivations for improving processes, goods and services, including their ability to lead, manage and collaborate

  Human capitals are needed for productive work. Enhancing human capital through education and training is central to a flourishing entity and wider economy.

- **Social and relationship capital** – The institutions and the relationships within and between communities, groups of stakeholders and other networks, and the ability to share information to enhance individual and collective well-being.

  Social and relationship capital includes:

  - shared norms, and common values and behaviours

  - key stakeholder relationships, and the trust and willingness to engage that an organisation has developed and strives to build and protect with external stakeholders

  - intangibles associated with the brand and reputation that an organisation has developed

  - an organisation's social licence to operate

- **Natural capital** – All renewable and non-renewable environmental resources and processes that provide goods or services that support the past, current or future prosperity of an organisation. It includes:

  - air, water, land, minerals and forests

  - bio-diversity and eco-system health.

  Natural capital within an entity will consider those factors that absorb, neutralise or recycle wastes and processes – e.g. climate regulation, climate change, CO_2 emissions.

6 Benefits and limitations

Benefits and limitations of integrated reporting

Benefits	Limitations
• Increase in the level of forward-looking information provided enabling more informed user decisions	• Potential for bias as reports are not required to be audited
• Disclosure of new previously undisclosed information increases users understanding	• Reluctance to disclose information for fear of losing competitive advantages
• Improved stakeholder reputation due to increased transparency	• May provide too much information for users to digest
• Integrated thinking may lead to improved efficiencies within organisations	

Benefits and limitations of the <IR> framework

Benefits	Limitations
• Provides guidance for preparers as to concepts and contents of the integrated report	• Principle based rather than rule based leads to increased subjectivity and potential bias
• Being principles based enables the application of the framework by entities operating in any industry	• Difficult to compare across different entities and sectors
• Increases user familiarity with the terminology and structure used within the <IR>	• Requires experienced staff to apply concepts properly

7 Examples of actual integrated reports

The IIRC website includes a section with examples of actual integrated reports published by a variety of companies across many sectors including BP, BAE Systems, Marks and Spencer, Fujitsu, HSBC and the Italian FA.

This database can be accessed here:

http://examples.integratedreporting.org/home

> **Test your understanding 3 (Objective test questions)**
>
> 1 **Which THREE of the following are objectives of integrated reporting, as identified by the International Integrated Reporting Council (IIRC)?**
>
>   A   To support integrated thinking and decision making
>
>   B   To communicate the impacts of economic, environmental and social and governance performance
>
>   C   To improve the quality of information available to providers of financial capital
>
>   D   To increase the quantity of information available to providers of financial capital
>
>   E   To provide a more cohesive and efficient approach to corporate reporting
>
> 2 The <IR> framework outlines 6 capitals that are used and affected by an organisation.
>
>   **Which of the following are identified by the <IR> framework as types of capital? Select all that apply**
>
>   A   Human
>
>   B   Animal
>
>   C   Social and relationship
>
>   D   Educational
>
>   E   Economic
>
> 3 **Which of the following organisations produced the <IR> framework?**
>
>   A   The International Accounting Standards Board
>
>   B   The Integrated Reporting Corporation
>
>   C   The Global Reporting Initiative
>
>   D   The International Integrated Reporting Council

4   Lucas Co is a well-established manufacturing company with operations in many countries. Its products have an excellent reputation.

In Lucas Co's Integrated Report, how would it present this information?

A   It would not disclose this information explicitly

B   As part of its disclosure of social and relationship capitals

C   As part of its disclosure of intellectual capitals

D   As part of its disclosure of manufactured capitals

5   **Which one of the following could be construed as a limitation of <IR>?**

A   increased integrated thinking

B   Competitors obtain improved levels of understanding regarding the entity

C   <IR> creates an over-emphasis on value creation and long-term prospects

D   <IR> requires disclosure of information regarding capitals not reflected within the financial statements

6   Banana Co is an entity operating at the luxury end of the technology sector. The business incurs a lot of research expenditure and has numerous patented innovations not shown as assets within their financial statements.

Based on the information provided, which of the following capitals would require significant disclosure within Banana's <IR>?

A   Intellectual

B   Manufacturing

C   Human

D   Financial

Test your understanding answers

Test your understanding 1 (OTQ style)

B

Investing in on-site crèche and leisure facilities for staff usage shows an entity valuing staff well-being which, in turn, will motivate staff. This will help the business to benefit from improved staff performance, loyalty and productivity. This indicates that the director's value their staff and not just financial performance, appreciating how business units will interact with appreciation of the capitals of the entity.

Preparing financial statements are a legal requirement so isn't an illustration of integrated thinking. Option A would not be appropriate.

Focussing on financial performance through cost cutting, particularly regarding costs relating to staff well-being and charitable donations, illustrates a lack of integrated thinking. The directors are oblivious to, or apathetic towards, the benefits of giving back to society and their staff. Option C would not be an appropriate example.

Deliberate manipulation of financial accounts to hit profit targets displays a proclivity towards self-interest. Option D does not illustrate integrated thinking.

Test your understanding 2 (OTQ style)

B

The role of the International Integrated Reporting Council is to create the Integrated Reporting Framework from which the preparation of integrated reports will be based.

Test your understanding 3 (Objective test question)

1   The answer is **A**, **C** and **E**.

     (B) is an objective of sustainability reporting but not <IR>

     (D) is irrelevant – investors are more interested in the quality, not the quantity, of information available.

2   The answers are **A** and **C**

3   **D**

     The IIRC produced the <IR> framework. IIRC stands for International Integrated Reporting Council.

4   **B**

     Social and relationship capitals include intangibles associated with the brand and reputation that an organisation has developed.

5   **B**

     Increased information given to competitors may create strategic disadvantages to the entity.

     The remaining options would be deemed benefits of integrated reporting.

6   **A**

     Intellectual capitals include organisational, knowledge-based intangibles and intellectual property, such as patents, copyrights, software, rights and licences.

Analysis of financial statements

Chapter learning objectives

Lead outcome	Component outcome
E1: Analyse financial statements of organisations	Analyse financial statements to provide insight on: (a) Performance (b) Position (c) Adaptability (d) Prospects
E2: Recommend actions based on insights from the interpretation of financial statements	(a) Recommend actions
E3: Discuss the limitations of the tools used for interpreting financial statements	Discuss (a) Data limitations (b) Limitations of ratio analysis

1 Session content

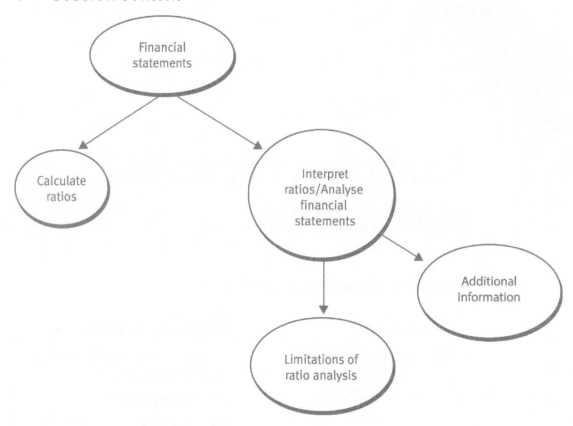

2 Introduction

Previous studies and chapters within this textbook focus on how to prepare the financial statements of an entity.

This chapter focusses on the skills required to analyse and interpret these financial statements. This is a separately defined syllabus area of F2, covering 25% of the examination.

Big data

One of the most striking and obvious changes arising in business during the digital age is the reliance upon, utilisation of and monetisation of data gathered by companies. Data relating to various stakeholders (e.g. customers, competitors, suppliers) is gathered by entities through their everyday operational interactions. Developments in hardware and software capabilities have led to the ability to store vast amounts of this data. This storage of data has coined the term '**Big data**'. The interpretation of this data is described as **data analytics**. Data analytics are of huge prevalence for corporations when striving to create and preserve value. The concepts of gathering data, big data and data analytics are further investigated in E2 and are revisited in strategic level papers.

With widespread technological developments enabling the accurate and easy collation of huge amounts of specific data, everyday life is becoming awash with the ability to analyse, interpret and conclude upon all sorts of different sources of data. The applications can be seen on a daily basis and affect all walks of life e.g:

– Improved analysis of sporting events e.g. distances covered, misplaced passes, number of fairways hit (or missed) in golf

– Political implications e.g. improved polling and approval assessments, targeted cyber-attacks and viral campaigns to create political instability

– Fitness and well-being data enabling monitoring of personal performance and targeted goal-setting

– Meteorology trends predicting behaviours in weather patterns.

– Tracking of coronavirus case numbers and death rates during the pandemic.

Corporations have been quick to take advantage of the new opportunities presented as a result of modern data analytics within their strategies for wealth and value creation e.g. targeted marketing campaigns using search engine results and trending social media topics to provide personalised consumer pop-ups and advertising.

Analysts often use analytical models to help with the process of making conclusions and in developing applications for the findings from their gathered data.

One such approach is the Gartner Data Analytics Maturity model.

Gartner Data Analytics Maturity model

The Gartner Data Analytics Maturity model groups data analytics into 4 separate stages. The stages outline the evolution of the use of data analytics by an entity. The stages are:

– Descriptive (what happened?)

– Diagnostic (why it happened?)

– Predictive (what is going to happen?)

– Prescriptive (how can we make it happen/prevent it happening?)

These stages enable analysts to improve the conclusions made, maturing from conclusions created with hindsight (within the descriptive and diagnostic stages), to providing insight about the potential future effects of the data (within the predictive stage) and cumulating in proactive decisions which focus upon applying foresight (within the prescriptive stage).

The financial statements include significant financial data regarding a particular entity. Data analytics can be used to help with the analysis of the financial statements and to improve user understanding of the content provided within them. The analysis of the financial statements forms the context as to how data analytics is relevant for CIMA F2.

The 4-step approach utilised by the Gartner Data Analytics Maturity model can be applied to analysing the financial statements. Before understanding how the Gartner model can be applied to financial statement analysis, the methods that underpin financial statement analysis must firstly be considered. The next sections investigate these areas at depth. Section 7 then includes examples that illustrate how the Gartner model can be applied to financial statement analysis.

Analysis of financial statements

The IASB®'s Conceptual Framework for Financial Reporting states:

'The objective of financial reporting is to provide financial information about the reporting entity that is useful to existing and potential investors, lenders and other creditors in making decisions about providing resources to the entity' *(IASB Conceptual Framework para 1.2).*

Interpretation and analysis of the financial statements is the process of arranging, examining and comparing the results in order that users are equipped to make such decisions.

Key areas to consider when performing an analysis of the financial statements are:

- identification of the user of the analysis

- an understanding of the nature of the business, industry and organisation

- identification of relevant sources of data for analysis

- numerical analysis of the data available

- interpretation of the results of the analysis.

3 Users of the analysis

It is important to identify the type of user for whom an analysis is being prepared, as different users have different needs. For any analysis exercise to be relevant and worthwhile, whether performed by a professional third party or internally within an organisation, it must be oriented towards the needs of the particular user who requires the analysis.

There is a wide range of user groups that may be interested in an entity's financial statements. Historically the financial statements have been prepared for investors. However, other users will also be interested in them.

Users of financial statements

Present and potential investors

Both present and potential investors are interested in information that is useful in making buy/sell/hold decisions. Will the entity be able to generate cash in the future? How risky is the investment? Does its financial performance exceed that of other potential investee entities? How much is the investment likely to yield in capital growth and/or dividend? Analysis of the financial statements can help to answer these questions.

Analysis of profits and liquidity will enable estimation of the likelihood of dividend pay-outs and future growth in share prices. Also, certain financial ratios are of particular interest to the investor group; most of which are out of the scope of the F2 examination (e.g. P/E, dividend yield). However, other more commonly used ratios, for instance, performance and asset management ratios like return on capital employed (ROCE), still supply information that is pertinent to the investors.

Lenders and potential lenders

Lenders are principally interested in assessing whether or not loans requested or provided, and any related interest, are likely to be repaid by the borrowers. Potential lenders require analysis of financial statements in order to assist them in deciding whether or not to lend. Lender groups are likely to be particularly interested in ratios such as interest cover and gearing, and will be interested in the nature and longevity of other categories of loan already provided to the entity.

Suppliers and other creditors

This group is interested in information that helps them to decide whether or not to supply goods or services to an entity. Availability of cash to enable continued repayment will be of particular interest, together with evidence about the entity's record in paying its creditors on time. Liquidity ratios, working capital ratios and the working capital cycle may be appropriate calculations to undertake when analysing financial statements for the benefit of this class of user.

Employees

Employees will want to be able to assess the stability and performance of the entity in order to gauge how reliable it is likely to be as a source of employment in the longer term. Employee's areas of interest will centre on the ability of the entity to continue as a going concern. Liquidity and profitability will be analysed in detail. Employees are also likely to be interested in disclosures about retirement benefits and remuneration. In a post-coronavirus economy, the going concern status of an employer will be paramount to the concerns of employees. The importance of this factor will be exacerbated due to the economic impacts of the closure or businesses and reduced revenue earning activities.

Customers

Customers may be in a vulnerable position if there are few potential suppliers in a market for goods. They may, therefore, be interested in assessing the risks which threaten their supplier. Again, liquidity and profitability will be analysed in detail in this assessment. Potentially they may also be interested in takeover opportunities in order to ensure the continuing supply of a particular raw material.

Governments and their agencies

The reason that a ruling government could be interested in an entity's financial statements are diverse and can be complex. The objectives of the government as a user of the accounts often depend upon the public interest in the company and the industry in which it operates. An obvious reason for governmental analysis of the financial statements lies in the assessment of the tax position of the entity. Is the amount of tax paid reasonable in comparison to its profits? In modern times, with the increase in global reaching entities, controversy regarding the tax bills of these large corporations is widely reported upon. The likes of Google, Starbucks and Amazon have all come under scrutiny regarding the amounts of tax that they pay in the UK alone. Hence, governments are under pressure to ensure that reasonable amounts of tax are recovered from trading in their jurisdictions and could use financial statements filings to help in their investigations.

The level of interest by governmental departments will be influenced by changes in the tides of public perception. Business practices are often investigated as a result of the importance of the issue to the population. In recent times, corporate failures have required governmental investigations to protect the interests of the general public (e.g. BHS pension scandal, the liquidation of Thomas Cook and Carillion, bail-outs of high street banks, manipulation of libor rates). Public inquiries can be held in which financial statement analysis could be integral.

Governments are in a position to require special-purpose reports across entire sectors, industries or on specific entities. Tax computations would fall into this category. However, general-purpose reports may also be of use, for example in gathering statistics on particular industries (e.g. in the analysis of GDP).

The general public

Members of the public may have special interests in the activities of certain entities, especially where, say, an individual entity dominates the local employment market. Pressure groups and their members would also fall under the umbrella category of 'general public', and their needs will vary according to their special interest. Environmental issues are of increasing concern to many people, and it is likely that pressure groups will take a particular interest in firms that are perceived as polluters. Analysis of the financial statements for this type of user would tend to focus on any additional voluntary disclosures made about the

> entity's environmental policies, on provisions and contingent liabilities related to environmental damage, and on capital investment (e.g. investment in new plant). For more on voluntary disclosures see Chapter 18 on Integrated reporting.
>
> The use of furloughing during the coronavirus pandemic by businesses has also created public scrutiny of how entities utilise public funds. Many premier league football clubs attempted to place non-playing staff on furlough schemes despite paying many thousands of pounds per week to playing staff. This created a back-lash in public perception causing many of these clubs to reverse their decisions.

4 Understanding the entity

It is often thought that financial analysis involves purely the application of a standard set of numerical calculations to a set of published accounts. This is not the case. Standardisation of analysis is not appropriate as users of the analysis and the specific industries, sectors and entities analysed, all have unique characteristics which must be considered when performing an analysis.

Having a comprehensive understanding of the markets and industry an entity operates within will improve the conclusions made from analysing the accounts.

Financial statement analysis should look beyond the numbers to provide narrative insight into the performance and position of an entity. The financial statements could be used in conjunction with <IR> (if available) to garner a detailed understanding of the overall developments within an entity (providing both a financial and non-financial perspective).

The history of the entity underlies the current position and future outlook. Furthermore, the owners and their individual characteristics will influence factors such as the level of risk in the entity and dividend policy. Knowledge of the quality, qualifications and experience of management will assist in evaluating the performance and position of the entity.

Financial analysis requires an understanding of the products, services and operating characteristics of the specific entity. This will assist in understanding data such as revenue, profitability, inventories and working capital. For example, despite operating in the same industry, the financial statements of a low-budget airline (e.g. easyJet, Ryan-air) will have different characteristics when compared to that of a luxury airline (e.g. British airways, Emirates).

An entity will operate within an industry consisting of other entities with similar operating characteristics. If the analysis requires comparison of the entity with the industry norms, it is important to identify the key characteristics of the industry and to establish benchmarks such as gross profit ratios, receivables collection days etc. For example, manufacturers would be expected to have high receivables, as the industry sells on credit. Retailers (Supermarkets, clothes stores) would have low receivables as customers typically pay immediately for their goods. These differences must be considered to enable effective analysis of financial statements taken from such industries.

5 Relevant sources of data

In practice, the analyst needs to consider carefully the possible sources of information available about an entity, starting with the annual report. This will contain financial information but there may be additional voluntary disclosures that will be helpful to the analyst, such as the entity's environmental impact, employment reports, graphs, pie charts and ratio calculations.

These 'extra' disclosures may be collated from the sources of 'big data' discussed in Section 2.

In the management level case study, pre-seen material will be provided in advance of the assessment and it will be important to consider how this information might be helpful in performing any analysis requirements that appear in the assessment.

6 Numerical analysis of the data

Financial statements can be used to analyse:

- Performance - how profitable the entity is during the year, mainly via its statement of profit or loss.

- Position - the entity's ownership of assets and obligations, mainly via its statement of financial position.

- Adaptability - how easily an entity can adapt to take advantage of opportunities that may arise (whether expected or unexpected), mainly through assessment of cash positions, working capital structure and profitability.

- Prospects - what does the future hold for the entity? How successful are investments and projects anticipated to be? Profits, cash flows, asset base and financing structure are all used to analyse whether the entity will operate successfully and continue going forward.

This section focusses on introducing and explaining the calculation of ratios derived from the financial statements as part of this analysis.

However, do not forget that these ratios are there to help with the analysis and are not always necessary. The same conclusions are often made by reviewing the movements in figures or looking for unusual fluctuations in the data e.g. operating profit margins can lead to a conclusion of improved performance but so could simply reviewing the actual operating profit figures!

Big data could be used to provide analysis on financial information in greater depth than could be gleaned from the aggregated financial statements e.g. GP% per product line, sale quantities per location and product.

Ratios

There are a variety of ratios that can be used when assessing an entity's financial statements. They fall into four broad categories:

- Profitability/performance ratios
  - Gross profit margin, operating profit margin, net profit margin
  - Return on capital employed
- Liquidity ratios
  - Current and quick (acid test) ratios
- Efficiency/activity ratios
  - Working capital ratios
  - Asset turnover ratios
- Capital structure ratios
  - Gearing
  - Interest cover

The financial statements provided below will be used to demonstrate how to calculate and interpret these ratios across test your understandings (TYUs) 1 to 4.

Financial information for TYUs 1 to 5

Below are the financial statements for T for the years ended 30 June 20X5 and 20X6:

Statement of profit and loss and other comprehensive income

	20X6	20X5
	$000	$000
Revenue	180	150
Cost of sales	(65)	(60)
Gross profit	115	90
Operating expenses	(40)	(29)
Share of profit of associate	59	–
Finance costs	(24)	(10)
Profit before tax	110	51
Tax	(14)	(13)
Profit for the year	96	38

Other comprehensive income:

Items that may be reclassified subsequently to profit or loss:

Gains on revaluation of FVOCI financial assets	14	5

Items that will not be reclassified to profit or loss:

Revaluation of PPE	30	–
Total comprehensive income	140	43

Summarised statements of changes in equity

	20X6	20X5
	$000	$000
Opening balance	100	82
Issue of shares	3	–
Total comprehensive income for the year	140	43
Dividends	(25)	(25)
Closing balance	218	100

Statements of financial position

		20X6		20X5
Non-current assets		$000		$000
Property, plant and equipment		266		190
Investment in associate		250		–
Other financial assets		31		17
		547		207
Current assets				
Inventory	15		12	
Receivables	49		37	
Cash and cash equivalents	–		1	
		64		50
		611		257

Equity

Share capital	12	10
Share premium	5	4
Revaluation surplus	30	–
FVOCI reserve	21	7
Retained earnings	150	79
Total equity	218	100

Non-current liabilities

Long term borrowings	335		110
Deferred tax	14		15
		349	125

Current liabilities

Trade payables	12		11
Overdraft	9		–
Taxation	13		11
Provisions	10		10
		44	32
		611	257

Test your understanding 1 – Profitability

Required:

For each of the two years, calculate the following ratios for T and suggest reasons why the ratios have changed.

	20X6	20X5

Gross profit margin

$$\frac{\text{Gross profit}}{\text{Revenue}} \times 100\%$$

Operating profit margin

$$\frac{\text{Operating profit}}{\text{Revenue}} \times 100\%$$

Profit before tax margin

$$\frac{\text{Profit before tax}}{\text{Revenue}} \times 100\%$$

Effective tax rate

$$\frac{\text{Tax expense}}{\text{Profit before tax*}} \times 100\%$$

* Share of profit of associate should be excluded from profit, as it is already net of tax

Return on capital employed

$$\frac{\text{Operating profit}}{\text{Capital employed}} \times 100\%$$

Operating profit = Gross profit less operating (admin and distribution) expenses

Capital employed = equity (share capital plus reserves) + interest bearing borrowings – non-current assets that do not contribute to operating profit (such as financial assets and investments in associates)

Analysing profitability ratios and data

Start by looking at the first line in the statement of profit or loss and other comprehensive income: revenue. Has it gone up or down and what is the percentage increase or decrease? A change in revenue may be due to a change in selling price or sales volume or both.

Gross profit margin is the percentage of revenue retained after costs of sale are deducted. Entities will aim to sell many products with a low margin or potentially fewer products with a high margin. A change in gross profit margin may be due to a change in product mix, for example, selling more of a product with a higher margin or conversely bringing a new product to market with a low margin to gain market share.

The operating profit margin is the trading or operating profit in relation to revenue, expressed as a percentage. The difference between gross profit margin and operating profit margin is the operating costs of the entity, such as administration costs, telephone costs and advertising costs. In assessment questions use background information provided to assess how these expenses may differ to the prior year or to another entity e.g. if a scenario suggests a business has been struggling or the market it operates in has deteriorated, an increase in operating costs could be caused by redundancy payments as a consequence of any restructuring performed. Operating margins would be expected to decline compared to prior years.

Profit before tax margin expresses the relationship between profit before tax and sales. Profit for this purpose would be after deduction of finance costs. An alternative is to calculate profit after tax margin.

Non-current asset policies (see Illustration 1) can have a substantial effect on ratios and comparisons between entities. For example, whether assets are measured at historical cost or are revalued will impact any analytical conclusions. Depreciation charges and reserves will be higher for revalued assets despite no actual change to the assets held. Policies regarding categorisation of expenses is another example that could distort analysis e.g. depreciation may be categorised as a cost of sale or an operating expense.

Exceptional items are one-off or irregular events that may distort the picture presented within the financial statements. Examples such as a profit on disposal of a non-current asset, costs caused by natural phenomena (e.g. volcanic ash clouds, pandemics) should be removed from the analysis to enable comparisons to be made.

Effective tax rate assesses the extent of the impact that tax has on the entity's profit.

Return on capital employed (ROCE) is a very useful measure when analysing performance. It assesses the efficiency with which the entity uses its assets to produce profit.

Consideration of any changes in capital employed and the causes of such changes will be required. For example, whether an increase caused by acquisition of new non-current assets occurred towards the end of an accounting period. If so, there has not yet been an opportunity for the entity to use the capital to generate increased profit. ROCE has been reduced but not due to any deterioration in performance compared to previous years. Changes in reserves during a period (e.g. revaluations) can also distort the conclusions made simply by comparing the ROCE figures from one year to the next.

Further analysis of profitability

Revenue

Problems can arise in making a valid interpretation of movements in revenue. For example:

- Accounting policies on revenue recognition may vary between entities. There may be inconsistencies between accounting periods, especially where the entity derives some or all of its revenue from long-term contracts.

- Inflation may account for some of the increase in price.

- A detailed breakdown of revenue for the entity may not be available.

Understanding the reasons for movements in revenue may help to explain movements in costs such as cost of sales, advertising, selling and distribution costs. If revenue increases, then a similar increase in these revenue-related costs could be expected. Conversely, an increase in, say, marketing and advertising expenditure might help to explain an increase in revenue.

Gross profit margin (GP%)

This ratio is expected to be more or less constant from one year to the next within an entity. Even if there is an increase in direct costs, an efficient entity could be expected to pass on the increases in the form of increased sales prices. However, this may not be the case in reality.

GP% will be impacted by changes in selling prices, changes in cost prices, changes in production wastage and efficiencies, changes in sales mix and changes in cost allocation policy. These examples are not an exhaustive list but provide some common causes to GP% fluctuations.

The gross profit margin requires a detailed breakdown in order to gain an understanding of movements. Ideally, the analyst requires information relating to opening and closing inventories, purchases, direct wages and overheads. Further information as to the following items would be required in order to evaluate gross profit margin fully:

- breakdown by product, geographical area or other segment

- inventory valuation policies

- overhead allocation methods

- purchasing details such as bulk discounts, purchasing errors, wastage or theft

- selling prices of different products over the period.

Obviously, much of this information is not available from an entity's annual report. Some entities do not even report gross profits.

Operating profit margin (OP%)

Operating profit is the profit from the trading activities of the business; it comprises profits after operating costs, but before finance costs, tax, investment income and any share of profits from an associate. Note that IAS 1 revised does not encourage the reporting of operating profit as a separate line item, although there is nothing to prevent entities providing additional information.

OP% is particularly useful for analysis when used in conjunction with GP%. If OP% performs in a similar fashion to GP%, then whatever causes the movement in GP% will be the driving force behind the OP% movements. Sales prices cause GP% increases, OP% margins will also see an increase assuming the operating costs structure is retained.

However, if OP% is not consistent with GP%, further investigations as to the causes are required. The entity has incurred greater operating costs than in the previous period and the reasons for these increased operating costs should be determined e.g. GP% due to increased selling prices but OP% has decreased. What extra operating costs have been incurred that were not previously present? The potential answers to this question are vast, but an obvious hypothesis could be that extra marketing costs were incurred. The analyst will strive to determine the root causes of the fluctuations arising.

The recent coronavirus pandemic could cause distorted operating margins in comparison to previous periods. For instance, operational cost increases caused by implementing lock-down working conditions or cost savings through salary reductions due to the use of government provided furloughing schemes

Profit before/after tax margin

Where comparing profit year on year, it is important to allow for any exceptional charges or credits. Also, it would be sensible when calculating profit after tax margin to take into account any large adjustments in respect of under or over-provided tax provisions.

Effective tax rate

This will help to understand the impact that tax has on the overall profit for the year. Tax is a consequence of being profitable and, to a certain extent, the impact of tax on profits is outside the control of the entity, however it should be considered when making investment decisions.

Return on capital employed

Return on capital employed (ROCE) shows the overall performance of the entity, expressed as a percentage return on the total investment. It measures management's efficiency in generating profits from the resources available.

Consistency of numerator and denominator is important in this ratio. Therefore, in calculating ROCE, the numerator should include profit before any deductions for finance costs. If capital employed includes a bank overdraft, the profit figure used in the calculation should exclude interest paid and payable on the overdraft.

The basic capital employed figure (the denominator) is equity (including share capital, reserves and NCI) and interest bearing borrowings. An adjustment should then be made to remove the carrying amount of any non-current asset that does not contribute to operating profit (the numerator) in order to provide consistency. A classic example of this is an investment in associate. The share of associate profit is presented in the statement of profit or loss below operating profit, therefore the value of the investment in associate should be deducted from the capital employed figure.

EBITDA

EBITDA is an acronym for earnings before interest, tax, depreciation and amortisation.

In recent years, many large entities have adopted EBITDA as a key measure of financial performance. Sceptics suggest that they do this in order to publicise a higher measure of earnings than profit from operations (this type of measurement is sometimes cynically referred to as EBBB – earnings before the bad bits).

However, it does make some sense to measure EBITDA, provided that the user fully understands what is included and what is left out. Depreciation and amortisation are accounting adjustments, not representing cash flows and are determined by management. It can be argued that excluding these items in assessing earnings eliminates a major area where management bias can operate.

Unfortunately, EBITDA is consequently often misunderstood as being a measurement of cash flow, which it is not. Even though EBITDA eliminates two categories of non-cash adjustment from profit, the earnings are still prepared on an accruals basis. EBITDA makes no adjustments in respect of other aspects of accrual accounting, such as accruals or working capital movements, and so is emphatically not a cash flow measurement.

Test your understanding 2

Required:

Using the financial information for TYUs 1 – 5, calculate the EBITDA for 20X6 and 20X5.

The following further information is also available:

	20X6	20X5
Depreciation	6	3

Illustration 1 – Effect of non-current asset policies on ratios

The following information has been extracted from the financial statements of A, B and C for the year ended 30 September 20X4:

	A	B	C
Statement of profit or loss	$000	$000	$000
Revenue	200	200	200
Operating costs	(160)	(190)	(170)
Profit from operations	40	10	30
Statement of financial position			
Share capital	50	50	50
Retained earnings	90	60	50
Revaluation surplus		210	
Capital employed	140	320	100
Operating profit margin	20%	5%	15%
Return on capital employed	28.6%	3.1%	30%

Entity A

A had purchased an asset costing $200,000 4 years ago. The asset is being depreciated on the straight-line basis over 10 years. Therefore, $20,000 of depreciation has been charged to this year's statement of profit and loss and the asset has a carrying amount of $120,000 in the statement of financial position.

B and C hold assets similar to that acquired by A. However, they adopt different accounting policies as described below. They are identical to A in all other respects.

Entity B

B revalued the asset to its current value of $350,000 at the start of the current year. As a result, a revaluation gain of $210,000 has been recognised and depreciation has been increased to $50,000 per annum, i.e. additional depreciation of $30,000 has been charged to the statement of profit and loss in the current year.

The revaluation has caused the operating profit margin to fall due to the extra depreciation. Return on capital employed has also fallen due to the revaluation surplus being included in capital employed.

Hence the entity looks to be generating a lower return.

Entity C

C has been leasing the asset under a 12 month rental agreement, paying an annual rental of $30,000 which has been charged to operating expenses. No right-of-use asset or lease liability is recorded for such a short lease.

This causes the operating profit margin to fall due to the lease payments being higher than depreciation. However, the return on capital employed is higher than A since the asset is not included on the statement of financial position but is still being used by the business to generate sales.

Test your understanding 3 – Liquidity

Required:

Using the financial statements provided for T, calculate the following ratios and suggest why the ratios may have changed.

	20X6	20X5

Current ratio (shown as ratio)

$$\frac{\text{Current assets}}{\text{Current liabilities}}$$

Quick ratio (shown as ratio)

$$\frac{(\text{Current assets} - \text{Inventory})}{\text{Current liabilities}}$$

Test your understanding 4 – Efficiency

Required:

Using the financial statements provided for T, calculate the following ratios and suggest why the ratios may have changed.

	20X6	20X5

Inventory holding period (in days)

$$\frac{\text{Inventory}}{\text{Cost of sales}} \times 365 \text{ days}$$

Receivables collection period (in days)

$$\frac{\text{Receivables}}{\text{Revenue}} \times 365 \text{ days}$$

Payables payment period (in days)

$$\frac{\text{Trade payables}}{\text{Cost of sales}} \times 365 \text{ days}$$

Asset turnover

$$\frac{\text{Revenue}}{\text{Capital employed}}$$

Non-current asset turnover

$$\frac{\text{Revenue}}{\text{Non-current assets (that contribute to revenue)}}$$

Analysing liquidity

The analysis of the liquidity of an entity should start with a review of the actual *bank balance* in absolute terms. This would be found in the statement of financial position under current assets. Has the bank balance increased or decreased significantly? If it has decreased dramatically, it may have entered an overdraft position (check current liabilities to confirm). If so, it could be that the overdraft is near to its permitted limit. This would cast doubt over the entity's ability to continue as a going concern. If the cash has increased significantly look out for details referred to in the scenario that could be used to explain the movement (e.g. disposal of non-current assets). Also, high cash resources indicate a good takeover prospect, so be vigilant for indications that the owners want to sell.

The **current ratio** compares current assets to current liabilities. A ratio greater than 1 indicates there are more current assets than current liabilities. The current ratio guides us to the extent that the entity is able to meet its current liabilities as they fall due.

The **quick ratio** compares current assets, excluding inventory, to current liabilities. The quick ratio gives a better indicator of liquidity as it removes the least liquid current asset, the inventory. Inventory can be difficult to sell. Quick ratio is particularly applicable to industries where inventory has long production times and cash is difficult to realise e.g. a whisky distillery that requires a number of months for its products to mature before being sold.

Analysing efficiency/activity

The **inventory holding period** is an average number of days that inventory is held before being sold. It indicates how much working capital is tied up in goods in the warehouse. An entity must balance the need to supply goods on time to customers with the risk of obsolescence. If inventory days are too high, then it could suggest inventory is struggling to be sold (and could be obsolete) or maybe it suggests then entity has a reason to stock pile as at the year-end (e.g. they recently received a large order from a customer for which they are in the process of preparing for despatch). If inventory days have decreased, it may suggest an increased risk of running out of inventory (referred to as a stock-out).

The **receivables collection period** tells us the number of days it takes on average to receive payment from credit customers. It should be based on the credit agreements with customers. Cash should be collected efficiently whilst bearing in mind customers in a strong negotiating position. If the receivable days have increased dramatically, it may suggest poor credit control or perhaps new terms with customer have been agreed.

The **payables payment period** is the length of time it takes to pay suppliers for goods bought on credit. This is effectively a free source of finance but the business should make sure suppliers are paid on a timely basis to avoid the risk of suppliers refusing to continue to supply.

Asset turnover measures how much revenue is being generated from the overall capital invested. It is a measure of the efficiency of the spending of the capital raised and the activity created by the total assets purchased.

Non-current asset turnover is a similar calculation but measuring the efficiency/activity of non-current assets only. There are many variations of this ratio that can provide useful information, such as total asset turnover and working capital turnover.

Over-trading

When an entity grows rapidly there is a risk of over-trading, i.e. expanding the entity without adequate long term or short term finance. Inventory, receivables and payables increase but there is a decline in cash and the entity may be unable to pay its suppliers as debts fall due.

Entities in this position should look to raise long-term finance. This will enable the entity to improve its inventory and credit control and, by reducing its inventory and receivable days, improve its cash-flow.

Other options to short-term financing arrangement may help such as factoring of receivables or invoice discounting facilities.

Further analysis of liquidity and efficiency/activity

Short term liquidity (current and quick ratios)

The quick ratio recognises that the time taken to convert inventory into cash can be significantly longer than for other current assets. The removal of inventory from the ratio gives a more conservative view of liquidity.

It is often useful to calculate current and quick ratio together. Current ratio may look healthy, presenting a positive picture of short-term liquidity. Upon calculating quick ratio, the discovery of a low quick ratio despite a heathy current ratio will put a different complexion upon the conclusions made. This result may be due to long production lead times on inventory lines or, more worryingly, could indicate obsolescence of inventory.

However, it is important to select ratios suitable for the circumstances of the entity. If inventory is an insignificant amount (as it would be, for example, in most service entities), there is little point in calculating the quick ratio, current ratio would be sufficient

There is no standard number that should be expected in these calculations; it should depend on the industry and should be linked to other areas of the analysis e.g. supermarkets have very low acceptable current ratios (less than 1), which would be of concern for most industries, but due to the expectation that receivables would be low (customers pay in cash) and payables very high (significant consumer power), low current ratios are the for the industry.

The higher the ratio, the more liquid the entity, but high liquidity can itself be a problem. It may mean that the entity is unable to utilise cash effectively by investing it profitably.

The working capital cycle

The total length of the working capital cycle is the inventory holding period plus the receivables days less the payables days, which approximates to the total time it takes to purchase the inventory, sell the inventory and receive cash.

The working capital cycle comprises cash, receivables, inventory and payables. The entity uses cash to buy inventory. Additional inventory may be purchased on credit. Inventories are sold and become receivables. Receivables pay and then the entity has cash available to repay payables or buy further inventory.

The length of the working capital cycle can assist in determining the immediate effects of the management of working capital on the bank balance and liquidity.

Inventory holding period

The ratio gives the number of days that inventory, on average, has remained in the warehouse. If only a closing figure is available for inventory, then that can be used. However, the result must be treated with some caution, as the closing figure may be unrepresentative, particularly if the nature of the entity's business is seasonal. An average stock level should be used if the closing stock figure is deemed not representative.

Receivables days

A retail or cash-based entity may have zero or very low receivables days. Note that, where an entity sells for both cash and on credit, it will be necessary to split revenue into the two types. Only the credit sales will be used within the receivable days calculation.

Payables days

Current payables comprise a form of finance which is very cheap but not totally free. Costs include loss of prompt payment discount and loss of supplier goodwill where excessive time is taken to pay. Efficiency is measured relative to industry norms, receivables days (if receivable days is long but payables days is short, the entity will be face cash flow pressures) and supplier terms.

In the above calculations, if figures are not available for credit sales and credit purchases (as may well be the case if the data source is a set of published accounts), an approximation may be obtained by using total revenue and cost of sales respectively, but the results of such ratio calculations must be treated with caution.

Asset turnover/utilisation

This calculation shows how much revenue is produced per unit of capital invested.

This ratio shows the productivity of assets in generating sales. It should be noted that, depending upon the specific circumstances, this ratio is not always useful or informative as it is easily distorted.

Where an entity is using assets that are nearing the end of their useful lives, having been subject to annual depreciation charges over a relatively long period, the ratio is likely to be rather high. Similarly, where an entity uses the historical cost convention, unmodified by revaluation, asset values are also likely to be relatively low, an effect which is more intrusive as the assets age. Also, in labour-intensive entities, where the non-current asset base is low, the ratio tends to lack significance.

For non-current asset turnover, where possible, the average asset figure over the year should be used in the denominator of the fraction. This is likely to give a more consistent and representative result.

External users of annual reports do not have access to monthly information with which to calculate an average, but opening and closing figures often give a reasonable approximation.

The denominator should exclude any assets that do not contribute to revenue as these would distort the ratio.

Test your understanding 5 (integration question) – Gearing

Required:

Using the financial statements provided for T, calculate the following ratios and suggest why the ratios may have changed.

	20X6	20X5

Gearing (%)

$$\frac{\text{Debt}}{\text{Debt + Equity}}$$

Gearing alternative (shown as ratio)

$$\frac{\text{Debt}}{\text{Equity}}$$

Interest cover (number of times covered)

$$\frac{\text{Operating profit}}{\text{Finance costs}}$$

Average rate of borrowing (%)

$$\frac{\text{Finance costs}}{\text{Borrowings}}$$

Dividend cover (number of times covered)

$$\frac{\text{Profit for the year}}{\text{Dividends}}$$

Analysing capital structure ratios and data

Gearing is an important measure of risk and a guide to the long term solvency of the entity. It is calculated by taking long term debt as a percentage of total capital employed. Alternatively it can be calculated by taking debt as a percentage of equity, or shareholders' funds.

Increased gearing indicates increased risk of default of loan finance. Debt finance will require minimum interest repayments periodically and any failure to meet these terms may cause the debt to be withdrawn.

Potential financers are always interested in the gearing of the entity. If the entity that is attempting to borrow money is already highly geared, it has a higher risk of default. In this circumstance, the financier will lend at inflated interest rates to reflect this increased risk and will strongly consider whether they should even lend at all. If the lender has a high asset base, despite the high gearing, then the debt could be issued with security taken against the assets of the lender.

It is important to assess the gearing ratio against the industry average and to ensure that any existing debt finance is put to good use to generate revenue and profits.

Interest cover indicates the number of times profits will cover the interest charge. The higher the ratio, the better. If it is too low, this indicates the entity is struggling to earn profits that cover its minimum interest payments. This can be a When looking at interest cover, the stability of profits is important as the interest must be paid consistently out of available profits otherwise the entity may default on its debt and may have to repay it at short notice.

Average rate of borrowings indicates the typical interest rate that the entity pays on its debt finance. A high rate would suggest that lenders consider the entity to be a relatively high risk.

Dividend cover indicates the number of times profits will cover the dividend. The higher the ratio the better as shareholders may expect a sustainable dividend payment.

Further analysis of capital structure

Capital structure is the composition of an entity's finance. Has the entity raised finance through debt or equity sources? It is important to analyse, particularly for users such as shareholders and creditors, the structure of finance as it can provide details regarding the ability of the entity to satisfy its longer term debts through repayment of capital and payment of interest.

The capital structure of the entity provides information about the relative risk that is accepted by shareholders and creditors. As long-term debt increases relative to shareholders' funds, then more risk is assumed by long-term creditors and so they would require higher rewards, thereby decreasing resources available for the shareholders. As risk increases, creditors require higher interest in order to compensate for the higher risk.

However, the use of debt by management in their capital structure can assist in increasing profits available to shareholders. Cash received into the entity from lenders will be used to generate revenue and profits. As interest costs are fixed and can be relatively cheap compared to dividends, any profits generated in excess of the interest costs will accrue to the shareholders. The negative side to the use of debt is that, if the cash from the debt does not raise sufficient profits, the fixed interest cost must be paid first and profits available to shareholders are decreased, and may be extinguished completely.

Gearing

The gearing (or leverage) ratio is an important measure of risk.

Gearing is calculated by taking long term debt as a percentage of total capital employed, i.e. long term debt plus shareholders' funds.

Long-term debt includes debentures, mortgages and other long-term debt, including redeemable preference shares. Any bank overdraft would be included to the extent that it is actually a source of long-term finance. Whether overdrafts are deemed long-term (used in gearing) or short-term (not used in gearing) would be explicitly stated within any exam question.

Shareholders' funds comprises of equity share capital and reserves.

Interest cover

Although the use of debt may generate higher profits for shareholders there is a limit to its use. This may be gauged from the statement of profit or loss by focusing on the profitability and interest repayments in the interest cover ratio.

Test your understanding 6 (OTQ style)

The return on capital employed of YK has increased from 12.5% to 16.4% in the year to 31 December 20X4.

Required:

Which one of the following would be a valid reason for this increase?

A   YK has acquired a significant amount of property, plant and equipment close to the year end.

B   YK has revalued its land and buildings for the first time this year, resulting in an increase in carrying amount.

C   YK raised long-term borrowings to finance the payment of a significant dividend.

D   A significant number of YK's assets were fully written down at the previous year end.

Test your understanding 7

The financial statements of DFG for the year ended 31 December 20X1 are provided below:

Statements of financial position at 31 December

	20X1		20X0	
	$m	$m	$m	$m
Non-current assets				
Property, plant and equipment	254		198	
Investment in associate	24		–	
		278		198
Current assets				
Inventories	106		89	
Receivables	72		48	
Cash and cash equivalents	–		6	
		178		143
Total assets		456		341
Equity				
Share capital ($1 equity shares)	45		45	
Retained earnings	146		139	
Revaluation surplus	40		–	
		231		184
Non-current liabilities				
Long-term borrowings		91		91
Current liabilities				
Trade and other payables	95		66	
Short-term borrowings	39		–	
		134		66
		456		341

Statement of profit or loss and other comprehensive income for the year ended 31 December

	20X1	20X0
	$m	$m
Revenue	252	248
Cost of sales	(203)	(223)
Gross profit	49	25
Distribution costs	(18)	(13)
Administrative expenses	(16)	(11)
Share of profit of associate	7	–
Finance costs	(12)	(8)
Profit before tax	10	(7)
Income tax expense	(3)	2
Profit for the year	7	(5)
Other comprehensive income:		
Items that will not be reclassified to profit and loss		
Revaluation gain on PPE	40	–
Total comprehensive income for the year	47	(5)

Required:

Calculate the following ratios for DFG for the year ended 31 December 20X1 and its comparative period:

- Gross profit margin
- Operating profit margin
- Profit for the year margin
- Gearing (debt/equity)
- Current ratio
- Quick ratio
- Receivables collection period
- Payables payment period
- Inventory holding period
- Return on capital employed
- Non-current asset turnover
- Interest cover.

Test your understanding 8 (case style)

You work as an accountant for XYZ. The finance director has asked you to analyse the financial statements of DFG, the entity whose financial statements are included in the previous TYU above, as the board of directors are considering acquiring the business. DFG supplies the building trade. The finance director commented that she had reviewed the information on DFG's website and there were lots of positive messages about the entity's future, including how it had secured a new supplier relationship in 20X1 resulting in a significant improvement in margins.

In addition to the financial statements, she has obtained the following information about DFG:

1   **Long term borrowings**

    The long term borrowings are repayable in 20X3.

2   **Contingent liability**

    The notes to the financial statements include details of a contingent liability of $30 million. A major customer, a house builder, is suing DFG, claiming that it supplied faulty goods. The customer had to rectify some of its building work when investigations discovered that a building material, which had recently been supplied by DFG, was found to contain a hazardous substance. The initial assessment from the lawyer is that DFG is likely to lose the case although the amount of potential damages could not be measured with sufficient reliability at the year-end date.

3   **Revaluation**

    DFG decided on a change of accounting policy in the year and now includes its land and buildings at their revalued amount. The valuation was performed by an employee of DFG who is a qualified valuer.

Required:

Using the financial information from the previous TYU and the additional information above, to assess the suitability of DFG as an acquisition target for XYZ, analyse the financial performance and financial position of DFG for the year to 31 December 20X1. Discuss your findings in a report address to the Board of Directors.

7 Financial statement analysis and the Gartner Data Analytics Maturity model

Users may apply the Gartner Data Analytics Maturity model to create focussed decision-making and improve conclusions from their financial statement analysis.

The 4 stages of the Gartner model could provide a framework for effective analysis. The following section, applies the Gartner model to an analysis made by a potential investor analysing the accounts of an entity they would like to acquire (the target company):

Stage 1 – Descriptive (what happened?)

Reviewing the financial statements from one year to the next or in comparison with another company would enable descriptive analysis.

 e.g. return on capital employed (ROCE) is lower in the target entity than in other potential acquisitions.

Stage 2 – Diagnostic (why it happened?)

Determining an explanation for why the movement occurred would provide diagnostic analysis.

 e.g. the target entity invested heavily in property, plant and equipment towards the end of the period leading to the lower ROCE.

Stage 3 – Predictive (what is going to happen?)

Consideration of future performance will provide greater insight into the potential of the target.

e.g. due to the significant investment already incurred, the likelihood of improved future performance is increased.

Stage 4 – Prescriptive (what can be done about it?)

Use the previous stages to develop a strategy or plan of action.

e.g. the decision as to whether or not to acquire the entity

Financial statement analysis can also provide prescriptive conclusions regarding future strategic decisions regarding the target. How can we make the investment a success? What strategies would improve the target company performance? For instance, if new products are required to boost sales, what new geographical locations should be operated within for maximum efficiency and wealth creation?

Overall, the Gartner Data Analytics Maturity model can enable proactive responses and strategies to be applied to financial statement analysis.

8 Actions resulting from financial statement analysis

It is important for any type of financial statement analysis to provide actions and conclusions specific to the needs of the user of the analysis. In doing so, using Gartner terminology, analysts will be considering the predictive stage to determine prescriptive solutions.

Actions are dependent upon the specific scenario provided within the exam but include:

– pursuing the acquisition of a particular target company

– deciding whether (or not) to continue to provide finance to a credit customer

– searching for alternative suppliers if it is considered that a current supplier may go bust

– deciding what strategic approach the business should take e.g. which product lines should continue to be offered?

– decisions regarding selling or retaining current investments in shares

– agreeing to provide new financing or to withdraw existing finance from borrowers.

9 Limitations of analysis of financial statements

Financial statements analysis has its limitations. These limitations are often inherent and can reduce the effectiveness and usefulness of analysis.

These limitations can be caused by internal factors (created by processes or choices within the entity e.g. accounting policy choices, strategic decisions) and also by external factors (ratios being incomparable between different entities and distortions due to geographic locations of operations).

It may be necessary to illustrate awareness of these limitations in your assessment (or discuss them in the management case study).

It is important to answer the question requirement carefully, i.e. are you asked for limitations of financial information or the limitations of using ratios for analysis?

Limitations of financial reporting information

- Only provide historic data.

- Only provide financial information.

- Filed at least 3 months after reporting date reducing its relevance.

- Limited information to be able to identify trends over time.

- Lack of detailed information.

- Historic cost accounting does not take into account inflation.

Difficulties in drawing comparisons between different entities

- Comparisons affected by changes in the entity's business, for example selling an operation.

- Different accounting policies between different entities, e.g. revaluations.

- Different accounting practices between different entities, e.g. debt factoring, lease v buy decisions.

- Different entities within the same industry may have different activities.

- Non-coterminous accounting periods.

- Different entities may not be comparable in terms of size.

- Comparisons between entities operating in different countries will be influenced by different legal and regulatory systems, the relative strength and weakness of the national economy and exchange rate fluctuations.

Limitations of ratio analysis

- Where ratios have been provided, there may be discrepancies between how they have been calculated for each entity/period, e.g. gearing.

- Distortions when using year-end figures, particularly in seasonal industries and when entities have different accounting dates.

- Distortions due to not being able to use most appropriate figures, e.g. total sales revenue rather than credit sales when calculating receivables days.

- It is difficult to identify reasons behind ratio movements without significant additional information.

Creative accounting

- Timing of transactions may be delayed/speeded up to improve results, e.g. not investing in non-current assets to ensure ROCE does not fall.

- Profit smoothing using IFRS compliant policy choices, e.g. inventory valuation method.

- Classification of items, e.g. expenses v non-current assets; ordinary v exceptional.

- Off-balance sheet financing to improve gearing and ROCE.

- Revenue recognition policies.

- Managing market expectations.

These are generic limitations that are not necessarily applicable to all entities in all circumstances. If asked to discuss limitations (in the case study) or when attempting a F2 examination question, your discussion or answer must be applied to the unique traits of an entity, for example: if you have been asked to compare two entities it makes sense to consider whether they use the same accounting policies (e.g. depreciation rates) and business methods (e.g. acquiring or leasing assets).

Limitations of financial reporting information

The objective of financial statements is set out in the IASB's Conceptual Framework for Financial Reporting:

'The objective of general purpose financial reporting is to provide financial information about the reporting entity that is useful to existing and potential investors, lenders and other creditors in making decisions about providing resources to the entity.' (*IASB Conceptual framework para 1.2*).

A rather substantial limitation of financial statements, is, however, then explained in the following paragraphs:

'... general purpose financial reports do not and cannot provide all of the information that existing and potential investors, lenders and other creditors need. Those users need to consider pertinent information from other sources, for example, general economic conditions and expectations, political events and political climate, and industry and company outlooks. (IASB Conceptual framework para 1.6).

Other parties, such as regulators and members of the public other than investors, lenders and other creditors, may also find general purpose financial reports useful. However, those reports are not primarily directed to these other groups.' (IASB Conceptual framework para 1.10).

It appears that although financial statements may be useful to a wide range of users, their usefulness is limited. The principal drawback is the fact that financial statements are oriented towards events that have already taken place. However, there are other significant limitations of the information contained in a set of financial statements as follows:

Timeliness

By the time financial statements are received by users, 2 or 3 months or longer may have elapsed since the year end date. The earliest of the transactions that contribute to the income and expense items accumulated in the statement of profit or loss will have taken place at least 15 months previously.

In some jurisdictions, there may be a requirement for large, listed entities to produce half-yearly or even quarterly financial statements. Where these are available, the timeliness problem is reduced. However, the comprehensiveness of the information may be limited in comparison to what is produced in the annual report. For example, quarterly statements may include only a statement of profit or loss without a statement of financial position or statement of changes in equity. Also, it is possible that they will have not been subject to verification in the form of audit.

Comparability

Comparisons over time for one entity

Comparisons over time between the financial statements of the same entity may prove to be invalid, or only partially valid, because significant changes have taken place in the entity. For example, an entity that makes an investment in a new non-current item, say a major addition to its production facilities, is not obliged to disclose any information about how well or badly the new investment has performed.

The analyst may, for example, be able to see that the entity's profitability overall has decreased, but the explanations could be as follows:

- The investment has proved to be very successful, but its success is offset by the rapidly declining profitability of other parts of the entity's productive capacity. As these elements are gradually replaced over the next 2 or 3 years, profitability is likely to increase overall.

- The investment has proved to be less successful than expected and is producing no better a return than the worn-out machinery it replaced.

- Although productive capacity has increased, the quality of goods overall has declined, and the entity has not been able to maintain its margins.

Financial statements simply do not provide sufficient information to permit the analyst to see these finer points of detail.

Comparisons over time and inflation

Comparability over time is often threatened by the effects of price inflation. This can, paradoxically, be particularly insidious where the general rate of inflation in the economy is comparatively low because analysts and others are not conscious of the effect. For example, suppose that the rate of price inflation applicable to a particular entity has been around 2.5 per cent per year over a 5-year period. Sales in 20X3 were reported at $100,000. A directly comparable level of sales in 20X4 would be $102,500 ($100,000 × 1.025). Therefore, sales in 20X4 would have to have increased to more than $102,500 before any real increase could be claimed. However, the analyst, seeing the two figures alongside each other on the statement of profit or loss, and knowing that inflation is running at a low level, may not take this factor into account.

Differences in accounting policy and accounting practices

Changes in accounting policy and accounting practices affect comparability over time of both a single entity's financial statements and in the comparison of multiple entities.

The type of differences which make comparisons difficult include the following:

- Different approaches to valuation of non-current assets, as permitted under IAS® 16 Property, Plant and Equipment. An entity that revalues its non-current assets on a regular basis, as permitted by that standard, is likely to have higher carrying amounts for its assets than an entity that carries non-current assets at depreciated historical cost. Also, the depreciation charges of the revaluing entity are likely to be higher. The two entities are therefore not strictly comparable.

- Different classifications of expenses in the statement of profit or loss. It is not always easy to decide whether should be classified as part of cost of sales or operating expenses. If entities classify similar expenses under different headings, the gross profit margins and operating profit margins will not be comparable.

- Varying approaches to judgements. For example, impairment reviews and quantification of provisions inevitably involves some degree of estimation.

Only the first of these three items relates to an accounting policy difference. The other two relate to variations in respect of judgemental issues. Where there is a difference in formal accounting policies adopted it is possible to discern this from the financial statements (through accounting policy disclosure notes) and to make some kind of adjustment to achieve comparability. However, judgemental matters are almost impossible to adjust for.

Entities in the same sector

Entities may appear to be comparable when operating in the same business sector. However, each sector has unique features, and a particular entity may not be strictly comparable with another from that same sector e.g. Waitrose vs Aldi.

Non-coterminous accounting periods

Financial statements are prepared to a particular date annually. The annual financial statements of an entity with a year-end of 31 December are not strictly comparable with those of an entity with a June year-end. The difference is only 6 months, but significant events may have occurred in the industry or the economy as a whole that affect the statements prepared to the later date but not those prepared to the earlier date. Seasonality will also influence the analysis.

Size of the entity

It may be inappropriate to compare two entities of very different sizes, or to compare a listed with a non-listed entity. A large entity may be able to take advantage of economies of scale that are unavailable to the small entity, making its performance ratios appear more favourable. However, that is not to say that the smaller entity is inefficient in comparison. It may, relatively speaking, be a better manager of the resources available to it. Conversely, a smaller entity may be able to react more rapidly to changes in economic conditions, because it can be easier to effect radical change within the smaller business.

Listed entities are subject to a great deal of additional regulation and their activities are far more likely than those of an unlisted entity to attract media coverage. Their share prices are widely advertised and are sensitive to alterations in market perceptions. It can be less acceptable for a listed entity to take risks or any course of action that might affect a regular flow of dividends to shareholders. By contrast, an unlisted entity whose shares are held by a limited number of people may be able to make investment decisions that result in a curtailment of dividends in the short term in exchange for projected higher returns in the long-term. So, operational flexibility varies between entities, and this may mean that their financial statement comparisons must be treated with caution.

Verification

Although regulations relating to audit vary from one country to another, it is likely that, in most jurisdictions, the financial statements of larger entities are audited. However, smaller entities' financial statements may not be subject to audit, and so the analyst has no external report on the fairness and validity of the accounts.

International issues

Where the financial statements of entities based in different countries are being compared:

- The entities may be subject to differing tax regimes.

- The financial statements may be based on different legal and regulatory systems. For example, traditionally, German, French and Spanish financial statements have been prepared in accordance with tax regulation (e.g. the depreciation allowances provided for in the financial statements are exactly those allowable for tax purposes). The preparation of British and Irish financial statements, by contrast, is focused much more upon the objective of achieving a true and fair view, and the links between accounts for tax purposes and accounts for filing and presentation purposes are few.

- The entities may use different exchange rates and operate in incomparable economic conditions. The relative strengths and weaknesses of a national economy, and of the national currency exchange rates, may produce cyclical differences in the profitability of businesses.

These effects will reduce comparability of the financial statements of two entities located in different countries.

Provision of non-financial information

It was noted earlier in this section that financial reports do not provide all the information needed for users to make decisions. Major listed entities have tended, in recent years, to provide more non-financial information in their financial statements e.g. disclosure of environmental issues. Regulations relating to non-financial disclosures are limited and users cannot rely on finding a consistent level of high quality information in annual reports.

Entities may adopt Integrated reporting <IR>, which goes some way to improving levels of non-financial disclosure. However, as <IR> is voluntary, not every entity will prepare an integrated report so the information cannot be relied upon to be available. Also, due to disclosures being non-compulsory, the content included does not always allow comparison between entities.

Limitations of ratio analysis

Calculation method

The only accounting ratio to have a prescribed method of calculation is earnings per share which is regulated through IAS 33. For other accounting ratios, there may be more than one valid method of calculation. There are, for example, two perfectly valid approaches to the calculation of gearing. When making comparisons between financial statements, it is important to ensure that the same method of calculation is used consistently, otherwise the comparison will not be valid.

Reliability

Many ratios are calculated using average figures. Often the average is based on only two figures: the opening and closing. These may not be representative of a true average figure, causing the calculations to be unreliable. This effect is noticeable in entities with seasonal operations.

For example, an artificial Christmas tree business starts building up its inventory from a low point at the beginning of February, gradually accumulating in order to build up to a maximum level at the beginning of November. Eighty-five per cent of its annual sales total is made in November and December .If the entity has an accounting year end of 31 January (which would make sense as there's not much going on at the time of year), inventory will be at its lowest level.

An average inventory figure may be used based upon (Opening inventory + closing inventory)/2 but it will not be representative of the entity's level of activity in the intervening months reducing the reliability of the ratio.

The idea of the norm

Sometimes we attempt to set norms for ratios: for example, that the current ratio should ideally be around 2, or 1.5 or 2.5. However, setting norms is both unrealistic and unhelpful. Some entities can, and do, operate successfully with a substantial excess of current liabilities over current assets. Such entities typically sell for cash, so don't have receivables, turn over their inventory very quickly (perhaps because it's perishable) but manage to take the maximum amounts of credit from their suppliers.

Inappropriate use of ratios

Not all ratios are useful or applicable in all business situations and the analyst must take care over the selection of ratios to use. For example, an entity may have a mixture of cash and credit sales, but it would normally not be possible to distinguish between them armed only with the information included in the annual financial statements. However, seeing a line for revenue and a line for receivables, the analyst might assume that it was sensible to work out the receivable days. The ratio would be inaccurate and the analyst could be seriously misled by it.

Limited usefulness of ratios

Ratios analysis may contribute to an understanding of an entity's business operations but often lead to more questions that cannot be answered due to lack of available information.

Stand-alone ratios are generally of very limited use. The analyst may be able to calculate that a business's gross profit percentage is 14.3 per cent for a particular year. In isolation, that piece of information is really quite useless. It's reassuring to know that the entity has actually made a positive gross profit, but without comparatives, it's hard to say much more than that.

Creative accounting

Defining the nature and scope of creative accounting is not straightforward. Despite the best efforts of accounting regulators there remains wide scope for the use of judgement in matters such as the determination of useful lives of assets and allowances for irrecoverable receivables.

The term 'creative accounting' is commonly used to suggest a rather suspicious approach to accounting. It carries connotations of manipulation of figures, deliberate structuring of series of transactions and exploitation of loopholes in the rules.

It should be noted that the directors have a legal responsibility to ensure that the financial statements reflect a fair presentation of the performance and position of the entity over the reporting period. Any creative accounting techniques would be likely to contravene this rule and would be considered highly unethical.

In addition, the auditors will consider the possibility of creative accounting carefully when forming their opinion on the financial statements. If they believe that a fair presentation is not reflected they will ask the directors to make amendments and, in the event that the directors refuse to do so, the auditors would be required to amend their opinion accordingly.

Methods employed by creative accountants

Financial statements can be manipulated in many ways, some more acceptable than others. Methods include the following:

Altering the timing of transactions

For example, the despatch of sales orders could be hurried up or delayed just before the year-end to either increase or decrease sales for the reporting period. An infamous example of this type of incident was reported at Tesco's where payments from suppliers were found to have been recognised early creating overstated revenues of £250m.

Other examples include delaying sales of non-current assets and the timing of research and development expenditure. If an entity needs to improve its results it may decide upon a lower level of research and development activity in the short-term in order to reduce costs. Delaying the replacement of worn-out assets falls into the same category. Some people would regard this type of 'manipulation' as falling outside the definition of creative accounting.

Artificial smoothing

This approach involves the exploitation of the elements of choice that exist in accounting regulation. Although the International Accounting Standards Board (the Board) has worked hard to reduce the number of allowed alternative treatments, there remains some scope for artificial adjustments in respect of, for example, the choice of inventory valuation method, the estimated useful lives of non-current assets, and the choice between valuation of non-current assets at revalued amounts or depreciated historical cost.

A change in accounting policy would, of course, have to be noted in the year in which it occurs, but its effects are not so easily discernible after that first year.

Classification

One of the grey areas that persists in accounting is the classification of debit items as either expenses of the current year or as non-current assets. If items are classified as non-current assets they do not impact on the reported income for the period (unless they are depreciated). A motive to capitalise the costs as non-current assets rather than expense exists.

One of the best known cases of misclassification occurred in the US long-distance phone company WorldCom. Over a 3 year period the entity improperly reported $3.8 billion of expenses as non-current assets, thus providing a considerable boost to reported earnings. The entity is also reported as having manipulated provisions in order to increase reported earnings. In this particular case, the scale of the irregularities has been such that senior officers were prosecuted, found guilty and subsequently jailed for fraud.

Other areas of the financial statements which provide opportunities for creative accounting via classification include the categorisation of expenses and income as exceptional. The recent liquidation of Thomas Cook saw the auditors involved grilled over why they allowed the regular exclusion of 'exceptional items' from Thomas Cook's SOPL. This enabled Thomas Cook director's to exclude $1.8bn of expenses over an 8 year period from operating profits and to continue to trade as a going concern for many years.

Exclusion of liabilities

Under-reporting liabilities in the statement of financial position can help to improve accounting ratios. For example, the calculation of gearing would be affected and total capital employed would be reduced, causing return on capital employed to appear to be higher. Entities have sometimes been able to take advantage of loopholes in accounting regulation to arrange off-balance sheet financing in the form of subsidiary undertakings that are technically excluded from consolidation. This was demonstrated in the Enron case, where so-called Special Purpose Entities (aka unconsolidated structured entities) were set up to provide finance to the business; these SPEs were, however, excluded from consolidation so that their liabilities did not appear in the group financial statements. Regulations have been revised to make this more difficult, with the recent introduction of IFRS 10: *Consolidated Financial Statements* being an example. However, off-balance sheet financing remains a problem.

The analyst must read the notes to the financial statements carefully to be aware of any contingencies. A contingent liability is where the probability of occurrence is less than 50% but it is not remote. Where an item is noted as a contingent liability together with a note of the estimated financial impact, it may be useful to calculate the impact on the entity's liquidity and to work out accounting ratios both with and without the item.

Recognition of revenue

Aggressive accounting often exploits revenue recognition rules. Some examples of inappropriate revenue recognition include:

- recognising revenue from sales that are made conditionally (i.e. where the purchaser has the right to return the goods for an extended period, or where experience shows that returns are likely)

- failing to apportion subscription revenue over the appropriate accounting periods but instead recognising it immediately

- recognising revenue on goods shipped to agents employed by the entity

- recognising the full amount of revenue when only partial shipments of goods have been made

- recognising revenue from future long-term sales earlier than appropriate e.g. longer term contracts were control passes at a point in time but recorded as if performance obligations are satisfied over time. This was a factor that caused the collapse of the construction company, Carillion, which was aggressively recording revenue despite delays in the progress of its biggest contracts (A contract linked to the Qatar World Cup 2022, the contract to build the Royal Liverpool Hospital) leading to Carillion being unable to recover cash from the work performed.

The adoption of IFRS 15 *Revenue from contracts with customers* attempts to utilise robust rules for recognising revenue and reduces the abilities for subjectivity surround revenue recognition.

Managing market expectations

This final category of manipulation has nothing to do with massaging an entity's figures, but it does involve the way the entity presents itself to the world. Reporting by listed entities, especially in the US market, is driven very much by analysts' expectations. It may be easier to massage their expectations rather than to improve the reported results by use of creative accounting techniques. Directors of listed entities meet analysts in briefing meetings where they have the opportunity to influence analysts' expectations by forecasting fairly poor figures. When the entity then proceeds to turn in a better result than expected, the market's view of the shares may be enhanced. This is a psychological game of bluffing which may backfire on the reporting entity if analysts become aware of what it is doing.

The motivation to use creative accounting

Various research studies have examined the issue of managerial motivation to use creative accounting. The following have been identified as significant factors:

Tax avoidance

If income can be understated or expenses overstated, then it may be possible to avoid tax.

Increasing shareholder confidence

Creative accounting can be used to ensure an appropriate level of profits over a long period. Ideally, this would show a steady upward trajectory without nasty surprises for the shareholders, and so would help to avoid volatility in share prices making it easier to raise further capital via share issues.

Personal gain

Where managerial bonuses are linked to profitability there is a clear motivation for managers to ensure that profits hit the necessary threshold to trigger a bonus payment.

Indirect personal gain

There is a market in managerial expertise in which demand often appears to outstrip supply. A manager's personal reputation in the marketplace will be enhanced by association with entities that have strong earnings records. By reporting strong performance, there is a long-term reward in terms of enhanced reputation and consequent higher earning power.

Following the pack

If managers perceive that every other entity in their sector is adopting creative accounting practices, they may feel obliged to do the same.

Meeting covenants

Sometimes, lenders insist on special covenant arrangements as a condition of making a loan e.g. they may stipulate that an entity's current ratio should not fall below 1.5:1, or that gearing never exceeds 35%. In such cases, if the entity cannot meet the covenants, the lender may be able to insist upon immediate repayment or to put the entity into liquidation. Where an entity is in danger of failing to meet its covenants, there is an obvious incentive for managers (especially if they genuinely feel that the difficulty is short-term in nature) to massage the figures so that the covenant is, apparently, satisfied.

---

10 Additional information

It is likely that the information available in the financial statements is not enough to produce a detailed and thorough analysis of the entity. This is particularly the case given the limitations of financial reporting information discussed in the previous section.

Additional information, financial and non-financial, will be required to develop a better understanding of the entity's business and its industry.

Some examples of additional information that could be useful to analysts are listed below:

Additional **financial** information

- budgeted figures
- other management information
- industry averages
- figures for a similar entity
- figures for the entity over a longer period of time.

Additional **non-financial** information such as:

- market share
- key employee information
- sales mix information
- product range information
- the size of the order book
- the long-term plans of management
- environmental policies
- third party documents e.g. solicitor's correspondence, contracts with customers and financiers,

In the assessment, it is imperative that you relate any additional information requested to the entity in the question, and to the user for whom the report is being prepared.

It is essential that any further information requested to aid the analysis would be reasonably available to the user. It is unreasonable to suggest that a non-controlling shareholder would be able to access board minutes or internal documentation. They can only access any publically available information like the financial statements.

Test your understanding 9 (OTQ style)

A colleague is looking to invest some surplus cash and has identified an entity that she believes has a promising future. However, having reviewed the financial statements she is a little concerned by the profit before tax margin which has fallen in the most recent financial year due to a significant increase in administrative expenses. She is also concerned that the cash position has worsened.

Which three of the following options would be considered realistic next steps for your colleague to take prior to making an investment decision?

A Write to the Chief Financial Officer and request a breakdown of administrative expenses to understand the cause of the increase.

B Review the narrative reports published alongside the financial statements to see whether they provide an explanation of the fall in margin.

C Obtain a copy of any interim financial statements published since the previous year-end to check whether the fall in profit is temporary.

D Review the financial press for any recent articles concerning the future prospects of the business.

E Review the cash flow forecasts of the business.

F Obtain confirmation from the entity's bank that it will continue to support the business.

Information for TYUs 10 and 11

MLR prepares its financial statements in accordance with IFRS and is listed on its local stock exchange. It is considering the acquisition of an overseas operation. Two geographical areas have been targeted, A-land and B-land. Entity A operates in A-land and entity B operates in B-land. Each entity is listed on its local stock exchange.

The most recent financial statements of entities A and B have been converted into MLR's currency for ease of comparison.

Financial data extracted from the financial statements of MLR, A and B are provided below:

	MLR	A	B
Revenue	$600m	$210m	$400m
Gross profit margin	32%	28%	19%
Profit before tax/revenue × 100	18%	10%	11%
Gearing	37%	66%	26%
Approx. rate of borrowings	8%	5%	10%

Test your understanding 10 (OTQ style)

Which one of the following statements is NOT a realistic conclusion that could be drawn from the above information?

A   A's higher gross profit margin suggests that it is benefiting from greater economies of scale than B.

B   A and B have similar profit before tax margins but different gross margins, which could be due to different classification of expenses.

C   A's high gearing may be a consequence of relatively low interest rates available.

D   B's approximate rate of borrowings suggest that lenders consider it to be higher risk than either MLR or A.

Test your understanding 11 (OTQ style)

The following statements concern the use of ratio analysis to make a decision about investing in A or B.

Which one of the statements is false?

A   The entities are listed on different stock exchanges and may be using different accounting standards. This will reduce the comparability of the financial indicators.

B   The entities may use different accounting policies and this could affect comparisons of specific ratios

C   Using only one year's worth of data gives no indication as to whether the entities are growing or in decline.

D   As A and B operate in differing geographical locations, they may pay different rates of tax and this will affect comparison of the margin ratios presented.

11   Analysis of the statement of cash flows

The cash flow of an entity is regarded by many users as being of primary importance in understanding its operations. After all, an entity that cannot generate sufficient cash will, sooner or later, fail.

The cash flow shows the cash coming in and cash going out and allocates the cash flows between categories identifying the nature and purpose of the different cash flow arising. The statement of cash flows prepared in accordance with IAS 7 *Cash flow statements* categorises cash flow under three principal headings: cash flows from operating activities, cash flows from investing activities and cash flows from financing activities.

To perform an effective assessment of an entity's cash flow, the following areas should be reviewed:

- cash generated from operations
- dividend and interest payments
- investing activities
- financing activities
- net cash flow.

There are also useful ratios that can be calculated – see expandable text below.

Cash generated from operations

Cash generated from operations gives the cash movements caused by day-day operational activities, such as cash received from cash sales, receipts from credit customer repayments, paid for cash purchases, paid to settle outstanding payables, paid to employees etc. Cash generated from operations is calculated using the indirect method, where profit before tax (from the SOPL) is reconciled to cash generated from operations.

A useful cash flow analysis exercise is to directly compare cash generated from operations to the profit from operations. These figures are shown in this reconciliation. The purpose of this is to determine how well the entity can turn its profits into physical cash flows. Businesses can appear profitable but may fail if they are overtrading.

Overtrading may be indicated by:

- high profits (PBT) and low cash generation (the cash generated from operations figure)

- large increases in inventory, receivables and payables (identified within the section highlighting movements in working capital).

Dividend and interest payments

These can be compared to cash generated from operations to see whether the normal operations can sustain such payments. If not enough cash is generated to cover the payments, the entity will be facing liquidity issues. The issue would be worse if caused by significant interest payments rather than dividends as interest payments are non-discretionary. The dividend payments could just be reduced going forward.

Investing activities

The nature and scale of an entity's investment in non-current assets is shown here.

A simple test may be to compare investment levels (cash paid to buy new non-current assets) and depreciation.

- If investment > depreciation, the entity is investing at a greater rate than its current assets are wearing out – this suggests expansion.

- If investment = depreciation, the entity is investing in new assets as existing ones wear out. The entity appears stable.

- If investment < depreciation the non-current asset base of the entity is not being maintained. This is potentially worrying as non-current assets are generators of profit.

Financing activities

The changes in financing (in pure cash terms) are shown here. Cash payments made to settle outstanding debt would identified here (or not if the repayments due have not occurred). New finance raised through loans or share issues are positive factors but consideration will be needed as to how these resources have been utilised. Look at other areas of the cash flow to ascertain if evidence exists regarding the purpose of the finance. Is there any evidence of investment in non-current assets within investing activities? This illustrates a commitment to growth. If not how has the money been spent? It would be worrying if long-term finance was being arranged to service day to day operations.

It would be useful to comment on the impact that such changes will have on the gearing ratio.

Net cash flow (movements in cash & cash equivalents)

The cash flow statement cumulates with the net cash flow for the year. Do not overstate the importance of this figure alone.

A decrease in cash in the year may be for very sound reasons (e.g. there was surplus cash last year as a new loan was raised just before the end of the accounting period) or may be the result of timing of transactions (e.g. new purchases of non-current assets were made just before the year-end).

Investigation into the causes of the overall movement is necessary through analysis of operating, investing and financing cash flows.

This section also provides the brought forward and carried forward cash figures. Carried forward cash balances will indicate if the entity is approaching specific pressure points negotiated applicable to the entity (e.g. possible breaches of overdraft terms). Large carried forward amounts are positive operational indicators but could also suggest that the entity is being primed for takeover.

Cash flow ratios

Cash return on capital employed

$$\frac{\text{Cash generated from operations}}{\text{Capital employed}} \times 100$$

For many external users, cash is a more significant indicator than profit.

Cash generated from operations to total debt

$$\frac{\text{Cash generated from operations}}{\text{Total long-term borrowings}}$$

This gives an indication of an entity's ability to meet its long-term obligations. The inverse ratio can also be calculated:

$$\frac{\text{Total long-term borrowings}}{\text{Cash generated from operations}}$$

This provides an indication of how many years it would take to repay the long-term borrowings if all of the cash generated from operations were to be used for this purpose.

Net cash from operating activities to capital expenditure

$$\frac{\text{Net cash from operating activities}}{\text{Net capital expenditure}} \times 100$$

This gives some idea of the extent to which the entity can finance its capital expenditure out of cash flows from operating activities. If it cannot meet its capital expenditure from this source, then longer-term financing is likely to be required.

Test your understanding 12 (case style)

SCF is considering the acquisition of FGH, one of its suppliers. SCF always looks carefully at the liquidity position of potential targets, having been exposed to cash flow problems in earlier acquisitions. If acquired, SCF would like to retain the existing management team of FGH.

You work as an accountant for SCF and the Managing Director has asked you to perform an analysis of FGH's most recent statement of cash flows to determine how well the management team is controlling cash.

FGH has been trading for a number of years and is currently going through a period of expansion of its core business area.

The FGH statement of cash flows for the year ended 31 December 20X0 is presented below.

	$000	$000
Cash flows from operating activities		
Profit before tax	2,200	
Adjustments for:		
Depreciation	380	
Gain on sale of investments	(50)	
Loss on sale of property, plant and equipment	45	
Investment income	(180)	
Interest costs	420	
	2,815	
Increase in trade receivables	(400)	
Increase in inventories	(390)	
Increase in payables	550	
Cash generated from operations		2,575
Interest paid		(400)
Income taxes paid		(760)
Net cash from operating activities		1,415

Cash flows from investing activities

Acquisition of subsidiary, net of cash acquired	(800)	
Acquisition of property, plant and equipment	(340)	
Proceeds from sale of equipment	70	
Proceeds from sale of investments	150	
Interest received	100	
Dividends received	80	
Net cash used in investing activities		(740)
Cash flows from financing activities		
Proceeds of share issue	300	
Proceeds from long term borrowings	300	
Dividend paid to equity shareholders of the parent	(1,000)	
Net cash used in financing activities		(400)
Net increase in cash and cash equivalents		275
Cash and cash equivalents at the beginning of the period		110
Cash and cash equivalents at the end of the period		385

Required:

Prepare a memo to the Managing Director assessing the cash management of FGH based on your analysis of the statement of cash flows.

Test your understanding 13 (further OTQs)

Note: there are TYUs earlier in the chapter that assess the calculation of ratios. This section concentrates on interpretation.

1   Anderson has a bank overdraft and a current ratio of 1:1.

   Which ONE of the following actions would increase the current ratio?

   A   Offering cash discounts to customers to encourage speedier payment

   B   Paying suppliers ahead of schedule to obtain cash discounts

   C   Selling inventory on credit at book value

   D   Increasing the allowance for doubtful receivables

2   The Port Erin fishmonger and the Port Erin bookseller both operate on a 50% mark-up on cost. However, their gross profit margins are:

   Fishmonger 25%

   Bookseller 33%

   Which one of the following statements would validly explain the higher gross profit margin of the bookseller?

   A   There is more wastage with inventories of fish than inventories of books

   B   The fishmonger has a substantial bank loan whereas the bookseller's business is entirely financed by family

   C   The fishmonger has expensive high street premises whereas the bookseller has cheaper back street premises

   D   The fishmonger's sales revenue is declining whereas the bookseller's is increasing

3   The following statements allegedly refer to the conclusions to be drawn when using ratio analysis to interpret the financial statements of an entity.

    Which two of the following statements are TRUE?

    A   An entity can only increase its gross profit margin by increasing its selling prices or reducing its costs per unit of production.

    B   With other things remaining equal, an upwards revaluation of non-current assets would lead to a reduction in the return on capital employed.

    C   An entity can increase its return on capital employed in the short term by postponing replacement of aged non-current assets.

    D   An upwards revaluation of non-current assets will result in an increase in the gearing of an entity.

4   JA and GB operate in the same industry and are of a similar size. The non-current asset turnover ratios of the two entities are as follows:

    JA 2.5

    GB 1.7

    Which of the following statements would be VALID explanations of the differences in the non-current asset ratio of the two entities? Select all that apply.

    A   JA has a policy of revaluing its non-current assets whereas GB uses the cost model. The revaluations normally reflect an increase in value.

    B   JA's non-current assets are older than GB's.

    C   GB's non-current assets are under-utilised at present.

    D   GB has acquired non-current assets in the final month of the accounting period, whereas JA last purchased significant non-current assets in the previous accounting period.

5   The following information has been obtained for two potential acquisition targets, A and B, who operate in the same industry.

	A	B
Revenue	$160m	$300m
Gross profit margin	26%	17%
Profit before interest and tax margin	9%	11%

Which two of the following statements are VALID conclusions that could be drawn from the above information?

A   A's gross profit margin is higher as A would be expected to have achieved more economies of scale than B.

B   The difference between gross profit margins could be due to the entities classifying their costs differently between cost of sales and operating expenses.

C   The difference between profit before interest and tax margins could be due to the entities classifying their costs differently between cost of sales and operating expenses.

D   B has lower operating expenses than A.

12 Chapter summary

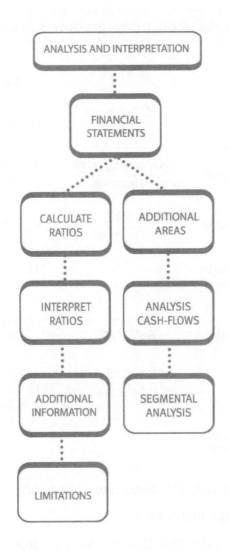

Test your understanding answers

Test your understanding 1 (integration question) – Profitability

Profitability:

		20X6	20X5
Gross profit margin	$\dfrac{\text{Gross profit}}{\text{Revenue}}$	115/180 = 63.9%	90/150 = 60%
Operating profit margin	$\dfrac{\text{Operating profit}}{\text{Revenue}}$	(115−40)/180 = 41.7%	(90−29)/150 = 40.7%
Profit before tax margin	$\dfrac{\text{PBT}}{\text{Revenue}}$	110/180 = 61.1%	51/150 = 34%
Profit before tax margin (excluding Associate)		(110−59)/180 = 28.3%	
Effective tax rate (excluding Associate)	$\dfrac{\text{Tax expense}}{\text{PBT} - \text{Assoc}}$	14/(110−59) = 27.5%	13/51 = 25.5%
Return on capital employed	$\dfrac{\text{Operating profit}}{\text{Capital employed}}$	(115−40)/ (218+335+9−250) = 24.0%	(90−29)/ (100+110) = 29.0%

(**Note:** CV of Associate is deducted from capital employed)

Possible reasons why T's ratios have changed:

Gross profit margin increased:

- Increase in sales due to increasing volume sold and so economies of scale result in lower costs per unit sold

- Increase in sales price per unit

- Changes in product mix.

Operating profit margin smaller increase (than GPM):

- Increase in expenses such as advertising to boost revenue

- Increased depreciation charges following acquisitions of non-current assets

- Poor control of costs since revenue increased by 20% but operating expenses increased by 38%.

Profit before tax margin significant increase:

- Due to share of profit of associate

- Removing this shows an actual reduction in margin

- Increased borrowing to fund expansion has resulted in 140% increase finance costs.

Effective tax rate increase:

- Effect of change in legislation

- Under-provision in previous year.

Return on capital employed:

- Fall due to significant increase in capital employed, not generating as significant an improvement in operating profit

- Large increase in long term borrowings to fund investment in non-current assets during year. If acquired near year-end, will not have generated returns yet

- Non-current assets also revalued – this increases capital employed but will not lead to an improvement in profit (it distorts the ratio).

Test your understanding 2

EBITDA = Earnings before interest, tax, depreciation and amortisation.

	20X6	20X5
Profit for the year (PAT)	96	38
Add back		
Tax	14	13
Interest (finance costs)	24	10
Depreciation	6	3
	140	64

Test your understanding 3 (integration question) – Liquidity

Liquidity ratios:

		20X6	20X5
Current ratio	$\dfrac{\text{Current assets}}{\text{Current liabilities}}$	64/44 = 1.5:1	50/32 = 1.6:1
Quick ratio	$\dfrac{(\text{Current assets} - \text{Inventory})}{\text{Current liabilities}}$	49/44 = 1.1:1	38/32 = 1.2:1

Overall liquidity situation has deteriorated:

- Current and quick ratios have both fallen slightly but not yet at levels that give cause for concern. The main reason for the reduction is the cash balance changing from positive to negative in 20X6.

- The increasing inventory holding and receivables collection periods (see efficiency ratios below) have been funded by an overdraft rather than an equivalent increase in the payables payment period.

Test your understanding 4 (integration question) – Efficiency

Efficiency/activity ratios:

		20X6	20X5
Inventory holding period	$\dfrac{\text{Inventory}}{\text{Cost of sales}} \times 365$ days	15/65 × 365 = 84 days	12/60 × 365 = 73 days
Receivables collection period	$\dfrac{\text{Receivables}}{\text{Revenue}} \times 365$ days	49/180 × 365 = 99 days	37/150 × 365 = 90 days
Payables payment period	$\dfrac{\text{Trade payables}}{\text{Cost of sales}} \times 365$ days	12/65 × 365 = 67 days	11/60 × 365 = 67 days
Asset turnover	$\dfrac{\text{Revenue}}{\text{Capital Employed}}$	180/(218+335+9– 250) = 0.58 times	150/(100+110) = 0.71 times
Non-current asset turnover	$\dfrac{\text{Revenue}}{\text{NCAs (that cont. to revenue)}}$	180/266 = 0.68 times	150/190 = 0.79 times

Possible reasons why T's ratios have changed:

Inventory holding period increased:

- Build-up of inventory levels as a result of increased capacity following expansion of non-current assets

- Increasing inventory levels in response to increased demand for product

- • Expectation of higher demand after year end

- • Lack of control over inventory.

Receivables collection period increased:

- • Deliberate policy to attract customers

- • Poor credit control procedures

Payables payment period unchanged.

Asset/non-current asset turnover:

- • Revaluation of non-current assets will reduce asset turnover but not a "real" deterioration in efficiency

- • Significant increase in non-current assets during year. If acquired near year-end, will not have generated returns/revenue for full year yet.

Test your understanding 5 (integration question) – Gearing

Capital structure

		20X6	20X5
Gearing	$\dfrac{\text{Debt}}{\text{Debt + Equity}}$	(335+9)/ (335+9+218) = 61.2%	110/(110+100) = 52.4%
Gearing (alternative)	$\dfrac{\text{Debt}}{\text{Equity}}$	(335+9)/218 = 1.6:1	110/100 = 1.1:1
NB. Gearing may be shown as a % or a ratio. The exam question make it explicit regarding how to present your answer.			
Interest cover	$\dfrac{\text{Operating profit}}{\text{Finance costs}}$	(115–40)/24 = 3.1 times	(90–29)/10 = 6.1 times
Average rate of borrowing	$\dfrac{\text{Finance costs}}{\text{Borrowings}}$	24/(335+9) = 7.0%	10/110 = 9.1%
Dividend cover	$\dfrac{\text{Profit for year}}{\text{Dividends}}$	96/25 = 3.8 times	38/25 = 1.5 times

Gearing increase and interest cover reduction:

- Significant increase in long-term borrowings – to finance acquisition of associate/PPE

- Increase in loan significantly greater than increase in equity finance

- Gearing ratio appears quite high and interest cover falling creates concern

- Interest cover may increase next year when full year's impact of investment reflected.

Average rate of borrowing has fallen:

- New borrowings at lower rate

- Loans taken out mid-way through year, so full year's cost not yet reflected.

Dividend cover significantly increases, principally due to associate profit.

Test your understanding 6 (OTQ style)

D is the valid reason.

A is incorrect. A significant investment close to the year-end would result in a large increase in capital employed with little increase in profit, therefore ROCE would reduce.

B is incorrect. A revaluation increases equity and therefore capital employed with no corresponding increase in profit.

C is incorrect. The reduction in retained earnings would be netted off against the increase in long-term borrowings so capital employed would not be affected.

Test your understanding 7 (integration question)

	20X1	**20X0**
Gross profit margin	49/252 × 100 = 19.4%	25/248 × 100 = 10.1%
Operating profit margin	(49 – 18 – 16)/252 × 100 = 6.0%	(25 – 13 – 11)/248 × 100 = 0.4%
Profit for year margin	7/252 ×100 = 2.8%	(5)/248 × 100 = (2.0)%
Gearing	(91+39)/231 × 100 = 56.3%	91/184 × 100 = 49.5%
Current ratio	178/134 = 1.3:1	143/66 = 2.2:1
Quick ratio	(178 – 106)/134 = 0.5:1	(143 – 89)/66 = 0.8:1
Receivable days	72/252 × 365 days = 104 days	48/248 × 365 days = 71 days
Payable days	95/203 × 365 days = 171 days	66/223 × 365 days = 108 days
Inventories days	106/203 × 365 days = 191 days	89/223 × 365 days = 146 days
Return on capital employed	(49 – 18 – 16)/ (231+ 91 – 24) = 15/298 × 100 = 5.0%	(25 – 13 – 11)/ (184 + 91) = 1/275 × 100 = 0.4%
Non-current asset turnover	252/254 = 1.0	248/198 = 1.3
Interest cover	(49 – 18 – 16)/ 12 = 1.3 times	(25 –13 – 11)/8 = 0.1 times

Test your understanding 8 (case style)

To: Board of Directors of XYZ

From: Accountant

Subject: Report on financial performance and position of DFG

The revenue of DFG has only marginally increased in the year by 1.6%, however profit margins have all increased significantly. In particular the gross profit margin has increased from 10% to 19%. This is likely to be as a result of reduced purchase prices from the new supplier contract that was secured in the year. Whilst this is a very positive and important step for DFG (given its low margin in the previous year) it will be important to establish whether this reduced cost also means a reduced level of quality. If quality is being compromised then this increase in margin may be short-lived as customers may be driven away in the longer term.

In addition, the switch in supplier may be responsible for the lawsuit. It is a risky strategy for DFG to pursue aggressive revenue and margin targets at the expense of supplying good quality products. Although a contingent liability of $30 million is included in the notes, the lawyer's assessment is that DFG is likely to lose the court case and the pay-out may be more. There is already serious pressure on DFG's finances and it may not survive if the pay-out is any more or if other customers decide to sue. There is a significant risk to the going concern of the entity.

Both administration and distribution costs have increased significantly when compared to a 1.6% increase in revenue. Whilst these costs are not that large in relation to revenues, it may suggest that management do not have good control of overheads. The impact of legal fees as a result of the court case may also be seen with the increase of expenses.

ROCE has increased overall due to the increases in operating margins described above. However, revaluation surplus recorded during the year would reduce ROCE. The increase in ROCE would be greater if the impact of the revaluation where to be removed. ROCE without the revaluation is calculated as = 5.8% (15/(298 – 40) × 100) compared to last years' ROCE of 0.4%.

The increase in total comprehensive income is largely due to the revaluation gain reported within other comprehensive income. The valuation was performed by an internal member of staff so an element of scepticism should be applied to the figures. However, the financial statements have been finalised and it can be assumed that they have been audited and that the valuations are fair.

Consideration is needed as to why the directors have chosen this year to change the policy. It could be an attempt to boost income and reduce gearing to make further borrowing easier, especially as the long term borrowings will need to be repaid or re-negotiated relatively soon.

However, it is good commercial sense to ensure that assets that are to be used as security for finance are at the most up-to-date valuation.

The overall liquidity of DFG is on the low side at 1.3:1 and has fallen significantly from 20X0. One contributing factor to the worsening liquidity is the significant increase in inventories in the year. This could be as a result of bad publicity about below standard goods and customer orders being cancelled. There is then an increased risk of obsolete inventories. This is reinforced by the inventory days which have increased from 146 days to 191 days. Receivable days have also increased from 71 days to 104 days, and this could be as a result of disputed invoices. DFG may then have a problem with slow/non-payment of these debts. Payable days have increased from 108 days to 171 days and this could be resulting from a deliberate attempt by DFG to improve cash flow by delaying payment, particularly in response to the struggle to recover cash from their customers, or extended credit terms given by the new supplier to attract DFG's business.

The cash position of DFG is clearly a concern as the cash has moved from a positive balance to an overdraft and the long term borrowings are soon to be repaid or re-negotiated. This, coupled with the poor working capital management, would indicate that DFG must raise some additional funding if it is to survive. The gearing ratio shows deterioration on the previous year, despite an increase in equity from the revaluation. However, it is likely to be the lack of interest cover that would put lenders off. It is unlikely that DFG could afford to pay interest on any additional funding.

Recommendation

I would recommend that you do not consider investing in DFG at this time. If they lose the court case and have a large settlement to pay this could result in the entity collapsing and despite the fact that details of this are only in the notes, its seriousness should not be overlooked. The entity may struggle to survive anyway as there is a lack of cash and funding options (and it should be noted that DFG did not pay a dividend in 20X1). The increases in profitability are not enough of an indicator of a stable/growing entity, especially an entity involved in the building trade which is known for its sensitivity to the economy around it.

Test your understanding 9 (OTQ style)

Realistic next steps are B, C and D.

Options A, E and F are not available to minority shareholders.

Test your understanding 10 (OTQ style)

A is not a realistic conclusion.

A has much lower revenue than B and, therefore, B should be achieving more economies of scale than A not vice versa.

Test your understanding 11 (OTQ style)

D is false.

The tax rate will have no effect on the ratios presented. The profits used in the margin calculations are **before** tax.

Test your understanding 12 (case style)

Memo to Managing Director

Firstly, FGH has managed to generate significant cash from operating activities which is a positive sign for any business wishing to be a going concern. This is particularly important since it appears that FGH is expanding as evidenced within the acquisitions shown in investing activities. In addition to the inflow of cash from trading, the directors have clearly made some good investment decisions as investment income of $180,000 has been included in the year and profits of $50,000 has been earned from the sale of these investments.

It does appear as if FGH needs to improve management of working capital as receivables have increased in the year by $400,000. The entity has, in turn, withheld payment to payables with an increase of $550,000. The increase in receivables may be a deliberate attempt to secure new customers by offering them favourable credit terms but it is essential that good working capital management is not compromised through poor credit control. It may be useful to compare our existing credit terms with FGH with those that they are offering to their other customers. This could be useful for our own negotiations with FGH next time our credit terms are discussed.

The increase in inventories has probably arisen in order to meet future expected demand from the expansion.

The expansion is shown in two areas of investment, with the acquisition of a subsidiary and in the purchase of property, plant and equipment. The sale of property, plant and equipment for $70,000 resulted in a loss of $45,000. It's possible that the expansion has resulted in the need for new equipment and hence management have taken the view to sell some of the old equipment whilst there is still a second hand market for it. The sale of investments for $150,000 may have been undertaken in order to generate funds for the expansion. The only note of caution is that these investments seem to be profitable and hence, given that a proportion has been sold during the year, future income from investments will be reduced.

A significant dividend has been paid out. The existing shareholders may be stripping cash out of the business prior to selling their shares to us. A good sign however is that FGH has managed to fund its expansion without increasing the overall gearing of the business, as equal amounts of debt and equity have been raised as new finance. It indicates good stewardship of assets when long term expansion is financed by long term financing. FGH appears to have used a mixture of long term financing and retained earnings generated in the year, together with the sale of some investments to fund the expansion. However, this is not to the detriment of shareholders as they have still received a significant dividend during the year. It's possible that the new investments will generate greater returns in the future than the investments which have been sold. In times of expansion, however, a more modest dividend may have negated the need for long term financing and the interest costs associated with it.

Overall, the cash position of the business has improved by $110,000 over the course of the year and therefore, even taking into account the expansion and significant dividend, FGH do not appear to have any significant liquidity issues.

Test your understanding 13 (further OTQs)

1 **B**

By paying suppliers ahead of schedule there would be a reduction in payables and a smaller increase in the overdraft (as the payment would be reduced by the discount). Therefore liabilities in total would decrease (by the amount of the discount) and the current ratio would increase.

A is not correct. The reduction in the overdraft would be lower that the reduction in the receivables and therefore the current ratio would decrease.

C is not correct. There would be a reduction in inventory and increase in liabilities therefore the current ratio would decrease.

D is not correct. This would reduce receivables and therefore the current ratio would decrease.

2 **A**

The fishmonger's inventories are perishable and some will therefore be written off, creating an additional expense within cost of sales and reducing the gross profit margin.

B is not correct. The bank loan would create finance costs but these are not expensed within gross profit.

C is not correct. The costs of the premises would be charged within operating expenses rather than cost of sales. GP% is untouched by these expenses.

D is not correct. Regardless of sales volumes, if the mark up is 50% then a change in volume would not affect the gross profit margin.

3 **B and C are correct.**

An upwards revaluation of non-current assets increases equity and, therefore, capital employed. It is also likely to reduce profit (if the assets are depreciable) as it will lead to higher depreciation charges.

When an entity continues to use fully depreciated assets, there will be a positive effect on return on capital employed. There will be no further depreciation charged as the assets will have nil carrying amount, but they may continue to generate profits. Profits would be expect to increase whilst capital employed remains constant.

A is not correct. An entity can improve its gross profit margin by changing its sales mix and selling greater proportional volumes of high margin products.

D is not correct. Revaluation would increase equity therefore reduce gearing.

4   **B, C and D are correct.**

Old non-current assets inflate the ratio as the carrying amount is low and is included in the denominator. B is correct.

A relatively low asset turnover also suggests that the assets are not generating sufficient revenue. They are under-utilised. C is correct.

ROCE would reduce if non-current assets have been acquired towards the end of the financial period, as the full cost would be included in the denominator but there wouldn't yet be a year's worth of revenue/profits in the numerator. D is correct.

A is incorrect. An upward revaluation would increase non-current assets and, as this is the denominator, would make non-current assets relatively low.

5   **B and D are correct.**

Different classification of expenses of two entities will affect any comparison of gross profit. B is correct.

D is correct. The operating expenses of both entities can be calculated from the information provided.

	A	B
	$m	$m
Gross profit (gross profit margin × revenue)		
(26% × $160m)	41.6	
(17% × $300m)		51
Operating profit (operating profit margin × revenue)		
(9% × $160m)	14.4	
(11% × $300m)		33
Operating expenses	27.2	18

A is incorrect. Economies of scale would not be a valid conclusion for A having the better gross margin as it is the smaller entity - its revenue is only 53% of B's and the two entities operate in the same sector.

C is incorrect. Different classification of expenses between cost of sales and operating expenses should have no effect on profit before tax (which includes both categories). It only affects gross profit.

References

The Board (2020) *Conceptual Framework for Financial Reporting.* London: IFRS Foundation.

The Board (2020) IAS 7 *Statement of Cash Flows.* London: IFRS Foundation.

The Board (2020) IAS 12 *Income Taxes.* London: IFRS Foundation.

The Board (2020) IAS 18 *Revenue.* London: IFRS Foundation.

The Board (2020) IAS 21 *The Effects of Changes in Foreign Exchange Rates.* London: IFRS Foundation.

The Board (2020) IAS 24 *Related Party Disclosures.* London: IFRS Foundation.

The Board (2020) IAS 27 *Separate Financial Statements.* London: IFRS Foundation.

The Board (2020) IAS 28 *Investments in Associates and Joint Ventures.* London: IFRS Foundation.

The Board (2020) IAS 32 *Financial Instruments: Presentation.* London: IFRS Foundation.

The Board (2020) IAS 33 *Earnings per Share.* London: IFRS Foundation.

The Board (2020) IAS 36 *Impairment of Assets.* London: IFRS Foundation.

The Board (2020) IAS 37 *Provisions, Contingent Liabilities and Contingent Assets.* London: IFRS Foundation.

The Board (2020) IAS 38 *Intangible Assets.* London: IFRS Foundation.

The Board (2020) IAS 39 *Financial Instruments:* Recognition and measurement. London: IFRS Foundation.

The Board (2020) IFRS 3 *Business Combinations.* London: IFRS Foundation.

The Board (2020) IFRS 7 *Financial Instruments:* Disclosure. London: IFRS Foundation.

The Board (2020) IFRS 8 *Operating Segments.* London: IFRS Foundation.

The Board (2020) IFRS 9 *Financial Instruments.* London: IFRS Foundation.

The Board (2020) IFRS 10 *Consolidated Financial Statements.* London: IFRS Foundation.

The Board (2020) IFRS 11 *Joint Arrangements.* London: IFRS Foundation.

The Board (2020) IFRS 12 *Disclosure of Interests in Other Entities.* London: IFRS Foundation.

The Board (2020) IFRS 13 *Fair Value Measurement.* London: IFRS Foundation.

The Board (2020) IFRS 15 *Revenue from contracts with customers.* London: IFRS Foundation.

The Board (2020) IFRS 16 *Leases.* London: IFRS Foundation.

Integrated Reporting framework (<IR> framework), IIRC

Index